CONCISE COLLEGE TEXTS

TORT

OTHER BOOKS IN THIS SERIES:

Public Law, by Professor G. Borrie
The Making of Business Contracts, by A. Harding Boulton
Public International Law, by D. J. Latham Brown
Criminal Law and Procedure, by I. G. Carvell and E. Swinfen Green
Administrative Law for Surveying Students, by H. W. Clarke
Constitutional and Administrative Law, by H. W. Clarke
Contract, by F. R. Davies
Sale of Goods and Consumer Credit, by A. P. Dobson
Labour Law, by C. D. Drake
The English Legal System, by K. J. Eddey
Hotel and Catering Law, by David Field
The Law of Arbitration, by William H. Gill
Family Law, by Judge H. B. Grant
Land Law, by E. Swinfen Green and N. Henderson
ONC/OND Commercial Law, by C. Hamblin and F. B. Wright
Advanced Level Law, by B. Jones
Estate Duty in England and Wales, by A. Douglas Lawton
(Adapted from *An Outline of Estate Duty in Scotland* by G. Herbert Brown and John M. Halliday)
Civil and Criminal Procedure, by J. R. Lewis
Landlord and Tenant, by J. R. Lewis and J. A. Holland
General Principles of Law, by C. R. Newton
Banking Law, by S. Twum
Patents, Trade Marks, Copyright and Industrial Designs, by T. A. Blanco White and Robin Jacob

AUSTRALIA
The Law Book Company Ltd.
Sydney : Melbourne : Brisbane

CANADA AND U.S.A.
The Carswell Company Ltd.
Agincourt, Ontario

INDIA
N. M. Tripathi Private Ltd.
Bombay

ISRAEL
Steimatzky's Agency Ltd.
Jerusalem : Tel Aviv : Haifa

MALAYSIA : SINGAPORE : BRUNEI
Malayan Law Journal (Pte.) Ltd.
Singapore

NEW ZEALAND
Sweet and Maxwell (N.Z.) Ltd.
Wellington

PAKISTAN
Pakistan Law House
Karachi

CONCISE COLLEGE TEXTS

TORT

By

C. D. BAKER, M.A., B.C.L.

of the Inner Temple, Barrister-at-Law

Lecturer in Law, University of Leicester

SECOND EDITION

LONDON

SWEET & MAXWELL

1976

Published in 1976 by
Sweet & Maxwell Limited of
11 New Fetter Lane, London
and printed in Great Britain
by Richard Clay (The Chaucer Press) Ltd.
Bungay, Suffolk

ISBN Hardback 421 21470 8
Paperback 421 21480 5

PREFACE

THE second edition of this book has been compiled while lawyers await the views of the Pearson Commission on the question of the desirability of the retention of a fault-based system of compensation for personal injuries. The feeling that legislative change is imminent may well explain the fact that there have been no revolutionary judicial changes since the first edition in the law relating to compensation for personal injuries. At the same time the courts have not been inactive, the most important decision being clearly *Dutton* v. *Bognor Regis U.D.C.* which has important implications for the law relating to negligent statements, omissions and purely pecuniary loss. In the intervening years we have also had the Defective Premises Act 1972 and, in 1975, a new Limitation Act. The book has been expanded, both to take account of change and to allow for a fair amount of rewriting and insertion of new material by the author. In so far as changes have resulted from suggestions made by colleagues, I would like to express my gratitude to them.

The law is stated in accordance with materials available to me on February 12, 1976. The following developments took place after the work went to the printers.

(i) The Trade Union and Labour Relations (Amendment) Act received the royal assent on March 25, 1976. Section 3(2) of the Act (reproduced as clause 2(2) of the Bill at page 269) has therefore replaced the defences available under section 13(1) of the Trade Union and Labour Relations Act 1974 with a much wider defence. The effect of this will be that the law of tort will have virtually no part to play in industrial disputes.

(ii) The Court of Appeal in *Esso Petroleum Co.* v. *Mardon* [1976]2 All E.R.5 approved the decision of Lawson, J. at first instance to the effect that *Hedley Byrne* liability is not excluded where a negligent misrepresentation has resulted in the making of a contract between representor and representee. The case indicates also that the limitation imposed by the Privy Council decision in the case of *Mutual Life and Citizens Assurance Ltd.* v. *Evatt* (1971) to the effect that the defendant must be in the business or profession of giving advice is unlikely to be accepted by English courts. In the words of Ormrod L.J., "If the majority view (in Mutual Citizens) were to be accepted the effect of Hedley Byrne would be so radically curtailed as to be virtually eliminated."

(iii) O'Connor J.'s decision in *Cummings* v. *Grainger* (1975) to the effect that the keeping of a ferocious alsatian dog for the purpose of protecting a scrap yard was unreasonable has been reversed by the Court of Appeal (*The Times*, May 29, 1976). The court thought that the defence under section 5(3) of the Animals Act 1971 was available to the defendant, and also that the plaintiff, since she knew of the dog's presence and had seen "Beware of the dog" notices outside the yard, had voluntarily accepted the risk within section 5(2) of the Act. But O'Connor J.'s ferocious dog with a particular aversion to coloured people had become, rather mysteriously, a normal guard dog which only became aggressive in the particular circumstances of carrying out its function to deter trespassers. This no doubt explains the difference in the decisions. There are indications in the judgments in the Court of Appeal that the keeping of a guard dog without a handler as required by the Guard Dogs Act 1975 would now be regarded as unreasonable and outside the protection of section 5(3).

June 11, 1976 C. D. BAKER

CONTENTS

		PAGE
Preface		v
Table of Cases		
Table of Statutes		
1.	Introduction	1
2.	Intentional Interference with the Person	8
3.	Intentional Interference with Chattels	21
4.	Trespass to Land	43
5.	Defences to the Intentional Torts to Person and Property	52
6.	Negligence	66
7.	Breach of Duty	90
8.	Causation and Remoteness of Damage	100
9.	Defences to Negligence	124
10.	Proof of Negligence	136
11.	Liability for Premises	142
12.	Liability for Chattels	158
13.	Employer's Liability towards Workmen	163
14.	Torts of Strict Liability—Introductory	168
15.	Nuisance	170
16.	The Rule in Rylands v. Fletcher	190
17.	Liability for the Escape of Fire	200
18.	Liability for Animals	202
19.	Breach of Statutory Duty	212
20.	Vicarious Liability	220
21.	Defamation	231
22.	The Economic Torts	255
23.	The Economic Torts: Passing Off	271
24.	The Economic Torts: Deceit and Inurious Falsehood	275
25.	Interference with Family Relationships	283
26.	Malicious Prosecution and Abuse of Process	289
27.	Innominate and Doubtful Torts	293
28.	Death in Relation to Tort	297

PAGE

29. Remedies 304
30. Extinction of Tortious Liability 315
31. Parties 321

Index 326

TABLE OF CASES

ABBOTT v. Sullivan [1952] 1 K.B. 189 294
ACROW (AUTOMATION) v. Rex Chainbelt [1971] 1 W.L.R. 1676 267
ACTON BOROUGH COUNCIL v. Morris [1953] 1 W.L.R. 1228 51
ADDIE (R.) AND SONS (Collieries) Ltd. v. Dumbreck [1929] A.C. 358 154
ALDHAM v. United Dairies Ltd. [1940] 1 K.B. 507 211
ALEXANDER v. North-Eastern Ry. Co. (1856) 6 B. & S. 340 242
ALLEN v. Aeroplane & Motor Aluminium Castings [1965] 1 W.L.R. 1244 .... 141, 216
—— v. Flood [1898] A.C. 1 4
AMBERGATE RY. CO. v. Midland Ry. Co. 55
AMERICAN CYANAMID CO. v. Ethicon [1975] A.C. 396 270
ANDERSON v. Oppenheimer (1880) 5 Q.B.D. 602 197
ANDERSON (W. B.) & SONS v. Rhodes (Liverpool) [1967] 2 All E.R. 850 .... 74, 278
ANDREAE v. Selfridge & Co. [1938] Ch. 1 .... 174, 176, 184
ANDREWS v. Freeborough [1967] 1 Q.B. 1 301
—— v. Hopkinson [1975] 1 Q.B. 229 .... 158, 160
ANGEL v. Bushell & Co. [1968] 1 Q.B. 813 251
ARENSON v. Casson, Beckman Rutley [1975] 3 W.L.R. 815 75
ARGYLL (DUCHESS) v. Argyll (Duke) [1967] Ch. 302 294
ARMORY v. Delamirie (1721) 1 Stra. 505 28
ARMSTRONG v. Strain [1952] 1 K.B. 232 276
ASHBY v. White (1704) 2 Ld. Raym. 938 .... 215, 218, 293, 304
ASHDOWN v. Williams and Sons [1957] 1 Q.B. 409 .... 150, 151
ASTLEY INDUSTRIAL TRUST v. Miller [1968] 2 All E.R. 36 40
ATKINSON v. Newcastle and Gateshead Waterworks Co. (1877) L.R. 2 Ex. D. 441 213
ATTENBOROUGH v. London and St. Katherine's Dock (1878) L.R. 3 C.P.D. 450 .... 37, 42
ATT.-GEN. v. Corke [1933] Ch. 89 193
—— v. Cory Brothers & Co. [1921] 1 A.C. 521 197
—— v. P.Y.A. Quarries [1957] 2 Q.B. 169 185
—— v. Sheffield Gas Consumers Co. (1853) 3 De G.M. & G. 304 185
—— v. Stone (1895) 12 T.L.R. 76 .... 179, 193
—— v. Times Newspapers [1974] A.C. 273 253

BAGOT v. Stevens, Scanlan & Co. [1966] 1 Q.B. 197 .... 3, 74
BAKER v. Bolton (1808) 1 Camp. 493 297
—— v. Hopkins (T. E. & Son [1959] 1 W.L.R. 966 114
—— v. Willoughby [1970] A.C. 467 102
BALFOUR v. Barty-King [1957] 1 Q.B. 496 200
BALL v. London County Council [1949] 2 K.B. 159 .... 157, 159
BALLETT v. Mingay [1943] K.B. 281 39
BARKWAY v. South Wales Transport [1950] A.C. 185 .... 139, 140
BARNES v. Lucille Ltd. (1907) 96 L.T. 680 203
BARNETT v. Chelsea and Kensington Hospital Management Committee [1969] 1 Q.B. 428 .... 100, 101

—— *v.* Cohen [1921] 2 K.B. 461 299
Batcheller *v.* Tunbridge Wells Gas Co. (1901) 84 L.T. 765 192
Bates *v.* Stone Parish Council [1954] 1 W.L.R. 1249 285
Bativala *v.* West [1970] 1 Q.B. 716 211
Batts Combe Quarry Ltd. *v.* Ford [1943] Ch. 51 258
Baume & Co. *v.* Moore (A. H.) [1958] Ch. 907 272
Beaman *v.* A.R.T.S. [1949] 1 K.B. 550 319
Beatty *v.* Illingworth (1898) 60 J.P. 740 56
Beaulieu *v.* Finglam (1401) 2 Hen. 4, 18, pl. 6 .... 200, 201
Behrens *v.* Bertram Mills Circus [1957] 2 Q.B. 1 203
Bellew *v.* Cement Co. [1948] Ir.R. 61 174
Benham *v.* Gambling [1941] A.C. 157 301
Bennett *v.* Allcott (1787) 2 T.R. 166 284
—— *v.* Tugwell [1971] 2 Q.B. 267 135
Berry *v.* British Transport Commission [1962] 1 Q.B. 306 292
Best *v.* Fox (Samuel) & Co. [1952] A.C. 716 .... 286, 288
Biakanja *v.* Irving (1958) 49 Cal. (2d) 647 282
Billings and Sons *v.* Riden [1958] A.C. 240 157
Birch *v.* Thomas [1972] 1 W.L.R. 294 135
Bird *v.* Fort Francis [1949] 2 D.L.R. 791 27
—— *v.* Holbrook (1828) 4 Bing. 628 .... 19, 20, 55
—— *v.* Jones (1845) 7 Q.B. 742 16
Blackham *v.* Pugh (1846) 2 C.B. 611 250
Blake *v.* Barnard (1840) 9 C. & P. 626 14
B.M.T.A. *See* British Motor Trade Association.
Boardman *v.* Sanderson [1964] 1 W.L.R. 1317 .... 86, 87
Bodley *v.* Reynolds (1846) 8 Q.B. 779 41
Bognor Regis U.D.C. *v.* Campion [1972] 2 Q.B. 169 236
Bollinger (J.) *v.* Costa Brava Wine Co. Ltd. (No. 2) [1961] 1 W.L.R. 277... 272
Bolton *v.* Stone [1951] A.C. 850 .... 69, 91, 92
Bonnington Castings *v.* Wardlaw [1956] 1 A.C. 613 .... 102, 216
Borthwick *v.* Evening Post (1888) 37 Ch.D. 449 273
Bourhill *v.* Young [1943] A.C. 92 .... 70, 86, 87, 88, 107
Bowater *v.* Rowley Regis Corporation [1944] K.B. 476 134
Bowmakers *v.* Barnet Instruments [1945] K.B. 65 62
Boyd *v.* G.N. Ry. Co. [1895] 2 I.R. 555 188
Boyle *v.* Kodak [1969] 1 W.L.R. 661 218
Bradburn *v.* Great Western Ry. (1874) L.R. 10 Exch. 1 309
Bradford *v.* Robinson Rentals Ltd. [1967] 1 W.L.R. 337 .... 108, 110
Bradford Corpn. *v.* Pickles [1895] A.C. 587 173
Brandon *v.* Osbourne, Garret & Co. [1924] 1 K.B. 548 129
Bray *v.* Palmer [1953] 1 W.L.R. 1455 139
Brekkes *v.* Cattel [1972] Ch. 105 .... 265, 267
Brew Brothers Ltd. *v.* Snax (Ross) Ltd. [1970] 1 Q.B. 612 182
Bridges *v.* Hawkesworth (1851) 21 L.J.Q.B. 75 .... 28, 29
Bridlington Relay Ltd. *v.* Yorkshire Electricity Board [1965] Ch. 436 176
Brimelow *v.* Casson [1924] 1 Ch. 302 262
Brinsmead *v.* Harrison (1872) L.R. 7 C.P. 547 120
British Celanese *v.* Hunt (A. H.) [1969] 1 W.L.R. 959 .... 177, 178, 194
British Economical Lamp Co. *v.* Mile End Theatre (1913) 29 T.L.R. 383 .... 34, 35
British Idustrial Plastics *v.* Ferguson [1940] 1 All E.R. 386 260
British Motor Trade Association *v.* Salvadori [1949] Ch. 556 258

British Railways Board v. Herrington [1972] A.C. 877 ...... 154, 155, 157
—— v. Liptrot [1969] A.C. 136 214
British Road Services v. Slater [1964] 1 W.L.R. 498 187
British Transport Commission v. Gourley [1956] A.C. 185 309
Brooke v. Bool [1928] 2 K.B. 578 119
Broom v. Morgan [1953] 1 Q.B. 597 222
Brunsden v. Humphrey (1884) 14 Q.B.D. 141 311
Bryanston Finance Co. v. Vries [1975] Q.B. 703 ...... 120, 251
Bryanston Finance Co. v. De Vries [1975] Q.B. 703 ...... 120, 251
Buckland v. Guildford Gas, Light and Coke Co. [1949] 1 K.B. 410 157
Buckle v. Holmes [1926] 2 K.B. 125 203
Buckpitt v. Oates [1968] 1 All E.R. 1145 ...... 52, 133, 134
Bunker v. Brand (Charles) & Son [1969] 2 Q.B. 480 149
Burnard v. Haggis (1863) 14 C.B. (n.s.) 45 ...... 22, 325
Burnett v. British Waterways Board [1973] 1 W.L.R. 700 ...... 135, 150
Burns v. Edman [1970] 2 Q.B. 541 298
Burrows v. Rhodes [1899] 1 Q.B. 816 275
Butterfield v. Forrester (1809) 11 East 60 124
Bux v. Slough Metals [1973] 1 W.L.R. 1358 212
Byrne v. Boadle (1863) 2 H. & C. 722 138
—— v. Deane [1937] 1 K.B. 818 ...... 235, 240

Calliope, The [1970] P. 172 117
Cambridge University Press v. University Tutorial Press [1928] 45 R.P.C. 335 ...... 274, 279
Caminer v. Northern and London Investment Trust [1951] A.C. 88 ... 97, 187
Campbell v. Paddington Borough Council [1911] 1 K.B. 869 321
—— v. Spottiswoode (1863) 3 B. & S. 769 246
—— v. Thompson [1953] 1 Q.B. 445 322
Candler v. Crane, Christmas & Co. [1951] 2 K.B. 164 ...... 72, 74, 77
Capital and Counties Bank v. Henty (1882) 7 App. Cas. 741 237
Carberry v. Davies [1968] 1 W.L.R. 1103 230
Carr v. Clarke (1818) 2 Chit. 260 284
Carslogie Steamship Co. v. Royal Norwegian Government [1952] A.C. 292 102
Cartledge v. Jopling (E.) & Sons [1963] A.C. 758 318
Cassell & Co. Ltd. v. Broome, *The Times*, February 24, 1972 ...... 253, 306
Cassidy v. Daily Mirror [1929] 2 K.B. 331 ...... 239, 241
—— v. Ministry of Health [1951] 2 K.B. 343 ...... 138, 223
Castle v. St. Augustine's Links (1922) 38 T.L.R. 615 178
Cattle v. Stockton Water Works Co. (1875) L.R. 10 Q.B. 453 ...... 83, 195
Cavanagh v. London Transport Executive, *The Times*. October 23, 1956 ... 127
—— v. Ulster Weaving Co. [1960] A.C. 145 99
Central Asbestos v. Dodd [1973] A.C. 518 319
Central Newbury Car Auctions v. Unity Finance [1957] 1 Q.B. 371 ... 61
Century Insurance Co. v. Northern Ireland Road Transport Board [1942] A.c. 509 224
Chadwick v. British Transport Commission [1967] 2 All E.R. 945 86
Chapman v. Honig [1963] 2 Q.B. 502 266
Chaproniere v. Mason (1905) 21 T.L.R. 633 138
Charing Cross Electricity Supply Co. V. Hydraulic Power Co. [1914] 3 K.B. 772 ...... 192, 196
Cheater v. Cater [1918] 1 K.B. 247 157

CHIC FASHION (WEST WALES) LTD. v. Jones [1968] 2 Q.B. 299 .... 47, 60
CHILDS v. Lewis (1924) 40 T.L.R. 870 18
CHRISTIE v. Davey [1893] 1 Ch. 316 173
—— v. Leachinsky [1947] A.C. 573 59
CHRISTOPHERSON v. Bare (1848) 11 Q.B. 473 12
CHURCH OF SCIENTOLOGY OF CALIFORNIA v. Johnson-Smith [1972] 1 Q.B. 522 248
CITY OF LONDON CORPORATION v. Appleyard [1963] 1 W.L.R. 982 28
CLARKE v. Brims (1947) C.L.C. 6814 213
—— v. Kirby-Smith [1964] Ch. 506 .... 3, 74
CLAY v. Crump (A. J.) & Sons [1964] 1 Q.B. 533 80
CLAYARDS v. Dethic and Davis (1848) 12 Q.B. 439 134
CLAYTON v. Le Roy [1911] 2 K.B. 1031 36
CLOSE v. Steel Co. of Wales [1962] A.C. 367 216
COATES v. Rawtenstall Borough Council [1937] 3 All E.R. 602 148
COLLINGWOOD v. Home and Colonial Stores [1936] 3 All E.R. 200 193
COLLINS v. Renison (1754) 1 Sayer 138 54
—— v. Hertfordshire County Council [1947] K.B. 598 223
COMMISSIONER FOR RAILWAYS v. Quinlan [1964] A.C. 1054 154
CONSTANTINE v. Imperial Hotels Ltd. [1944] K.B. 693 293
COOK v. Lewis [1952] 1 D.L.R. 1 .... 102, 103, 141
CONWAY v. Wimpey [1951] 2 K.B. 266 .... 222, 224
COOKE v. Midland Great Western Ry. of Ireland [1909] A.C. 229 153
COOKSON v. Harewood [1932] 2 K.B. 478 252
COOPER v. Railway Executive [1953] 1 W.L.R. 223 208
COPE v. Sharpe (No. 2) [1912] 1 K.B. 496 .... 56, 57
COVENTRY CITY COUNCIL v. Cartwright [1975] 1 W.L.R. 845 189
CRANLEIGH PRECISION ENGINEERING v. Bryant [1965] 1 W.L.R. 1293 294
CRESSWELL v. Sirl [1948] 1 K.B. 241 54
CROFT v. Day (1843) 7 Beav. 84 272
CROFTER HAND WOVEN HARRIS TWEED CO. v. Veitch [1942] A.C. 435 .... 262, 263
CROWHURST v. Amersham Burial Board (1878) 4 Ex.D. 5 193
CUMMINGS v. Grainger [1975] 1 W.L.R. 1330 .... 205, 207
CUNARD v. Antifyre [1953] 1 K.B. 551 157
CUNNINGHAM v. Harrison [1973] Q.B. 942 309
CUSHING v. Walker & Son Ltd. [1941] 2 All E.R. 693 187
CUTLER v. United Dairies Ltd. [1933] 2 K.B. 297 113
—— v. Vauxhall Motors [1971] 1 Q.B. 418 101
—— v. Wandsworth Stadium [1949] A.C. 398 213
CUTTS v. Chumley [1967] 1 W.L.R. 742 286

DABORN v. Bath Tramways Motor Co. [1946] 2 All E.R. 333 93
DAILY MIRROR v. Gardner [1968] 2 Q.B. 768 267
DAISH v. Wauton [1972] 2 Q.B. 262 309
DALLISON v. Caffery [1965] 1 Q.B. 348 59
DALY v. Liverpool Corporation (1939) 160 L.T. 128 96
DANIEL v. Ferguson [1891] 2 Ch. 27 314
DANIELS & DANIELS v. White & Sons Ltd. [1938] 4 All E.R. 258 162
DANN v. Hamilton [1939] 1 K.B. 509 133
DAVEY v. Harrow Corporation [1958] 1 Q.B. 60 .... 180, 183, 192
DAVID v. Abdul Cader [1963] 1 W.L.R. 834 294

DAVIE *v.* New Merton Board Mills [1959] A.C. 604 .... 164, 166
DAVIES *v.* Davies [1975] Q.B. 172 211
—— *v.* Mann (1842) 10 M. & W. 546 124
—— *v.* Swan Motor Co. Ltd. [1949] 2 K.B. 291 .... 125, 126
—— *v.* Whiteways Cyder Co. [1975] Q.B. 262 299
DAWRANT *v.* Nutt [1961] 1 W.L.R. 253 133
DE BEERS ABRASIVE PRODUCTS *v.* International General Electric [1975] 1 W.L.R. 972 279
DE FREVILLE *v.* Dill [1927] W.N. 133 16
DEEN *v.* Davies [1935] 2 K.B. 282 211
DELANEY *v.* Smith (T. P.) & Co. [1946] 1 K.B. 393 43
DENNY *v.* Supplies & Transport Co. [1950] 2 K.B. 374 161
DEYONG *v.* Sherburn [1946] K.B. 227 144
DILLWYN *v.* Llewellyn (1862) 4 De G.F. & J. 517 44
DIMOND MANUFACTURING CO. *v.* Hamilton [1969] N.Z.L.R. 609 .... 76, 77
DONAGHEY *v.* Boulton & Paul [1968] A.C. 1 216
DONALD *v.* Suckling (1886) L.R. 1 Q.B. 585 36
DONALDSON *v.* McNiven [1952] 2 All E.R. 691 .... 159, 325
DONNELLY *v.* Joyce [1974] Q.B. 454 .... 310, 312
DONOGHUE *v.* Stevenson [1932] A.C. 562 .... 4, 66, 158, 159
DOOLEY *v.* Cammell Laird & Co. and Mersey Insulation Co. [1951] 1 Lloyd's Rep. 271 86
DORSET YACHT CO. *v.* Home Office. *See* Home Office *v.* Dorset Yacht Co.
DOUGHTY *v.* Turner Manufacturing Co. [1964] 1 Q.B. 518 .... 105, 108
DOUGLAS VALLEY FINANCE CO. *v.* Hughes (Hirers) [1969] 1 Q.B. 738 32
DOYLE *v.* Olby (Ironmongers) [1969] 2 Q.B. 158 277
DULIEU *v.* White and Sons [1901] 2 K.B. 669 85
DUNNE *v.* North Western Gas Board [1964] 2 Q.B. 806 .... 192, 196
DUNWICH CORPORATION *v.* Sterry (1831) 1 B. & Ad. 831 23
DUTTON *v.* Bognor Regis U.D.C. [1972] 1 Q.B. 373 .... 80, 81, 82, 83, 84, 115, 155, 282, 318
DYMOND *v.* Pearce [1972] 1 Q.B. 496 .... 186, 187

EASSON *v.* L. & N.E. Ry. Co. [1944] K.B. 421 138
EAST SUFFOLK RIVERS CATCHMENT BOARD *v.* Kent [1941] A.C. 74 ... 82, 115
EAST AND SOUTH AFRICAN TELEGRAPH CO. [1902] A.C. 381 195
EAVES *v.* Morris Motors [1961] 2 Q.B. 385 214
EDGINGTON *v.* Fitzmaurice (1885) 29 Ch.D. 459 276
EDWARDS*v.* Railway Executive [1952] A.C. 737 153
EGGER *v.* Chelmsford (Viscount) [1965] 1 Q.B. 248 252
EGLANTINE INN *v.* Smith [1948] N.I. 29 240
ELECTROCHROME *v.* Welsh Plastics [1968] 2 All E.R. 205 .... 83, 84
ELIAS *v.* Pasmore [1934] 2 K.B. 164 47
ELLIS *v.* Home Office [1953] 2 Q.B. 135 67
ELVIN & POWELL LTD. *v.* Plummer Roddis Ltd. (1933) 50 T.L.R. 158.................... 34
ELWES *v.* Brigg Gas Co. (1886) 33 Ch.D. 562 28
EMANUEL (H. & N.) *v.* G.L.C. [1971] 2 All E.R. 835 201
EMERALD CONSTRUCTION CO. *v.* Lowthian [1966] 1 W.L.R. 691 260
ENGLAND *v.* Cowley (1873) L.R. 8 E. 126 .... 33, 35, 42
ERRINGTON *v.* Errington and Woods [1952] 1 K.B. 290 44
ESSO PETROLEUM CO. *v.* Mardon [1975] Q.B. 819 .... 73, 79

—— *v.* —— [1976] 2 All E.R. 5 *v.* Southport Corporation [1956] A.C. 218; reversing [1954] 2 Q.B. 182; restoring [1953] 3 W.L.R. 773 .... 45, 179

FAGAN *v.* Metropolitan Police Commissioner [1969] 1 Q.B. 439 12
FARR *v.* Butters Bros. & Co. [1932] 2 K.B. 606 161
FAY *v.* Beale (1701) 1 Ld. Raym. 339 311
FIELDING *v.* Variety Incorporated [1967] 2 Q.B. 841 281
FILLITER *v.* Phippard (1847) 11 Q.B. 347 200
FISH *v.* Kapur (1948) 64 T.L.R. 328 3
FITZGERALD *v.* Cooke Bourne (Farms) [1964] 1 Q.B. 249 203
FLEMINGTON *v.* Smithers (1826) 2 C. & P. 292 285
FLETCHER *v.* Autocar and Transporters [1968] 2 Q.B. 322 310
FLYING FISH, H.M.S. (1865) 34 L.J.P.M. & A. 113 311
FORRESTER *v.* Tyrell (1893) 57 J.P. 532 233
FORSDICK *v.* Collins (1816) 1 Stark. 173 .... 31, 36
FOULDES *v.* Willoughby (1841) 8 M. & W. 540 31
FOWLER *v.* Lanning [1959] 1 Q.B. 426 .... 9, 24, 53
FOWLEY MARINE (EMSWORTH) *v.* Gafford [1968] 2 Q.B. 618 44
FOXCROFT *v.* Lacy (1613) Hop. 89 238
FOXLEY *v.* Olton [1965] 2 Q.B. 306 309
FRANCE *v.* Parkinson [1954] 1 W.L.R. 581 139
FRANKLIN *v.* S.E. Ry. (1858) 3 H. & N. 211 299
FRASER *v.* Evans [1969] 1 Q.B. 349 295
FRENCH *v.* Auckland City Corporation [1974] 1 N.Z.L.R. 340 181
FROOM *v.* Butcher [1975] 3 W.L.R. 379 .... 129, 130

G.W.K. CO. LTD. *v.* Dunlop Rubber Co. Ltd. (1926) 42 T.L.R. 376 ... 259, 260
GALASHIELS GAS CO. *v.* O'Donnell (or Millar) [1949] A.C. 275 214
GAUTRET *v.* Egerton (1867) L.R. 2 C.P. 371 158
GAYNOR *v.* Allen [1959] 2 Q.B. 403 94
GEE *v.* Metropolitan Ry. (1873) L.R. 8 Q.B. 161 138
—— *v.* Pritchard (1818) 2 Swan. 402 294
GENERAL CLEANING CONTRACTORS *v.* Christmas [1953] A.C. 180 165
GHANI *v.* Jones [1970] 1 Q.B. 693 60
GILES *v.* Walker (1890) 24 Q.B.D. 656 .... 180, 181, 192
GINTY *v.* Belmont Building Supplies [1959] 1 All E.R. 414 218
GLASGOW CORPORATION *v.* Taylor [1922] 1 A.C. 44 146
GLENWOOD LUMBER CO. *v.* Phillips [1904] A.C. 405 41
GLINSKI *v.* McIver [1962] A.C. 726 291
GOLD *v.* Essex County Council [1942] 2 K.B. 293 223
GOLDMAN *v.* Hargrave [1967] 1 A.C. 645 .... 81, 94, 180, 181, 192
GOMBERG *v.* Smith [1963] 1 Q.B. 25 211
GORDON *v.* Harper (1796) 7 T.R. 9 22
GORLEY *v.* Codd [1967] 1 W.L.R. 19 .... 96, 324
GORRIS *v.* Scott (1874) L.R. 9 Ex. 125 215
GOUGH *v.* National Coal Board [1954] 1 Q.B. 191 147
—— *v.* Thorne [1966] 1 W.L.R. 1387 96
GRAHAM *v.* Peat (1861) 1 East 244 43
GRANT *v.* Australian Knitting Mills [1936] A.C. 85 .... 138, 161, 162, 223
GREAT LAKES S.S. CÆ. *v.* Maple Leaf Milling Co. Ltd. (1924) 41 T.L.R. 21 110
GREEN *v.* Chelsea Waterworks Co. (1894) 70 L.T. 547 196

GREENHALGH v. British Railways Board [1969] 2 Q.B. 286 144
GREENOCK CORPORATION v. Caledonian Railway Co. [1917] A.C. 556 195
GRIFFITHS v. Liverpool Corporation [1967] 1 Q.B. 374 188
GRINHAM v. Willey (1859) 4 H. & N. 496 289
GUAY v. Sun Publishing Co. [1953] 4 D.L.R. 577 88

HALE v. Hants and Dorset Motor Services [1947] 2 All E.R. 628 115
—— v. Jennings Brothers [1938] 1 All E.R. 579 .... 193, 194, 196
HALEY v. London Electricity Board [1965] A.C. 778 92
HALL v. Hollander (1825) 4 B. & C. 660 284
HALSEY v. Esso Petroleum Co. [1961] 1 W.L.R. 683 ... 174, 176, 177, 188, 193
HAMBROOK v. Stoke Bros. [1925] 1 K.B. 141 .... 86, 87
HAMMACK v. White (1862) 11 C.B. (N.S.) 588 137
HANNAH v. Peel [1945] K.B. 509 .... 28, 29
HARGREAVES v. Bretherton [1959] 1 Q.B. 45 .... 266, 292
HARNETT v. Bond [1925] A.C. 669 17
HARPER v. National Coal Board [1974] Q.B. 614 319
HARRIS v. James (1876) 45 L.J.Q.B. 545 179
HARRISON v. National Coal Board [1951] A.C. 639 213
—— v. Rutland (Duke) [1893] 1 Q.B. 142 45
HARTLEY v. Mayoh & Co. [1954] 1 Q.B. 383 214
HARTWELL v. Grayson, Rollo and Clover Docks [1947] K.B. 901 145
HARVEY v. O'Dell [1958] 2 Q.B. 78 .... 122, 123
HASELDINE v. Daw & Son [1941] 2 K.B. 343 151
HAY v. Hughes [1975] Q.B. 790 .... 300, 302
HAYNES v. Harwood [1935] 1 K.B. 146 .... 113, 114
HEATLEY v. Steel Co. of Wales [1953] 1 W.L.R. 405 300
HEDLEY BYRNE & Co. v. Heller & Partners [1964] A.C. 465 ....
72, 73, 74, 75, 76, 77, 78, 79, 80, 81, 82, 84, 256, 275
HEGARTY v. Shine (1878) 14 Cox C.C. 124 52
HELLAR v. Bianco (Cal. 1952) 244 P. 20 757 241
HEMMINGS v. Stoke Poges Golf Club [1920] 1 K.B. 720 64
HENDERSON v. Jenkins (H. E.) & Sons and Evans [1970] A.C. 282 ..... 137, 139
HENLEY v. Cameron [1948] W.N. 468 126
HERBERT v. Harold Shaw [1959] 2 Q.B. 138 214
HERD v. Weardale Steel, Coal and Coke Co. [1915] A.C. 67 .... 17, 19
HEYWOOD v. Wellers [1976] Q.B. 446 75
HICKMAN v. Maisey [1900] 1 Q.B. 752 295
HIGGINS v. Arfon B.C. [1975] 1 W.L.R. 524 318
HINZ v. Berry [1970] 2 Q.B. 40 85
HIORT v. Bott (1874) L.R. 9 Ex. 86 34
HOARE & Co. v. McAlpine [1923] 1 Ch. 167 .... 195, 198
HODGE & SONS v. Anglo-American Oil Co. (1922) 12 Ll. L. Rep. 183 159
HOLDMAN v. Hamlyn [1943] K.B. 664 147
HOLLIDAY v. National Telephone Co. [1899] 2 Q.B. 392 .... 228, 229
HOLLINS v. Fowler (1875) L.R. 7 H.L. 757 31
HOLLOYWOOD SILVER FOX FARM v. Emmett [1936] 2 K.B. 468 173
HOME FFFICE v. Dorset Yacht Co. [1970] A.C. 1004 67
HONEYWILL & STEIN v. Larkin Bros. [1934] 1 K.B. 191 227
HOPKINS v. Crowe (1836) 4 A. & E. 774 289
HORROCKS v. Lowe [1975] A.C. 135 251
HOUGH v. London Express Newspaper [1940] 2 K.B. 507 240
HOUGHLAND v. Low (R. R.) (Luxury Coaches) Ltd. [1962] 1 Q.B. 694 39

HUBBARD v. Pitt [1975] 2 W.L.R. 254 .... 170, 270
HUDSON v. Ridge Manufacturing Co. [1957] 2 Q.B. 348 164
HUGHES v. Lord Advocate [1963] A.C. 837 ... 107, 108, 109, 110, 118, 216
HULTON v. Jones [1910] A.C. 20 .... 238, 241
HUNT v. Great Northern Railway [1891] 2 Q.B. 189 249
HUNTLEY v. Thornton [1957] 1 W.L.R. 321 .... 269, 270
HYETT v. Great Western Ry. Co. [1948] 1 K.B. 345 114
I.C.I. v. Shatwell [1965] A.C. 656 .... 132, 133, 217
ILOTT v. Wilkes (1820) 3 B. & Ald. 304 55
INGRAM v. Little [1961] 1 Q.B. 31 61
INITIAL SERVICES v. Putterill [1968] 1 Q.B. 396 295
I.R.C. v. Hambrook [1956] 2 Q.B. 641 287
IQBAL v. London Transport Executive 225

KELLY v. W.R.N. Contracting [1968] 1 W.L.R. 921 213
KELSEN v. Imperial Tobacco Co. (of Great Britain and Ireland) [1957] 2 Q.B. 334 46
KEMSLEY v. Foot [1952] A.C. 345 244

KEARNEY v. Eric Waller [1967] 1 Q.B. 29 214

KEPPEL BUS CO. v. Sa'ad Bin Ahmad [1974] 1 W.L.R. 1082 225
KERR v. Kennedy [1952] 1 K.B. 409 234
KIDDLE v. City Business Properties [1942] 1 K.B. 269 .... 178, 183
KING v. Phillips [1953] 1 Q.B. 429 .... 87, 107
KIRK v. Gregory (1876) 1 Ex. D. 55 23
KIRKHAM v. Boughey [1958] 2 Q.B. 338 287
KUBACH v. Hollands (1937) T.L.R. 1024 161

LAGAN NAVIGATION CO. v. Lamberg Bleaching, Dyeing and Finishing Co. Ltd. [1927] A.C. 226 65
LAMPERT v. Eastern National Omnibus Co. [1945] 1 W.L.R. 1047 .... 130, 306
LANCASHIRE WAGGON CO. v. Fitzhugh (1861) 6 H. & N. 502 32
LANE v. Holloway [1968] 1 Q.B. 379 61
LANGRIDGE v. Levy (1837) 2 M. & W. 519 276
LASZCZYK v. National Coal Board [1954] 1 W.L.R. 1426 .... 127, 128
LATHAM v. Johnson and Nephew [1913] 1 K.B. 398 147
LATIMER v. A.E.C. [1953] A.C. 643 94
LATTER v. Braddel (1881) 50 L.J.Q.B. 448 12
LAUNCHBURY v. Morgans [1971] 2 Q.B. 245 229
LAURIE v. Raglan Building Co. [1942] 1 K.B. 152 138
LAWRENCE v. Biddle [1966] 2 Q.B. 504 286
LE FANU v. Malcolmson (1848) 1 H.L.C. 637 238
LEAKE v. Loveday (1812) 4 M. & G. 972 30
LEE v. Luper (1936) 81 S.J. 15 153
—— v. Showmen's Guild of Great Britain [1952] 2 Q.B. 329 294
LEE COOPER v. Jeakins (C. H.) & Sons [1967] 2 Q.B. 1 .... 38, 42
LEEDS INDUSTRIAL CO-OPERATIVE SOCIETY LTD. v. Slack [1924] A.C. 851 .... 185, 314
LEIGH v. Gladstone (1909) 26 T.L.R. 139 56
LEMMON v. Webb [1894] 3 Ch. 1 .... 45, 64, 177
LENNARD'S CARRYING CO. v. Asiatic Petroleum Co. [1915] A.C. 705 321

LETANG v. Cooper [1965] 1 Q.B. 232 .... 9, 11, 13, 15, 24, 317
LEVESLEY v. Thomas Firth [1953] 1 W.L.R. 1206 214
LEWIS v. Daily Telegraph [1964] 2 Q.B. 601 237
LEWIS (JOHN) & Co. v. Tims [1952] A.C. 676 59
LICHFIELD CORPORATION v. Simpson (1845) 8 Q.B. 65 219
LIESBOSCH DREDGER v. Edison [1933] A.C. 449 .... 111, 277
LIMPUS v. London General Omnibus Co. (1862) 1 H. & C. 526 224
LISTER v. Romford Ice and Cold Storage Co. [1957] A.C. 555 123
LLOYD v. Grace, Smith & Co. [1912] A.C. 176 226
LLOYDE v. West Midlands Gas Board [1971] 1 W.L.R. 749 139
LONDON ARTISTS v. Littler [1969] 2 Q.B. 375 246
LONG v. Hepworth [1968] 1 W.L.R. 1299 317
LORD v. Price (1874) L.R. 9 Ex. 54 27
LOTAN v. Cross (1810) 2 Camp. 464 22
LOUDON v. Ryder [1953] 2 Q.B. 202 .... 15, 305
LUMLEY v. Gye (1853) 2 E. & B. 216 ...... 256, 257, 258, 259, 260, 261, 262
LUMSDEN v. London Trustee Savings Bank [1971] 1 Lloyd's Rep. 114 61
LYNCH v. Knight (1861) 9 H.L. Cas. 577 234
LYNE v. Nicholls (1906) 23 T.L.R. 86 279
LYONS v. Wilkins [1899] 1 Ch. 255 .... 170, 295

MCCULLOCH v. May (Lewis A.) (Produce Distributors) [1947] 2 All E.R. 845 273
MCGHEE v. National Coal Board [1973] 1 W.L.R. 103, 141
MCKEW v. Holland & Hannen & Cubitts [1969] 3 All E.R. 1621 ..... 116, 117
MCKINNON INDUSTRIES LTD. v. Walker [1951] W.N. 401 176
MCLAREN v. Bradstreet (1969) 113 S.J. 471 110
MCNEILL v. Johnstone [1958] 1 W.L.R. 888 287
M'PHERSON v. Daniels (1829) 10 B. & C. 263 237
MCQUAKER v. Goddard [1940] 1 K.B. 687 .... 203, 204
MCWILLIAMS v. Arrol & Co. [1962] 1 W.L.R. 295 217
MAFO v. Adams [1970] 1 Q.B. 548 277
MALLETT v. Dunn [1949] 2 K.B. 180 285
MALZ v. Rosen [1966] 1 W.L.R. 1008 291
MARCROFT WAGONS LTD. v. Smith [1951] 2 K.B. 496 44
MARKET INVESTIGATIONS v. Minister of Social Security [1969] 2 Q.B. 173 ... 221
MASON v. Clarke [1955] A.C. 778 50
—— v. Levy Auto Parts of England [1967] 2 Q.B. 530 200
MATANIA v. National Provincial Bank Ltd. [1936] 106 L.K.J.B. 136 228
MEAD v. Clarke, Chapman & Co. [1956] 1 W.L.R. 76 302
MEAD'S CASE (1823) 1 Lew. C.C. 184 13
MEARS v. L. and S.W. Ry. (1862) 11 C.B. (N.S.) 850 42
MEERING v. Graham-White Aviation Co. (1919) 122 L.T. 44 18
MERCER v. S.E. Ry. Co. [1922] 2 K.B. 549 81
MERRYWEATHER v. Nixan (1799) 8 T.R. 186 121
MERSEY DOCKS AND HARBOUR BOARD v. Coggins and Griffith (Liverpool) [1947] A.C. 1 222
METROPOLITAN POLICE DISTRICT RECEIVER v. Croydon Corporation [1957] 2 Q.B. 154 309
MIDWOOD v. Manchester Corporation [1905] 2 K.B. 597 178
MILLARD v. Serck Tubes [1969] 1 W.L.R. 211 216
MINISTRY OF HOUSING AND LOCAL GOVERNMENT v. Sharp [1970] 2 Q.B. 223 .... 77, 281, 282

MINT *v.* Good [1951] 1 K.B. 517 182
MITCHELL *v.* Mulholland (No. 2) [1972] 1 Q.B. 65 308
MOGUL S.S. Co. *v.* McGregor Gow & Co. (1889) 23 Q.B.D. 598 .... 255, 267
MOHAMMED ANIM *v.* Bannerjee [1947] A.C. 322 290
MONK *v.* Warbey [1935] 1 K.B. 75 213
MOORE *v.* Fox & Sons [1956] 1 Q.B. 596 36
MORGAN *v.* Fry [1968] 1 Q.B. 710 268
—— *v.* Odhams Press [1971] 1 W.L.R. 1239 .... 231, 239, 241
MORREN *v.* Swinton and Pendlebury B.C. [1965] 1 W.L.R. 576 221
MORRIS *v.* Martin (C. W.) & Sons [1966] 1 Q.B. 716 .... 223, 226
MORRISON STEAMSHIP CO. LTD. *v.* Greystoke Castle [1947] A.C. 265 84
MORRIS *v.* Marsden [1952] 1 All E.R. 925 324
MUNRO *v.* Southern Dairies [1956] V.L.R. 332 174
—— *v.* Willmott [1949] 1 K.B. 295 41
MURRAY *v.* Harringay Arena [1951] 2 K.B. 529 132
MUSGROVE *v.* Pandelis [1919] 2 K.B. 43 .... 193, 200
MUTUAL LIFE AND CITIZENS' ASSURANCE CO. *v.* Evatt [1971] A.C. 793 .... 73, 74, 75

NAGLE *v.* Feilden [1966] 2 Q.B. 633 294
NASH *v.* Sheen, *The Times*, March 13, 1953 .... 11, 52
NATIONAL COAL BOARD *v.* England [1954] A.C. 403 .... 62, 63
—— *v.* Evans & Co. [1951] 2 K.B. 861 .... 9, 24
NATIONAL MERCANTILE BANK *v.* Rymill (1881) 44 L.T. 767 32
NETTLESHIP *v.* Weston [1971] 2 Q.B. 691 .... 97, 134
NEWCASTLE-UNDER-LYME CORPORATION *v.* Wolstanton [1947] Ch. 427 179
NEWSTEAD *v.* London Express Newspaper Ltd. [1940] 1 K.B. 377 .... 238, 241
NEWTON *v.* Edgerly [1959] 1 W.L.R. 1031 .... 159, 325
NICHOLS *v.* Marsland (1876) 2 Ex.D. 1 195
NIELD *v.* L. & N.W. Ry. (1874) L.R. 10 Ex. 4 56
NOBLE *v.* Harrison [1926] 2 K.B. 332 .... 180, 187, 193
NORTH GENERAL WAGON AND FINANCE CO. *v.* Graham [1950] 2 K.B. 7 27
NORTHWESTERN UTILITIES *v.* London Guarantee and Accident Co. [1936] A.C. 108 196

OAKLEY *v.* Lyster [1931] 1 K.B. 148 .... 34, 35
O'CONNELL *v.* Jackson [1972] 1 Q.B. 270 .... 129, 130
O'CONNOR *v.* British Transport Commission [1958] 1 W.L.R. 346 148
OGOPOGO, THE [1971] 2 Lloyd's Rep. 410 115
OLIVER *v.* Ashman [1962] 2 Q.B. 210 .... 308, 312
ORMROD *v.* Crossville Motor Services [1953] 1 W.L.R. 1120 .... 229, 230
OROPESA, THE [1943] P. 32 112
OSBORN *v.* Boulter & Son [1930] 2 K.B. 226 .... 233, 251
OTTO *v.* Bolton and Norris [1936] 2 K.B. 46 155
OWENS *v.* Liverpool Corporation [1939] 1 K.B. 394 87
OXLEY *v.* Watts (1785) 1 T.R. 12 47

PADBURY *v.* Holliday and Greenwood Ltd. (1912) 28 T.L.R. 492 229
PANNETT *v.* McGuinness & Co. [1972] 2 Q.B. 599 155
PARIS *v.* Stepney Borough Council [1951] A.C. 367 93
PARKER *v.* Miller (1926) 42 T.L.R. 408 230
PARKER-KNOLL *v.* Knoll International [1962] R.P.C. 243 272
PARRY *v.* Cleaver [1970] A.C. 1 309

PAYNE v. Rogers (1794) 2 H.B. 350 182
PEARSON v. North Western Gas Board [1968] 2 All E.R. 669 197
PEEK v. Gurney (1873) L.R. 6 H.L. 377 276
PENDER v. Lushington (1877) 6 Ch.D. 70 218
PENFOLD'S WINES PTY. LTD. v. Elliott (1946) 74 C.L.R. 204 .... 22, 36
PERERA v. Vandiyar [1953] 1 W.L.R. 672 45
PERRY v. Fitzhowe (1846) 8 Q.B. 757 64
—— v. Kendricks Transport [1956] 1 W.L.R. 85 196
—— v. Wrigley (Thomas) [1955] 1 W.L.R. 1164 147
PETERS v. Prince of Wales Theatre [1943] K.B. 73 197
PETRE (LORD) v. Heneage (1701) 12 Mod. 519 36
PHILCO RADIO AND TELEVISION CORPORATION OF GREAT BRITAIN v. Spurling [1949] 2 K.B. 33 113
PHILIPS v. Whiteley [1938] 1 All E.R. 566 97
PHILLIPS v. Britannia Hygienic Laundry Co. [1923] 2 K.B. 832 213
PHIPPS v. Rochester Corporation [1955] 1 Q.B. 450 .... 147, 148
PIGNEY v. Pointers Transport Services [1957] 1 W.L.R. 1121 .... 116, 298
PLATO FILMS v. Speidel [1961] A.C. 1090 .... 253, 254
POLAND v. Parr (John) & Sons [1927] 1 K.B. 236 225
PONTARDAWE R. D. C. v. Moore-Gwyn [1929] 1 Ch. 656 .... 180, 181, 192
POLEMIS & FURNESS WITHY & Co., *Re* [1921] 3 K.B. 560 .... 88, 100, 104, 105, 109, 110, 118
POULTON v. L. & S.W. Ry. (1867) L.R. 2 Q.B. 534 312
POWELL v. Birmingham Vinegar Brewery Co. (1896) 14 R.P.C. 1 271
PULLMAN v. Hill and Co. [1891] 1 Q.B. 524 240
PURSELL v. Horn (1838) 8 A. & E. 602 12

QUINN v. Leathem [1901] A.C. 495 263

R. v. Blave [1975] 1 W.L.R. 1411 117
—— v. Dudley and Stevens (1884) 14 Q.B.D. 273 56
—— v. Inwood [1973] 1 W.L.R. 647 59
—— v. Kulynycz [1971] 1 Q.B. 367 59
—— v. Latimer (1886) 17 Q.B.D. 359 13
—— v. St. George (1840) 9 C. & P. 483 14
RAINHAM CHEMICAL WORKS v. Belvedere Fish Guano Co. [1921] 2 A.C. 465 192
RAND v. Craig [1919] 1 Ch. 1 224
RANDALL v. Tarrant [1955] 1 W.L.R. 255 45
RANDS v. McNeil [1955] 1 Q.B. 253 .... 204, 207
RAPIER v. London Tramways Co. [1893] 2 Ch. 588 178
RATCLIFFE v. Evans [1892] 2 Q.B. 524 .... 236, 278, 280
READ v. Coker (1853) 13 C.B. 850 13
—— v. Croydon Corporation (1938) 108 L.K.J.B. 72 213
—— v. Lyons (J.) & Co. [1947] A.C. 156 .... 6, 168, 170, 191, 193, 194
READY-MIXED CONCRETE Co. v. Ministry of Pensions & National Insurance [1968] 2 Q.B. 497 221
REDDAWAY v. Banham (George) & Co. Ltd. [1896] A.C. 199 272
REFFELL v. Surrey County Council [1964] 1 W.L.R. 358 213
RICKARDS v. Lothian [1913] A.C. 263 .... 193, 196
ROACH v. Yates [1938] 1 K.B. 256 310
ROBINSON v. Balmain New Ferry Co. [1910] A.C. 295 19
—— v. Kilvert (1889) 41 Ch.D. 88 176

Robinson v. Post Office [1974] 1 W.L.R. 1176 109
Robson v. National Coal Board [1968] 3 All E.R. 159 214
Rodriguez v. Parker [1967] 1 Q.B. 116 317
Roe v. Minister of Health [1954] 2 Q.B. 71 223
Roles v. Nathan [1963] 1 W.L.R. 1117 .... 148, 149
Rondel v. Worsley [1969] 1 A.C. 191 75
Rookes v. Barnard [1964] A.C. 1129 ... 253, 262, 264, 65, 66, 267, 277, 06
Rose v. Matt [1951] 1 K.B. 810 .... 22, 25, 26
—— v. Plenty [1976] 1 All E.R. 97 224
Ross v. Associated Portland Cement Manufacturers [1964] 1 W.L.R. 768... 217
—— v. Fedden (1872) L.R. 7 Q.B. 661 197
Rouse v. Gravelworks Ltd. [1940] 1 K.B. 489 193
Roy v. Prior [1970] 1 Q.B. 283 292
Ruddiman & Co. v. Smith (1889) 60 L.T. 708 226
Rushton v. Turner Bros. Asbestos Co. [1960] 1 W.L.R. 96 126
Ryan v. Youngs [1938] 1 All E.R. 522 96
Rylands v. Fletcher (1868) L.R. 3 H.L. 330 ...... 1, 5, 6, 60, 168, 170, 171
190, 191, 192, 193, 194, 195, 196, 197, 198, 199, 200, 227

Sachs v. Miklos [1948] 2 K.B. 23 39
St. Anne's Well Brewery Co. v. Roberts (1928) 140 L.T. 1 181
St. Helens Smelting Co. v. Tipping (1865) 11 H.L. Cas. 642 175
Sales Affiliates Ltd. v. Le Jean Ltd. [1947] Ch. 295 .... 273, 274
Salford City Council v. McNally [1975] 3 W.L.R. 87 189
Salsbury v. Woodland [1970] 1 Q.B. 324 228
Savile v. Roberts (1698) 1 Ld. Raym. 374 291
Sayers v. Harlow U.D.C. [1958] 1 W.L.R. 623 .... 15, 17, 129
Scala Ballroom (Wolverhampton) v. Ratcliffe [1958] 1 W.L.R. 1057 ... 263
Schneider v. Eisovitch [1960] 2 Q.B. 430 88
—— v. Heath (1813) 3 Camp. 506 276
S.C.M. v. Whittall [1971] 1 Q.B. 337 84
Scott v. Shepherd (1773) 2 W.Bl. 892 .... 8, 56, 112
Seager v. Copydex [1967] 1 W.L.R. 923 295
—— v. —— (No. 2) [1969] 1 W.L.R. 809 295
Searle v. Wallbank [1947] A.C. 341 211
Sedleigh-Denfield v. O'Callaghan [1940] A.C. 880 .... 178, 181
Seligman v. Docker [1949] Ch. 53 180
Sharp v. Avery and Kerwood [1938] 4 All E.R. 85 .... 80, 83
Sheridan v. New Quay Co. (1858) 4 C.B. (n.s.) 618 32
Shiffman v. Order of St. John [1936] 1 All E.R. 557 .... 112, 193, 194
Sim v. Heinz (H. J.) Co. Ltd. [1959] 1 W.L.R. 313 273
Simms v. Leigh Rugby Football Club [1969] 2 All E.R. 923 133
Singleton Abbey. S.S. v. S.S. Paludina [1927] A.C. 16 .... 117, 118
Siveyer v. Allison [1935] 2 K.B. 403 62
Slater v. Clay Cross Co. [1956] 2 Q.B. 264 144
Slim v. Daily Telegraph [1968] 2 Q.B. 157 246
Smeaton v. Ilford Corporation [1954] Ch. 450 .... 192, 193
Smith v. Baker & Sons [1891] A.C. 325 .... 131, 134
—— v. Central Asbestos Co. [1972] 1 Q.B. 244 310
—— v. Chadwick (1844) 20 Ch.D. 27 276
—— v. Johnson & Co. (1897) unreported 86
—— v. Kenrick (1849) 7 C.B. 515 180
—— v. Leech Brain & Co. [1962] 2 Q.B. 405 109

—— *v.* Moss [1940] 1 K.B. 424 222
—— *v.* Scott [1973] Ch. 314 180
—— *v.* Stone (1647) Style 65 46
—— *v.* Supreme Wood Pulp Co. [1968] 3 All E.R. 753 215
SOCHACKI *v.* Sas [1947] 1 All E.R. 344 .... 193, 200
SOUTH HETTON COAL CO. *v.* North Eastern News Association [1894] 1 Q.B. 133 236
SOUTH STAFFS. WATER CO. *v.* Sharman [1896] 2 Q.B. 44 .... 28, 29
SOUTHERN PORTLAND CEMENT CO. *v.* Cooper [1974] A.C. 155
SOUTHPORT CORPORATION *v.* Esso Petroleum Co. Ltd. *See* Esso Petroleum Co. Ltd. *v.* Southport Corporation.
SOUTHWARK LONDON BOROUGH *v.* Williams [1971] Ch. 734 56
SPACKMAN *v.* Foster (1883) 11 Q.B.D. 99 33
SPARHAM-SOUTER *v.* Town and Country Developments (Essex) [1976] 2 W.L.R. 493 318
SPARTAN STEEL ALLOYS *v.* Martin [1973] Q.B. 27 84
SPICER *v.* Smee (1946) 175 L.T. 163 178
SQUARE *v.* Model Farms Dairies Ltd. [1939] 2 K.B. 365 213
STANLEY *v.* Powell [1891] 1 Q.B. 86 9
STANSBIE *v.* Troman [1948] 2 K.B. 48 112
STAPLEY *v.* Gypsum Mines [1953] A.C. 663 127
STAVELEY IRON AND CHEMICAL CO. *v.* Jones [1956] A.C. 627 128
STEARN *v.* Prentice Brothers [1919] 1 K.B. 394 .... 180, 192
STENNETT *v.* Hancock and Peters [1939] 2 All E.R. 578 .... 160, 161
STEVENS *v.* Midland Counties Ry. Co. (1854) 10 Ex. 352 291
STONE *v.* Taffe [1974] 1 W.L.R. 1575 225
STOTT *v.* West Yorkshire Road Car Co. [1971] 2 Q.B. 651 121
STRAND ELECTRIC CO. *v.* Brisford Entertainments [1952] 2 Q.B. 246 41
STRATFORD (J. T.) & SON *v.* Lindley [1965] A.C. 269 ...... 257, 259, 260, 261, 267, 268, 269, 270
STUPLE *v.* Royal Insurance Co. [1971] 1 Q.B. 50 141
STURGES *v.* Bridgman (1879) 11 Ch.D. 852 .... 175, 183
SUMMERS *v.* Frost [1955] A.C. 740 214
SUMNER *v.* Henderson (William) & Sons [1963]1 W.L.R. 823 166
SUNBOLF *v.* Alford [1838] 3 M. & W. 311n 18
SUTCLIFFE *v.* Thackrah [1974] A.C. 727 75
SWADLING *v.* Cooper [1931] A.C. 1 124
SYKES *v.* N.E. Ry. (1875) L.J.C.P. 191 299

TARLETON *v.* McGawley (1794) 1 Peake 270 267
TARRY *v.* Ashton (1876) 1 Q.B.D. 314 187
TAYLOR *v.* Bristol Omnibus Co. [1975] 1 W.L.R. 1054 308
—— *v.* Liverpool Corporation [1939] 3 All E.R. 329 157
—— *v.* O'Connor [1971] A.C. 115 308
—— *v.* Rover Car Co. [1966] 1 W.L.R. 1491 161
TENNENT *v.* Earl of Glasgow (1864) 2 Macq. (H.L.) 22 195
TEXAS TUNNELLING CO. *v.* City of Chattanooga, 204 Fed. Supp. 821 (D.C.) (1962) 78
THEAKER *v.* Richardson [1962] 1 W.L.R. 151 239
THOMAS *v.* Bradbury, Agnew & Co. [1906] 2 K.B. 627 247
THOMPSON-SCHWAB *v.* Costaki [1956] 1 W.L.R. 335 171
THOMSON (D. C.) & Co. *v.* Deakin [1952] Ch. 646 260
THORNS CASE (1466) 6 Edw. IV, V, p. 18 63

THUROGOOD v. Van den Berghs and Jurgens [1951] 2 K.B. 537 .... 141, 216
THURSTON v. Charles (1905) 21 T.L.R. 659 305
TINSLEY v. Dudley [1951] 2 K.B. 18 144
TOLLEY v. Fry (J. S.) and Sons Ltd. [1931] A.C. 333 .... 237, 295
TOOHEY v. Hollier (1955) 92 C.L.R. 618 286
TORQUAY HOTEL v. Cousins [1969] 2 Ch. 106 .... 257, 258, 262, 268
TRAVERS v. Gloucester Corporation [1947] K.B. 71 156
TREMAIN v. Pike [1969] 1 W.L.R. 1556 .... 108, 110, 118
TRUTH (N.Z.) v. Holloway [1960] 1 W.L.R. 997 245
TUBERVILLE v. Savage (1669) 1 Mod. Rep. 3 14
TUSON v. Evans (1840) 12 A. & E. 733 250
TWINE v. Bean's Express (1946) 175 L.T. 131 .... 224, 226

UDDIN v. Associated Portland Cement Manufacturers [1965] 2 Q.B. 582 ... 215
UNITED AUSTRALIA v. Barclay's Bank [1941] A.C. 1 .... 315, 316
UNITED DOMINIONS TRUST LTD. v. Parkway Motors Ltd. [1955] 1 W.L.R. 719 40
U.S.A. AND FRANCE v. Dollfuss Mieg [1952] A.C. 582 37
UNIVERSITY OF WARWICK v. De Graaf [1975] 1 W.L.R. 1126 50

VACWELL ENGINEERING CO. v. B.D.H. Chemicals [1971] 1 Q.B. 88 111
VAN OPPEN & CO. LTD. v. Tredegars Ltd. (1921) 37 T.L.R. 504 .... 32, 34
VICTORIA PARK RACING AND RECREATION GROUNDS CO. LTD. v. Taylor (1937) 58 C.L.R. 479 .... 171, 274
VIDEAN v. British Transport Commission [1963] 2 Q.B. 650 114
VIZETELLY v. Mudie's Select Library Ltd. [1900] 2 Q.B. 170 241
VOLUTE, THE [1922] 1 A.C. 129 125

WAGON MOUND, THE [1961] A.C. 388 ...... 100, 104, 105, 109, 118, 198
WAGON MOUND, THE (No. 2) [1967] 1 A.C. 617 ...... 92, 97, 184, 186, 188
WAH TAT BANK v. Chang Cheng Kum [1975] A.C. 507 120
WAKELIN v. L. & S.W. Ry. Co. (1886) 12 App. Cas. 41 141
WALSH v. Holst & Co. [1958] 1 W.L.R. 800 140
WALTER v. Selfe (1851) 4 De G. & S. 315 174
WALTERS v. Smith (W. H.) [1914] 1 K.B. 595 58
WARD v. James [1966] 1 Q.B. 273 6
WARDER v. Cooper [1970] Ch. 495 219
WARREN v. Henleys [1948] 2 All E.R. 935 225
WATSON v. Buckley, Osborn, Garret & Co. [1940] 1 All E.R. 174 160
WATT v. Hertfordshire County Council [1954] 1 W.L.R. 835 94
—— v. Jamieson, 1954 S.C. 56 174
—— v. Longsdon [1930] 1 K.B. 130 .... 249, 250
WELLER & CO. v. Foot and Mouth Disease Research Institute [1966] 1 Q.B. 569 84
WELLS v. Cooper [1958] 2 Q.B. 265 97
WEST AND SON LTD. v. Shephard [1964] A.C. 326 307
WEST LONDON COMMERCIAL BANK LTD. v. Kitson (1884) 13 Q.B.D. 360 ... 276
WESTWOOD v. Post Office [1974] A.C. 1 215
WHALLEY v. Lancashire and Yorkshire Ry. Co. (1884) 13 Q.B.D. 131 192
WHEAT v. Lacon & Co. [1966] A.C. 552 145
WHEATLEY v. Lodge [1971] 1 W.L.R. 29 59
WHITE v. Blackmore [1972] 2 Q.B. 651 .... 150, 151
—— v. Mellin [1895] A.C. 154 .... 279, 280

—— v. Stone Lighting and Radio Ltd. [1939] 2 K.B. 827 239
WHITELEY v. Hilt [1918] 2 K.B. 808 39
WHITWHAM v. Westminster Brymbo Coal and Coke Co. [1896] 2 Ch. 538 ... 48
WHYCHERLEY v. Grave, unreported, February 9, 1967 204
WICKHAM HOLDINGS v. Brooke House Motors [1971] 1 W.L.R. 295 40
WIELAND v. Cyril Lord Carpets [1969] 3 All E.R. 1006 .... 109, 118
WIFFEN v. Bailey and Romford U.D.C. [1915] 1 K.B. 600 292
WIGLEY v. British Vinegars [1964] A.C. 307 215
WILCHICK v. Marks and Silverstone [1934] 2 K.B. 56 182
WILKES v. Hungerford Market Co. (1835) 2 Brig. N.C. 281 188
WILKS v. Cheltenham Car Club [1971] 1 W.L.R. 668 98
WILKINSON v. Downton [1897] 2 Q.B. 57 .... 11, 19, 20, 24, 37, 52, 85
WILLIAMS v. Archer (1847) 5 C.B. 318 40
—— v. Hursey (1959) 103 C.L.R. 30 266
—— v. Settle [1960] 1 W.L.R. 1072 295
WILLIS v. Brooks (1947) 62 T.L.R. 745 236
WILSON v. Lombank [1963] 1 W.L.R. 1294 .... 23, 24, 30
WOLSONS AND CLYDE COAL CO. LTD. v. English [1938] A.C. 57 165
WIMPEY (GEORGE) & CO v. B.O.A.C. [1955] A.C. 169 .... 120, 121, 122
WINKFIELD, THE [1902] P. 42 42
WINSTANLEY v. Bampton [1943] K.B. 319 251
WISE v. Kaye [1962] 1 Q.B. 638 307
WOODWARD v. Mayor of Hastings [1945] K.B. 174 151
WOOLDRIDGE v. Sumner [1963] 2 Q.B. 43 .... 98, 132, 133
WOOLLERTON & WILSON v. Richard Costain [1970] 1 W.L.R. 411 46
WORMALD v. Cole [1954] 1 Q.B. 614 208
WRIGHT v. Wilson (1699) 1 Ld. Raym. 739 16
WRINGE v. Cohen [1940] 1 K.B. 229 .... 178, 182, 187

YORKSHIRE ELECTRICITY BOARD v. Naylor [1968] A.C. 529 301
YOUSOUPOFF v. Metro-Goldwyn-Mayer Pictures [1934] 50 T.L.R. 581... 233, 235

TABLE OF STATUTES

1381 Forcible Entry Act (5 Ric. 2, Stat 1, c. 7) 64

1774 Fires Prevention (Metropolis) Act (14 Geo. 3, c. 78) 184, 200

1843 Libel Act (6 & 7 Vict. c. 96)
s. 2 252

1846 Fatal Accidents Act (9 & 10 Vict. c. 93) 297, 298, 299

1858 Chancery Amendment Act (Lord Cairns' Act) (21 & 22 Vict. c. 27) 185, 294, 314

1861 Offences Against the Person Act (24 & 25 Vict. c. 100)
s. 45 61

1875 Supreme Court of Judicature Act (38 & 39 Vict. c. 77) 6

1882 Married Women's Property Act (45 & 46 Vict. c. 75)
s. 17 324

1891 Slander of Women Act (54 & 55 Vict. c. 51). 234

1893 Sale of Goods Act (56 & ˜ Vict. c. 71)
s. 14 (2) 2
s. 18 ...:.............. 26
s. 25 (1) 33

1906 Dogs Act (6 Edw. 7, c. 32). 207

1911 Coal Mines Act (1 & 2 Geo. 5, c. 50) 213

Maritime Conventions Act (1 & 2 Geo. 5, c. 57) 125

1914 Bankruptcy Act (4 & 5 Geo. 5, c. 59)
s. 30 (1) 325

1925 Law of Property Act (15 & 16 Geo. 5, c. 20)
s. 40 44

Supreme Court of Judicature (Consolidation) Act (15 & 16 Geo. 5, c. 49)
s. 45 312

1928 Dogs (Amendment) Act (18 & 19 Geo. 5, c. 21) 207

1934 Law Reform (Miscellaneous Provisions) Act (24 & 25 Geo. 5, c. 41) 297, 300, 302

1935 Law Reform (Married Women and Tortfeasors) Act (25 & 26 Geo. 5, c. 30) ... 324
s. 6 (1) (*a*) 120
s. 6 (1) (*c*) 120, 121, 122
s. 6 (2) 123
s. 6 (3) (*b*) 120

1937 Factories Act (1 Edw. 8 & 1 Geo. 6, c. 67)
s. 14 (1) 126, 214

1938 Trade Marks Act (1 & 2 Geo. 6, c. 22) 271

1939 Limitation Act (2 & 3 Geo. 6, c. 21) 316, 317, 318, 319

1945 Law Reform (Contributory Negligence) Act (8 & 9 Geo. 6, c. 28) 124, 125, 126, 207
s. 1(1).................. 125
s. 4 126

1947 Crown Proceedings Act (10 & 11 Geo. 6, c. 44) 322
ss. 2 (5), 10 323

1948 Law Reform (Personal Injuries) Act (11 & 12 Geo. 6, c. 41) ... 309

1949 Civil Aviation Act (12, 13 & 14 Geo. 6, c. 67)
s. 40 .... 46, 47

National Parks and Access to the Countryside Act (12, 13 & 14 Geo. 6, c. 97) 143

1952 Defamation Act (15 & 16 Geo. 6 & 1 Eliz. 2, c. 66) 233
s. 2 234
s. 3 (1) 280, 281
ss. 4, 5 242
s. 6 245
s. 7 248

1954 Law Reform (Limitation of Actions, etc.) Act (2 & 3 Eliz. 2, c. 36) 317
s. 2 (1) 10

Mines and Quarries Act (2 & 3 Eliz. 2, c. 70)
s. 48 (1) 214

1956 Restrictive Trade Practices Act (4 & 5 Eliz. 2, c. 68) 265, 267

1957 Occupiers' Liability Act (5 & 6 Eliz. 2, c. 31) 2, 142, 323
s. 1 (1) 143, 145
(2) 143, 145
(3) (*a*) 146
(*b*) 144
(4) 143
s. 2 (1) 143, 150
(2) 143
(3) 146
(*b*) 148
(4) 149
(*b*) 151
(5) 148
(6) 144
s. 3 (1) 151, 152
(4) 152
s. 4 (1) 156
s. 5 (1) 151

1959 Highways Act (7 & 8 Eliz. 2, c. 25)
s. 44 188

1961 Highways (Miscellaneous Provisions) Act (9 & 10 Eliz. 2, c. 63)
s. 1 (3) 187, 228

Housing Act (9 & 10 Eliz. 2, c. 65) 182

1962 Law Reform (Husband and Wife) Act (10 & 11 Eliz. 2, c. 48) ... 324

1963 Limitation Act (c. 47) ... 318
s. 4 (2) 122

1965 Rent Act (c. 75)
ss. 31, 32 64

1967 Misrepresentation Act (c. 7)
s. 2 (1) 78, 79
(2) 79

Criminal Law Act (c. 58) 58–59
s. 2 (2) 57, 58
(3) (4) 57, 58
(5) 57, 58
(6) 58
s. 3 58

1968 Trade Descriptions Act (c. 29) 213

Theatres Act (c. 54) 233

Theft Act (c. 60) 213, 242

Civil Evidence Act (c. 64)
s. 11 .... 141, 243

1969 Employers' Liability (Defective Equipment) Act (c. 37) 164, 166

1970 Proceedings against Estates Act (c. 17)
s. 1 320

Law Reform (Miscellaneous Provisions) Act (c. 33)
s. 4 283

1971 Animals Act (c. 22) .. 204–211
s. 2 .... 205, 206, 207
(1) (2) (*a*) 205
(*b*) (*c*) 206
s. 3 207
s. 4 .... 209, 210
(1) (*a*) (*b*) 209
(2) 210
s. 5 (1) 207, 210
(2) (3) 207
(5) (6) 210
s. 6 .... 204, 205
(2) (*b*) 205
(5) 207
s. 7 .... 55, 209, 210
s. 8 (1) (2) 211
s. 9 .... 54, 207
s. 10 207
s. 11 209

1971 Unsolicited Goods and Services Act (c. 30)
s. (1) (2) 34

Law Reform (Miscellaneous Provisions) Act (c. 43)
s. 4 (1) 299

1972 Road Traffic Act (c. 20)
s. 148 (3) 133, 134

Defective Premises Act (c. 35)
s. 1, 3 (1) 156
s. 4 (1) (2) (4) 156

1973 Supply of Goods (Implied Terms) Act (c. 13)
s. 4 2

1974 Trade Union and Labour Relations Act (c. 52)
s. 13 (1) (*a*) 261
(*b*) 266
(3) (*a*) (*b*) ... 261, 268
(4) 264

Rehabilitation of Offenders Act (c. 53) 243

1975 Limitation Act (c. 54)
s. 2 317
(*a*) (*b*) 319

1976 Trade Union and Labour Relations (Amendment) Act (c. 7)
s. 3 (2) .... Preface

CHAPTER 1

INTRODUCTION

MEANING OF "TORT"; PURPOSE OF THE LAW OF TORT

THE difficulty of defining the word "tort" is well recognised. In the words of an American authority (*Prosser on Torts*, 3rd ed., p. 1), "the numerous attempts which have been made to define the term [*i.e.* tort] have succeeded only in achieving language so broad that it includes other matters than torts, or else so narrow that it leaves out some torts themselves." The main reason for this difficulty is the extreme variety of behaviour which may constitute a tort. Intentionally or negligently to cause physical injury to another, to interfere with this enjoyment of his land, to defame him, or to conspire with another to cause him financial loss are examples of such behaviour. Such cases appear to have three elements. The first is human behaviour which the law categorises as wrongful. The second is that such behaviour infringes an interest of another person which is considered worthy of protection by the law. The third is that the person suffering the wrong is allowed to seek redress for it in the civil courts—it is a civil wrong. The law of tort may therefore be stated to be concerned with the protection of certain interests against certain types of wrongful conduct. Two points may be made in further elaboration of this. In the first place, in order that a tort be committed, it is essential that the relevant interest be protected against the particular type of wrongful conduct. Certain interests, for example the interests in personal security and property, are protected against both intentional and negligent conduct on the part of another, and in some cases against conduct which is free from fault. Other interests, such as the interest in economic security, are less well protected, being protected, generally speaking, only against their deliberate infringement by another. The second point is that, apart from the wrongfulness of the conduct involved in the tort, the type of person responsible for the conduct, and in some cases the relationship between the tortfeasor and his victim, may also be relevant. So, for example, to commit the tort known as *Rylands* v. *Fletcher* (*infra*, p. 190), it is necessary to be an occupier of land, and one who allows a dangerous thing to escape from land he does not occupy does not commit that tort. An example of relationship affecting the "wrongfulness" of conduct is the liability of an occupier of premises towards a visitor on those premises. Liability for negligent acts in relation to those premises under the Occupiers' Liability Act 1957 exists only when the relationship of occupier and lawful visitor is established between defendant and plaintiff.

It is recognised that the above in no sense provides a definition of tort. It fails to distinguish tort from other civil wrongs such as breach of contract, quasi-contract, and breach of trust. Each of these is definable in a broad sense by reference to some basic underlying principle (that underlying breach of contract and trust is obvious; in the case of quasi-contract the principle is that of unjustified enrichment). Tort, however, has no basic identifying principle and can therefore only be defined so as to include within itself the other categories of civil wrong. So, for example, the same act may be both a tort and a breach of contract. If a taxi-driver drives negligently and causes injury to his passenger, this is both the tort of negligence and a breach of the contractual duty to drive carefully. The same overlapping may occur with quasi-contract and with breach of trust. There are at first sight some obvious differences between contractual and tortious obligations. Tortious obligations are said to be imposed by law, contractual obligations by the agreement of the parties to the contract. There are, however, many examples of contractual obligations which are imposed by law. For example, the seller of goods has a duty under section 14 (2) of the Sale of Goods Act 1893, to supply goods of merchantable quality, a duty which under section 4, of the Supply of Goods (Implied Terms) Act 1973 has been rendered incapable of exclusion by the agreement of the parties to the contract. Furthermore the contractual agreement is merely an essential precondition to the existence of the obligation—the obligation to perform the agreement is imposed by the law itself.

Many other differences between contract and tort are typical but not identificatory. The interest protected by a contract is generally speaking an expectation of gain, whereas torts protect a person in the enjoyment of what he already possesses, such as his bodily security. The latter interest may, however, be protected by a contract and it is perfectly possible for a tort to protect an expectation of gain, the best example being the tort of inducement of a breach of contract in which the tortious interest is identical with the contractual interest. Winfield and Jolowicz, *Tort* (10th ed., 1975) p. 14 appears to suggest that the right to bring action for unliquidated damages is an identifying feature of tort. This is unsatisfactory since the right to sue for unliquidated damages exists also in cases of breach of contract and breach of trust. It is, however, true that the right to sue for unliquidated damages may serve to identify as tortious those claims (for examples, see p. 293) whose exact nature is in doubt but which are clearly not within any of the other categories of civil wrong. Because of the elasticity of tort, it tends to act as residual category for civil wrongs which cannot be fitted in elsewhere.

Although no essential difference exists between tort and breach of contract, there are many important incidental differences between actions in tort and in contract which make it important to be able to say whether the cause of action is one or the other (for example, the measure of damages may differ). That actions in tort or contract may be alternative to each other has already been mentioned. But in some cases the court insists that the claim is of one type or the other, though such differentiation rarely has anything other than established dogma to support it. Thus in *Fish* v. *Kapur* (1948) it was held that the plaintiff's claim against a dentist for negligence was tortious only. Recently it has been held that claims against a solicitor and an architect for professional negligence lie only in contract (*Clark* v. *Kirby-Smith* (1964); *Bagot* v. *Stevens, Scanlan & Co.* (1966)).

Between the law of tort and the criminal law, the difference is essentially one of purpose. The law of tort exists in order to give private redress to wrongs suffered by individuals. Criminal law exists for the public interest in the suppression of certain behaviour. There is, however, considerable overlapping between tortious and criminal behaviour. Most crimes are also torts. One tort, breach of statutory duty, requires proof of behaviour by the defendant which will normally be criminal. Even negligence, not normally a ground of criminal liability has its counterpart in crimes such as dangerous and careless driving of a motor vehicle and breaches of factory legislation.

Classification of Torts

Something must be said about classification in order to explain the order of treatment in this book. The emphasis of the courts has tended to be placed on the interest that is infringed, and on whether this was worthy of being protected against the defendant's conduct. This book has therefore adopted a classification of torts based upon the interest protected, beginning with the tortious infringement of the most important interests, those in personal security and property, and continuing with the protection of interests in reputation, in economic security, in domestic relationships and in various miscellaneous matters such as the right to vote. In view of the central importance at the present day of the tort of negligence, a classification based upon the mental element involved in the defendant's conduct into torts of intention, negligence and strict liability might seem logical. But negligence is pre-eminently of importance in protecting interests in person and property. It will therefore be treated as a whole in the part of the book dealing with torts to person or property, though this leads to a discussion of the negligent infringement of economic interests before such interests are dealt with as a whole. Otherwise, however, the classification of torts by reference to the interest protected is maintained. The difficulty with proceeding on the basis of a classification of torts by reference to the mental element required by the tort is that this fails to reflect the way in which the law developed and leads to completely disparate material being treated together. For example, the rules relating to the intentional invasion of economic interests are very different from those relating to the intentional invasion of bodily security.

No Unitary Principle of Liability

It has been stated above that tortious liability is referable to no single principle. Mention must be made, however, of two attempts in which an attempt has been made to establish a principle which would constitute a sufficient though not a necessary condition for the existence of tortious liability. In *Allen* v. *Flood* (1898) it was argued that the malicious threat by the defendant trade unionists, lawfully to terminate their contracts unless the plaintiff was dismissed from his employment was not actionable in tort by the plaintiff who was dismissed by his employer. The presence of malice did not therefore make tortious what was otherwise a lawful act.

In the light of this case it would be surprising if any other general principle of liability could be established. In *Donoghue* v. *Stevenson* (1932) (for the ratio of this case, see *infra*, p. 66) the judgments of the majority in the House of Lords, in particular that of Lord Atkin, were susceptible of the interpretation that the negligent infliction of damage or loss upon another person was invariably actionable by that person. Despite the extent of the tort of negligence, however, there are still exceptions to this rule (*infra*, p. 71), and it is therefore impossible to regard negligence as a universal ground of liability in tort.

Reasons for Failure of Tortious Action

An action in tort may fail for substantive or procedural reasons. The action will fail for substantive reasons where the facts relied on by the plaintiff do not in law amount to a tort. Generally speaking, this will mean the failure of the plaintiff's action, although there is the unlikely possibility of the court being willing to recognise a new tort. The most recent examples of such recognition appear to be of the tort of deceit, in 1789, of a general right to sue for inducing a breach of contract in 1853, and of the tort known as the rule in *Rylands* v. *Fletcher* in 1868.

The second substantive reason for failure of the action is that the defendant has a defence. Since the essence of a defence is that the defendant is alleging facts which make conduct of his harmless which would otherwise be tortious, the burden of proving the defence lies on the defendant.

An example of the failure of an action in tort for procedural reasons is failure in the plaintiff's evidence. Such evidence may fail to prove facts on which the plaintiff relies, or those facts which the plaintiff proves do not justify the court in reaching a certain conclusion, for example, that the defendant was negligent or malicious. In the case of those torts in which damage has to be proved as part of the cause of action the plaintiff's action may fail through his inability to show that he has suffered damage. Thus a passenger in a car which has been involved in a collision through its driver's negligence does not establish a cause of action by proof of this. He must show also that he suffered damage in the form of personal injury or damage to his property. In the case of torts actionable *per se* (*i.e.* without proof of damage) the plaintiff succeeds upon proof of the commission of the tort by the defendant.

One procedural reason for failure that no longer exists is incorrect choice of the form of action. The forms of action were abolished in 1852, and under the Judicature Act of 1875, the plaintiff need only state the facts on which he relies without specifying any particular tort or torts. He will succeed if these facts are proved by him and show the commission of a tort by the defendant.

The failure of the plaintiff's action because of the expiry of a limitation period upon the action seems clearly procedural rather than substantive. This matter must be raised by the defendant as a defence; the court will not of its own motion take account of such expiry.

Jury Trial in Tortious Actions

Jury trials are now rare in actions in tort. They can be demanded by either party in actions for libel, slander, malicious prosecution, or false imprisonment, and by the defendant when the action against him contains an allegation of fraud. In all these cases the court may refuse jury trial if it considers that the trial will involve a prolonged examination of documents or accounts or a scientific or local investigation. In all other cases the court has a discretion to order trial by jury, but this discretion is exercised sparingly especially in actions for personal injury in the case of which the Court of Appeal in *Ward* v. *James* (1966) laid down that there must be special circumstances before the court may order jury trial. The reason for this was the fear of excessive awards of damages against defendants on the ground that they were insured. *Ward* v. *James* also laid down as a general rule that the discretion to order jury trial is not a completely unfettered discretion but is one that must be exercised judicially. As a result of this case, jury trial in actions of tort, already uncommon, will become increasingly so.

FAULT AND COMPENSATION

In the majority of cases under English law, the plaintiff must show fault on the part of the defendant or someone for whose acts the defendant is in law responsible. Despite the advent of the age of machinery, and such inherently dangerous objects as industrial plant and high-speed locomotives, the courts have not adopted the view that those who carry on enterprises or activities in which such machinery plays a part should be liable without fault for the damage they cause. "Our law," said Scott L.J. in *Read* v. *Lyons* (1945, in the Court of Appeal), "is concerned not with [the defendant's] activities but with [his] acts." This rejection of enterprise or activity liability seems doubly unfortunate. First, it discards the justice of holding liable those who, though no fault can be proved against them in the individual case, have increased the risk of injuries by carrying on a certain activity. Secondly, the enterprise is normally in a better position than the victim to absorb the loss suffered by having to pay damages, either by passing it on to the public in the form of prices it charges for its product or by insuring against it. *Read* v. *Lyons* is significant in this respect. In it, the House of Lords rejected an attempt to argue a principle of strict liability for the carrying on of hazardous activities postulated on the basis of the rule in *Rylands* v. *Fletcher* (1868) which established that under certain conditions strict liability existed for the escape of dangerous things from the defendant's land. From the time of this decision, therefore, strict liability in the English law of tort could only exist in the logically unsatisfactory form of the rule in *Rylands* v. *Fletcher* itself, and in a few other unconnected instances (*infra*, p. 169).

Another problem which the law of tort has to face is that though liability in tort may be established, the means of the defendant may be insufficient to satisfy the judgment. Although no general rule of

English law exists to avert this possibility, two important provisions ensure that in the large majority of tortious claims, the judgment will be satisfied. Under the provisions of various Road Traffic Acts the owner of a motor vehicle is compelled to insure against tortious liability to third parties. The master of a servant is at common law liable for torts committed by that servant in the course of his employment. These rules have the desirable effect of ensuring that in road and industrial accident cases, numerically the most important area of tort, the tortfeasor's liability will normally be met by a solvent person. These provisions do not cover the whole of tortious liability; and they are only applicable when tortious liability can be established. Accordingly some have argued for the introduction of a comprehensive system of state insurance for the victims of accidents operative without the necessity of establishing the legal responsibility of someone for the injury (argued for the victims of road accidents by Professor Street in Elliott and Street's *Road Accidents*; for accident victims in general by Atiyah, *Accidents, Compensation and the Law*). The Royal Commission on Compensation for Personal Injuries (for its terms of reference, see *infra*, p. 166) will undoubtedly consider the merits of these suggestions.

CHAPTER 2

INTENTIONAL INTERFERENCE WITH THE PERSON

IN this chapter the law concerning intentional interferences by the defendant with the plaintiff's person will be considered. The law on this subject is still to some extent bound up with the former distinction between the action of trespass and that of case. It is therefore necessary as a preliminary matter to consider the distinction between the two.

TRESPASS AND CASE

The action of trespass had a requirement that the interference complained of by the plaintiff must be the direct or immediate result of the defendant's act. Case lay, on the other hand, where the interference was only a consequential result of the defendant's act. For example, if the defendant threw a log into the highway, striking the plaintiff, trespass was the appropriate action; if the log lay in the highway and the plaintiff rode his horse into it, the proper action was case. The distinction between the two actions, though clear-cut in many cases, might give rise to argument. In the well-known case of *Scott* v. *Shepherd* (1773) the defendant threw a lighted squib into a crowded market-place. The squib was thrown on by two persons acting in self-preservation and for the protection of property. The second time it was thrown it hit the plaintiff in the face and exploded causing him to lose an eye. The majority of the court held the defendant liable in trespass, but Blackstone J. dissented on the ground that the action should properly have been one of case. This uncertainty was made more serious by the fact that an incorrect choice penalised the plaintiff by the failure of his action.

The distinction between trespass and case was not of purely procedural significance. Trespass was actionable *per se*, that is, without proof of damage; case needed such proof. There was however no association of any particular mental state with either form of action. Trespass may have involved strict liability, in other words, have been actionable without proof that the defendant either intended or should have foreseen the interference with the plaintiff's interest, but the matter is controverted. In any case it lay where the defendand had acted either intentionally or negligently. Case tended to be more closely connected with negligence, because the types of harm for which it lay were more likely to be committed negligently rather than intentionally, for example, actions for nuisance and for damage by fire. But it could lie for intentional injury; thus the modern tort of deceit evolved from the action on the case.

Trespass and Negligence

After the nineteenth-century legislation which abolished the forms of action and allowed a plaintiff merely to recite the facts of his case in his statement of claim provided these facts disclosed a cause of action, the plaintiff could no longer lose by making an incorrect choice of the form of action. From then on the term "trespass" came to be used in a substantive rather than a procedural sense; to describe a tort, rather than the form of action for enforcing the tort. There have been two important developments in the tort of trespass since that time. The first is that a number of cases have decided that trespass with the possible exception of trespass to land is no longer, if it ever was, a tort of strict liability (decided for trespass to the person by *Stanley* v. *Powell* (1891); for trespass to chattels by *National Coal Board* v. *Evans* (1951)). Furthermore, it has been decided that the onus of proof is upon the plaintiff to show that the defendant either intended the trespass or was negligent in committing it, rather than upon the defendant to show that he acted without fault. In *Fowler* v. *Lanning* (1959) the plaintiff in his statement of claim alleged that "the defendant shot the plaintiff." It was held that the facts stated did not disclose a cause of action. The plaintiff also needed to allege (and therefore to prove) that the defendant shot him either intentionally or negligently.

The second development concerns the relationship between trespass and negligence. The frequency of actions in which negligence is the gist of the action, due to the increased mechanisation and industrialisation of society and the consequent multiplication of cases of personal injury caused by negligence, has led to the idea of negligence as a tort in itself, and not simply as a means of committing trespass or case. The tort of negligence has thus taken over much of the former area of trespass, namely, where it lay for personal injuries caused negligently though directly. Although trespass has been recognised as theoretically still available in such cases as the causing of personal injuries through the negligent driving of a motor vehicle, in practice such actions have usually been described as actions of negligence. Furthermore, the phrase "trespass to the person" has been more commonly applied to intentional invasions of the interest in bodily security such as assault, battery, and false imprisonment. In *Letang* v. *Cooper* (1965) this distinction appears to have gained Court of Appeal approval: the plaintiff was sunbathing in the car-park of a hotel. The defendant drove his car over her legs injuring her. Over three years later the plaintiff sued the defendant in negligence and trespass. There was no doubt that the claim in negligence was barred by the lapse of over three years after the accident under section 2 (1) of the Law Reform (Limitation of Actions etc.) Act 1954, which sets up a three-year limitation period on actions for negligence, nuisance, or breach of duty, when the plaintiff has suffered personal injuries. The question in the action was whether the plaintiff's action in trespass was also barred under this subsection. The Court of Appeal held that it was, on the ground that it was an action for breach of duty within the meaning of the subsection.

The Court of Appeal also thought that the plaintiff's action could be dismissed on the ground that it was an action for negligence within the meaning of the subsection, since negligence was the basis of the plaintiff's allegation against the defendant. They made, during their judgments, observations about the relationship between trespass and negligence. Lord Denning M.R. thought that the old distinction between trespass and case had been replaced by a distinction between trespass, which lay only for intentional and direct invasions of the plaintiff's interest and was actionable *per se*, and negligence which lay only for negligent invasions and was actionable only upon proof of damage by the plaintiff. Diplock L.J. thought that it was still possible to call an action trespass where it was based on negligence. But no advantage could be gained by so doing. Where negligence was the gist of the cause of action, a plaintiff suing in trespass would still have to satisfy the requirements of the tort of negligence, for example, that the defendant owed him a duty of care or that he had suffered actual damage. Moreover, such an action was an action for negligence within the meaning of section 2 (1) of the Law Reform (Limitation of Actions) Act 1954, since the law looked to the substance rather than the form.

The width of these expressions of opinion may make them *obiter*, but they point the way to the law in the future. If followed, they would finally remove possible anomalies arising from the fact that a plaintiff injured by negligence might gain an advantage by framing his action in trespass. Although it is too early to conclude that trespass in all its forms can only be committed intentionally, it is suggested in this book that this should be the law. If followed they would finally remove possible anomalies arising from the fact that a plaintiff injured by negligence might gain an advantage by framing his action in trespass. Although it is too early to conclude that trespass in all its forms can only be committed intentionally, it is suggested in this book that this should be the law.

Battery and Assault

In the remainder of this chapter, various forms of intentional interference with the person will be considered. Of these, battery, assault, and false imprisonment are forms of trespass. Liability under the *Wilkinson* v. *Downton* (1897) principle (*infra*, p. 20) is on the other hand derived from the action on the case.

Assault and battery are both crimes as well as torts. It does not appear that the criminal law as to what constitutes an assault or a battery differs from the civil, with the exception that it is certain that neither crime can be committed negligently. Consequently many of the relevant precedents in civil actions of assault or battery are decisions in criminal cases.

Battery

Where the defendant, intending this result, does an act which directly and physically affects the person of the plaintiff, he commits battery.

It will be noticed that battery is here defined as an intentional tort. This reflects the views of the Court of Appeal expressed in *Letang* v. *Cooper* (1965). The effect is that where the defendant negligently though directly injures the plaintiff, by driving his motor-car against him, the plaintiff's action is not battery but negligence.

The battery need not be forcible but must be direct

Battery can be committed without the use of force. For instance it would be battery to move a sleeping man. But the requirement of directness excludes from the category of battery many intentional inflictions of physical harm upon another person. Thus it is not battery to poison another's drink, or to dig a hole intending another to fall into it, even though in each case the intended harm occurs. These cases are, however, clearly remediable by action based on the principle of *Wilkinson* v. *Downton* (1897) (*infra*, p. 20).

Consent

Many events of everyday occurrence such as a haircut, a surgical operation, and a passionate embrace would be batteries but for the fact that consent operates as a defence to an action of battery. But in order that consent should operate as a defence, it must be given to the act complained of by the plaintiff. A case illustrating this principle is *Nash* v. *Sheen* (1953): the plaintiff went to the defendant, a ladies' hairdresser for a permanent wave. The defendant applied a tone-rinse to the plaintiff's hair, which not only changed its colour but caused a rash all over the plaintiff's body. The plaintiff recovered damages for battery, since her consent did not extend to the application of the tone-rinse.

Implied consent appears to be the reason why a person who receives numerous physical contacts with his person of a trivial nature while standing in a large crowd, for example, at a football match, cannot sue those who touch him in battery.

It is assumed that consent in battery as in the case of other torts operates as a defence, the burden of establishing it therefore resting on the defendant. Certain nineteenth-century authority (*Christopherson* v. *Bare* (1848); *Latter* v. *Braddell* (1881)) appears to suggest, however, that the plaintiff must establish his own want of consent. The matter awaits an authoritative decision.

Method of commission of battery

The battery need not be committed with the person of the defendant; it is battery to strike the plaintiff by throwing a stone at him. Equally provided the force used has its effect against the person of the defendant, it is not necessary that it should be aimed against his person, though to satisfy the definition of battery given above, the effect on the plaintiff's person must be intended by the defendant. For instance, it would be battery to throw over the chair in which the plaintiff is sitting. Equally it is probably sufficiently direct to constitute battery to remove the chair on which the plaintiff is about to sit, or to cut the rope up which he is climbing. It is more difficult when the defendant's act is committed against something in close proximity to the plaintiff, but has no effect upon his person, for example, to remove his hat or to throw water upon his clothes. In *Pursell* v. *Horn* (1838) it was held that the defendant's throwing of boiling water over the plaintiff's clothes, which he was wearing, was not a battery, but the judgment gives little indication of the principles upon which it was decided. In any case such acts are actionable as trespass to chattels.

A positive act by the defendant is needed for the commission of a battery. Trespass could not be committed by an omission to act. In *Fagan* v. *Metropolitan Police Commissioner* (1969) the defendant accidentally drove his car on to the foot of a police constable. He then delayed in reversing the car in order to allow the constable to escape, knowing that his foot was trapped. The majority of the court held the accused liable for criminal assault, but one judge dissented on the ground that at the time the accused did the act complained of, he had no *mens rea*, and after he had formed the *mens rea*, he did not act. The decision seems justifiable, however, on the ground that at the time the accused formed a wrongful intention, the effects of his act in the form of a physical contact with the constable's person still persisted.

One situation that may cause difficulty arises where A intends to commit battery against B, but instead and by mistake strikes C. In criminal law, it appears that a battery is committed (in *R.* v. *Latimer* (1886) it was held that in similar circumstances the crime of malicious wounding was committed by the accused). In America such conduct is regarded as tortious on the ground that A's wrongful intent towards B is transferred to C. But it is doubtful whether English courts should adopt this doctrine. In every case, it appears, A's conduct will be negligent towards C. The doctrine of transferred intent, though necessary in criminal law because of the absence of a general principle of criminal liability for negligence, is unnecessary in tort.

Assault

A person commits assault if he intentionally and directly causes the plaintiff to apprehend that he is going to commit a battery against the plaintiff.

Although this tort, like the other variants of trespass, has the requirement of directness, in practice it seems that difficulties about directness are unlikely to arise. As in the case of battery, it is suggested that after *Letang* v. *Cooper* (1965) assault can only be committed intentionally. The interest protected by assault, that is, freedom from apprehension of a battery, is unusual. The reason for the existence of a tort of assault separate from battery is that, where two persons have fought, the law can regard the aggressor as a tortfeasor and the other as acting in self-defence, even though the aggressor does not succeed in landing the first blow.

Can assault be committed verbally?

In *Meade's Case* (1823) which was a criminal prosecution for murder, it was said, "no words or singing are equivalent to an assault." It seems unsatisfactory to exclude the mere threat as a means of committing assault, on the basis of this flimsy *obiter dictum*, although if assault by threat is held actionable it would be a question of fact in each case whether the defendant intends to implement the threat. In *Read* v. *Coker* (1853) the defendant, who had paid rent on behalf of the plaintiff, visited the plaintiff with some of his workmen, and threatened the plaintiff with physical violence in order to make him leave the premises. The workmen clustered round the plaintiff and committed such threatening actions as tucking up their sleeves and aprons. This was held to be an assault, but in the judgment of Jervis C.J. there is no indication that the threat by itself was not enough. He said, "There was a threat of violence, exhibiting an intention to assault, and a present ability to carry the threat into execution."

Words may qualify or explain an otherwise threatening action, so as to render it no assault. In *Tuberville* v. *Savage* (1669), the defendant did not commit assault by placing his hand on his sword in the plaintiff's presence, because he said the word, "If it were not assize-time, I would not take such language from you." Where, on the other hand, the words take the form of a conditional threat ("Your money or your life"), this seemingly constitutes assault, nor should it matter that the defendant has committed no threatening action.

Must the defendant intend to commit battery?

The old view of assault was that it was an incomplete battery. The question arose, if the defendant did not intend to commit battery, but nevertheless induced a reasonable belief in the plaintiff's mind that he was about to do so, would this amount to assault? The usual example is that of the defendant who points an unloaded gun at the plaintiff. This behaviour complies with the definition of assault given above, and in principle it seems that it ought to amount to assault. It is therefore to be hoped that a criminal case, *R.* v. *St. George* (1840) which holds it to be assault, should be preferred to a civil case, *Blake* v. *Barnard* (1840) which holds it not to be. The analogy between assault and battery can, it seems, be overstated. Battery, for instance, can take place without prior apprehension of harm by the plaintiff, as, for example, where he is struck from behind. If battery is not necessarily a completed assault, there is no reason why assault should necessarily be an incomplete battery.

Must the plaintiff's apprehension be reasonable?

Suppose the plaintiff to be an unusually timorous person in whom the defendant's act has induced a fear of an imminent battery, though a reasonable man would not have feared in such circumstances. Does the defendant commit assault? The answer involves an examination of the mental element required of the defendant in assault. One answer is to say that the defendant is liable because he has intentionally done an act which has directly brought about apprehension of a battery in the plaintiff, whether or not the defendant knew or should have known that this would be the result. Another possible answer is to say that the defendant is liable only if he has intended to arouse such apprehension in the plaintiff, and, if he has so intended, he is liable whether or not he knew of the plaintiff's timorousness. An intermediate approach is to say that the defendant is liable only if he has intentionally acted in such a way as to cause apprehension in a reasonable person, an approach which would excuse the defendant in the case posed. The problem with the third approach is that liability in assault is made to depend upon negligence. Whether the first or second answer is correct seems to depend upon how specific the intention in trespass must be. In other forms of trespass (for example, trespass to land), an intention to do the act constituting the tort rather than an intention to commit the tort is sufficient.

Damages in assault and battery

Both torts, being forms of trespass are actionable *per se*. Where the defendant's act has caused no damage to the plaintiff, the plaintiff may in fact get only nominal damages. But it is quite possible for the court to give high damages in such a case because of the way in which the defendant acted. For instance, in *Loudon* v. *Ryder* (1953) the defendant entered the plaintiff's flat by climbing a ladder and entering through a window. He beat the plaintiff on her shoulders and head and dragged her downstairs. The plaintiff was not seriously injured. The following damages were awarded: £1,500 for the trespass, £1,000 for the assault and battery and £3,000 exemplary damages.

The exemplary damages could not now be awarded, but the other awards, consisting of aggravated damages for the manner in which the trespass and assault were committed, could still be made.

False Imprisonment

This tort is committed by one who intentionally and directly places a total restraint upon the liberty of the plaintiff. It is a form of trespass to the person, and is actionable *per se*.

Intention and directness

The tort is defined to exclude negligent imprisonment of another person. This is a reflection of the views of the Court of Appeal in *Letang* v. *Cooper* (1965) (*supra*, p. 9). There is also a requirement that the tort should be committed directly. This is of course a requirement of trespass to the person. Where for either reason the plaintiff cannot establish false imprisonment, an action in negligence may still be available. Thus in *Sayers* v. *Harlow U.D.C.* (1958) the plaintiff, she recovered £50 damages from him. Since no damage because of the negligent maintenance of the door lock by the defendants' servants. In trying to climb out of the lavatory, she fell and was injured. She recovered damages from the defendants because it was a reasonable act on her part to attempt to escape from the situation in which the defendants by their negligence had placed her. An action for false imprisonment was not available because there was not a sufficiently direct act of imprisonment.

Where the plaintiff has been imprisoned by the negligence of the defendant, but has suffered no damage, it seems that he has no remedy if we define false imprisonment to exclude negligence. This may cause hardship to a person who has suffered a fairly lengthy period of imprisonment. Even if such a person has suffered financial loss, for example, in the form of loss of wages, it seems that he could not recover these in an action of negligence since negligence will not lie for purely pecuniary loss. The solution may be to regard the period of imprisonment itself, if it is not of merely trivial duration as damage, loss of wages being then recoverable as consequential loss. Some support for this exists in the case of *De Freville* v. *Dill* (1927). The defendant, a doctor, negligently certified the plaintiff to be insane, as a result of which she was detained in a lunatic asylum for two days. Although false imprisonment was probably not committed, because the defendant had not directly imprisoned the plaintiff, she recovered £50 damages from him. Since no damage other than the actual detention was suffered, the court seems to have regarded this as sufficient damage to support the action, though since the action was on the case rather than a simple action for negligence, it is unwise to draw the conclusion that it would count as damage for the latter tort. In the tort of malicious prosecution, imprisonment counts as special damage.

The act of imprisonment

There must be a total restraint placed upon the plaintiff's freedom of action. In *Bird* v. *Jones* (1845) the defendant closed off the public footpath over one side of Hammersmith Bridge. The plaintiff, wishing to use the footpath, was prevented by the defendant. In the plaintiff's action one of the questions it was necessary to decide was whether the defendant's act amounted to a false imprisonment. The court held that it did not (if the plaintiff could have proved special damage arising from the defendant's act he could have sued successfully on the case).

Provided the area of restraint is total, it does not seem to matter that it is very large. False imprisonment on a large estate or in a town seems possible. But there must be limits to this. A wrongful deportation order which has the effect of excluding the deportee from a particular country could hardly be regarded as false imprisonment in the rest of the world.

Reasonable escape

There is no false imprisonment if a reasonable escape route is available to the plaintiff. In *Wright* v. *Wilson* (1699) false imprisonment was not committed where the plaintiff could escape by trespassing on the land of a third party.

What is a reasonable escape route depends upon the circumstances of the case. The mere fact that the plaintiff is *able* to take advantage of an escape route does not mean that he must do so. An expert swimmer might be justified in not taking advantage of an escape route offered by swimming if he thought that release by other means would soon become available.

Although an escape route which involves a risk of injury to the plaintiff may be regarded as unreasonable for the purpose of establishing the tort of false imprisonment it appears that an imprisoned person may not have acted unreasonably in taking that means of escape and suffering injury as a result. Thus in *Sayers* v. *Harlow U.D.C.* (1958) (*supra*) though it was regarded as reasonable, and therefore not a *novus actus* (*infra*, p. 111), for the plaintiff to attempt to escape from a lavatory in which she was locked by climbing over the wall, it seems likely that such an escape route would not have been held a reasonable one for the purpose of preventing her detention from amounting to false imprisonment. A person locked by the defendant in a room from which the only possibility of escape is a hazardous climb down a drain-pipe, is falsely imprisoned, and yet if he risks the climb and suffers injury, it seems that he might be held to have acted reasonably and therefore recover damages from the defendant. But whether he has acted reasonably depends upon a number of factors, in particular the possible duration of his detention and the degree of risk involved in trying to escape.

Despite the fact that false imprisonment is a form of trespass to the person, it does not require a physical act aimed against the person of the plaintiff. Imprisonment by show of authority is sufficient, for example, arrest by a constable, or restraint by persuasion used by a Commissioner of Lunacy to prevent the plaintiff, whom he believed to be insane, from leaving the room as in *Harnett* v. *Bond* (1925).

False imprisonment by omission to act

In *Herd* v. *Weardale Steel, Coal and Coke Co.* (1915) the plaintiff miners refused to complete their shift because they considered the work to be dangerous. The defendants' manager refused for some time to allow the lift to be used to take the men up the lift-shaft. The defendants were not in breach of contract because there was no obligation to remove men from the shaft except at certain times.

The House of Lords held that this did not amount to false imprisonment. The ratio appears to be that the defendants had committed no positive act of detention upon the plaintiffs and the plaintiffs were in breach of contract in asking for their liberty before the end of the shift. But the original imprisonment had been committed by an act of the defendants, to which admittedly the plaintiffs had given their consent. It would clearly have been false imprisonment to have refused to take up the miners *at the end of their shift*. This being so, it is not clear why the fact that the miners were in breach of contract should have made a difference, since the fact that a workman is in breach of contract in leaving his work early is no justification for imprisoning him. The case is probably wrongly decided.

What interest does this tort protect?

Although the obvious answer to this question appears to be, the interest in freedom, there is some force in the idea that it is the plaintiff's belief in his freedom that is protected. If the defendant informs the plaintiff that he is to be confined to his house, and that armed guards are placed outside the house with instructions to shoot the plaintiff if he attempts to leave, this appears to be false imprisonment even if no armed guards are present. In the same way, a police officer who induces in another person a belief that he is arresting him imprisons him even if he had no intention of preventing the departure of that person.

More difficult is the case where the plaintiff does not know that he is imprisoned. In *Meering* v. *Graham-White Aviation Co.* (1919) the plaintiff was being questioned at the defendants' factory in connection with certain thefts from the defendant company. He did not know of the presence outside the room in which he was being questioned of two works police who would have prevented his leaving if necessary. He succeeded in an action of false imprisonment against the defendants. It appears that the case can be supported on the ground that such imprisonment may conceivably affect the plaintiff's reputation. There seems little doubt that damages may be awarded in false imprisonment for loss of reputation caused by the imprisonment. This is a reasonable deduction from *Childs* v. *Lewis* (1924) in which it was held that damages might be awarded for the fact that the plaintiff, a director, had been compelled to resign by his co-directors, because of his wrongful detention in custody by the defendant.

Justification of imprisonment

It is clear that it is not in every case in which one person detains or imprisons another that such detention is wrongful. The detention may be justified because of a lawful arrest, or because there may have been a consent to the detention by the person detained.

There is, however, no power to arrest for a purely civil offence, for example the non-payment of a debt (*Sunbolf* v. *Alford* (1838)—

defendant landlord committed false imprisonment by detaining guest for non-payment of his bill). The case of *Robinson* v. *Balmain New Ferry Co.* (1910) does not conflict with this principle—the forcible detention of the plaintiff for refusal to pay a penny as the price of exit from the defendant's wharf was not false imprisonment since the plaintiff was attempting to leave the wharf by the exit on the side he had entered and in the words of the Privy Council "there is no law requiring the defendants to make the exit from their premises gratuitous to people who come upon a definite contract which involves their leaving by another way." The case is thus merely an illustration of the principle stated earlier that the restraint must be total (for a criticism of the *Herd* and *Robinson* decisions, see G. Williams, *Justice, Equity and the Law*, Essays in tribute to G. W. Keeton, p. 47).

Intentionally Causing Physical Harm

In *Bird* v. *Holbrook* (1828) a trespasser succeeded in an action on the case against an occupier of land who had set a spring-gun on his land and thus caused injury to the trespasser. The principle underlying the case must have been liability for intentionally causing injury—there could have been no question of liability for mere negligence towards a trespasser.

A similar principle was applied in *Wilkinson* v. *Downton* (1897). The defendant, as a joke, told the plaintiff falsely that her husband had been seriously injured in an accident and that she was to take a cab with two pillows to fetch him home. The plaintiff suffered severe nervous shock as a result. The defendant was held liable under a principle which Wright J. expressed as follows: "where the defendant has intentionally done an act or made a statement calculated to cause physical harm to the plaintiff, and in fact causes physical harm, the plaintiff has a good cause of action."

The principle on which the case was decided gives rise to difficulty. The main trouble is with the words "calculated to cause." If these words mean no more than that harm was foreseeably likely as a result of the act or statement, there is great difficulty in distinguishing the *Wilkinson* v. *Downton* (1897) principle from negligence. If the words mean more than foreseeable, such as certain or substantially certain, there is difficulty with the case itself since nervous shock, as distinct from mental distress, though a foreseeable result of the news imparted to the plaintiff, was hardly a certain or a substantially certain result. Only if the case is interpreted in this way, however, does it seem that the principle can have a separate existence independent of the tort of negligence.

It is clear that the law must impose liability for the intentional, non-trespassory infliction of personal injury, *i.e.* the *Bird* v. *Holbrook* situation. It is doubtful, however, whether the law needs a rule of liability so wide as that stated by Wright J. in *Wilkinson* v. *Downton*, which, according to the likeliest interpretation of his judgment, has a considerable overlap with the tort of negligence. On the other hand, the liability imposed by the actual decision in *Wilkinson* v. *Downton* is defensible, since no duty of care exists in relation to the publication or utterance of words causing shock and accordingly there could be no liability in negligence in this situation. In America a further use has been found for the *Wilkinson* v. *Downton* principle by extending it to cases of the intentional infliction of emotional distress, as opposed to nervous shock, by insulting behaviour or language, but no such development seems likely in this country.

CHAPTER 3

INTENTIONAL INTERFERENCE WITH CHATTELS

THE term "chattel" is generally taken to mean all forms of tangible property not regarded as realty, including goods, money, cheques, and other negotiable instruments.

The law relating to interference with chattels is full of difficulties, many of them arising from its evolution from three different forms of action, trespass, detinue, and conversion. Although each of these actions has a different function, there is a great deal of overlapping between them, and particularly in the case of detinue and conversion it is often a moot point whether the rules of one tort or the other should be applied.

There is no doubt that the person principally protected by these tortious remedies is the owner of the chattel. He will normally be the person with a right to the immediate possession of the chattel as is required in conversion and detinue. He will also normally, though less often, be the person in actual possession of it as required in trespass. But the emphasis of the law on possession rather than title means that many others besides the owner of the chattel can sue in tort for interference with the chattel. These may include the wrongful possessor, even the thief. The extent to which the law has gone in protecting actual possession may be derived from the fact that such possession is a means of establishing a right to the chattel's possession, so that the person deprived of it may bring conversion or detinue. This fact has also meant a certain amount of overlapping between the latter two remedies and trespass.

TRESPASS TO CHATTELS

The tort may be defined as an intentional and direct act of interference by the defendant with a chattel of which the plaintiff was in possession at the time of the interference.

Plaintiff's interest; possession

The defendant's act must disturb the plaintiff in his possession of the chattel. Therefore it will be necessary for the defendant to prove his possession in order to succeed in trespass. Generally in order to prove possession of a chattel, it is necessary to prove that it is within one's control, either because it is in one's physical grasp or by other means. Thus a person continues to possess the goods that he has left in his house or car despite the fact that he himself is not in the house or car. It is also possible for possession to exist through another person; thus a master is in possession of goods held on his behalf by his servant.

It appears to be the law that there is no requirement in trespass that the possession should be lawful. Thus a thief may sue in trespass. But there must be some limits to this. The owner, or one with some genuine proprietary right over the chattel, cannot be successfully sued in trespass by a thief. This does not mean that an owner can never commit trespass to his own chattel. In *Rose* v. *Matt* (1951) the purchaser of some goods pledged his clock with the seller of the goods as security for a loan of the purchase price. Later he returned and took the clock away secretly. The owner of the clock was convicted of larceny. Since larceny (now called theft) was an offence which involved a trespassory taking, there is no doubt that the owner of the clock could have been sued in trespass by the pledgee.

Exceptions to the rule that the plaintiff must have possession

(i) *Bailment* is a transaction by which A, the bailor, transfers possession of a chattel to B, the bailee, both intending that at some future date, it should be transferred back to A. If no term is fixed for the bailment, it is said to be at will, and the bailor can demand possession from the bailee at any time. If a term is fixed, the bailor cannot demand possession from the bailee until the term has expired (or the bailment has otherwise been determined).

The bailor-at-will is allowed to sue for trespasses to his bailee's possession (*Lotan* v. *Cross* (1810); *Johnson* v. *Diprose* (1893)). The justification of this is normally expressed to be that the bailor here has a right to the immediate possession of the chattel, and in consequence may be regarded as being in actual possession through his bailee. The bailor for a term, who has no right to immediate possession of the chattel, cannot sue in trespass (*Gordon* v. *Harper* (1796)). It seems contrary to principle that the bailor can ever sue his bailee in trespass for doing an act contrary to the terms of the bailment, since there can be no question of the bailee infringing his own possession. There is support for this view in the Australian case of *Penfold's Wines Pty.* v. *Elliott* (1946), but in the English case of *Burnard* v. *Haggis* (1863) the court held that an act of the bailee which was not merely a wrongful performance of the bailment but went completely outside its terms was trespassory at the suit of the bailor. The case seems difficult to support.

(ii) The title of *executors and administrators of estates* relates back to the death of the deceased. This is the case with possession of chattels forming part of the estate. They are thus enabled to sue for trespass to such chattels committed before they actually take possession of the estate.

(iii) The *owner of a franchise* in wrecks has been allowed to sue in trespass one who seized a cask of whiskey from the wreck (*Dunwich Corporation* v. *Sterry* (1831)).

(iv) A *trustee* may sue for trespass to chattels in the possession of a beneficiary.

Jus tertii

The weight that is attached to possession in the action of trespass is also shown by the fact that *jus tertii*, the right of a third person, is not a defence.

In *Wilson* v. *Lombank* (1963) the defendants' servant took a car, which was in the plaintiff's possession, thinking it belonged to the defendants. The latter, on finding a third party to be the owner of the car, delivered it to him. They were held liable in trespass to the plaintiff for the full value of the car. The court refused to allow the defendants to set up the title of the true owner of the car as a defence to the plaintiff's action.

Acts constituting trespass

The defendant's act need not dispossess the plaintiff. A mere moving of the chattel, called an asportation, is sufficient.

In *Kirk* v. *Gregory* (1876) the defendant, the sister-in-law of a person recently deceased, removed his jewellery from the room where he lay dead to another room in the house, in order to safeguard it. The jewellery was stolen by some unknown person. She was sued successfully in trespass by the executor of the estate, although the damages awarded against her were nominal.

Clearly a dispossession will amount to a trespass. Indeed it is the usual ground of complaint for which trespass is brought. It is uncertain whether a mere touching of the chattel, not amounting to an asportation or a dispossession is a trespass. If it causes damage it is clearly actionable as trespass, as for example where poison is administered directly to another's dog. Where no damage is caused, it is a little difficult to imagine circumstances in which the action of trespass would serve a purpose. It has been suggested that it might be useful for the purpose of preventing the handling of museum exhibits, but the action of trespass seems a somewhat heavy-handed way of dealing with this. Nevertheless the theoretical possibility of an action of trespass for mere touching probably should be preserved.

The defendant's act must directly cause the trespass

If the defendant has put poison down for the plaintiff's dog which the dog consumes, or placed a barrier across the highway into which the plaintiff drives his car, damaging the car, these acts will not amount to trespass because they are insufficiently direct. The courts have not yet decided whether, under an analogous principle to that on which *Wilkinson* v. *Downton* (1897) (*supra*) was based, a person can be sued for causing intentional, non-trespassory, damage to a chattel. There is probably liability here (*cf. infra*, p. 42).

As in battery, there is no need for the defendant himself to come into physical contact with the chattel. To throw a stone at a window and break it is therefore a trespass.

State of mind of defendant

It is suggested that after *Letang* v. *Cooper* (*supra*, p. 9) this form of trespass requires an intentional act on the defendant's part. It is true that *Letang* v. *Cooper* (1965) concerned trespass to the person, but there seems no reason why this should be treated differently from trespass to chattels.

National Coal Board v. *Evans* (1951) is authority for the proposition that in the absence of intention or negligence on the defendant's part, trespass to chattels will not lie. In that case the defendant's servant in the course of excavating the foundations of a building damaged the plaintiff's cable which was situated beneath the land surface. Because the presence of the cable could not have been foreseen by the defendant's servant, the defendant was held not liable in trespass.

It is assumed that after *Fowler* v. *Lanning* (*supra*, p. 9) the burden of proving fault in this form of trespass rests on the plaintiff.

Damages in trespass to chattels

The successful plaintiff who has actually been permanently deprived of the chattel by the defendant is entitled to its full value (even where as in *Wilson* v. *Lombank* (1963) the plaintiff has no title to the chattel, and the defendant's trespass involves restoring the chattel to its true owner). It may be assumed that consequential damages due to the plaintiff's being deprived of the chattel will also be awarded in trespass. Where the defendant has not deprived the plaintiff of the chattel, but has damaged it, the damages awarded will be measured by the extent of the damage.

CONVERSION

This tort requires an intentional dealing with a chattel by the defendant serious enough to be regarded as a denial of the plaintiff's right to possess that chattel.

Conversion is both more various in its methods of commission than trespass, and more exacting in its requirement that the defendant's act must amount to a denial of the plaintiff's right to possess the chattel. Thus an infringement of actual possession is always trespass, but whether it is conversion depends upon the seriousness of the infringement (see the cases on asportation, *infra*, p. 23). Conversion may take many forms other than an infringement of actual possession.

Conversion is the primary remedy by which proprietary interests in chattels are protected. Its reputation for difficulty owes something to this, since many disputes over title to chattels involve difficult questions of commercial law. Although it is largely an accident of history that proprietary claims to chattels are protected by actions in tort, the tortious aspect of conversion causes it to have characteristics which a purely proprietary action would not possess. Thus the judgment in conversion is for the value of the chattel, rather than for the return of the chattel itself. Where the plaintiff is the owner of the chattel, his title in the chattel passes to the defendant when the latter has satisfied a judgment obtained against him in conversion; for this reason conversion operates like a compulsory sale of the chattel to the defendant. A further distinctive feature of conversion is that it lies against anyone who has had dealings with the chattel provided they are sufficiently serious to amount to conversion; a purely proprietary action would lie only against the actual possessor of the chattel.

It must also not be overlooked that because the interest protected in conversion is the plaintiff's right to possess the chattel rather than his title to it, and because such right to possess may be established in other ways than by showing title to the chattel (*infra*, p. 26), the interest protected is more extensive than a merely proprietary one.

The distinction between right to possession and title can be observed in those cases where the owner has no right to possess his own chattel. On the facts of *Rose* v. *Matt* (1951) (*supra*, p. 22) for instance, the pledgee could certainly have sued the owner of the clock in conversion. This is because the pledgor, as a bailor for a term, had lost the right to possess the clock for the period of the pledge.

Plaintiff's interest; concept of right to possession

The plaintiff in conversion must have a right to the chattel's immediate possession. The force of the word "immediate" is that it serves to exclude cases where the plaintiff has some right over the chattel which will entitle the plaintiff to its possession at some future date. For example, the bailor for a term of a chattel will eventually become entitled to its possession. Since, however, his right is to eventual rather than immediate possession, he cannot sue in conversion.

The plaintiff may prove his right to immediate possession of the chattel in one of two ways:

1. He may show that he was in actual possession of the chattel at the time of the defendant's act. The mere fact of possession peacefully held is usually enough to confer a right to possession as against one who disturbs it. But this will not be the case where the person interfering with possession is the true owner or some other person with a title to the chattel which entitles him to its immediate possession. In some cases, however, even the owner can commit conversion against one in actual possession (the facts of *Rose* v. *Matt* (*supra*, p. 22) again present an example).

2. Where the plaintiff was not in possession at the time of the defendant's act, he must show that he has some right in relation to the chattel, entitling him to its immediate possession. Again ownership is the best example, with the proviso that as already explained, the owner does not always have the right to immediate possession of his chattel. It is difficult to state with certainty what, apart from ownership, confers the right to immediate possession of a chattel. Certain cases are clear. The bailee for a term of a chattel has such a right. The pledgee also has the right to immediate possession of the pledge; indeed pledge is a special type of bailment for a term. The holder of a lien also has the right to immediate possession of the subject-matter of the lien. For example, the seller of a chattel has a lien over it until the buyer has either paid or tendered the purchase price. Until that time, the buyer, though he normally acquires ownership of the chattel (section 18 of the Sale of Goods Act 1893) does not have the right to its immediate possession.

The following examples show the working of the law:

1. A bails a chattel for a term to B. It is stolen by C who sells it to D.

Under the principles laid down above, A has no action in conversation against anyone. B can sue either C or D in conversion (the receipt by D under a sale amounts to conversion).

2. A buys a chattel from B. It is stolen from B by C. The buyer of a chattel normally acquires ownership once the contract of sale has been concluded (Sale of Goods Act 1893, section 18) and therefore has the right to possession of the chattel. But he only has this right if he has paid or tendered the purchase-price to the seller;

until that time the seller has a lien over the chattel. In the above example B could sue C in conversion, since C has infringed his actual possession. A could sue C in conversion if he has paid or tendered the purchase price to B, since only then does B's lien over the chattel terminate. (*Cf. Lord* v. *Price* (1874) where the facts were similar to this example.)

Although the bailee for a term of a chattel has no right to its immediate possession during the term, at the end of the term or at the termination of the bailment, for example, where the bailee has committed an act repugnant to the bailment, the bailor acquires the right to the immediate possession of the chattel and can sue in conversion. If, for example, the bailee sells the chattel, the bailor may sue the bailee or the buyer in conversion. Complicated problems arise in the case of hire-purchase contracts in determining whether the hirer's disposal of the goods has the effect of determining the contract of hire-purchase, so allowing the hire-purchase company to sue in conversion (this normally depends upon the court's interpretation of the hire-purchase agreement—see *North General Wagon and Finance Co.* v. *Graham* (1950)).

Apart from these specific cases, there appears to be a general rule that possession of a chattel confers a right to possession of that chattel as against a later possessor. The clearest example of such so-called possessory title is that of the finder, but the doctrine does not appear to be limited to this case. So if A is in possession of a chattel, he has a right to its possession, not only as against B who steals it from him but as against C who buys it from B.

Right to possession of a wrongdoer

There appears to be no English authority upon whether a thief and other wrongful possessors can sue in conversion, but academic opinion leans in favour of their being able to do so where the thief is suing for an infringement of his actual possession, but less so where they are suing on the basis of a possessory title. In the Canadian case of *Bird* v. *Fort Frances* (1949) the plaintiff who had found money on land while trespassing on that land, was allowed to recover it from the police in an action of conversion. The court thought that whether or not he committed larceny as a finder was immaterial, since a thief could sue in conversion.

Finder

The finder is a somewhat special case. In those cases in which he gets possession, he can sue in conversion for an infringement of his actual possession, or on the basis of his possessory title.

In *Armory* v. *Delamirie* (1721) a chimney-sweep's boy found a jewel and handed it to the apprentice of a goldsmith for valuation. The latter extracted the jewl from its setting, and handing back the setting the boy, offered him 1½d. for the jewel. This offer the boy refused and later sued the goldsmith in conversion. This action was successful, the court ruling that "the finder has such a property as will enable him to keep it against all but the rightful owner."

This went further than was necessary for the decision. In the first place, by property the courts clearly meant possession. In *Armory* v. *Delamirie* (1721) there was an infringement of an existing possession, which the plaintiff had not surrendered by handing over the jewel for valuation. Secondly, the finder's possession will not always avail against all but the owner; for example, a previous lawful possessor from whom the goods had been stolen previous to the find could successfully bring conversion against the finder. Finally the courts have limited the possession of finders to cases where the finding is on the surface of land. Thus in *Bridges* v. *Hawkesworth* (1851) the plaintiff, a customer in the defendant's shop, found some bank-notes on the floor of the shop. He then handed them to the defendant for the purpose of trying to discover the owner, but the notes were never claimed. The plaintiff successfully sued in conversion for the notes. The facts clearly illustrate the underlying principles. The plaintiff had obtained possession of the notes by finding, and although he surrendered them under a bailment to the defendant for the purpose of discovering the owner, the bailment became determinable on demand by the bailor when it was clear that the owner would make no claim. After this the rule that the bailee commits conversion by denying his bailor's title came into play, with the result that the defendant was liable for conversion of the money. To the same effect is *Hannah* v. *Peel* (1945) (finder, a soldier, entitled to possession of brooch he found in house which had been requisitioned by the military authorities as against the defendant who was the owner of the house, and to whom the brooch had been handed by the police).

On the other hand, where the chattel is attached to or lying beneath the surface of land, the possessor of land has possession of it. On this ground the possessor of land has been held entitled as against the finder to a pre-historic boat buried beneath the land surface (*Elwes* v. *Brigg Gas Co.* (1886)), two rings lying on the mud at the bottom of a pool (*South Staffs. Water Co.* v. *Sharman* (1896)) and bank-notes found by workmen in the wall safe of demolition premises (*City of London Corporation* v. *Appleyard* (1963)). It should be emphasised that possession of the land *at the time of the finding* is not necessary. Thus in *Elwes* v. *Brigg Gas Co.* (1886) the boat was found by the actual possessor of the land who had possession under the lease from the plaintiff. As it was clear, however, that the boat had been under the land at the beginning of the lease, the plaintiff was entitled to it.

The law on this matter is not particularly logical. The distinction between finding something on the surface of land, and finding something attached to it makes quite trivial matters important. If the chattel is lost on a dry patch of land the finder gets possession; if dropped into mud, the possessor of land. To allow the finder possession will encourage the finder to be honest and report his find, since otherwise he has no incentive for so doing. (He may have a further incentive since a finder in certain circumstances commits theft if he decides to keep the thing for himself—sections 3 (1) and 2 (1)(*c*) of the Theft Act 1968.) This is particularly necessary in the case of finding on land to which the public has access, and for this reason the explanation of *Bridges* v. *Hawkesworth* (1851), in *South Staffs. Water Co.* v. *Sharman* by Lord Russell of Killowen, that the notes were found in the public part of the shop, though not justified by the judgment in the case, seems the most rational explanation of it. The policy argument in favour of allowing a finder possession of something found on the surface of private land seems weaker. Here it seems that the possessor of land should possess the chattel—*Hannah* v. *Peel* (1945) can be distinguished on the ground that the owner of the house had never been in possession of it prior to its requisition. (The Law Reform Committee has given its support to the view that in the case of a finding on land of a public character, the finder should acquire possession—Eighteenth Report of the Law Reform Committee, Cmnd. 4774 (1971).)

Jus tertii

This defence only has relevance where the plaintiff has, as against the defendant, a right to possess the chattel, but a third party has a better right than either of them. As its scope is controverted, it is best to state first what is settled. *Jus tertii* cannot be set up by a bailee against his bailor—he is estopped from relying on the defence. There are two exceptions to this: (1) where the bailee has been evicted by one with a title paramount to that of the bailor, and (2) where the bailee is defending the action on behalf of one with title paramount. Where the bailee cannot rely on either of these two exceptions, he is in a difficult position, since he commits conversion by refusing to recognise his bailor's title to the goods, yet may have a claim made against him for the goods by another person, who, if he has title to the goods, can treat the bailee's refusal of his demand as conversion. The bailee's solution is to institute interpleader proceedings, the effect of which is that the court determines as between bailor and third party who has the right to the chattel, and the bailee who hands over to whichever the court holds entitled, has a good defence against an action by the other.

In cases other than bailment it seems clear that the *jus tertii* will be available as a defence in the same two exceptional cases where it is available to the bailee. Apart from these, the extent to which *jus tertii* is available as a defence is in doubt. It is clear that *jus tertii* is not available where the defendant has infringed the plaintiff's actual possession of the chattel (*Jeffries* v. *G. W. Ry. Co.* (1856)). Where the defendant is suing on the basis of his right to possession rather than infringement of his possession, there is text-book support for the view that *jus tertii* should form a defence (Salmond, p. 143; Winfield, p. 506). But the case on which they rely (*Leake* v. *Loveday* (1812)) appears to turn on the plaintiff's being unable to establish a right to possess the goods in question, rather than on the existence of a better right elsewhere. It seems undesirable that where the plaintiff has a right to possession of the chattel as against the defendant, he should be defeated by the superior title of one who may make no claim to the chattel, or be untraceable. On the other hand the absence of the defence may work unfairly as far as defendants are concerned since a double liability is incurred if the third party subsequently makes a claim for the chattel (this is so even where the defendant has returned the chattel to the true owner and is being sued by one with a mere possessory title—*Wilson* v. *Lombank* (*supra*, p. 23). Accordingly the Law Reform Committee in its Report on Conversion and Detinue (Cmnd. 4774) has recommended that the defence should be available provided the third party is served with notice of the action by the defendant and is joined as a party. Failure by the third party to appear after being served with notice in these circumstances would prevent him from making any subsequent claim against the defendant.

Mental state of defendant in conversion

The defendant must intend to do the act which is relied on by the plaintiff as a conversion. This is quite different from intending to commit conversion. Where A does an act amounting to a conversion of B's chattel, in the mistaken belief that it belongs to him, he commits conversion. For this reason, conversion often operates like a tort of strict liability, in the sense that the defendant may be altogether free from fault.

Acts amounting to conversion

In order to constitute a conversion, the defendant's act must deny the plaintiff's right to possess the chattel. Around this somewhat vague requirement have centred most of the difficulties of conversion. Although there will be no argument about most of the forms that conversion may take, there will always be a peripheral category of acts about which doubt must be felt. The following is a classification of the chief ways in which conversion can be committed. It is recognised that conversion may take other forms not here described.

Dispossession

Dispossession of another person is normally both a trespass and a conversion, since an infringement of another person's possession is usually sufficient to amount to a denial of that person's right to possess the chattel. Thus a thief commits both torts. Asportation, though invariably a trespass is not necessarily a conversion.

Thus in *Fouldes* v. *Willoughby* (1841) the defendant, in order to induce the plaintiff to leave the defendant's ferry-boat, removed the plaintiff's horses from the boat to the shore. The plaintiff remained in the boat and was transported across the river. This did not amount to a conversion; the defendant had done nothing inconsistent with the plaintiff's right to possess the horses. Where loss of the chattel is foreseeably likely as a result of the asportation, however, the defendant will be liable in conversion if such loss occurs.

In *Forsdick* v. *Collins* (1816) the defendant took possession of land on which was lying a block of Portland stone belonging to the plaintiff. He removed the stone off the land to another place, and subsequently the stone was lost; the defendant was held liable in conversion to the plaintiff.

Destruction

Intentional and total destruction of another's chattel is a conversion. Partial or negligent destruction will normally be actionable either in trespass or in negligence.

Dealing

1. *After obtaining possession.* The first problem arises where the defendant has obtained possession of the plaintiff's chattel, knowing of the plaintiff's right, and then dealt with it, for example, by selling it to or pledging it with a third party. This is an obvious example of conversion. The law goes further by making the defendant liable in conversion, even where he is in ignorance of the plaintiff's right. Thus in *Hollins* v. *Fowler* (1875) the defendant, a cotton broker, sold and delivered some cotton belonging to the plaintiff, acting on behalf of a rogue who had obtained possession of the cotton fraudulently from the plaintiff. He was held liable for converting the

cotton, despite the fact that he acted in the bona fide belief that he was acting on behalf of the owner.

The rigour of this principle is to some extent mitigated by the fact that it appears that the defendant is only liable if he himself has negotiated the transaction under which the goods are disposed of to a third party. Where he has only acted to facilitate another's transaction he is not liable in conversion, despite the fact that he knows the transaction affects the title of the goods. In *National Mercantile Bank* v. *Rymill* (1881) goods were given to the defendant, an auctioneer, for sale at his auction. The goods were sold privately by the seller himself, and the defendant handed them over to the buyer on the seller's instructions, knowing they had been sold. He was held not liable in conversion to the true owner of the goods.

Similarly a carrier of goods does not convert them, even where the carrier knows that his act is a delivery of the goods under a sale or other transaction which affects the title to them (*Sheridan* v. *New Quay Co.* (1858)).

Whether a defendant who has himself negotiated the transaction under which possession of the goods passes to a third party is liable in conversion depends upon whether the transaction purports to create rights over the goods inconsistent with those of the plaintiff. Sale, pledge, and hire-purchase are obvious examples. A bailment-at-will by way of loan or deposit would not be. But if the bailment is for repair of the goods, the fact that the repairer has a lien over the goods for the amount of the repairs would probably make the act of bailment a conversion.

2. *Without a physical dealing.* Normally a physical dealing with a chattel is required for conversion to be committed. *Van Oppen* v. *Tredegars* (1921) shows, however, that it is not always necessary. In that case the plaintiff delivered goods by mistake to a firm. The defendants' managing director purported to sell the goods to the firm, claiming to act on behalf of the defendants. The firm used and disposed of the goods in the course of their business. The defendants were held vicariously liable for their servant's conversion of the goods. In this case, although the managing director did not physically deal with the goods, he clearly caused their ultimate loss, since he induced a belief in the firm that it could deal with the goods as its own. A mere sale of another person's goods does not amount to conversion by itself (*Lancashire Waggon Co.* v. *Fitzhugh* (1861)). There is some difficulty in reconciling *Douglas Valley Finance Co.* v. *Hughes* (*Hirers*) (1969) with this. In that case, the defendants, who had possession of the plaintiffs' lorries under contracts of hire-purchase, sold them to third parties in order to enable the latter to obtain the special A-licences attaching to the lorries. The lorries

never left the defendants' possession, and after the third parties had obtained the A-licences, they resold the lorries to the defendants. Nevertheless, it was held that the sale of the lorries was conversion.

Receipt

To receive another's chattel under a sale amounts to a conversion of it, even though the recipient is ignorant of the other's right. This rule clearly reflects the view on which the tort of conversion is based, that ownership, even of chattels, should be inviolable. In a predominantly commercial society, however, a greater need is felt to uphold transactions, to protect the person who for value and in good faith has acquired the chattel. Thus numerous exceptions to the principle that receipt is a conversion have been established, principally by statute. For example, section 25 (1) of the Sale of Goods Act 1893 allows a seller of goods who has remained in possession of them to transfer a title to the goods under a disposition to one who takes them in good faith with the result that such a person is protected against an action of conversion by the buyer.

Receipt under a transaction which does not involve the assertion of any proprietary right over the chattel is not a conversion. For example, a carrier or warehouseman does not convert the chattel he receives. Pledge causes more difficulty. There is authority (*Spackman* v. *Foster* (1883)) that the receipt of a chattel by way of pledge does not amount to a conversion, on the ground that the pledgee does not claim a title to the chattel. But as a normal incident of pledge is the pledgee's right of sale should the debt be unpaid, it seems that this assertion of a right inconsistent with those of the owner should make the receipt by the pledgee conversion.

Involuntary receipt

Where the defendant has taken receipt of a chattel involuntarily (for example, unwanted goods sent through the post), he is called an involuntary bailee of it. The term must be limited to cases where, although the recipient does not want the chattel, he may be taken to have consented to its being in his possession (as when it is delivered through the post). If there is no question of consent to the acquisition of possession, for example, if the chattel is placed in a person's pocket without his knowledge, or thrown on to his land, different considerations arise (*infra*, p. 34).

The legal position of the involuntary bailee is a question of some importance in view of the increasing use by high-pressure salesmanship of the practice of sending unwanted goods through the post and then claiming their price if they are not returned. The involuntary bailee does not commit conversion by his receipt of the goods, nor by taking no steps to return them to the sender. He is not bound to take steps to return the goods, nor by failing to return the goods does he become bound to pay for them. He is probably not liable for negligence in their safekeeping. He would no doubt convert if he unreasonably refused to return the goods to the sender on request by the latter. He formerly had no right to use or dispose of the goods, but now under section 1 of the Unsolicited Goods and Services Act 1971, he has a right, after six months from receipt, or 30 days after giving notice to the sender, to use, deal with or dispose of the goods as if they are an unconditional gift to him.

An involuntary bailee who takes reasonable steps to return the goods to the sender is protected if they are lost. In *Elvin and Powell Ltd.* v. *Plummer Roddis Ltd.* (1933) the delivery by the bailee to a rogue who posed as the plaintiff's agent for collection of the goods was held not to be conversion since the bailee had acted reasonably and without negligence. But in *Hiort* v. *Bott* (1874) where goods had been sent to a railway station, and were deliverable to the order either of the plaintiff or defendant, the defendant committed conversion by indorsing the delivery order to the rogue who posed as the plaintiff's agent. The defendant was here not in the position of an involuntary bailee, and his intermeddling had caused the plaintiff to lose the goods. It was irrelevant that his action may have been reasonable.

Interference with the exercise of the plaintiff's rights

It is clear that the defendant's act may be a conversion even though the defendant has not physically dealt with the plaintiff's chattel (see *Van Oppen & Co. Ltd.* v. *Tredegars Ltd.* (1921) (*supra*)). But in such a case it must be quite clear that the defendant's act constitutes a repudiation of the plaintiff's right to possess the chattel. In *British Economical Lamp Co.* v. *Mile End Theatre* (1913) the defendants' refusal to allow their tenant to enter their premises and remove some lamps which the tenant had left behind at the termination of the lease was held to be neither conversion nor detinue. The lamps were not present by the defendants' act nor was the mere refusal to allow the plaintiffs to enter their land a sufficient interference with the plaintiffs' right to possess the lamps (see *infra*, p. 63, for the right of recaption of chattels). *Oakley* v. *Lyster* (1931) shows that a refusal to allow the plaintiff to exercise his rights over the chattel coupled with other acts of the defendant may be actionable. The plaintiff had leased some land for the purpose of depositing on it a quantity of material which he owned. The defendant acquired the freehold, and subsequently wrote to the plaintiff, informing him that he would not be allowed to remove the material, claiming that it belonged to the defendant; he also used part of the material. The Court of Appeal held that he had converted all the material. He clearly converted the material he had used, but the judgments in the case do not make clear whether his conversion of the rest of the material was based on the totality of his actions, or whether individually they amounted to conversion. If the latter view is correct, there may be a conflict with the *British Economical Lamp* case, though in *Oakley* v. *Lyster*, the defendant's act interfered with the plaintiff's possession rather than merely denying him the opportunity to take possession. *England* v. *Cowley* (1873) shows, however, that a mere interference with possession does not necessarily constitute conversion. The facts in that decision were that the defendant landlord refused at night to allow the plaintiff to remove furniture belonging to the tenant, which the plaintiff had a right to possess under a Bill of Sale, the purpose of the defendant's action being that the defendant should be able to levy a distress over the furniture, which he could only do during the hours of daylight. This was held to be no conversion, on the ground that all the defendant had prevented was a particular use of the goods by the plaintiff. The case would not have been differently decided, it appears, if the plaintiff had actually owned the furniture. But it seems clear that on proof of damage there would be actionability under the residual principle (p. 42).

Demand and refusal

An action of conversion can be based on a demand for the return of the chattel, and a refusal to surrender it by the defendant. The action of detinue was the more typical remedy in this situation, and it was only by treating the defendant's refusal as evidence of a conversion by him that the availability of conversion could be justified by the courts.

Two conditions are necessary for the defendant's refusal to operate as a conversion:

1. The defendant must be in possession of the chattel. Where the defendant has not possession, this may be because of his prior act of conversion. In such a case, the conversion dated for the purpose of the limitation period on the action from the act of conversion, detinue only from the demand and refusal (but see Limitation Act 1939, *infra*, p. 319). Where the defendant has lost possession in circumstances not amounting to a conversion by him the plaintiff's only possibility is detinue, since merely losing possession, even if negligent, is not conversion.

2. The defendant's refusal to surrender the chattel to the plaintiff must be unreasonable. In *Clayton* v. *Le Roy* (1911) where the defendant refused to return the plaintiff's watch on demand to the managing clerk of the plaintiff's solicitors, it was held that the refusal was not unreasonable because the clerk had shown no evidence of authority from the plaintiff to make the demand.

User

There is a certain amount of ancient authority (for example, *Petre* v. *Heneage* (1701)) to the effect that to use another's chattel without destroying or consuming it is conversion, and Australian authority as modern support (*Penfold's Wines Pty. Ltd.* v. *Elliott* (1946)). The desirability of following these cases seems doubtful. If the defendant has caused damage to the chattel by using it, this would seem to be actionable under the residual principle mentioned below at page 42. Where the defendant has used the chattel without making any assertion of title to it (for example, where one person takes another's horse, rides it, and redelivers it to its owner), his act does not appear to be inconsistent with the owner's right to its possession, and should not expose him to an action for the chattel's value. The problem of use is more difficult in the case of bailment because of the introduction by the courts of the nebulous concept of an act repugnant to the bailment. If such an action of user is committed by the bailee, this terminates the bailment and the bailee can be sued in conversion. If the bailee's user is not repugnant to the bailment but is contrary to its terms, it is actionable on the case under the residual principle provided it causes damage (*Donald* v. *Suckling* (1866)).

Conversion and negligence

Although there is normally a great difference between the torts of conversion and negligence, it appears that negligence may have the effect of turning an otherwise innocent act into a conversion. One example of this is *Forsdick* v. *Collins* (1816) (*supra*) where the purely trespassory act of asportation was made into a conversion by the likelihood of loss of the chattel which it caused. Another example is *Moorgate Mercantile Co.* v. *Finch & Read* (1962). The defendant borrowed a car from a hirer at a time when the plaintiff hire-purchase company had the right to immediate possession of the vehicle because of the hirer's default in payment of instalments. The defendant used the car for the purpose of carrying smuggled watches, and when he was caught and convicted, the car was confiscated (permanently) by the customs under statutory powers.

The defendant was liable for conversion because he had intentionally done an act which was foreseeably likely to lead to the car's loss. The similarity of the ground on which this case was decided to the principle established in *Wilkinson* v. *Downton* (1897) may be noticed. It may give rise to difficulties in separating conversion from negligence.

Effect of judgment in conversion

In an action of conversion the plaintiff can only claim the value of the chattel, not the chattel itself. This reflects the tortious rather than proprietary nature of the action. Where the plaintiff wants the chattel itself, he must use detinue.

Satisfaction of a judgment in conversion by the defendant vests the plaintiff's title in the defendant. A successful action of conversion therefore operates as a compulsory sale of the chattel to the defendant (the defendant because of his act of conversion being forced to buy out the plaintiff's interest). Where the action is brought successfully by one without title (*i.e.* one with a possessory title), the defendant will of course not acquire title, and may therefore still be liable to the true owner (*Attenborough* v. *London and St. Katherine's Dock* (1878)—for the effect of satisfaction made to a bailee see, *infra*, p. 41). Once the plaintiff has been divested to his title to the chattel by means of the satisfaction of a judgment in conversion, he loses the right to possession of the chattel and cannot bring any further actions against those who may have converted his chattel.

Although the plaintiff may not claim the chattel itself when suing in conversion, it appears that the defendant has the alternative of surrendering the chattel to the plaintiff rather than paying its value. The court will therefore stay an action in conversion once surrender of the chattel has been made by the defendant to the plaintiff; the defendant must pay the plaintiff's costs up to that moment, and any damages he has suffered through being deprived of his chattel (for these propositions see the judgment of Lord Radcliffe in *U.S.A. and France* v. *Dollfuss Mieg* (1952)).

Detinue

The basis of the cause of action in detinue is that the defendant is wrongfully detaining the plaintiff's chattel. In order to establish this, it is essential that the plaintiff should demand the return of his chattel from the defendant and that the defendant should refuse this demand. Where the defendant is in possession of the plaintiff's chattel at the time of the plaintiff's demand, the defendant commits both conversion and detinue by refusing the demand, and the two torts are here identical. Where the defendant is no longer in possession, however, there is a difference. Conversion cannot be based on a demand and refusal when the defendant no longer has possession of the chattel at the time of the demand. Detinue can be based on such demand and refusal provided the defendant ought to be in possession of the chattel, for example, by virtue of a contract under which the chattel has been bailed to him by the plaintiff.

Example. A hires a chattel to B who sells it to C.

A's action of conversion against B is based upon his sale of the chattel to C. His action of detinue is based upon his demand for the return of the chattel and B's refusal to comply.

In some circumstances detinue will lie where conversion does not.

Example. A hires his chattel to B who loses it negligently.

In this situation the plaintiff can sue the defendant in detinue, having made his demand for the chattel and having had this refused by the defendant. Conversion is not available (because the negligent loss of the chattel does not amount to conversion).

A further difference between conversion and detinue is that in the latter tort, the plaintiff must, with a few exceptions such as the bailee or pledgee, show both a right to possession of the chattel and a right of property in it (*Jarvis* v. *Williams* (1955)).

In some circumstances neither conversion nor detinue will lie, for example where the defendant has had possession of the plaintiff's chattel, but has lost possession of it without converting it, and there is no contractual relationship between the plaintiff and defendant. The only possible cause of action available to the plaintiff here is negligence. An example is *Lee Cooper* v. *Jeakins* (1965). The plaintiffs, who had sold goods to a firm in Eire, arranged with X, another firm, for the reshipment and delivery of the goods, on arrival in port in England, to Eire. The defendants, road-haulage contractors agreed with X to carry the goods from the English port of arrival to X's warehouse. The goods were lost in course of transit owing to the defendants' negligence. The court held that this negligence was actionable by the plaintiffs. Neither conversion nor detinue was available because the plaintiffs had lost the right to possession of the goods.

Detinue and contract

An action in detinue will often be alternative to an action in contract. Subject to variation by the terms of the contract, the test of liability for loss of the chattel will be the same whatever action is brought, the defendant being liable if he acted deliberately or negligently. But in detinue, proof of the bailment and the loss of the chattel raises a prima facie case of negligence requiring an explanation against the defendant—this is not so in contract (*Houghland* v. *Low* (*Luxury Coaches*) *Ltd.* (1962)). Detinue may be available where no contractual action lies (see *Ballett* v. *Mingay* (1943)—action against a minor). But detinue will not lie where the defendant has caused a damage to the chattel rather than its loss. Only a claim in contract is possible here.

Specific restitution in detinue

If the plaintiff wishes to get the chattel itself back rather than its value, he must sue in detinue. The judgment in conversion is always for the value of the chattel, although as we have seen, the defendant is given the option of surrendering it in mitigation of damages. Even where the defendant is successful in an action of detinue, the court will not always order specific restitution of the chattel. The court will not normally award specific restitution where the chattel "is an ordinary article of commerce and of no special value or interest, and not alleged to be of any specific value to the plaintiff, and where damages would fully compensate" (*Whiteley* v. *Hilt* (1918)). It is also assumed, although authority is lacking, that specific restitution would not be ordered against a defendant no longer in possession of the chattel.

Measure of Damages in Conversion and Detinue

In both torts, where the defendant is paying a sum of money to the plaintiff rather than returning the chattel, the damages awarded will be based on the value of the chattel together with any damage the plaintiff has suffered as a result of being deprived of it. The first problem is that of assessing the value of the chattel. The date of assessment is clearly of importance, since the value of the chattel can fluctuate between the commission of the wrong and the date of judgment. Most textbooks support the view that in conversion the value is assessed as at the date of conversion; in detinue the date of the judgment in the action is appropriate. This is because conversion is regarded as complete once the act of conversion has been committed, whereas detinue, which is based on wrongful detention of the chattel, is thought of as continuing until judgment is given. But in one case (*Sachs* v. *Miklos* (1948)), a plaintiff suing in conversion was allowed an increment in the value of the goods converted as at the date of judgment, provided it appeared from the evidence the plaintiff did not delay her action in order to take advantage of this increase. There is some support in the judgment of Goddard L.J. for the view that the increased value would only be given in conversion where detinue also was available, as it was in that case. It is hoped, however, that this case will be given a wider interpretation. A plaintiff suing in detinue has been allowed the value of the goods at the date of demand and refusual where there has been a fall in their value at the date of judgment (*Williams* v. *Archer* (1874)). These cases are not so much exceptional as pointers to the true rule of law, whereby the plaintiff gets damages based on his loss, it being assumed in his favour as against a wrongdoer that had he had the goods in his possession, he would have retained them in the event of a rise in prices, whereas he would have sold before a fall in the market. The date of the commission of the tort and the date of judgment are the outer extremes within which fluctuations in value will be taken into account. Thus if the chattel was worth £100 at the date on which the cause of action in conversion or detinue arose, and rose to £120 before falling to £100 at the date of judgment, there is no reason why the plaintiff should not recover as damages such intermediate rise in value.

The value is taken as the market value of the chattel, although where such a chattel is unobtainable on the market, the replacement cost must be awarded. Hire-purchase contracts again cause difficulties in this connection. Does a finance company suing for conversion of the chattel recover the value of the chattel or only the amount of the unpaid instalments? If the former the company may make a profit from the commission of a wrong against itself, often at the expense of a defendant who has acted innocently. But this was the measure of damages allowed in *United Dominions Trust Ltd.* v. *Parkway Motors Ltd.* (1955) on the ground that the hirer who had disposed of the goods in breach of a term in the contract of hire-purchase was expressly prohibited by the contract from transferring the benefit of the agreement. But this was disapproved by the Court of Appeal in *Wickham Holdings* v. *Brooke House Motors* (1967) in which the plaintiff company recovered only the amount of the unpaid instalments from the defendants. Lord Denning M.R. thought that a hire-purchase contract creates two proprietary interests in the goods, that of the finance company, and that of the hirer. In other words the finance company's interest in the goods gradually diminishes and that of the hirer gradually increases with the payment of instalments.

In some cases the amount of the unpaid instalments will exceed the present value of the chattel. In *Astley Industrial Trust* v. *Miller* (1968) the defendant was allowed to return a car or pay its present value together with damages for its detention, rather than pay the outstanding hire-purchase instalments on the car. The *Wickham Holdings* case was distinguished on the ground that it involved a claim for conversion and the present action was one of detinue. But it seems that the option of returning the chattel plus the payment of damages for its detention exists in conversion also (*supra*, p. 37). It is to be hoped that the judgment does not give countenance to a further anomalous distinction between conversion and detinue whereby the defendant can be made to pay the value of the car in detinue even though this exceeds the amount of the unpaid instalments.

The value of any improvement to the chattel carried out by the defendant is not allowed in an action of conversion (*Munro* v. *Willmott* (1949)). There seems no reason why it should make a difference if the plaintiff sues in detinue, but in the case of *Glenwood Lumber Co.* v. *Phillips* (1904) it was held that the defendant could not be allowed the expenses of improvement where specific restitution of the chattel had been ordered against him, although the court considered that such expenses might but would not necessarily be taken into account in assessing the damages to be awarded where the defendant was given the alternative of paying damages to specific restitution.

In both conversion and detinue the plaintiff may recover special damages arising from being deprived of his chattel. Thus where a carpenter whose tools were converted by the defendant was thereby rendered unable to work, he recovered in conversion his loss of wages as special damages in addition to the value of the tools (*Bodley* v. *Reynolds* (1846)). In *Strand Electric Co.* v. *Brisford Entertainments* (1952) the plaintiffs who sued in detinue for the return of some switchboards which they had hired to the defendants were allowed to recover as special damages a hiring charge for the equipment during the period of detention (despite the fact that the plaintiff could not have hired out all of the equipment during this period). There seems no reason why these damages should not also be awarded in conversion, where the action is based on the defendant's refusal to return the plaintiff's chattel.

Plaintiffs with limited interests

Where the plaintiff has a limited interest in the chattel, such as that of a bailee, pledgee or carrier, the law appears to be that he still recovers the full value of the chattel in conversion or detinue where he is relying on an infringement of his actual possession and probably also where he is relying on a mere right to possession. Of course he is only entitled to keep the amount representing his interest in the chattel—the remainder he holds for the benefit of the person with the residual interest in the chattel. In the case of a person suing on the basis of a mere possessory title, the rule is that satisfaction to the plaintiff by the defendant does not bar an action by the true owner of the chattel (*Attenborough* v. *London and St. Katharine Docks* (1878)). In the case of bailment, on the other hand, the rule is that satisfaction made to the bailee prevents any action by the bailor (*The Winkfield* (1902)—the rule is presumably the same for the pledgee and the carrier). This, together with the rule that the bailee in his action can recover the full value of the chattel, has the effect of throwing the risk of the bailee's insolvency on the bailor rather than on the wrongdoer. It is an essential rule that the bailee should be able to recover full value where the bailment is for a term, since in this case the bailor cannot sue in conversion or detinue at all. Where the bailment is at will, however, there seems little point in allowing the bailee to recover full value unless he is instructed to sue for that amount to the bailor. It follows that the bailor's action here should not be barred by the fact that satisfaction has been made to the bailee (no doubt, the defendant should be given the right to have the bailor joined as a party to the action).

Residual Forms of Tortious Interference with Chattels

Trespass, conversion, and detinue do not exhaust the forms which a tortious interference with chattels may take. In these torts the plaintiff must prove either an infringement of his possession or a denial of his right to possession by the defendant. Where the plaintiff cannot fulfil these requirements, he may still be able to sue. Thus, if the defendant has damaged or destroyed the chattel, the owner may sue for the damage to his reversionary interest in the chattel. This rule may be of benefit to the bailor for a term (*cf. Mears* v. *L. & S.W. Ry.* (1862)), the purchaser of a chattel where the seller has a lien over it for its price, and other holders of reversionary interests in chattels. Under a similar principle, the bailee who has deviated from the terms of the bailment and thereby caused damage to the chattel can be sued by the bailor by what was formerly action on the case (*supra*, p. 36). Case was also available where the defendant's act did not constitute conversion but had nevertheless caused damage, for example by interfering with the owner's freedom of using the chattel (*cf. England* v. *Cowley*, *supra*). It is suggested that liability under this principle extends to the causing of damage to the chattel by wrongful user (*cf. supra*, p. 36).

Where the owner has no reversionary interest in the chattel (*i.e.* is not entitled in future to its possession), he may be able to rely on negligence. *Lee Cooper* v. *Jeakins* (*supra*, p. 38) is an example of this.

CHAPTER 4

TRESPASS TO LAND

THIS tort, which is also called trespass *quare clausum fregit*, is committed by one who intentionally makes entry on the land of another in possession of that land. It is also committed by one who enters in circumstances not amounting to a trespass, but who commits an act of trespass while on the land, for example, by refusing to leave when required to by the occupier.

Plaintiff's interest; actual possession of the land

The plaintiff must show that he was in actual possession of the land at the time of the defendant's act. It is clear, therefore, that the remedy of an owner of land out of possession of it against one who has entered it cannot be trespass. In this situation the owner must sue the intruder with the action of ejectment (*infra*, p. 48). The requirement of possession of the land in the plaintiff means also that trespass is available to persons other than the owner of the land. For example, a lessee who under the lease has possession of the demised premises may sue for trespass to them. So also may a mortgagee in possession of mortgaged land.

The law does not insist upon any legally recognised interest in the land entitling the plaintiff to possession of the land. To put the plaintiff to proof of his title to the land would penalise many persons whose peaceable and long-enjoyed occupation of land has been disturbed by a third party. But the wrongful possessor gets the benefit of the same rule, even seemingly the person who gained possession by his ejection of another person. Thus in *Graham* v. *Peat* (1861) the plaintiff who was in possession of land under a lease which was wholly void by statute was allowed to sue in trespass. But there are limitations to this doctrine. An unlawful possession, though sufficient against a third party, is not so against the true owner of the land. In *Delaney* v. *T. P. Smith & Co.* (1946) the plaintiff and defendant had orally agreed that the plaintiff was to acquire the tenancy of the defendant's premises. The plaintiff entered the premises secretly before a tenancy agreement had been executed, and was ejected forcibly by the defendant a week later. The plaintiff's action against the defendant in trespass failed. The oral agreement could not be relied on by the plaintiff as giving him the right to the possession of the premises since it was not evidenced by writing as required by section 40 of the Law Property Act 1925. Furthermore, the plaintiff's actual possession of the premises did not justify him in bringing an action of trespass against the owner of the premises.

Title to the land, though not conferring a right to bring trespass, is therefore nevertheless relevant in providing the holder of such title with a defence to an action of trespass. This does not mean that an owner of land cannot commit trespass thereto, *e.g.* a lessor can trespass against his lessee. Another limitation upon the rule that possession of the land confers title to bring trespass is that actual possession gained as a result of ejecting another is not sufficient to allow the possessor to treat a later entry of that other as trespass. The law allows the ejected person a reasonable time to reinstate himself in possession. If he succeeds in this, he does not commit trespass.

Title to the land also appears to be relevant where the exclusiveness of the plaintiff's possession is disputed by the defendant; if the plaintiff has title it will be more readily assumed in his favour that his actions in relation to the land show him to be in possession of it. Thus in *Fowley Marine* (*Emsworth*) *Ltd.* v. *Gafford* (1968) the plaintiffs were seeking an injunction against the defendant's trespassing on their tidal creek. Having found first of all that the plaintiffs could not establish a "paper title" to the creek, the court then ruled that the plaintiffs' actions in relation to the creek did not establish them to be in exclusive possession so that their action of trespass failed.

A certain amount of difficulty surrounds the question whether a licensee can sue in trespass. It seems certain that the person who has a licence coupled with an equity to remain on the land (as in *Errington* v. *Errington* (1952); *Dillwyn* v. *Llewellyn* (1862)) can sue for trespass to the land. Such a licence cannot be revoked by the licensor, and the licensee enjoys exclusive occupation of the land and security of tenure. On the other hand, the bare licensee, for example, the lodger who takes a room for a night, or the person who takes a seat in a cinema or a train has no possession and cannot sue a third party who disturbs his occupation in trespass. It now seems possible, however, for a bare licensee to be given such exclusive occupation of land as to amount to possession of the land enabling the licensee to sue a third party in trespass if he has entered. Thus where the parties wished to avoid the creation of a tenancy to which the Rent Restriction Acts applied they were able to create a licence giving the licensee exclusive possession with a right to sue in trespass (*Marcroft Wagons Ltd.* v. *Smith* (1951)). Previously it had been thought that such a relationship must give rise to a tenancy. Whether the idea of exclusive possession in a licensee would be extended beyond the case of a licence to avoid the application of the Rent Restriction Acts is unsettled.

The act of trespass

The defendant by his act must cause a direct invasion of the plaintiff's land. Where the invasion is indirect, trespass will not lie, although nuisance or negligence may be available. In *Lemmon* v. *Webb* (1894) roots and branches of the defendant's trees projected from the defendant's land on to the plaintiff's. This was held to be nuisance and not trespass. In *Esso Petroleum Co.* v. *Southport Corporation* (1956) oil discharged from the defendants' ship was carried by the tide on the plaintiffs' foreshore. It was held that this was not trespass.

The entry on the land need not be that of the defendant. If he has thrown a stone on the land this is a trespass. But there must be some entry. In *Perera* v. *Vandiyar* (1953) the defendant turned off the plaintiff's gas and electricity from the meter in the defendant's cellar. This was not trespass because the defendant had caused no entry of anything into the plaintiff's premises although the effects of what he did were experienced there.

Trespass to the highway

The highway is in legal analysis a public right of way over land which remains in the ownership and possession of the adjoining landowners (although by statute ownership and possession of the surface and so much of the land above and below the surface as is necessary for the effective maintenance of the highway is often vested in a highway authority).

The public right over the highway is one of passage merely. One who uses the highway for a purpose other than that of passage may thereby commit a trespass against the adjoining landowners. Thus in *Harrison* v. *Duke of Rutland* (1893) the defendant who had scared off grouse as they were approaching a shooting-party on the Duke's land was successfully sued in trespass by the Duke. In *Randall* v. *Tarrant* (1955) the parking of a car on the highway was held not to be a trespass to the highway despite the fact that the occupants of the car after parking it committed trespasses on the plaintiff's adjoining land. The test appears to be whether the act committed on the highway can in itself be fairly objected to by the adjoining landowner.

State of mind of the defendant

The entry by the defendant on to the plaintiff's land will normally be intentional. This will be a trespass even if the defendant is under a reasonable though mistaken belief that he is entitled to enter (for example, because he thinks the land belongs to himself).

Trespass to land is not available where the defendant has acted neither intentionally nor negligently in entering the land. Support for this is provided by the ancient case of *Smith* v. *Stone* (1647) in which it was held that one thrown by another on to the plaintiff's land did not commit trespass, although he who threw did. It is also likely that after *Letang* v. *Cooper*, trespass to land cannot be committed negligently.

Subject-matter of trespass

The subject-matter of this form of trespass is land. This is wide enough to cover buildings, rooms in buildings, plants, and vegetables; indeed, anything attached to the land and capable of being separately possessed.

Possession of land is normally *usque ad coelum*, *usque ad inferos*. The possession extends to the air-space above the land, as well as to the land beneath the surface. Of course it is possible that such possession may be in different hands. Thus the possession of the surface may be in one person, while that of the land below in another. In the case of the highway, the possession is often vested in a local authority so that it is proper plaintiff in an action of trespass to the highway. On the other hand the subsoil and minerals beneath the surface of the highway will be in the possession of the adjoining landowners.

In *Kelsen* v. *Imperial Tobacco Co.* (1957) the plaintiff obtained an injunction against the defendant to remove an advertisement which infringed the air-space above a shop of which the plaintiff was the lessee. In the later case of *Woollerton and Wilson* v. *Richard Costain* (1970), an injunction was granted against the defendants' infringement of the plaintiffs' air-space but its operation was suspended until certain building operations carried on by the defendants and which had given rise to the necessity to trespass, were concluded. The discretionary nature of the injunction makes it possible for the court to ensure that the right to freedom of air-space is not unreasonably enforced. The *usque ad coelum* principle clearly causes difficulty in the case of aircraft flights, and has been modified by statute. The Civil Aviation Act 1949 provides that no action shall lie in respect of trespass or nuisance by reason only of the flight of an aircraft over any property at a height above the ground which, having regard to wind, weather and all the circumstances of the case, is reasonable.

On the other hand, under the same section the owner of an aircraft is liable for all material loss or damage caused by it, or by a person in, or by an article or person falling from it, while in flight, taking off or landing, whether the damage is to person or property, and without proof of negligence or intention or other cause of action.

The Act now applies to aircraft belonging to the Crown, except for military aircraft.

Trespass ab initio

Under the common law doctrine of trespass *ab initio*, one who has entered land under authority of law is liable as a trespasser in respect of his original entry if he commits some act on the land not justified by the authority under which he entered.

There is no doubt that the doctrine at its genesis was intended as a means of restraining abuse of power by officials who had a legal right to enter premises, and in particular sheriffs and bailiffs appointed to levy a distress on property within the premises. The fact that they could be treated as trespassers from the time of entry justified the award of greater damages. The same purpose can in many cases be achieved by the award of exemplary damages (*infra*, p. 303). The only importance of the doctrine apart from this is to make trespassory what is not in itself trespassory. So in *Oxley* v. *Watts* (1785) the defendant had worked a horse which he had taken as a lawful distress. It was held that this made him a trespasser *ab initio*, although the working of the horse was not trespass to chattels. But where the wrongful conduct is an omission, trespass *ab initio* cannot apply. It is also ruled out where a ground justifying entry remains, despite the misfeasance (*Elias* v. *Pasmore* (1934)—police lawfully entered premises to arrest plaintiff, and while there took documents some of which they were not entitled to take, but were not trespassers *ab initio* because of the arrest of the plaintiff). In *Chic Fashions Ltd.* v. *Jones* (1968) it was held that seizure by police lawfully on premises of goods on the premises reasonably believed by them to have been stolen was not trespass to chattels and the police were therefore not trespassers *ab initio*. The Court of Appeal appeared to doubt whether the doctrine of trespass *ab initio* had any continuing existence.

Defences

It is a defence that the defendant was on the land by permission or licence of the occupier. Such licence may be revoked by the occupier, and the entrant, having been given reasonable time to remove himself, ejected as a trespasser (the problems arising from revocation of contractual licences are not considered in this book).

The entrant also may have a legal right to enter, apart from the occupier's permission. This may be conferred by statute (for example, the powers given to officials of Gas and Electricity Boards), or may exist at common law (for example, public and private rights of way, and the right of recaption of chattels).

Remedies

The action of trespass to land, like that of conversion, is not a means of recovering the plaintiff's property. The remedies available to the plaintiff for trespass, damages, or an injunction, will not suffice to restore possession of the land to the plaintiff if at the time of the action the defendant rather than the plaintiff has possession. Furthermore, the measure of damages in trespass to land assumes the plaintiff either to have or to be able to recover possession of the land, since the plaintiff gets not the value of land but the diminution in value as the result of the trespass. The difference between conversion, on the one hand, where the plaintiff recovers the whole value of his chattel, and trespass, where he recovers only the reduction in value of his land, derives from the difference between chattels and land. Land is always identifiable—the plaintiff out of possession cannot therefore get the value of the land from the defendant but must bring action for the recovery of the land itself. All this points to the existence of another remedy if the plaintiff wishes to recover possession of the land rather than damages for an infringement of possession. This is the action of ejectment. It may be combined with an action for damages, called an action for mesne profits, which is merely another form of trespass *quare clausum fregit*. Where, therefore, the plaintiff is out of possession at the time of the action, even where he has been dispossessed by the defendant's act of trespass, he will sue in ejectment for recovery of the land and claim damages in the action of mesne profits. Where, on the other hand, he has possession at the time of the action, he will sue in trespass, claiming either damages from the defendant, or an injunction against further disturbance of his possession.

Measure of damages in trespass

The rule is that the plaintiff recovers from the defendant the loss he has suffered as a result of the trespass. Thus he will get the depreciation in the market value of the land (though not the cost of restoring it to its original condition). The plaintiff is further entitled to a reasonable rental for the land where the defendant has been in occupation of the land and has made use of it (*Whitwham* v. *Westminster Brymbo Coal and Coke Co.* (1896)—the two claims are cumulative—thus in the case itself the defendant had tipped refuse on part of the plaintiff's land. It was held that he must pay damages for the depreciation in the value of the land plus a reasonable amount of rental for that part of the land which the defendant had made use of for tipping).

Ejectment and the action for mesne profits

In all cases in which the plaintiff wishes to recover possession of his land from the defendant, he must use the action of ejectment. The action is wider in scope than trespass since it lies against a defendant who has come into possession of the plaintiff's land by other means than by committing trespass.

The action for mesne profits, as already pointed out, is merely a form of trespass *quare clausum fregit*. It is a claim in respect of damage of a trespassory nature done to the land by the defendant, together with a claim for profits taken from the land by the defendant during his occupancy, but unlike trespass is available where the plaintiff had a right to possession rather than possession at the time of the defendant's act. Since it is available in similar circumstances to the action of ejectment, it is normally combined with that action. The theoretical justification for allowing the plaintiff to sue in the action of mesne profits, which is a form of trespass, for acts of the defendant committed when the plaintiff had not possession of the land, is the doctrine of trespass by relation. Under this doctrine, the possession of one with a right to possession of land, who has recovered possession of it, is deemed to extend back to the date when the right to possession came into existence with the result that such a person can sue for trespass committed during the interim period. The theoretical objection against combining the action of mesne profits with the action of ejectment, *viz.* that possession of the land is not recovered until *after* the action of ejectment, with the result that the doctrine of trespass by relation cannot then operate, is now overlooked by the courts.

It may be helpful to set out the possibilities of action available to a person whose possession of land has been disturbed (it is assumed that he also has title to the land):

1. Trespass *quare clausum fregit* lies against the person who has actually infringed the plaintiff's possession, whether his act has dispossessed the plaintiff or not, and if he has dispossessed the plaintiff whether or not he is now in possession.

2. Where the plaintiff has been dispossessed of his land, it will be more normal to sue the person now in possession with the action of ejectment for recovery of the land, combining this with an action for mesne profits which lies against the present possessor whether or not he is the person who dispossessed the plaintiff.

3. Where the plaintiff has recovered possession of his land without suing in ejectment, or where he did not claim damages in the

action of ejectment, it seems that he can now proceed in a claim for damages, either, in the case of the dispossessor, by an action of trespass, or against subsequent possessors, by the action for mesne profits.

4. Finally, there is a new summary procedure for the recovery of land laid down by R.S.C. Ord. 113 which was brought in in 1970 as a result of various "squatting" cases (as to which see *University of Warwick* v. *De Graaf* (1975), the last of the cases). Where a person or persons have entered into or remained on land of which they are in *sole* occupation, a person claiming possession of such land may do so by means of an originating summons supported by an affidavit. This procedure is not only much quicker than the more traditional methods outlined above, but it has the advantage of being available against unidentifiable defendants (one of the features of the "squatters" cases being that the defendants refused to identify themselves thus making it impossible or at least very difficult for proceedings to be commenced against them). However, when recovery of land is sought by this method, no other claim, *e.g.* for mesne profits or damages, can be joined with the originating summons, and the procedure is in any case not available against a tenant holding over after the expiration of the tenancy.

Actions by those without possession or a right to immediate possession of the land

The first case is that of the reversioner, for example the landlord or the person with an interest in remainder in land. The landlord has contractual protection against the tenant under the lease for damage to the premises. The remainderman is protected against damage done by the tenant for life under the rules of waste. Reversioners also have an action against third parties who have damaged the land in such permanent fashion that the reversioner's interest is prejudiced.

The next case is the licensee. As already explained, he is normally unable to sue for trespass to the land. An exception to this is That where the defendant has interfered with a profit *à prendre* possessed by the plaintiff, the plaintiff can bring trespass against him (as in *Mason* v. *Clarke* (1955), the defendant interfered with the plaintiff's right to catch rabbits on another's estate). The rule that a bare licensee cannot sue in trespass may cause hardship where a third party has caused damage to fixtures erected by the licensee on the land, or defaced advertisements displayed by the licensee on another's wall, since these acts are not actionable at the instance of the licensee.

Declaratory judgment

If for any reason it is impossible to prove the requirements of the tort of trespass, it may still be possible for a plaintiff to obtain a declaration of his rights in a declaratory action. A declaratory judgment, though not enforceable by the plaintiff, is of use in cases where the parties are in genuine doubt about their rights and wish the courts to remove this doubt. It therefore seems likely to be of use in disputes over title to land. In *Acton Bor. Council* v. *Morris* (1953) the defendant locked the door of his house thereby depriving the plaintiffs of access to their flat on the upper storey of the house. The defendant's act was not trespass, but the plaintiffs obtained a declaration from the court of their right of access to the flat.

CHAPTER 5

DEFENCES TO THE INTENTIONAL TORTS TO PERSON AND PROPERTY

THE defences that will be discussed in this chapter are those available where the defendant has committed an intentional invasion of the plaintiff's interest. Although some of these defences (for example, consent, contributory negligence) are equally applicable in the case of negligence and other non-intentional torts, most of the defences discussed here assume an intentional act by the defendant. The effect of the defence is that the defendant while admitting the commission of what would be a tort now seeks to adduce in evidence additional facts which will excuse what he has done. For this reason the burden of proving the facts that will establish the defence rests on the defendant.

CONSENT

The term consent is used to describe the defence available when the plaintiff has agreed to the commission of an intentional tort against himself. *Volenti non fit injuria* or voluntary assumption of risk is the defence available when the plaintiff has agreed to run the risk of being injured by the defendant's negligence. Consent may be express or implied. Whether it is implied will often be a difficult question of fact. The plaintiff in *Wilkinson* v. *Downton* (*supra*, p. 20) would no doubt have impliedly consented to being told the news about her husband had it been true. Consent must be given to the act complained of (for an example where consent was not a defence for this reason, see *Nash* v. *Sheen* (*supra*, p. 11)). Consent is invalid if it is obtained by fraud, duress or improper show of authority. In *Hegarty* v. *Shine* (1878) it was held that the consent of the plaintiff to having intercourse with the defendant, who did not reveal he was suffering from syphilis, was not obtained by fraud. The defendant had made no representation about his condition, and the plaintiff could therefore not establish that the terms of her consent excluded intercourse with syphilitic males.

In *Buckpitt* v. *Oates* (1968) it was held perhaps suprisingly that an infant of seventeen, though incapable of giving a contractual consent, could give a consent to another's negligence for the purpose of establishing the defence of *volenti non fit injuria*.

Mistake

Mistake appears to be no defence to the commission of an intentional tort against the plaintiff. The constable who mistakenly arrests the wrong man, however reasonable his mistake, has no defence to an action of false imprisonment. The rule is well settled but there is no doubt that it can cause hardship. Several examples of this have already been noted in the case of conversion, where it is clearly no defence that the defendant thinks that he has a right to do the act constituting the conversion.

Another case where hardship may be caused is where the defendant commits a battery through a reasonable though mistaken belief that he was acting in self-defence or to eject a trespasser—such belief is no defence.

Inevitable Accident

In an action of trespass, it appeared to be the law that the burden of proving that he acted neither intentionally nor negligently rested on the defendant—he had to prove inevitable accident. After *Fowler* v. *Lanning* (1959) (*supra*, p. 9) this defence no longer exists.

Defence of Person

The fact that the defendant was acting in the defence of his person may be a valid defence to an action of battery brought by the plaintiff. The defence is made out if the defendant shows that he used no more than reasonable force in the protection of his person. Force may be unreasonable either because it is more than necessary to repel the plaintiff's attack, or because though necessary it is disproportionate to the harm the plaintiff threatened to inflict on the defendant.

Thus, suppose that the plaintiff repeatedly ruffles the hair of the defendant, a much smaller man, against his will, and the defendant eventually stabs the plaintiff. Although there is no authority on the use of disproportionate force, it seems doubtful whether the defendant could here rely on self-defence.

A case for self-defence must exist; a reasonable though mistaken belief by the defendant in his right to act in self-defence is not enough. But it may in this connection be pointed out that one who induces in another a reasonable belief that he is about to use force against him, even if he does not intend to use that force, probably commits assault. In such a case there is no doubt that a right of self-defence exists, as when the plaintiff has pointed an unloaded gun at the defendant, and the defendant has then used force against the plaintiff.

The courts have also recognised that a person may be justified in acting in the defence of his wife, his family, and his servants. Whether this would be extended to other persons is doubtful. The rule is probably that provided the defendant has acted reasonably in defending another person, he can use this as a defence.

Defence of Property

It is well established that reasonable force may be used by one in possession of land to eject a trespasser from that land. A reasonable though mistaken belief that the person ejected is a trespasser is not sufficient. This may give rise to hardship, because there is often difficulty in drawing a line between the trespasser and the entrant under an implied licence. The occupier who ejects such a licensee thinking he is a trespasser, may it seems be acting perfectly reasonably, and yet be liable in tort.

Defence of property generally

As a matter of principle, it seems right that force might legitimately be used in the defence of one's own property in other cases than the ejection of a trespasser; for example against one who threatens a trespass, or where an owner of property not in possession of it uses force in its defence. The only decisions appear to be on the defence of property against the attacks of animals.

Thus in *Cresswell* v. *Sirl* (1948) the defendant, acting under the authority of the owner of livestock, shot the plaintiff's dog, which he believed to be about to renew an attack on the livestock. The court held that if the defendant's belief was reasonable, and if he acted reasonably in regarding the shooting as necessary to protect the livestock, he had a good defence. Under section 9 (3)(*b*) of the Animals Act 1971, the defendant is also provided with a defence if he has killed or injured a dog when it "has been worring livestock, has not left the vicinity and is not under the control of any person and there are no practicable means of ascertaining to whom it belongs". *Creswell* v. *Sirl* remains authority for a common law defence of defence of property.

The force used must be reasonable

As a general proposition it seems true that reasonable force in the defence of property means something less than reasonable force in the defence of person, but there is very little authority on how much force may be justifiable. In *Collins* v. *Renison* (1754) in which the defendant pulled away a ladder on which the plaintiff a trespasser was standing this was held to be an unreasonable use of force. In

Bird v. *Holbrook* (*supra*, p. 20) in which the defendant set a spring gun on his land which went off and injured the plaintiff, a trespasser, the force clearly was not used for the purpose of ejection, and was therefore unreasonable. The defendant was therefore held liable. On the other hand, in *Ilott* v. *Wilkes* (1820) where the plaintiff, a trespasser, knew of the presence of spring guns on the land, recovery against the defendant was not allowed. In so far as this case suggests that any amount of force is reasonable provided the occupier gives prior warning of it or the trespasser has notice that it may be used, it seems to go too far. The use of a spiked wall or one with broken glass seems, however, clearly justifiable. The purpose is deterrent not retributory and the trespasser has only himself to blame if he takes the risk (as to keeping a savage dog, see, *infra*, p. 205).

Distress damage feasant

This may be regarded as part of the protection which the law gives to an owner of property acting in its defence. If the plaintiff's chattel is unlawfully on the defendant's land, and has caused or is causing damage there, the defendant may seize the chattel and retain it until the plaintiff compensates him for the damage. This form of distress operates therefore as a defence to the plaintiff's action of conversion or detinue, which would otherwise be available if the defendant refused to return the chattel. The defence now applies only to the seizure of inanimate objects. In *Ambergate Ry. Co.* v. *Midland Ry. Co.* (1853) the plaintiffs' railway engine which was encumbering the lines of the defendants' railway was distrained damage feasant by the defendants. The common law right of distress damage feasant in respect of trespassing animals has been abolished by section 7 of the Animal Act 1971, which provides, however, a new statutory defence based on similar principles except that the detainer of the animal is also given a right to sell it and to retain out of the proceeds his costs and the amount of any claim for damages he may have arising from the trespass.

The chattel must have come on the land in circumstances amounting to a trespass or other tort. It must not be in use at the time of seizure, and the right to seize is only available as long as the chattel remains on the land.

Necessity

This defence differs from defence of person and property in that it purports to justify the infliction of harm on a person who is not himself threatening the person or property of the defendant.

The limits of this defence are ill-defined. The necessity of saving life was recognised as a defence in *Leigh* v. *Gladstone* (1909) in which it was held that prison warders, who forcibly fed the plaintiff, a suffragette, who was fasting in prison, were not liable in battery. Necessity would no doubt also be a defence to the surgeon who performs a necessary operation without consent (*cf. Beatty* v. *Illingworth* (1896) in which the defendant surgeon removed both the plaintiff's diseased ovaries though she had given consent to the removal of only one; the plaintiff was held to have impliedly consented to the removal. But necessity here appears a better ground for the decision). Where the defendant has acted in self-preservation, there is no authority on the availability of the defence. The two who threw on the squib in *Scott* v. *Shepherd* (*supra*, p. 8) could presumably have pleaded necessity, although the fact that they acted in the agony of the moment seems additionally important. What of cannibalism, where this is the only means of supporting life (*cf. R.* v. *Dudley and Stevens* (1884))? Certainly, homelessness does not give rise to a sufficient necessity to provide a defence to an action of trespass to land (*Southwark London Borough* v. *Williams* (1971)). The Court of Appeal in that case thought that the defence must be confined to an "urgent situation of extreme peril".

Where the defendant has acted to save property, necessity may be a defence. In *Cope* v. *Sharpe* (No. 2) (1912) the Court of Appeal excused for this reason the action of a gamekeeper who set fire to heather on the plaintiff's land in order to prevent a fire on that land from spreading to land over which his master had shooting rights. The case is unsatisfactory since the question of the liability of the plaintiff for the fire on his land is not considered so that defence of property cannot be ruled out. As a decision on necessity the case appears to be authority for two principles. The first is that the court will make a value-judgment as to which property deserved protection—the shooting-rights were valuable, the heather far less so. Secondly, it was important that the defendant was not a mere volunteer, being treated as having the same right to act as his master. It is uncertain whether a mere volunteer could ever rely on necessity as a defence in these circumstances.

Many cases which are sometimes explained as turning on this defence are better regarded as cases in which the defendant has committed no tort. Thus the defendant who erects barricades in order to keep flood-water out of his land, where the inevitable result of this is that the plaintiff's land is flooded (as in *Nield* v. *L. & N.W. Ry.* (1874)) is not liable to the plaintiff not because of the necessity of his action but because he has not committed any tort recognised by our law.

In order to establish this defence the defendant must have acted reasonably, firstly in deciding that his intervention was necessary, secondly in the steps he took to deal with the danger. *Cope* v. *Sharpe* shows that the necessity must be judged at the time of the defendant's action. In that case, the fire died out before reaching the land over which the sporting rights existed.

DISCIPLINE

It is recognised that parents and schoolteachers have a common law power, for the purposes of discipline, to inflict corporal punishment on children within their care. In all cases the force used must be for the purposes of discipline and correction and must be reasonable.

LAWFUL ARREST

The fact that the defendant is arresting the plaintiff for the commission of an offence is a defence to the plaintiff's action of battery or false imprisonment, provided the arrest is lawful. The powers of arrest of private citizens and police officers are now almost entirely statutory. The Criminal Law Act of 1967 has codified and to some extent extended the powers of arrest that existed at common law. The Act allows arrest only where the offence is "arrestable." This means an offence for which the punishment is fixed by law, or one for which under statute a sentence of five years' imprisonment may be imposed or an attempt to commit such offences. When an offence is non-arrestable, arrest for such an offence is only possible if a power to arrest for that offence has been created by statute. There is now a common law power of arrest only in the case of one crime, breach of the peace.

Arrest under warrant

A policeman who arrests under a warrant issued by a magistrate is not liable for the arrest even if the magistrate had no jurisdiction to issue the warrant, or if it was defective in form. The policeman must however act within the terms of the warrant; he is not protected if, for example, he arrests the wrong person.

Arrest by policeman without warrant

The effect of section 2, subsections (2), (4), and (5) of the Act is to empower a policeman to arrest without a warrant in three cases:

(1) where he has reasonable cause to suspect that an arrestable

offence has been committed and that the person he arrests is guilty of that offence (section 2 (4));
(2) where he has reasonable cause to suspect that the person he arrests is about to commit an arrestable offence (section 2 (5));
(3) where he has reasonable cause to suspect that the person he arrests is in the course of committing an arrestable offence (section 2 (2)).

It may be noted that in none of these subsections is it necessary for the policeman to show that his suspicion was correct, only that it was reasonable.

Section 2 (6) gives a policeman a power of entering and searching any place for the purpose of exercising these powers of arrest.

Powers of arrest of the private person

The private person has the same power as the policeman to arrest one whom he has reasonable cause to suspect to be guilty of an arrestable offence, but he has this power only if the offence has actually been committed (section 2 (3)). The common law rule in *Walters* v. *W. H. Smith* (1914) is therefore preserved. The private person has the same power as the constable under section 2 (2) to arrest one in the course of commission of an arrestable offence, but the power of arrest under section 2 (5) can only be exercised by a constable.

Reasonable cause

Where the power to arrest is dependent upon the person making the arrest having reasonable cause to suspect certain facts, it appears that he has the burden of proving reasonable cause in any action against him by the person whom he arrested.

Reasonable force

The Act of 1967 enacts the common law rule that reasonable force may be used in "effecting or assisting in the lawful arrest of offenders or suspected offenders" (section 3). It seems that a number of obvious factors are relevant to the degree of force that may be used, the seriousness of the offence, the likelihood of its repetition if the offender is allowed to escape, the seriousness of the harm the arrest inflicts upon the offender, the availability of other means of arrest. It appears that the burden of proving that the force used was reasonable rests upon the person making the arrest.

Manner of arrest

The arrest may be tortious, not because it is unjustified according to the principles discussed previously, but because it is conducted in an improper manner. *Christie* v. *Leachinsky* (1947) established that the person arrested is entitled to be informed of the offence for which he is arrested, unless this is in the circumstances obvious. Where the person making the arrest does not comply with this rule, he commits false imprisonment even if the arrest was justifiable for other reasons. In *Christie* v. *Leachinsky* itself the defendant policeman purported to arrest the plaintiff under a local Act. There were no grounds for making the arrest under this Act, but grounds did exist for arresting the plaintiff on reasonable suspicion of his commission of a crime. The defendant was held liable in false imprisonment. In *R.* v. *Kulynycz* (1970) the Court of Appeal held that though an arrest was unlawful because of a contravention of *Christie* v. *Leachinsky*, a lawful arrest could subsequently be made by informing the arrested person of the reason for which he was being held. *R.* v. *Inwood* (1973) shows that in order to effect a lawful arrest the fact of arrest must be made clear to the arrested person. If this is not done, any detention is unlawful and a false imprisonment. On the other hand, when arresting a deaf person who cannot lip-read, the arrester need do only what is reasonable in the circumstances to convey the fact of arrest and the reason for it to the person being arrested (*Wheatley* v. *Lodge* (1971)).

Another factor which can make an otherwise lawful arrest improper is the time taken before charging the plaintiff, or in the case of a private person, before bringing the plaintiff before a constable or magistrate.

In *Lewis & Co.* v. *Tims* (1952) it was held that a wait of between twenty minutes and an hour by the defendants before deciding to call the police in to charge the plaintiff who had been detained by the defendants on suspicion of shoplifting at their store, was reasonable. The police may go further than a private person and conduct inquiries and collect evidence before charging one whom they have arrested. So in *Dallison* v. *Caffery* (1965) the action of the defendant policeman in taking the plaintiff after arresting him to the plaintiff's house to see if any stolen property was there was held justifiable. But both these cases presuppose the lawfulness of the original arrest. Where, for example, the police have insufficient evidence to arrest upon reasonable suspicion in the first place, they cannot justify the arrest by the fact that it has allowed the collection of further evidence which would have made their suspicion reasonable.

Police Powers Other Than Arrest

The police possess a number of powers, in addition to their power of arrest, which may provide them with a defence to an action in tort.

For example, they may lawfully enter premises in order to carry out an arrest which they are empowered to make under the Criminal Law Act 1967; or they may lawfully enter premises under the authority of a search warrant issued by a judge or magistrate. There is no general power to search persons without arresting them, although particular statutes such as the Metropolitan Police Act 1839 (stolen goods), and the Misuse of Drugs Act 1971, have conferred such powers on the police. There is some difficulty in deciding what the police are entitled to seize on premises which they have lawfully entered. Where they have entered under warrant to search for stolen goods, section 26 (3) empowers the seizure of any goods belived to have been stolen (whether or not the belief is reasonable, and whether or not the occupier appears to be the thief or handler of such goods, so extending the common law power of seizure conferred by *Chic Fashions* (*West Wales*) v. *Jones* (1968)). In a later case (*Ghani* v. *Jones* (1969)), Lord Denning thought that where the police were lawfully on premises, they could seize any article on the premises which was reasonably believed to be the fruit of a crime, or the instrument of a crime's commission or to provide material evidence of the commission of the crime. Furthermore, although there must be reasonable grounds for thinking that the person in possession of the premises has committed the crime, this is not necessary if his refusal to surrender the article would be quite unreasonable. Thus although there is no general police power to enter a person's house in order to search for evidence that he has committed a crime, there are quite extensive common law powers of search and seizure once the police are lawfully inside the premises.

Acts Done Under Authority of Law

The immunity of officials and other participants in the judicial process is considered below at page 322. Statutory authority may be a defence to an action in tort under the following circumstances: (1) the statute must confer either a duty or a power on the defendant to commit the act complained of; (2) the commission of the tort must be the inevitable result of acting under the duty of power. Statutory authority is thus no defence where the authorised act is committed negligently, unless the statute clearly excludes liability for negligence. Statutory authority is of chief importance in relation to the torts of nuisance and *Rylands* v. *Fletcher*, and receives separate consideration in the chapters dealing with those torts.

Contributory Negligence

The chief scope of this defence will be where the tort complained of is one of negligence (*infra*, p. 125). It will rarely, for obvious reasons, be available where the defendant has acted intentionally, and no English case has yet applied it in such a situation. In *Lane* v. *Holloway* (1968), the Court of Appeal refused to make any deduction for contributory negligence where the plaintiff, a man of 64, had insulted and made a feeble attempt to strike the defendant in answer to which the defendant, aged 24, struck the plaintiff a very severe blow thus injuring him. The defendant acted disproprtionately to the provocation received. In the case of a lesser blow the requisite causal connection between the provocation and the blow might have been established. On the other hand, in *Lumsden* v. *London Trustee Savings Bank* (1971), the defendant bank had negligently paid out on a forged cheque, which had been defectively drawn by the plaintiff in such a way as to give an opportunity for forgery. The plaintiff's damages for conversion were reduced by 10 per cent because of his contributory negligence. It may be possible to explain this case on the ground that the defendants did not intentionally convert the cheque (see, for example, Street, p. 77), but in earlier similar cases it seems to have been assumed that contributory negligence was no defence even here (*Ingram* v. *Little* (1961); *Central Newbury Car Auctions* v. *Unity Finance* (1957)).

Torts which are also Crimes

It is now not a defence that criminal proceedings are yet to be instituted for the crime (the common law rule which made this a defence where the crime was a felony has disappeared with the abolition of felonies under the Criminal Law Act 1967).

It is in one case a defence that the defendant has actually been convicted of, or prosecuted for, an offence. Where the defendant has been convicted of an assault, section 45 of the Offences against the Person Act 1861 gives him a defence to a subsequent civil action arising out of the assault under these conditions:

1. The criminal proceedings must have been summary. This limits the rule to those assaults which are fairly trivial.

2. The justices must either convict the defendant, and he must either serve a term of imprisonment or pay a fine, or they must dismiss the complaint against him on the merits of the case. Such certificate of dismissal may be granted because the assault was not proved, or was justified or was too trivial to merit punishment.

ILLEGALITY

The principle of this defence is that no one can establish a right if it is necessary for him to rely on his own illegal act or one contrary to public policy. The authorities on this seemingly simple matter are bewildering and the treatment of it here can only be brief. The first problem arises where an illegal contract exists. Such contract is unenforceable, but it is settled that where a cause of action in tort can be established without reliance on the contract or the plaintiff's illegal conduct, illegality is no defence. Thus in *Bowmakers* v. *Barnet Instruments* (1944) the plaintiff company had let machine tools to the defendants under hire-purchase agreements which were illegal because they infringed a statutory order. The defendants sold all the machines except one, which they refused to return to the plaintiffs. They were held liable for the conversion of all the machines because the plaintiffs' cause of action in tort could be established without reliance on the illegal contracts. In the case of those machines which were sold, the decision is explicable on the ground that the court treated the sale as determining the bailment without reference to the terms of the agreement and the right to immediate possession of the machines therefore revested in the plaintiffs. In the case of the machine which was not sold, the mere refusual to return it would not seem *ipso facto* to determine the bailment, and the decision can therefore only be justified on the ground that a term in the contract caused it to have this effect. If this is so, it seems that, while reliance on the illegal contract may not be made by the plaintiff, he can at least refer to its terms in order to establish his cause of action. If the plaintiff cannot establish a cause of action in tort without disclosing his own illegal or immoral conduct, no action will lie. So in *Siveyer* v. *Allison* (1935) the plaintiff could not succeed in an action of deceit against the defendant, a married man who had promised to marry her (an illegal contract), because in establishing her cause of action she had to disclose her immoral association with the defendant.

Where no contract is involved, illegality may still be a defence. Much depends upon whether the illegality is a casual or incidental part of the main cause of action, or whether it is an integral part. So a person driving an unlicensed car could clearly sue another driver for his negligence in causing a collision. Also if one burglar picks another's pocket while proceeding to the premises they intend to burgle, that other may sue. If, however, they have agreed to open a safe by means of explosives, and one negligently handles the explosive charge so injuring the other, no action will lie (the latter examples are taken from *obiter dicta* of Lord Asquith L.J. in *National Coal Board* v. *England* (1954)).

So far the courts have made little attempt to distinguish the effects of different types of illegality. But such distinction is conceivably important. Would the decision in the *Bowmaker* case have been the same had the illegality been more than a breach of a fairly trivial statutory rule? In one case at least, the type of illegality is important. Where an employee who has aided and abetted his employer's breach of statutory duty is suing his employer for personal injury caused by that breach, illegality is no defence(*National Coal Board* v. *England* (1954)).

Entry on Land

In certain circumstances there is a right to enter another's land with a consequent defence to any action arising out of that entry. Three cases may be considered in all three of which the element of self-help as a *remedy* for tort is present, although the defence may be available where no tort has been committed by the occupier of the land which the defendant enters.

1. Recaption of chattels

An owner of a chattel may sometimes enter another's land in order to recapt it. The so-called right of recaption here operates as a defence to the owner of the land's action of trespass. This right of entry, however, appears to be limited to three situations:

(*a*] Where the chattel comes on the land by the act of the occupier.

(*b*) Where it comes on the land by the felonious act of a third party. How this will be interpreted with the abolition of the distinction between felonies and misdemeanours is uncertain.

(*c*) Where it comes on the land accidentally. In the case of *Thorns* (1466) thorns fell from a tree growing in a hedge on to another's land, and it was held that as they came there accidentally, they could be recapted. But there is room for doubt as to the meaning of "accidentally." Would it cover the situation where the chattel came on the land by the negligence of its owner or a third party? Can an owner ever recapt it when it is his act that has caused the entry of the chattel, whether negligent or not?

Recaption of the chattel may be a defence to an action of battery as well as trespass to land, since reasonable force may be used to effect recaption.

Where the right of recaption does not exist, the owner of the chattel may be without remedy, since the mere refusal by the occupier either to surrender the chattel, or to allow the owner to retake it does not appear to be conversion or detinue (*supra*, p. 34).

2. Re-entry on land

A person entitled to the possession of land can enter it and eject, using only reasonable force, the person in possession, in the same way as he can remove a licensee, after revoking his licence. The defence of re-entry operates not as a defence to trespass to land, which is in any case not available against one entitled to possession, but to assault and battery. The entrant may be guilty of the criminal offence of forcible entry under an Act of 1381 if he does not enter in a "peaceable manner" but his civil liability is unaffected provided the force he uses is not unreasonable. The right of a landlord to enter premises to the possession of which he is entitled and, using reasonable force, evict the tenant as in *Hemmings* v. *Stoke Poges Golf Club* (1920) is now removed by sections 31 and 32 of the Rent Act 1965, which compel the landlord to take court proceedings for this purpose.

3. Abatement of nuisance

The right of abatement of a nuisance enables one affected by the nuisance to take steps of his own in order to remove the nuisance. Where the abatement is effected by an entry on the land on which the nuisance exists, it affords a defence to the owner's action of trespass.

Abatement is not always advisable. The abater must be careful not to do any unnecessary damage, and where there is more than one method of abatement, he must choose the least mischievous. Furthermore, where he has exercised his right to abate, he cannot then sue for damages.

Notice of the abatement need not be given where there is no entry on the land on which the nuisance exists. Thus in *Lemmon* v. *Webb supra*, p. 45), abatement could be performed without notice because it simply required lopping off the offending branches. Notice is also not required in cases of emergency. Notice is required where the nuisance has not been created by the occupier of the land but by a predecessor in title of the occupier.

So far it does not seem to have been stated by the courts that the abatement must be reasonable; that the harm inflicted by abatement must not be disproportionate to the harm caused by the nuisance. But such a requirement seems likely. Thus in *Perry* v. *Fitzhowe* (1846) the defendant purported to justify the pulling down of the plaintiff's house on the ground that the house interfered with the defendant's easement of pasture over the plaintiff's land and was therefore a nuisance. But the court held that abatement was not justified in these circumstances since it might lead to a breach of the peace.

It has been said that abatement is a remedy which the law does not favour (in *Lagan Navigation Co.* v. *Lambeg Bleaching Co.* (1927)). This appears to go too far. There may, however, be a tendency by the courts to decide matters of uncertainty (for example, as to the necessity of notice, reasonableness of the abatement) against the abater.

CHAPTER 6

NEGLIGENCE

NEGLIGENCE is a universal concept in legal systems. But as a ground of liability in itself for causing damage it is not so common. The evolution of negligence as a tort separate from trespass has already been considered (pp. 8–9, *supra*). It is now time to look at the tort of negligence itself.

At one time, although there were numerous instances of liability in negligence, there was no connecting principle formulated which could be regarded as the basis of all of them. In 1932, in *Donoghue* v. *Stevenson*, the House of Lords had to decide on appeal from the Scottish courts if there was a cause of action where the pursuer (the Scottish term for plaintiff) alleged that, owing to the negligence of the defender (the Scottish term for defendant), a manufacturer of soft drinks, a bottle of lemonade manufactured by the defender, purchased for the pursuer by a friend, contained a snail which had appeared in decomposed form when the pursuer poured the contents of the bottle into the glass from which she was drinking. As a result of drinking the lemonade and seeing the snail the pursuer alleged that she had suffered gastro-enteritis and shock. The House of Lords decided that on proof of these facts the pursuer was entitled to succeed against the manufacturer. The case has an importance going beyond the obviousness of its so-called narrow ratio, that a manufacturer of products owes a duty of care to the consumer of those products. It also decides that the parties to a contract may owe duties of care in the performance of the contract to persons who are not parties (for example, in the case itself, the contract between manufacturer and wholesaler did not preclude a duty owed to the consumer). The House of Lords thus disposed of the objection to liability based upon privity of contract.

The case owes its chief importance, however, to the fact that it contains an attempt by the chief appellate court to provide a general formulation of liability in negligence. Lord Atkin's judgment is most important in this respect. He said that negligence depends upon proof that one person has committed a breach of a duty of care binding upon himself and owed to another and has thereby caused injury to that other. Whether a duty of care is owed to another depends upon whether that other is in law a neighbour and Lord Atkin described a neighbour as a person "so closely and directly affected by [my] act that I ought reasonably to have [him] in contemplation as being so affected when I am directing my mind to the acts or omissions which are called in questions." This statement is often described, for convenience's sake, as "the neighbour principle." It is clear that Lord Atkin considered that a person was under a duty of care in respect of his actions or omissions whenever it could be foreseen that as a result of those actions or omissions another might be injured.

The existence of a separate tort of negligence was thus conclusively established. In the years since 1932, the tort has developed to such an extent that it is clearly now the most important tort. Quantitatively, actions in negligence far exceed those brought for any other tort. Besides this, negligence is in the process of absorbing other areas of tortious liability. Thus liability for defective premises and chattels is now governed almost exclusively by negligence. Negligence has taken over much of the area of liability formerly occupied by trespass, and appears at the moment to be in the process of doing the same thing to nuisance. On the other hand, the breadth of Lord Atkin's statement in *Donoghue* v. *Stevenson* has not received total acceptance. It is not universally true that whenever there is foreseeability of harm the defendant is under a duty to so regulate his conduct that such harm is not produced. A number of so-called exceptions to the neighbour principle, the extent of which will be discussed in this chapter, have been established by the courts. In *Home Office* v. *Dorset Yacht Co.* (1970), the House of Lords gave its consideration to the question of the basis upon which such exceptions rest. In that case it was held by a majority of four to one that the Home Office owed a duty of care to the plaintiffs in respect of the detention of certain borstal trainees who had escaped from a borstal institution and had caused damage to the plaintiffs' yacht. Of those in the majority, Lords Reid, Morris and Pearson clearly thought that the neighbour principle of Lord Atkin had the status of a rule of law, subject only to exceptions based upon a "justification or valid explanation," or upon matters of policy. Lord Diplock thought, however, that foreseeability was only one element in determining the existence of a duty of care. In deciding whether to recognise a new duty, the court must also look at previous decisions by way of analogy and at the policy aspects of the case. Applying this to the facts of the case before him, Lord Diplock was prepared to extend the duty that already existed in respect of actions of prisoners committed inside the prison (*Ellis* v. *Home Office* (1953) to actions committed by the prisoner on escape in the vicinity of the prison. To the other judges in the majority, therefore, foreseeability as a determinant of duty has the force of a rule of law subject to exceptions, whereas Lord Diplock sees it as only an element in establishing such a rule. It is doubtful, however, whether there is much practical difference between Lord Diplock and the rest of the judges in the majority in the House of Lords. The broad basis upon which the latter rest the recognition of exceptions to the neighbour principle makes it clear that new duties will not be lightly imposed.

Constituent Requirements of Negligence

The tort of negligence is not merely carelessness. There must be a duty of care recognised by law in the situation in which the defendant finds himself. There must be a breach of that duty. There must be damage resulting from that breach. The damage that results must not be too remote a consequence of the breach. These constituent requirements of the tort will be examined in this and the succeeding chapters beginning with the examination of the requirement of duty of care.

Duty of Care

The concept of duty of care has come under criticism for being unnecessary in the tort of negligence. The main reason for the criticism is that the criterion for existence of a duty of care, reasonable foreseeability, is also that for establishing breach of duty and therefore liability. The existence of a duty of care can therefore only be ascertained at the same time as the breach of duty is ascertained. The concept of duty of care can therefore only be used to express a given result, rather than as a means of prescribing conduct. Of course, it is possible to argue that a duty of care can be expressed and therefore can operate prescriptively, as in the statement that a motorist owes a duty of care to other road users. But whether a *particular* motorist owes a duty of care to a *particular road user* can only be determined by deciding whether that road user was within the range of that motorist's reasonable foresight of harm. This matter can only be determined (at least by a court) retrospectively. The question must therefore be asked why it is necessary to express the result of such a determination by saying that X, the motorist, was in breach of a duty of care owed to Y, rather than by saying that X by his careless driving caused Y injury. In other torts, the existence of a duty not to commit the tort is assumed. For instance, if A has defamed B, it is not necessary to say that A was in breach of a duty not to commit defamation.

The answer to this question lies in the fact that two questions are concealed within the question whether a duty of care exists in a particular case. The first question is whether in the factual situation concerned, a duty of care is in law capable of existing. The second is whether on the actual facts of the case before the court the duty existed. Some light on the difference between these two questions may be derived from a statement of Lord Normand in the case of *Bolton* v. *Stone* (1951). In that case the occupiers of a cricket ground were held not liable in negligence to the plaintiff who was struck and injured by a ball hit out of the ground by a batsman. Lord Normand in the House of Lords said: "It is not questioned that the occupier of a cricket ground owes a duty of care to persons on an adjacent highway or on neighbouring property.... But it is necessary to consider the measure of the duty owed." The first statement clearly does not arise from an examination of the actual facts of the case since it might be possible to play cricket in a place from which it was quite inconceivable that a ball would ever be struck and yet the statement would still be true. The statement can mean only therefore that as a matter of law occupiers of cricket grounds owe a duty of care to those outside the ground. This is certainly a prescriptive statement, but it says nothing about the duty of a particular occupier towards a particular person outside the ground. It does not preclude a decision by the court that on the actual facts of the case the occupier owed no duty to the plaintiff (this was the actual decision in *Bolton* v. *Stone*). This decision by the court is an answer to the second question involved in deciding whether the defendant owed the plaintiff a duty of care. The answer depends upon whether, on the facts found by the court, the defendant ought to have foreseen that, unless he took or refrained from a certain action, the plaintiff would suffer harm. An answer to this question can clearly be given only retrospectively by a court, so that the statement by the court that on the facts found by it X owed Y a duty of care is expressive of a legal result rather than of a rule of conduct to which X must conform. The legal result is expressed in the same way by saying that X was in breach of a duty of care owed to Y—in fact the inquiry involved in deciding whether a breach of duty has been committed is exactly the same as that involved in deciding whether a duty arose on the actual facts of the case. The expression "duty in fact" is sometimes used to represent the second aspect of the duty of care.

Were negligence a tort in which the imposition of a duty of care depended as a matter of law solely upon the issue of foreseeability of harm, the first question involved in deciding whether there was a duty of care would be unnecessary; indeed, the duty of care itself would be redundant, since the court could go straight to the question whether the defendant had foreseeably endangered the plaintiff. We have seen already, however, that the neighbour principle admits exceptions. These exceptions are expressed through the device of the duty of care which may therefore be seen as a curb on or control over the growth of the tort of negligence. That the duty of care is a mere device for the purposes of control may be illustrated by those cases in which a person has a duty in respect of certain types of harm which may result from his conduct but not others. For example, a motorist may be in a position to foresee that if he drives negligently he may cause to other road users physical injury, damage to property or pecuniary loss. If, however, he causes only pecuniary loss, he is not liable because although he has a duty of care in relation to damage to person and property, he has no such duty in relation to purely pecuniary loss. The law is here therefore in the curious position of requiring him to drive carefully and not requiring him to drive carefully in relation to the same act of driving. Here again, and in the very aspect of the duty of care which has a more obviously prescriptive function, the duty of care simply seems to express a legal result rather than to prescribe conduct.

Duty of care owed to plaintiff

It is sometimes said that the duty of care must be owed by the defendant to the plaintiff. On examination, however, this requirement seems no more than an obviously essential step in establishing that a "duty in fact" existed, or, which is the same thing, that the defendant was in breach of a duty of care. The plaintiff cannot establish negligence towards himself without showing that the defendant should have foreseen that he would suffer harm. *Bourhill* v. *Young* (1943) illustrates the point. In that case, the defender, a motorcyclist, was by his careless driving involved in an accident in which he himself was killed. The pursuer was on the other side of a tramcar at the time of the collision and so did not observe the accident, although she heard a loud noise and subsequently saw the pursuer's blood on the road. As a result she suffered nervous shock, which caused her child to be still-born. The House of Lords held that she could not succeed in negligence against the defender's estate, since the defender could not have foreseen nervous shock to a person placed in the position of the pursuer, although he was clearly in breach of his duty to drive carefully to other persons in the vicinity. It is important to note what this case did not decide. It did not decide that, as a matter of law there is no duty to a casual spectator of an accident who suffers nervous shock. The case was concerned with "duty in fact"; whether the defender should have foreseen shock to *this spectator*. The case did not decide, although it is true that certain of the judgments may receive this interpretation, that Mrs. Bourhill could not recover for her shock because she was outside the foreseeable range of impact produced by the negligent driving. In other words the test of liability for shock is foreseeability of shock, not of physical injury. This must receive some qualification where the plaintiff receives shock because of fear of injury to himself. In such a case it appears that the test of liability for shock is whether the defendant has foreseeably caused the plaintiff to feel endangered which is tantamount to asking whether physical injury to the plaintiff was foreseeable. If Mrs. Bourhill had in fact feared injury to herself, the result of the case may have been different, since the court could well have found that a freakish physical injury to her was foreseeable. Because she had no such fear, the only question was as to the foreseeability of shock to her.

Situations in which no Duty of Care has been Recognised

In certain cases, the courts have refused to impose a duty of care even where there was foreseeability of harm. In this way, a number of so-called exceptions to the neighbour principle have been established. First of all, it must be realised that there is no finite list of exceptions to Lord Atkin's formulation. Since the recognition of exceptions turns very much upon matters of policy, as explained above, new exceptions are always a possibility. In the same way, as society's view of policy changes, some of the old exceptions will disappear. In the past few years, for example, the law has fundamentally changed its attitude to the principles determining the existence of a duty of care in relation to negligent statements and to liability to trespassers. Finally, it will be observed that in some cases, of which the duty in relation to statements is again an example, the law now recognises a duty of care but it is a limited or qualified duty, one not entirely determined by principles of foreseeability. Liability for causing nervous shock is another example of this.

1. Negligent statements

The courts have been reluctant to establish a rule that a defendant who negligently makes a false statement is always liable if the plaintiff foreseeably suffers loss as the result of the statement. This has been because it was thought that to some extent different considerations applied to words than to acts. The statement may be made without any intention that it should be acted on; the loss might be considered more remote in that it usually arises from the plaintiff's acting in reliance on the statement, rather than from the statement itself; finally "words travel faster than deeds"—to make the defendant liable for all the foreseeable loss arising from the statement might involve him in excessive liability. Thus until recently the courts had refused to award damages for negligent statements causing financial loss to the plaintiff unless the false statement constituted a breach of a contract made between plaintiff and defendant, or unless the defendant was in a fiduciary relationship towards the plaintiff. Where the defendant's statement did not amount to a breach of contract but had induced the plaintiff to contract with the defendant (called a misrepresentation) the plaintiff could not recover damages from the defendant but was allowed the equitable remedy of rescission of the contract. The position differed if the false statement was made fraudulently by the defendant. Then the plaintiff could get damages for the amount of his loss in the tortious action of deceit.

The position thus summarised has been altered by two important changes in the law, by means of which it is now possible for the courts to make an award of damages for a negligent statement. The first change was brought about by the decision of the House of Lords in *Hedley Byrne & Co. Ltd.* v. *Heller and Partners Ltd.* (1964). The second change was the enactment of the Misrepresentation Act 1967.

The Hedley Byrne case

The facts of the case were:

The plaintiffs, *Hedley Byrne & Co.* who were advertising agents, asked their bank to inquire into the financial position of one of their clients, a company on behalf of which they wished to undertake certain advertising orders. The bank made inquiries of the defendants, the company's bank, which gave favourable references about the company, stating that these were made "without responsibility." As a result of relying on this advice, the plaintiffs lost money when the company went into liquidation. The plaintiffs' action in negligence against the defendants failed because of the defendants express disclaimer of responsibility for their reference.

The importance of the decision lies in the fact that all the members of the House of Lords thought that in appropriate circumstances an action for a negligent statement would lie, thus disagreeing with the contrary decision of the Court of Appeal in *Candler* v. *Crane, Christmas & Co.* (1951). The principle that negligent statements may be actionable in tort is therefore generally taken as established. It is a more difficult matter to deduce from the speeches what circumstances are necessary in order to make the statement actionable.

All members of the House of Lords were agreed that it is not enough that the maker of the statement can foresee financial loss arising to the plaintiff if the statement is untrue. The statement may be made in circumstances where it is unreasonable to expect care to have been taken by its maker, for example, a recommendation of the shares of a particular company, or a medical diagnosis given at a party. Lord Reid spoke of the need for a special relationship between plaintiff and defendant, and of such a relationship arising where the "party seeking the information or advice was trusting the other to exercise such a degree of care as the circumstances required, where it was reasonable for him to do that, and where the other gave the information or advice when he knew or ought to have known that the inquirer was relying on him."

Lords Morris and Hodson on the other hand required an assumption of responsibility by the defendant that care has been taken, although, as it seems clear that such an assumption could be implied from the circumstances of the case, there is not very much difference between their formulation and that of Lord Reid. Lord Devlin thought that a relationship akin to contract must exist between plaintiff and defendant. All these views may be seen as attempts to formulate a criterion of liability which allows the courts to take into account the element of policy in deciding whether care ought to be taken by the defendant.

The Mutual Citizens case—a gloss upon Hedley Byrne?

In *Mutual Life and Citizen's Assurance* v. *Evatt* (1971), the Privy Council held that a pleading which alleged that the defendant insurance company had negligently misrepresented the financial condition of one of its subsidiaries, in which as a result the plaintiff had invested and thereby lost money, disclosed no cause of action, since there was no allegation that the statement was made in the "ordinary course of the adviser's business or profession," nor that the insurance company had expressly undertaken responsibility for the statement's accuracy. The Privy Council left open the question whether it might be sufficient to establish the validity of the cause of action that the adviser had a financial interest in the advice being acted on. The case appears to place a qualification of dubious value upon the *Hedley Byrne* decision, the authority of which would have recognised a cause of action on these facts (a view reinforced by the dissent of Lords Reid and Morris, both members of the House of Lords in *Hedley Byrne*). The English courts have not yet needed to choose between the judgments of the House of Lords and that of the Privy Council in *Mutual Citizens*. In *Esso Petroleum Co.* v. *Mardon* (1975) Lawson J. imposed liability in tort upon the defendants who had negligently misrepresented the amount of petrol which was likely to be sold at a certain garage in reliance on which the plaintiff bought the garage. The statement was not made in the ordinary course of the defendants' business or profession, but Lawson J. held that since the defendants had a financial interest in the plaintiff's acting on the statement, liability was established under the third category referred to in the Privy Council's judgment. Lawson J. thought that in any case liability existed under the ordinary principles established by *Hedley Byrne* and that, if he had had to choose between the judgment of the House of Lords in *Hedley Byrne* and that of the Privy Council in *Mutual Citizen's*, he would have preferred to follow *Hedley Byrne*. It is suggested that his views are sound. In an earlier decision (*W. B. Anderson* v. *Rhodes* (*Liverpool*) (1967)) liability was imposed upon a defendant for a negligent statement which was not made in the ordinary course of the defen dant's business although here again the defendant appears to have had a financial interest in the plaintiff's acting on the statement.

Effect of the decision in Hedley Byrne

One of the chief effects of the decision in *Hedley Byrne* is that those whose professions involve them in giving advice, for which they are expected to possess expert skill or knowledge, such as accountants, architects, surgeons, solicitors, valuers and estate agents, may be liable in tort for the giving of negligent advice. Whether *Hedley Byrne* has had or will have much practical effect upon the position of such persons is doubtful. Very often their advice is given under contract so that they also owe a contractual duty of care. In some cases the existence of the contractual duty precludes an action in tort (*Clark* v. *Kirby-Smith* (1964) (solicitor); *Bagot* v. *Stevens, Scanlan* (1966) (architect)—these cases do not of course prevent an action in tort against such persons when no contractual relationship exists. It seems likely also that professional persons will be particularly likely to take advantage of the possibility of excluding liability in tort for misstatements. If, as *Mutual Citizens* suggests, *Hedley Byrne* is more or less limited to persons who are in the profession or business of giving advice, it may turn out to be an unimportant decision.

The *Mutual Citizens* case may even be unduly restrictive as far as the liability of professional persons is concerned since the requirement is that the statement must be made in the ordinary course of the adviser's business or profession and it might be difficult for a court to hold that a statement not made as part of a contract fulfilled this requirement. So, in *Candler* v. *Crane, Christmas* (1951), a case thought to be fundamentally affected by *Hedley Byrne*, the defendants. a firm of accountants, had been told to prepare the balance sheet of a company rapidly so that it could be shown to a potential investor. The defendants prepared the balance sheet negligently and the plaintiff lost money through investing in the company. Under *Hedley Byrne* principles the decision of the Court of Appeal that there was no liability would clearly be reversed, but it is at least open to doubt whether such a statement was made in the ordinary course of an accountant's profession so as to attract liability under *Mutual Citizens*.

It was decided soon after *Hedley Byrne* itself that, despite that decision, barristers are not liable for negligence in relation to litigation, whether such negligence occurs during proceedings in court or in preliminary matters such as the drafting of pleadings (*Rondel* v. *Worsley* (1967)). The opinion was expressed in that case that solicitors were entitled to immunity in respect of the same matters (though solicitors may be liable for failure to commence an action in time so that a limitation period expires; or for giving incorrect advice concerning the cost, length and suitability of particular legal proceedings—*Heywood* v. *Wellers* (1975)). The reason for this is policy-first, that in relation to litigation, both barristers and solicitors have a duty to present to the court the facts of the case, not just those favourable to their client; secondly, the undesirability of allowing disgruntled litigants a "second go" by suing their legal advisers; thirdly, the difficulty involved in speculating whether a decision would have gone to the other way but for the negligence. On the other hand, barristers, as well as solicitors, may be liable for negligence in relation to non-litigious work such as the drafting of wills and settlements and the giving of opinions. It need hardly be said that a judge is immune from liability for negligence in relation to the performance of his judicial duties. The same is true of an arbitrator over whom the courts exercise control by reason of the right of either party to demand a case to be stated for the opinion of the court. The mere fact, however, that a person is to decide a question, rather than resolve a dispute, as between two parties does not give him the status of an arbitrator (*Arenson* v. *Casson, Beckman Rutley* (1975)). Thus a person who agrees to value shares owes a duty of care in respect of the valuation to the seller and prospective buyer (*Arenson* case). So also the House of Lords held in *Sutcliffe* v. *Thackrah* (1974) that an architect, employed to certify to his client that building work undertaken for his client by a building contractor had been properly completed, owed a duty of care to the client in respect of the certification.

Duty of honesty

In some cases, it will be unreasonable to expect that care should be taken by the defendant. For example, if advice about investment or medical diagnosis is given at a party, it is normally unreasonable to rely on this as careful advice and therefore no special relationship will exist between adviser and advisee. *Hedley Byrne* itself may have been such a case. In the words of Lord Morris: "There was in the present case no contemplation of receiving anything like a formal and detailed report such as might be given by some concern charged with the duty (probably for reward) of making all relevant inquiries concerning the nature, scope and extent of a company's activities and of obtaining and marshalling all available evidence as to its credit, efficiency, standing and business reputation." Does this duty mean that the defendant must merely make what appears to him to be a correct statement, that he must not commit deceit? It has been argued that more may be required of a defendant than mere truthfulness; that he has a duty to warn the plaintiff that the reply is given impromptu, without a careful sifting of the relevant material. When the defendant fails to do this he is in breach of a duty of honesty. There certainly appears to be a need for such a warning in those circumstances where it is not clear to the plaintiff whether a duty of care or honesty is owed to him. In this situation it seems dishonest for a defendant to invite the plaintiff to believe that a careful statement has been made, while knowing that this is not the case. (In the *Hedley Byrne* case itself it was probably apparent to the plaintiffs, or should have been, that the defendants' reply was not a careful one.)

To whom is the duty under Hedley Byrne owed?

The House of Lords in *Hedley Byrne* did not enter into the question of the extent of the duty of care in relation to statements. They appeared to have no doubt that had a duty of care arisen in the case itself, it would have been owed to the plaintiffs, although it appears that the defendants had no knowledge of the identity of the plaintiffs nor even that the inquiring bank intended to transmit the statement to its customer (though such transmission would be an obvious inference). On the other hand, the judgments in the case appear to require knowledge by the maker of the statement that it will be acted upon by another person. There appear to be two possible tests for determining the extent of the *Hedley Byrne* special relationship. The first is that the defendant should intend that the statement should be acted on by the plaintiff. This is difficult to reconcile with the actual facts of *Hedley Byrne*, unless such an intention on the part of the defendants in that case could have been presumed. The test of intention seems the best explanation of the New Zealand case of *Dimond Manufacturing Co.* v. *Hamilton* (1968) in which it was held that an accountant preparing the balance sheet of a company owed no duty of care towards persons who purchased shares in the company in reliance on the accuracy of the balance sheet, because although such purchases could have been foreseen, the defendant did not know they would be made. A variant, and more restrictive version, of this test would require the defendant to have both the plaintiff, and the particular transaction to be entered into by the plaintiff, in his mind at the time of making the statement. This test has the judicial support of Lord Denning in *Candler* v. *Crane, Christmas* (1951), in which, in the course of his dissenting judgment, he adverted to the hypothetical example of the marine cartographer whose careless omission of a dangerous reef from his map causes a shipwreck. The cartographer would not be liable according to Lord Denning because he drew the map with no particular voyage in mind. It is questionable whether this test is not unduly restrictive. It would prevent newspapers, for example, from being held liable for negligent financial advice offered in their columns.

The second possible test is that the defendant is liable to anyone whom he ought to foresee would act on the statement to his loss. This seems an unjustifiably wide interpretation of the special relationship, and apart from certain statements of the Court of Appeal in *Ministry of Housing* v. *Sharp* (1970) to the effect that all the foreseeable loss arising from a negligent statement is recoverable has no judicial support. The *Sharp* case was in fact concerned with a different factual situation from that in *Hedley Byrne*, namely, liability for a negligent statement made by A to B as a result of which B acts to C's loss. The issues raised by this are somewhat different from those arising in relation to the typical *Hedley Byrne* liability and are discussed elsewhere in this book (*infra*, p. 281).

Exclusion of liability

In the *Hedley Byrne* case, the defendants escaped liability because they had expressly excluded responsibility for the statement. The House of Lords has thus recognised the logical force of the argument that, since liability for the statement rests upon the defendant's assumption of responsibility for it, liability is negatived where the defendant makes it clear that he is not assuming responsibility. This serves to distinguish liability under *Hedley Byrne* from other types of tortious liability. Liability in tort is generally imposed by law; it does not, like contractual liability, depend upon the consent of the person liable, and it is therefore normally impossible to exclude it by a notice or other unilateral indication of intent. But *Hedley Byrne* liability, since it only arises if the defendant has expressly or impliedly consented to it, is more like contractual than tortious liability, and can therefore be excluded.

The logical force of the argument can only be countered if it is accepted that the defendant's assumption of responsibility, which is in any case implied, is an assumption of law arising from the circumstances of the case rather than from the defendant's implied consent. The defendant's express disclaimer of responsibility would then only amount to evidence that no assumption of responsibility for the carefulness of the statement could be expected of him. It is perhaps unfortunate that the House of Lords has recognised the effectiveness of a disclaimer of responsibility for the statement by the defendant. One clear possibility is that this will lend to the considerable erosion of this important new form of liability. In the United States liability has been imposed for a negligent statement, even though an express disclaimer of responsibility (or what was tantamount to one) had been made by the defendant (by the Federal District Court in *Texas Tunnelling Co.* v. *City of Chattanooga* (1962)).

There are two probable limits upon the power of exclusion: (1) it seems necessary that for the exclusion to be effective, it must be communicated to the plaintiff by the defendant; (2) it seems clear that there can be no exclusion of the duty of honesty, breach of which is akin to committing deceit (liability for which cannot be excluded).

Misrepresentation Act 1967

The common law did not allow an action for damages for an innocent misrepresentation, even where it was made negligently. Any contract entered into by the representee with the representor as a result of the misrepresentation could be rescinded in equity, subject to the various limitations upon that right. But rescission remained the only remedy until the *Hedley Byrne* decision allowed an action for damages where the misrepresentation was negligent. Further changes have been made by the Misrepresentation Act 1967. Section 2 (1) of the Act provides as follows:

Where a person has entered into a contract after a misrepresentation has been made to him by another party thereto, and as a result thereof he has suffered loss, then if the person making the misrepresentation would be liable to damages in respect thereof had the misrepresentation been made fraudulently, that person shall be so liable not withstanding that the misrepresentation was not made fraudulently, unless he proves that he had reasonable ground to believe and did believe up to the time that the contract was made that the facts represented were true.

The effect of this section is to prove an additional remedy by way of an action for damages where the misrepresentation is negligent. The following points may be noted about it:

(*a*) The subsection only applies where the defendant has made a misrepresentation. As will be seen when considering the rules of deceit (*infra*, p. 275) the term "misrepresentation" has acquired legal limitations which it may be assumed are not shared by the term "statement" used in connection with liability under *Hedley Byrne*. For example, it seems that no reason exists for excluding the statement of future intention as a cause of liability under the latter principle.

(*b*) The subsection only applies where the misrepresentation has induced the making of a contract between representor and representee. Where this is not the case, a person who suffers damage by acting on the misrepresentation must continue to rely on the *Hedley Byrne* case.

(*c*) The plaintiff suing on the bases of section 2 (1) has the advantage that he does not need to prove that the defendant was negligent, since the burden of proving lack of negligence is put upon the defendant. An additional advantage is that the plaintiff does not need to show the existence of a special relationship between himself and the defendant. The fact that the misrepresentation has induced the making of a contract between the defendant as representor and the plaintiff as representee is sufficient.

(*d*) The fact that the defendant is to be liable as if the misrepresentation had been made fraudulently means that the other conditions of the tort of deceit must be satisfied. This means, *e.g.* that the subsection imports the deceit rules as to damages into the cause of action.

It has now been held (*Esso Petroleum* v. *Mardon* (1975)) that where a negligent misrepresentation induces the making of a contract between defendant and plaintiff, the plaintiff can base his action upon *Hedley Byrne*, so that in this situation he has the alternative of suing in tort or basing his action on section 2 (1) of the Misrepresentation Act. Where the misrepresentation does not induce the making of a contract between representor and representee, liability for negligence will continue to depend on *Hedley Byrne* principles. The 1967 Act made a further change in that section 2 (2) allows the court in its discretion, having regard to the nature of the misrepresentation and the loss that would be caused by it if the contract were upheld, as well as to the loss that rescission would cause the other party, to declare the contract subsisting and award damages in lieu of rescission. In particular, this allows the court to award damages for a non-negligent misrepresentation. There is as yet uncertainty about the measure of damages to be applied under this subsection; the Act does not make it clear whether it is to be the tortious or the contractual measure.

Liability for misstatement causing physical injury

Although no case seems directly to confirm this point, it seems clear that there may be liability in negligence when the statement causes physical injury or damage. A case such as *Clay* v. *A. J. Crump* (1964) comes close to confirming such liability. The defendant architect was held liable for leaving a wall on a demolition site standing without making a proper inspection of it, and thereby causing injury to the plaintiff, a workman on the site, when the wall fell. The defendant's conduct is clearly interpretable as a statement that the wall was safe. And the conduct of the defendant in *Sharp* v. *Avery* (*infra*, p. 83) can be regarded as a misdirection. The *Hedley Byrne* judgments were considered in *Clay's* case but the special requirements of liability under *Hedley Byrne* were not applied. It may, however, be unsafe to regard liability for negligent statements causing physical injury as turning entirely upon questions of foreseeability. Similar problems of limiting the extent of liability will occur as in the case of the negligent statement causing pecuniary loss (see, for example, the discussion of the problem of the cartographer's liability, *supra*, p. 77). It may be that despite *Clay* v. *Crump*, a special relationship between plaintiff and defendant is necessary.

Dutton v. Bognor Regis U.D.C.—an offshoot of Hedley Byrne

In the above case, a building inspector employed by the defendant local authority negligently failed to notice that the foundations of a house under construction had been laid over a former rubbish tip and accordingly the local authority gave its approval to the building of the house. The builder then completed the building and sold the house. The plaintiff, who bought the house from its original owner, suffered damage when the walls subsided because of the inadequacy of the foundations. The plaintiff brought action for this damage against the builder and the local authority. In the case of the latter, the Court of Appeal thought that it was liable whether it had been acting under a statutory duty or a mere power. The liability thus imposed upon the local authority is clearly closely akin to liability under *Hedley Byrne*, but the court was agreed that it was distinguishable in principle, though the difference which the members of the court relied on, namely, that there must be reliance on the statement by the plaintiff, causes some difficulty because of the Court of Appeal decision in *Ministry of Housing* v. *Sharp* which appeared to base liability on *Hedley Byrne* principles in a case where a third party had acted upon the statement to the plaintiff's loss. There is some doubt, however, about whether that case was an application of *Hedley Byrne* principles (*infra*, p. 82), and the *Dutton* case appears to confirm this doubt. A further difference between *Dutton* and *Hedley Byrne* is that in the former the builder was not misled by the statement made by the council to act to Mrs. Dutton's loss. He knew about the defectiveness of the foundations. The local authority approval simply operated as a green light to him to build.

The *Dutton* case also raises problems in relation to omissions and pecuniary loss. These will be discussed in the relevant sections of this chapter (*infra*, pp. 82, 84).

2. Omissions and undertakings

The problem of liability for an omission to act is not necessarily connected with the tort of negligence. The conduct of the person who, seeing a drowning man and being capable of saving him, makes no effort to do so, is deliberate rather than negligent. But since most of the problems concerning omission arise in connection with negligence, the topic will be treated here. The rule of English law is that pure omissions to act are not actionable in tort. The reason for this reluctance to impose liability for omissions (shared by other legal systems) is that legal obligations to take affirmative action ought not to be imposed upon people without their consent.

It must be emphasised that the omission must be a pure omission. When a person by some positive action has incurred a duty of care towards other persons, he may be liable for omissions in the performance of that duty. Thus a motorist by the act of driving incurs a duty of care towards other road-users and the fact that his negligence consists in an omission to give a signal will not prevent his being liable. Similarly the act of employing other persons puts the employer under a duty of care towards those persons; his obligation to provide proper machinery is not discharged by the provision of initially proper machinery which becomes defective through his failure to have it serviced. An example of this type of liability is *Mercer* v. *S.E. Ry.* (1922) in which the defendant railway company had made a practice of locking the gates of a level crossing upon the approach of trains and, when the plaintiff was injured by a train while using the crossing with the gates open, it was held that the company was liable for its failure to lock the gates because of its previous practice of doing so on which the plaintiff relied.

Similarly, a person who acquires the ownership of land may be liable for a negligent failure to remedy a state of affairs on that land, although he did not create the state of affairs. Thus, in *Goldman* v. *Hargrave* (1967), the defendant was held liable for failing to prevent the spread of fire from his own land to that of the plaintiff, the fire having begun because of the ignition by lightning of a tree on the defendant's land.

Where a person who is under no duty to act in fact does so, the law takes the view that his only obligation is not to make matters worse by acting—he does not need to bring about an improvement. In *East Suffolk Rivers Catchment Board* v. *Kent* (1941) the defendants were emplowered by statute but had no duty to repair a sea wall. They exercised their power in such a way that the plaintiff suffered flooding of his land for five months, whereas had proper skill been shown the flooding would have been limited to fourteen days. The plaintiff's action failed because the defendants had merely failed to improve matters rather than made them worse; the plaintiff had suffered no damage.

In this case there was a dissent by Lord Atkin who thought that the failure to put things right amounted to damage. In the *Hedley Byrne* case (*supra*) Lord Morris considered that a doctor who treated an unconscious patient whom he came across unexpectedly lying by the roadside must show reasonable care and skill in so doing. He did not distinguish the case of failure to diagnose (*i.e.* failure to improve the patient's condition) from that of applying an incorrect remedy and making things worse. There seems force in these conclusions. Although it may be objected that the plaintiff should not be able to insist on the defendant's improving matters where he has no contract with the defendant, the defendant by acting may have deterred the plaintiff (or those acting for him) from remedying the situation by securing contractual assistance, and in this sense the plaintiff has suffered loss. Furthermore, there is now the difficulty of distinguishing the East Suffolk decision from *Dutton* v. *Bognor Regis U.D.C.* (*supra*, p. 80). In that case, the Court of Appeal found it unnecessary to decide whether the defendant local authority was acting under a duty or a mere power in carrying out inspection of a building site, since there was liability even if they were acting under a power. All three members of the Court of Appeal thought that the *East Suffolk* case was distinguishable but gave different reasons for thinking this. Sachs L.J. thought that the *Dutton* case involved positive misfeasance, whereas the earlier case had involved simple non-feasance. This explanation does not seem to coincide with the facts of the *East Suffolk* case. Stamp L.J. thought the distinction between the cases to be that in the *Dutton* case there was a failure to *avert* damage whereas in the *East Suffolk* case there was a failure to deal effectively with damage which had already happened. The negligence in the *Dutton* case could thus be seen as a cause of the damage the plaintiff suffered. This seems to present a distinction without a difference. It seems implicit in the House of Lords judgments in the earlier case that the real question is whether the damage suffered by the plaintiff as the result of the defendant's action was any greater than that which he would have suffered had the defendant taken no action at all. If not, the plaintiff could not succeed. This reasoning does not allow a distinction to be drawn according to whether the defendant's negligence has failed to avert damage or failed to remedy a situation which has already occurred. Lord Denning M.R. thought that there was an intermediate concept between duty and power, that of control, which was enjoyed by the council in this case and which involved it in liability for negligent omissions. Despite the nebulousness of the concept of control, this is perhaps the best approach to cases where there is a general duty imposed with attendant powers for the purpose of carrying out the duty. Little confidence, however, can be reposed in the grounds on which the two cases were distinguished by the Court of Appeal and although the result of the *Dutton* case is supportable, the law it lays down awaits review by the House of Lords.

Where the performance of the gratuitous undertaking has caused the plaintiff damage he has a cause of action. Thus, in *Sharp* v. *Avery and Kerwood* (1938), the defendant undertook to guide the plaintiff from London to Southend by road at night, both travelling on different motor-cycles and the defendant travelling eight yards ahead of the plaintiff. The defendant negligently left the road at some stage, and the plaintiff followed him, and as a consequence suffered injury when his motor-cycle crashed. The plaintiff recovered damages from the defendant for the personal injuries he suffered.

3. Purely pecuniary loss

The courts have, generally speaking, refused to impose a duty of care where, as a result of negligence, the plaintiff has suffered purely pecuniary loss. A number of reasons of policy appear to explain and support this refusal (not all of which are articulated in the cases). The recovery of purely pecuniary loss will lead to difficult problems of limiting the extent of liability. If, for example, A negligently fails to deliver machinery to B, a manufacturer, ought A to be liable in negligence to all those employees of B who lose wages through having in consequence to be laid off work? (this ground of excessive liability was particularly relied on by Lord Blackburn in *Cattle* v. *Stockton Water Works* (1875)). Another argument against imposing liability in negligence for such loss is that the person suffering the loss may be in a better position to absorb it than the person inflicting it. This seems the best explanation of a case such as *Electrochrome* v. *Welsh Plastics* (1968) in which it was held that the financial loss suffered by the plaintiffs whose factory had to be closed down for several hours because of the stopping of their water supply after the defendants' servant had negligently damaged a fire hydrant was not recoverable from the defendants. Such loss can be covered by consequential loss insurance, and it seems more reasonable to expect a factory to take out such insurance than for persons to have to take out liability insurance against causing such loss. Finally, in view of judicial reluctance to establish a general principle of liability for intentional invasion of economic interests (*infra*, p. 255) a refusal to establish such a principle for negligence is not surprising.

One major exception to the rule is provided by the *Hedley Byrne* case. Another more limited exception is evidenced by the facts of *Morrison Steamship Co. Ltd.* v. *Greystoke Castle* (1947). In this case owners of undamaged cargo were allowed to recover for their financial loss in having to pay general average expenditure when the defendants' ship had by negligence been brought into collision with the ship carrying the cargo. The most acceptable explanation of this case is that given by Widgery J. in *Weller* v. *Foot and Mouth Disease Research Institute* (1966): if A can foresee direct physical injury to B resulting from his action, B can recover for purely pecuniary loss resulting from that action. This explanation meets objections based upon fear of excessive liability, but gives little indication of what principles should determine the recognition of further exceptions. In *S.C.M.* v. *Whittall* (1971) Lord Denning M.R. said *obiter* that purely pecuniary loss should be recoverable when it was the immediate consequence of the defendant's negligence, but this, apart from the difficulties of "immediacy," ignores the question of to whom the duty is owed and in respect of what. In *Spartan Steel & Alloys* v. *Martin* (1973), which affirmed the existence of the rule, he appears to have changed his mind and said that existing concepts of duty and remoteness were inadequate for dealing with pecuniary loss cases, and that the whole issue should be looked at as one of policy. He applied the rule, however, in the same way as it had been applied before.

The concept of purely pecuniary loss raises difficulties of classification. If a person has bought an article which is defective through negligence in its manufacture, it had generally been thought that no action lay against the manufacturer unless the article has caused damage of a physical nature. Unless that happens, the buyer's loss is purely pecuniary. But in *Dutton* v. *Bognor Regis U.D.C.* (*supra*, p. 80), the Court of Appeal regarded the damage the plaintiff had suffered as physical damage to property, although the house was defective at the time of its purchase by the plaintiff. If it is correct to draw an analogy between the *Dutton* situation and that of the manufacturer (Lord Denning expressly did so, and Stamp L.J.

expressly refused to accept the analogy), a further result of this decision will be to revolutionise the law relating to consumer protection.

Isolated exceptions to the general rule stated in the text concerning negligence causing purely pecuniary loss will be considered in other parts of this book (Chapter 25 and pp. 297–298).

4. Nervous shock

The reasons for the courts' restrictions upon the right to recover damages for nervous shock are different from those denying a claim for purely financial loss. For a long time the courts doubted the genuineness of nervous shock as a head of damages. When finally the force of medical opinion could admit of no further doubt as to the genuineness of physical symptoms produced by nervous shock, the courts' recognition of this was still somewhat gradual with the result that inconsistencies still exist in the law. Even now, the courts refuse to recognise extreme distress or grief as compensable damage. The term "nervous shock" means actual illness, whether in the form of physical symptoms produced by the shock, or genuine psychiatric illness (as in *Hinz* v. *Berry* (1970)—morbid depression produced by plaintiff witnessing death of her husband and simultaneous injury to her children).

Actions for nervous shock were first allowed:

1. When it accompanied actual physical injury, where the courts were less inclined to doubt the genuiness of the symptoms of shock.
2. Where the plaintiff was put in fear of physical injury through the defendant's negligence and suffered nervous shock though not physical injury as a result (*Dulieu* v. *White and Sons* (1901)).
3. Where the defendant had intentionally done an act calculated to cause nervous shock to the plaintiff (*Wilkinson* v. *Dowton* (1897)).

One authority has argued that the law should go no further than these three cases, on the ground that where nervous shock is suffered in other situations, it is because of some abnormality in the person suffering the shock (Havard, 19 M.L.R. 478). But nervous shock actions have now been allowed in situations other than these, and the fact that the plaintiff in some cases was suffering from some condition such as pregnancy or neurosis which created a greater susceptibility to shock has not precluded recovery.

The nervous shock cases appear to fall into a twofold division. In some the plaintiff has suffered a shock as the result of witnessing or being present at, an accident brought about by the defendant's negligence. In others the plaintiff has suffered shock in other circumstances. In the first type of case, it is probable that the law has reached the point where liability is governed by the ordinary principles of foreseeability, and for this reason it is perhaps inappropriate to discuss this form of nervous shock as an exception to the neighbour principle. About the second type of case, there is more argument, and unfortunately very little authority.

Plaintiff viewer of or present at accident caused by defendant's negligence

Whether the plaintiff was inside the area of foreseeable risk of physical injury seems relevant only where the plaintiff suffers nervous shock through fear of injury to herself, which was not the case in *Bourhill* v. *Young*. Accordingly, it is suggested that the case lays down a simple test for deciding whether nervous shock was recoverable, namely, whether nervous shock to a person in the position of the plaintiff was foreseeable. The plaintiff in *Bourhill* v. *Young* was unable to establish that it was. The case also does not establish that a mere casual spectator of an accident can never recover from nervous shock. It is true that both the cases which have concerned liability to casual spectators, *Bourhill* v. *Young* itself and *Smith* v. *Johnson* (1897), have denied liability. But *Bourhill* v. *Young*, a House of Lords decision, clearly contemplated that an action by a casual spectator would be successful if nervous shock to him was foreseeable.

Where the plaintiff bears some relationship to the person injured in the accident, it seems clear that he is more likely to suffer nervous shock than a mere casual spectator, and therefore that a court would be more likely to hold that nervous shock to him was foreseeable. The cases have generally speaking borne this out. In *Hambrook* v. *Stokes* (1925) the plaintiff, a mother, recovered damages for shock she suffered when she saw the defendants' runaway lorry coming down the hill up which her children had just travelled on their way to school. In *Boardman* v. *Sanderson* (1964), the defendant was held liable to the plaintiff for causing him nervous shock by driving his car into the plaintiff's child so that the plaintiff, who was known by the defendant to be in the vicinity, heard the screams of the child and later saw it to be injured. An emotional as opposed to a blood relationship is sufficient. In *Dooley* v. *Cammell Laird* (1951), the plaintiff, a crane-driver, recovered damages for nervous shock as the result of witnessing what appeared to be a serious accident to his workmates (who were in fact uninjured), involving the crane he was operating and caused by the negligence of the defendants. A "relationship" brought about by close proximity to the accident was found sufficient in *Chadwick* v. *British Transport Commission*

(1967). In that case a rescuer recovered damages for nervous shock which he suffered as a result of performing rescue work at a train accident caused by the defendants' negligence.

These decisions seem sound and it is unfortunate that some doubt is thrown upon them by the decision of the Court of Appeal in *King* v. *Phillips* (1953). In that case it was held that shock suffered by a mother who saw from her bedroom window the defendants' taxi being negligently reversed over her child did not give rise to liability. Singleton L.J. thought that the mother's presence at the window was unforeseeable; Denning L.J. that the slow backing of the taxi was not likely to cause shock in the same way as the runaway lorry in *Hambrook* v. *Stokes*; Hodson L.J., that damages for nervous shock could only be recovered when the plaintiff was in fear for his own safety. The last two reasons are clearly not supportable, and the reasoning of Singleton L.J. requiring foreseeability of the relative's presence by the defendant places an obstacle in the way of actions for nervous shock by relatives, since it is difficult to see in what circumstances the defendant ought to foresee the presence of a relative. The test should be whether, granted the presence of a relative, nervous shock to the relative was foreseeable (*N.B.* in *Boardman* v. *Sanderson* the presence of the relative was *known* by the defendant). There appears therefore to be a conflict between the Court of Appeal decisions in *Hambrook* v. *Stokes* and *King* v. *Phillips* which it is hoped will eventually be resolved in favour of the former case.

There are dicta in *Bourhill* v. *Young* to the effect that the test is whether a person of ordinary phlegm and fortitude in the plaintiff's position would suffer shock. Yet some successful plaintiffs have been either temporarily more susceptible to shock through pregnancy (such as Mrs. Hambrook), or suffering from a nervous illness (Dooley) or a history of psychic disturbance (Chadwick) both creating a greater susceptibility to shock. The courts have not yet answered the question whether the test is whether a person of ordinary phlegm and fortitude in the position of the plaintiff would have suffered shock, or whether the defendant is liable for failing to foresee the presence of a person with characteristics which predispose him towards suffering nervous shock.

Other cases of nervous shock

There are few English cases on nervous shock suffered in a different manner to that already described. In *Owens* v. *Liverpool Corporation* (1939) the plaintiffs who were mourners at a funeral and saw the hearse overturned by the negligent driving of the defendants recovered damages for nervous shock. But this case was disapproved by three members of the House of Lords in *Bourhill* v. *Young* and is now doubtful law. Where the shock is caused by grief, rather than by the witnessing of an accident, it is unlikely that it is actionable. Thus in *Schneider* v. *Eisovitch* (1960), Paull J. assumed as the basis of his decision that a person who by his negligent driving caused the death of someone's spouse was not liable for the nervous shock suffered by the other spouse when this was reported to her.

In the Canadian case of *Guay* v. *Sun Publishing Co.* (1953) an action for negligence for causing nervous shock against the defendant newspaper which had published an erroneous report that the plaintiff's husband and three children had been killed in an accident was unsuccessful. The ground of the decision was that the newspaper, though negligent, had published the news in good faith, and was therefore under no duty towards the plaintiff. If this decision represents English law it appears that the reasons for not imposing a duty in this situation can only be those of policy. The genuineness of the plaintiff's shock cannot be questioned after *Wilkinson* v. *Downton*, and, further, there seems no doubt that it was foreseeable. On the somewhat special facts of *Schneider* v. *Eisovitch*, *supra*, recovery was allowed for nervous shock suffered when the news of the death of one spouse was imparted to the other. In that case the plaintiff was knocked unconscious and her husband killed in a car accident between a car in which she and her husband were travelling and one driven negligently by the defendant. When the plaintiff was given the news of her husband's death on recovering consciousness, she suffered nervous shock attributable to the effect of the news on her. She was allowed to recover damages for this shock from the defendant. Although the reason for the decision seemed a mistaken application of *Re Polemis* (on the ground that the shock was treated as a direct consequence of the plaintiff's injury—but the husband's death could not have been a consequence of the injury done to the plaintiff) the decision seems supportable on the ground that one who by negligent driving kills one spouse can foresee the presence of the other spouse at the time of the accident, and that this fact and that of her injury in the same accident will render her more susceptible to shock caused by the news of her husband's death.

Other exceptional cases

In other cases formerly recognised as clear exceptions to the neighbour principle, the exceptions have recently either been removed or have weakened in force. Thus, although an occupier still owes a trespasser on his land no duty of care, he now owes him a duty of humanity which is quite a stringent duty (*infra*, p. 154). Many of the exceptions relating to premises which existed at common law have been removed by the Defective Premises Act, 1972 (*infra*, p. 156). There is now, under section 8 of the Animals Act, 1971, a duty of care in relation to the straying of domestic animals on to the highway from private land (*infra*, p. 211). It seems likely though it has not yet been conclusively established, that there is aduty of care in relation to a chattel not dangerous in itself (*infra*, p. 158).

CHAPTER 7

BREACH OF DUTY

Introduction

In the case of some torts, of which battery may be given as an example, the definition of the tort allows us to form a clear mental picture of the defendant's conduct in committing it. Negligence is not like this. To say that a person has acted negligently tells us nothing about the type of conduct involved. It merely evaluates that conduct as against some ideal standard. The standard against which the defendant's actions are judged is that of *reasonableness*; to be more precise, the question is asked whether the defendant has acted as a reasonable man would have acted in the situation in which he found himself. If the defendant's conduct fails to pass this test, he is said to be in breach of his duty of care. The phrase, "standard of care," which is often used to indicate the standard of reasonable conduct by which the defendant's conduct is measured is misleading in that it suggests that a pre-existing standard is available to determine whether or not the defendant is negligent. In fact, the court always reaches its decision by an *ex post facto* adjudication that on the actual facts of the case the defendant acted reasonably or unreasonably. Previous decisions on similar facts, though they are evidence of what has in the past been regarded as reasonable or unreasonable conduct will not bind the court in its decision in the instant case.

How breach of duty is established

The vagueness of the rule that the judge has to apply in deciding whether a person was negligent and the lack of binding force in previous judicial determinations of the same question inevitably create a measure of judicial discretion and therefore of uncertainty in the law. Negligence is not alone in this respect—unreasonableness (though not necessarily the unreasonableness of the defendant's conduct) is the central requirement of the tort of nuisance. Furthermore, the uncertainty is mitigated by the existence of certain guiding principles of law which control the exercise of the judicial discretion. Thus, in arriving at his decision, the judge must take into account:

1. The degree of risk to the plaintiff created by the defendant's conduct. In this matter, the question of the foreseeability of the

plaintiff's injury by the defendant is important.

2. The seriousness of the harm that the plaintiff may suffer.

3. The social utility of the defendant's action.

4. The expense and practicability of taking precautions against the risk.

These criteria for deciding the reasonableness of the defendant's conduct are interrelated, and cannot therefore be separately assessed. Thus, it is impossible to decide the question whether the degree of risk created by the defendant is sufficient to involve him in liability without also examining the seriousness of the harm that may result from the risk materialising. Equally the social importance of the defendant's conduct may justify the creation of a higher degree of risk than is normally permissible. Essentially the court's decision is an attempt to strike a balance between these various factors.

(1) *Degree of risk*

In order to decide whether the defendant has created a sufficient risk of the harm which the plaintiff suffers, it is not enough to ask whether this harm was a foreseeable result of the defendant's conduct. The harm must be *reasonably* foreseeable: it must therefore result from a risk which a reasonable man would regard as one against which precautions ought to be taken. Here, more than in any other aspect of negligence, questions of degree enter into the court's decision. If injury to the plaintiff is too remote a possibility of the defendant's conduct, the defendant is not liable.

For example, in *Bolton* v. *Stone* (1951), the defendants were occupiers of a cricket ground. The plaintiff who was standing on the highway outside the ground was struck by a cricket ball hit during the course of a match on the ground. The plaintiff's action of negligence against the defendants was unsuccessful.

The House of Lords took the view that in view of the distance from the wicket to the fence which marked the perimeter of the ground, the upward slope from the wicket to the fence, the infrequency with which balls had been hit into the road (estimated at six times in the previous thirty years), the plaintiff had not established that the defendant had created a sufficient risk of the injury she suffered happening. It may be noted that in this case the defendants took no precautions whatsoever to prevent balls being struck into the road. This shows again that the expression "standard of care" may be misleading since the defendant may have acted reasonably although he has taken no precautions whatsoever against the risk. If the risk is sufficiently slight he is justified in ignoring it altogether.

In recent cases the courts have taken a more stringent attitude where the defendant has created only a slight risk of harm.

In *The Wagon Mound* (No. 2) (1967) the defendants' servants discharged furnace oil into the waters of Sydney harbour. The oil drifted towards a wharf (owned by the plaintiffs in *The Wagon Mound* (No. 1)) where oxyacetylene welding was being carried out by their servants, in the course of repairing a ship belonging to the present plaintiff. The oil was ignited by the fall of pieces of hot metal from the welding operations. The plaintiff's ship was damaged in the resulting fire. The defendants were held liable to the plaintiff for this damage in negligence. The finding of fact by the trial judge in Australia was that a reasonable man in the position of the defendants' servant would have regarded the ignition of furnace oil on water as a possibility but one which could become an actuality only in very exceptional circumstances. This did not excuse the defendants. In the words of Lord Reid, delivering the judgment of the Privy Council: "If a real risk is one which would occur to the mind of a reasonable man in the position of the defendants' servant, and which he would not brush aside as far-fetched, and if the criteria is to be what that reasonable man would have done in the circumstances, then surely he would not neglect such risk if action to eliminate it presented no difficulty, involved no disadvantage and required no expense."

This raises the problem of distinguishing this case from *Bolton* v. *Stone*. It seems impossible to separate the two cases on the question of the degree of likelihood of the harm occurring. Equally it seems wrong to regard the damage in *The Wagon Mound* (No. 2) as more serious than that in *Bolton* v. *Stone*—the cricket ball could have caused serious injury. The difference seems to be that in *Bolton* the defendants were carrying on a lawful activity, arguably of social benefit, and would have been put to expense in providing precautions against the risks of the activity. The discharging of oil by the servants of the *Wagon Mound* was on the other hand anti-social, unnecessary and unlawful (as a public nuisance). In the circumstances the defendants were not entitled to ignore any risk involved provided they should have foreseen it. This comparison shows how factors 3 and 4 (*supra*) can impinge on the question whether the degree of risk created by the defendant was sufficient.

Another case which shows that a court may be prepared to find negligence though the risk of injury is slight is *Haley* v. *London Electricity Board* (1965). In that case a blind person recovered damages in negligence from the defendants for personal injuries received through falling into an excavation made by the defendants' servants in the pavement. The House of Lords found that the defendants' duty of care was not discharged by safeguarding, as they had, normal persons from falling into the excavation; they must also take into account the use of the pavement by blind persons, for whom the excavation was not reasonably safe.

(2) *The seriousness of the injury*

It is an obvious proposition that the defendant's obligations become greater with the greater seriousness of the injury his actions may threaten. The more serious the injury or damage, the less the defendant will be entitled to argue that the degree of risk involved in his actions was insufficiently large, or that he would have needed to incur considerable expense in order to avoid the risk.

In *Paris* v. *Stepney Borough Council* (1951) the House of Lords held that the defendants' omission to provide protective eye goggles for their servants while not negligent in the case of a two-eyed man was negligent in the case of the plaintiff who had only one eye. Such omission clearly did not increase the risk of injury to the plaintiff but only the risk that if he did suffer injury it would be more serious.

(3) *The social utility of the defendant's action*

It has become apparent in the present century that certain inventions, such as the train, the motor-car and various forms of industrial machinery, though by and large regarded as beneficial to humanity, inevitably by their operation involve danger to human life and limb. When the first cases of train and motor-car accidents came before the court, it would have been possible for them to have laid down a rule that the mere operation of the train or motor-car involved so great a risk of injury that it was in itself negligent. Instead the courts decided that there was no negligence provided the vehicle was operated with proper care. The courts reached this result by balancing the social utility of the inventions against the risk of injury where they were operated with due care. Cases in which the defendant is excused on the ground of the usefulness of the activity he is carrying on are therefore somewhat rare, because it will be unusual for such a consideration to excuse what would otherwise be negligence in the activity itself. The only English case in which a plea of utility has been unequivocally recognised is *Daborn* v. *Bath Tramways* (1946) (and even this is a decision on contributory negligence rather than negligence itself). In that case the driver of a left-hand drive ambulance in wartime was held not contributorily negligent in failing to signal a right turn prior to a collision with a bus driven by the defendants' servant, because the shortage of ambulances in wartime conditions justified the use of a vehicle in which it was impossible to give such a signal. In *Watt* v. *Hertfordshire* Corporation (1954) the plaintiff, a fireman, was injured when a heavy jack in a lorry belonging to his employers, the defendants, and in which he was travelling, moved on to him. Although the jack was insecurely tied on, the court held that there was no negligence because the jack was urgently needed in order to save a person trapped under a lorry, and the emergency justified the risk of travelling with the jack insecurely tied. The most acceptable explanation for the case appears to be that given in the judgment of Singleton L.J. to the effect that firemen are deemed to accept the risks incidental to dealing with such an emergency as part of their employment. It seems doubtful whether the emergency would have justified the defendants' action had the jack injured a member of the public. In *Gaynor* v. *Allen* (1959) a police constable who knocked down a pedestrian while riding a motorbicycle in excess of the speed limit was held liable although he had been riding his motorbicycle in pursuance of his police duties.

(4) *The expense and practicability of taking precautions*

From the dearth of decisions where the relevance of the practicability and expense of taking precautions against the risk has been discussed, it appears that the courts do not look with favour upon an argument by the defendant along these lines. In *Latimer* v. *A.E.C.* (1952) it was argued on behalf of the plaintiff that the defendants should have have shut down their factory, the floor of which had been flooded in a thunderstorm, rather than subject the night-shift workers, who included the plaintiff, to the risks caused by the resulting slipperiness of the floor, on which the plaintiff slipped and suffered injury. The House of Lords accepted this argument in principle, though finding that insufficient evidence had been presented by the plaintiff to show that such a step was necessary.

Where the defendant is being sued in negligence for failing to remedy the state of affairs on his land, where that state of affairs arose without his default, the expense of remedying the state of affairs is a relevant factor in deciding whether a defendant is negligent. Thus, in *Goldman* v. *Hargrave* (*supra*, p. 81) since the fire could have been extinguished at nominal expense, the defendant was held liable for its spreading from his land to that of the plaintiff. It seems reasonable to regard expense as a relevant factor where the defendant has done nothing to create the risk, but is liable merely because of his occupation of land upon which the risk spontaneously arises. It has also been held that expense is a relevant factor in deciding whether an occupier has committed a breach of his duty of humanity towards a trespasser on his land (*infra*, p. 154).

The objective standard; the reasonable man

In imposing a requirement on a defendant that he should have acted reasonably, the law is judging him by a standard external to himself. The standard by which the defendant's conduct is assessed is that of a reasonable man in the same situation as that in which the defendant finds himself. It is sometimes said that the standard is an objective rather than a subjective one; but the defendant could hardly be judged by his own standards—this would not be a standard at all. It is important to note that the standard by which the defendant is judged though objective is also hypothetical; the court must imagine what a non-existent reasonable person in the position of the defendant would have done. In effect the court must make up its own mind as to what is reasonable in the light of the evidence.

Difficulty arises where the defendant has some defect, whether physical or mental, which makes it impossible for him to show the same standard of care as a normal person. Are these defects engrafted upon the reasonable man, so that the question is what is it reasonable to expect of a person with those defects? On this matter it seems there are two competing viewpoints. The first is that, unless the defect is taken into account, the "fault" basis of negligence will be ignored, and it will operate as a tort of strict liability. Against this it is argued that unless the test is largely objective, liability in negligence will be hard to establish because all sorts of trifling defects might be put forward in excuse for what is in fact a careless act. To a great extent the problem may be solved by application of the principle that one who, with knowledge of his own defects put himself into a position where those defects made it impossible to display a proper standard of care, is negligent. So a car-driver with slow reactions cannot plead that in an accident caused by his slowness of reaction he was not negligent. On these matters there is a dearth of English authority, and a paucity of discusssion of principle in those authorities that exist. The cases, such as they are, tend to support those who argue for a subjective interpretation of negligence. Many of the decisions are, however, on contributory negligence rather than negligence itself and it may be that different considerations apply (a court might excuse a child for failure to look after itself—but what of a failure to look after the safety of other people?). The following is a discussion of the more common factors which might defeat an allegation of negligence.

Defects caused by immaturity

Clearly very young children have a different standard of care from adults both in matters of negligence and of contributory negligence. But the courts have also applied a different standard of care, at least in contributory negligence cases, to older children. In *Gough* v. *Thorne* (1966) a thirteen-year-old child was held to be not contributorily negligent in crossing the road on a signal from a lorry driver without checking that the way was clear beyond the lorry. Where the child is nearing adulthood, however, the same leniency will not be shown him. In *Gorely* v. *Codd* (1967) the court held a boy of $16\frac{1}{2}$ liable for his negligence in "larking about" with an air-rifle as a result of which he shot the plaintiff.

Defects caused by age

There is little authority about the effect of old age. Old people are not expected to show the same agility as the young (*Daly* v. *Liverpool Corporation* (1939) in which an old person who was struck by a bus while crossing a street was held to be not contributorily negligent where a younger person would have succeeded in crossing). Clearly, however, an old person must not put himself in a position which calls for the reactions or agility of a younger person; also he must make allowances for the slowing-up processes of age (for example, when driving a car).

Ilness

In *Ryan* v. *Youngs* (1938) a driver who had a heart attack at the wheel prior to an accident was held not negligent in causing the accident. Although it has been argued that even in such a case the defendant should bear the loss because he is insured against it, there does not seem any sense in which the defendant's conduct could be described as negligent. The case would be different if the illness were foreseeable, for example, if the driver knew himself to be an epileptic and was seized by a fit.

Intelligence and character

It seems certain, although there is no authority, that a defendant, is not excused by such defects as stupidity, absent-mindedness, accident-proneness, inability to learn from experience, and the like. This is not surprising because if these were regarded as excusing factors few actions in negligence would succeed.

Knowledge

Every adult is expected to possess a certain quantum of knowledge. That petrol is highly inflammable, that dynamite explodes, that acid burns, that toadstools are dangerous, are matters of common knowledge. Apart from this a person may be expected to acquire knowledge by observation from his surrounding circumstances. Expert knowledge is not required of a defendant unless he has acted on the footing that he is an expert. A landowner who has trees growing on his estate is not expected to possess scientific knowledge of diseases that may affect the trees—the knowledge required of him is "somewhere between that of an urban observer and a scientific arboriculturist" (*Caminer* v. *Northern and London Investment Trust* (1951)). But such a landowner also owes a duty to call in experts to inspect the trees from time to time to assess their safety, especially where, as in that case, one of the trees is an elm, which a reasonable landowner ought to know possesses special hazards and the elm in question overhangs or adjoins the public highway. Equally, although expert knowledge is not required of a ship's engineer, he is expected to know that furnace oil might in exceptional circumstances be ignited on water (*The Wagon Mound* No. 2) (1967)), knowledge that clearly would not be expected of the average person.

Skill

Skill is very often interrelated with knowledge, although of course a skill may exist which does not require a body of knowledge. Sometimes the skill and knowledge of an expert is required of a person, for example, a surgeon in performing an operation. In other cases only ordinary skill or knowledge is required, for example, that required of a motorist in driving a car. In general it may be said that the person who holds himself out as possessing the skill and knowledge required for performing a certain task must show that skill and knowledge in the exercise of the task.

The courts have not been too ready to decide that a person must show more than ordinary skill. In *Philips* v. *Whiteley* (1938) it was held that a jeweller who pierced the plaintiff's ears at her request was not liable for showing proper medical skill in performing the operation, since he need only show the standard of care of a reasonably competent jeweller. In *Wells* v. *Cooper* (1958) the defendant was held not negligent in fitting a new door-handle, the plaintiff suffering injury because it came away when he pulled on it and he fell down some steps. The defendant had shown the standard of care of a reasonably competent amateur carpenter, and professional expertise was not required of him. Both cases seem open to the objection that they encourage the doing by amateurs of tasks which involve danger to others. In *Nettleship* v. *Weston* (1971), on the other hand, the Court of Appeal held that a learner-driver must show the standard of driving skill of a reasonably competent qualified driver and was therefore liable to a passenger for injuries the passenger received through his failure to do so. The case is a strong pointer towards "objectifying" the fault element in negligence, although the fact that the defendant was insured against liability clearly influenced the decision (there can be no real objection towards this decision now that insurance against liability towards passengers is compulsory).

Superior qualities

There seems no English authority on the question whether the person of superior intelligence or skill is liable for failing to use those qualities in a situation where such person is not holding himself out as possessing these qualities. Is a racing driver liable for causing an accident in ordinary traffic in which he showed the skill of an ordinary motorist, but had he driven with the skill to be expected of a racing driver the accident would have been averted? The answer to this question depends upon a resolution of the uncertainty as to whether the fault element in negligence is assessed subjectively or objectively.

Sportsmen

There is authority that participants in a sport are not required to show the same standard of care as is normally required. In *Wooldridge* v. *Sumner* (1963) Diplock L.J. said, "if the participant does so concentrate his attention and consequently does exercise his judgment and attempt to exert his skill in circumstances of this kind which are inherent in the game or competition in which he is taking part, the question whether any mistake he makes amounts to a breach of duty to take reasonable care must take account of these circumstances." Thus in that case, the defendant who was riding a horse in a competition was held not liable to the plaintiff, a photographer, standing inside the competition area, who was injured when the horse took a wrong turn as the result of an error of judgment on the part of the rider. This decision, which appears to impose liability upon the sportsman only if he has acted in reckless disregard of the spectator's safety, has been criticised (by Goodhart (1962) 78 L.Q.R. 490), and in *Wilks* v. *Cheltenham Car Club* (1971), Edmund Davies L.J., speaking *obiter*, disapproved the rule laid down and said the proper test should be whether the spectator's injury was caused by an error of judgment that a reasonable competitor, being a reasonable man of the sporting world, would not have made." The criticism seems sound, particularly since the plaintiff will often have difficulty in establishing liability on the part of the organisers of the sporting event (*infra*, pp. 132, 150).

General practice of those engaged in the activity

It is relevant evidence of the fact that the defendant acted reasonably to show that he acted in accordance with the general practice of those who carried on the same activity. For example, in order to decide whether he showed proper medical skill, it is relevant to show that the defendant acted in accordance with approved medical practice. But such evidence is not necessarily conclusive. It is not enough to act in accordance with general practice if it ought to be apparent to a reasonable man that it is a negligent practice. In *Cavanagh* v. *Ulster Weaving Co.* (1960) the plaintiffs employers were held to be negligent in providing him with an unsafe system of work despite the fact that the system was in accordance with accepted practice.

CHAPTER 8

CAUSATION AND REMOTENESS OF DAMAGE

THE question of remoteness of damage in negligence arises when it has been established that the defendant is in breach of a duty of care which is owed to the plaintiff. The rules of remoteness of damage are concerned with the problem for what consequences of that breach the defendant ought to be held liable. While *Re Polemis* remained good law, problems of remoteness of damage were, generally speaking, causal problems, since the plaintiff had to show that his damage was a direct consequence of the defendant's breach of duty (this was not universally true—in some cases the defendant might be liable for indirect consequences of his act, provided they were foreseeable—see cases on ulterior harm, *infra*, p. 111). When *The Wagon Mound* (No. 1) replaced the *Polemis* test with one of liability only for the foreseeable consequences of the defendant's negligence, causation and remoteness of damage became distinct concepts. Thus, although a plaintiff may now be able to prove that the defendant's act caused him damage, he must also show that this particular damage was foreseeable. This has not entirely reduced the importance of causation in the question of deciding for what consequences the defendant is answerable. In general, the plaintiff must still prove that the defendant's act caused the damage that he suffered as well as that this was foreseeable, and the plaintiff will fail if he is unable to prove causal connection. For example, in *Barnett* v. *Chelsea Hospital Management Committee* (1969), the defendant's servant, a doctor, negligently failed to examine the plaintiff who attended for treatment, complaining of vomiting. The plaintiff later died from arsenical poisoning. The action of the plaintiff's estate against the defendants failed because there was little or no chance that the arsenical poisoning would have been diagnosed in time by a proper examination so that an effective antidote could not have been administered.

The topic of causation and remoteness of damage is one that is common to all torts, but will be discussed in connection with negligence because problems of remoteness are most commonly produced by that tort and are there at their most difficult. In the case of other torts, questions of remoteness will be discussed when dealing with the tort itself.

The question of remoteness of damage must be distinguished from that of measure of damages. The rules of remoteness are concerned with whether the defendant is liable for damage he has inflicted upon the plaintiff. Measure of damages is concerned with the question of the *amount* the defendant must pay for damage he has inflicted on the plaintiff and for which his liability is unquestioned. It is also necessary to note that as a matter of terminology some writers use the term "remoteness of damage" to refer only to the issue of foreseeability and not to include the issue of causation as well. Whether to adopt this terminology is really a matter of choice. If the term remoteness of damage is used to include both questions of foreseeability and of causation, however, it must be borne in mind that certain issues of remoteness are purely causal questions to which foreseeability is not relevant (*infra*, pp. 108, 115).

Legal cause-causation in fact and in law

(1) *Causation in fact*

The first question in relation to causation is whether, factually speaking, the defendant's conduct caused the damage the plaintiff suffered. Sometimes the answer to this question is supplied by answering another question, whether, but for the defendant's conduct, the damage to the plaintiff would have occurred. If the answer is yes, then the defendant's conduct is not a cause in fact; if no, then it is a cause in fact (see, *e.g.*, *Barnett* v. *Chelsea Hospital Management Committee*, *supra*). While serving in some cases to exclude and in other cases to admit events as causes in fact, the so-called "but for" test fails to give a ready answer in many difficult cases of factual causation. The answer to the question often depends upon how the question is framed. Thus in *Cutler* v. *Vauxhall Motors* (1971), the plaintiff, an employee of the defendants, grazed his right ankle in an accident at work for which the defendants were legally liable. The graze caused an ulcer to form, and because the plaintiff had been suffering from varicose veins in both legs, an immediate operation was necessary. The plaintiff claimed damages for the pain and discomfort of the operation, but the Court of Appeal held that since the plaintiff would very probably have needed a similar operation within five years, the defendants' negligence could not be regarded as its cause. The Court of Appeal thus asked itself whether the plaintiff would have needed an operation but for the defendant's careless and concluded that he would. If however the question had been whether but for the defendants' carelessness the plaintiff would have needed an operation at the time he did, the answer would have been that he would not. This is not to say that the decision is wrong.

On the second approach, however, the necessity for an operation apart from the defendants' carelessness would have been relevant to measure of damages rather than causation.

Another case which shows the difficulty of formulating the question is *Baker* v. *Willoughby* (1970). In that case the defendant through his negligent driving caused the plaintiff severe injuries to his leg. The plaintiff was later shot in the leg in the course of an armed robbery and in consequence the leg had to be removed. The House of Lords held that the second injury did not have the effect of rendering the defendant liable only for the plaintiff's disability until the time of removal of the leg. In applying the "but for" test to the facts of this the difficulty lies in describing the plaintiff's first injury for the purposes of the question. If described as injury to his leg, then clearly it would not have occurred but for the conduct of the defendant. The subsequent removal of the leg might still have been relevant to the measure of damages. If described as loss of use of, or partial disability in, the leg after its removal, the question becomes meaningless, since a non-existent leg cannot be partially disabled. The House of Lords decision that there was causal connexion between the defendant's negligence and the plaintiff's disability after the amputation seems therefore one of policy. If the first tortfeasor were released from further liability after the amputation, and the second tortfeasor liable only for causing the removal of an already damaged leg, the plaintiff would receive less compensation than he deserved. If, however, the event causing removal of the leg had been a natural event, there are grounds for thinking that the first tortfeasor would have been liable for disability only until the time of removal of the leg. In *The Carslogie* (1952), for example, a ship received damage in a collision due to the negligent navigation of another ship, and subsequently received storm damage. Thirty days were necessary for the repair of the storm damage, but during this period the collision damage (estimated at 10 days repair) was also repaired. The period of loss of use of the ship was held by the House of Lords to be wholly attributable to the storm damage.

A slightly different problem in relation to factual causation is that in which the evidence makes it impossible to say whether or not the defendant's act caused the plaintiff's damage. Normally this will mean that the plaintiff's action will fail—the burden of proof of causation is on the plaintiff (*Bonnington Castings* v. *Wardlaw* (1956)). Sometimes, however, the issue is more complex. In the Canadian case of *Cook* v. *Lewis* (1952), for example, the plaintiff was shot by one of two members of a hunting party both of whom had negligently fired their rifles in the plaintiff's direction at the same time. Both members of the party were held liable in negligence to the plaintiff, despite the fact that the plaintiff could not show which of the two had hit him, and had therefore not established factual causation between the breach of duty by the two defendants and the damage he suffered. The decision can be supported on the ground that where the plaintiff can show that he has been injured as the result of a tort, and where he can prove an incipient tort (*i.e.* breach of duty) against him by a number of persons one of whom must actually have committed the tort, and where the commission of the incipient tort is the reason for the plaintiff's inability to prove the real tort, the plaintiff should not be prejudiced by such inability. It has remained doubtful whether the English courts would follow *Cook* v. *Lewis* but in *McGhee* v. *National Coal Board* (1975) the House of Lords appeared to go one step further. In that case the plaintiff had contracted dermatitis through working in some brick kilns belonging to the defendants. He alleged that the defendants had been negligent in not installing showering facilities. Because of the state of medical knowledge concerning dermatitis it was impossible for the court to say whether the taking of showers after work would have prevented the plaintiff's contracting dermatitis. Nevertheless the defendants were held liable by the House of Lords. The court refused to draw a distinction between materially increasing the risk of injury by failure to provide showering facilities, and materially contributing to injury. This distinction seems, however, to be fundamental. Unless the law relating to proof of negligence has been rewritten to the extent that the plaintiff need establish only a breach of duty by the defendant, it seems necessary to explain the case as being limited to factual situations of the type with which it dealt. Comparison between it and *Cook* v. *Lewis* is of interest. In both cases the defendant's act had prevented the plaintiff from knowing the real cause of his damage. But in *Cook* v. *Lewis* is was clear that a tort had been committed whereas in *McGhee* the other possible cause (*i.e.* dermatitis caught from working in the kiln and incurable by washing) was not a tort. The defendants' negligence did not therefor prevent the plaintiff from establishing the commission of a tort by someone else. Secondly the plaintiff's inability to establish the real cause of his damage was not due, solely, to the combination of events but also to the defective medical knowledge of the real cause of dermatitis.

(2) *Causation in law*

If a defendant were held liable for all the consequences of his act of which that act was a cause in fact, his liability would be excessively wide. The "but for" test is useful for establishing causal connection, but this is not the same as deciding the defendant's legal responsibility for what he has caused. For this purpose it is necessary to decide whether the defendant's conduct is a cause in law of the plaintiff's damage. The test laid down by *Re Polemis* (*infra*) for deciding this was that the damage had to follow sufficiently directly or immediately from the defendant's act. This test of legal causation has not been disapproved by the decision of the Privy Council in the *Wagon Mound* (*No. 1*) (*infra*). That case merely added an additional requirement that the damage be a foreseeable consequence of the defendant's act. Even while *Re Polemis* was still law the defendant might be held liable in certain cases for the indirect consequences of his act, provided these were foreseeable (for examples of this see, *infra*, p. 110), and the *Wagon Mound* (*No. 1*) has made no change here. Furthermore certain cases appear to involve pure issues of causation to which foreseeability is not relevant. In particular, where liability in tort on the defendant's part has already been established and the question is for what consequences of that tort he is liable, this is a purely causal question to which foreseeability is not relevant (*infra*, pp. 108, 115).

Remoteness of damage—the test of foreseeability

In order to succeed in negligence the plaintiff must show that the damage he suffered was a not too remote consequence of a careless act by the defendant. At one time he achieved this by showing that the damage was a direct consequence of the defendant's careless act. In *Re Polemis* (1921) the defendants were held liable in negligence when one of their servants carelessly allowed a plank to fall into the hold of the plaintiff's ship. The fall of the plank caused a spark which ignited petrol vapour present in the hold, and the ship was destroyed by fire. Although the fire was not foreseeable the Court of Appeal held the defendants liable, because their servant committed a breach of duty in allowing the plank to fall (since damage to the ship of some kind was foreseeable) and the fire was a direct consequence of that breach of duty.

During the intervening years between the decision in *Re Polemis* and that in *The Wagon Mound* (No. 1) remarkably few cases needed a direct application of the *Polemis* rule of liability for direct consequences of negligence. But there was much dissatisfaction with the rule it laid down for remoteness problems in tort. There were two chief reasons for this dissatisfaction. It was felt unjust that a person should be held liable for more damage than he should have foreseen. Furthermore foreseeability was the basis of liability for ulterior harm and two different tests for remoteness of damage were therefore recognised by the law. There was also a feeling that a test of foreseeability would give a court greater scope for taking into account issues of policy in their decisions on remoteness of damage.

In *The Wagon Mound* (No. 1) (1961) the Privy Council gave its approval of a test of foreseeability in deciding for what consequences of his negligence the defendant ought to be liable.

The facts in *The Wagon Mound* (No. 1) were as follows: ship engineers, who were servants of the defendants who owned the ship, the *Wagon Mound*, discharged into Sydney harbour a quantity of furnace oil. The oil floated on the surface of the water and was ignited by the fall of pieces of hot metal from the wharf belonging to the plaintiffs, on which welding operations were being carried on by the plaintiffs' servants. The wharf was substantially damaged in the fire that ensued. The trial judge's finding of fact (which was accepted by the appellate courts—*cf.* the finding of fact in *Wagon Mound* (No. 2), *supra*, p. 92) was that, though damage to the wharf by the fouling of the plaintiffs' slipways was foreseeable, damage by fire was not reasonably foreseeable. The Privy Council held on appeal from the Australian courts, that the defendants were not liable because the fire was not a foreseeable consequence of their negligence.

Although strictly speaking the case is only persuasive authority in the English courts, it appears to have been accepted by subsequent cases as good law and as in effect overruling *Re Polemis*. (The case was applied by the Court of Appeal in *Doughty* v. *Turner Manufacturing Co.* (1964) but has not yet received the full consideration of the House of Lords. A return by the latter to *Polemis* seems, however, unlikely.) It seems safe, therefore, to conclude that the defendant's liability in negligence is limited to the foreseeable consequences of that negligence.

(1) *Effect of the rule*

To some it is not self-evident that the *Polemis* rule produces injustice whereas the *Wagon Mound* rule does not. Where it is a question as between plaintiff and defendant of who shall bear the loss, it is arguable that the defendant who has been guilty of some carelessness should be the one. This argument seemed to have been settled in 1961 by the Privy Council's limiting the defendant's liability to foreseeable damage. But cases decided after the *Wagon Mound* suggest that the courts have not departed so widely from the *Polemis* rule as was thought. The "injustice" of the *Polemis* rule, therefore, to some extent still remains.

(2) *The working of the rule*

Foreseeability is a more flexible notion than that of causation. It will be easier for the courts to take into account matters of policy in their decisions than before, and on the whole this seems desirable. But the flexibility of foreseeability is both its strength and its weakness. The unpredictability of foreseeability as a test of duty of care has been seen, in particular, in the nervous shock cases. With foreseeability now the test both of breach of duty and of remoteness of damage there is a real danger of uncertainty in the law producing lack of confidence in the courts' decisions.

It has also been suggested that, now that the test both of the defendant's breach of duty and of remoteness of damage is one of foreseeability, there is no longer any need to answer the two questions, "What should the defendant have foreseen?" and "was the plaintiff's damage a foreseeable consequence of the defendant's act?" in order to decide the defendant's liability. A single question such as "Was the plaintiff's damage a foreseeable consequence of the defendant's act?" should be sufficient. But it may be too early to conclude that the two questions of breach and of remoteness have become merged. Into the question of breach questions of degree (has the defendant created a sufficiently great risk of damage to the plaintiff?) and of social policy (was the defendant's action justified by its utility?) enter, which have no place in the decision whether the consequence the plaintiff suffered ought to have been foreseen by the defendant. Thus it seems obvious that many of the consequences of negligence which courts have held foreseeable would not in themselves involve a sufficiently great risk to justify holding the defendant in breach of duty in not taking care to avoid them. This point is illustrated by remarks of Prosser (taken from an article "*Palsgraf* revisited," 52 Mich. L.R. 1, 17–18): "It is clearly foreseeable that the speeding driver may hit another car and kill another man. But what of the possibility that he may only bruise a shin, and cancer may develop from the bruise? ... Or that the person he injures may be left helpless in the street and be run over by another car? Or that he will hit a power line pole, mix up electric wires, and start a fire, or kill a woman operating a machine two miles away? Or that he will hit a man carrying a shotgun, and the gun will be discharged, and a bystander be shot in the leg? There is a mathematical chance of all these possibilities. All of them have occurred, and can occur again, and all of them have been held 'proximate' (*i.e.* not too remote) by some court. But which of them are foreseeable in the sense of being a significant part of the risk recognisable in advance?" In other words, it is wrong to say that the defendant is held liable for the risk that materialised because he created a sufficiently substantial risk of its happening. He is liable because he has created a sufficiently substantial risk of one type of harm (which may be defined as injury or damage to other road users by impact) and the harm that occurs can be regarded as a foreseeable consequence of his negligence in creating that risk. If this is so, it seems that there ought to be different meanings accorded to the term "foreseeability" according to whether it is being used in connection with a question of breach of duty or of remoteness of damage. Once the question of remoteness of damage has been reached, it seems that the quantity of risk of the consequence occurring is irrelevant, and the only question is whether it can be foreseen that the consequence might occur.

The example given by Prosser of the woman killed two miles away from where the car has struck the electric pylon creates more difficulty. Even if this eventuality is regarded as foreseeable, it could hardly be regarded as a sufficiently real risk to make the defendant's driving negligent in respect of *that* risk. The defendant's driving is negligent because it involves a risk of injury to other road users, a class which does not include the plaintiff. If English law were to hold the defendant liable here, it would have to abandon its requirement that the defendant must owe a duty of care to the plaintiff and must be in breach of that duty, a recognition of "negligence in the air." The attitude of English law towards problems such as these is as yet uncertain. Many of the workings of foreseeability as a test for remoteness of damage have not had sufficient time up to now to be formulated by the courts.

Foreseeability and risk

Certain statements in the judgment of the Privy Council in *The Wagon Mound* (No. 1) adopt a broad approach to the problem of remoteness. For example, as Denning L.J. said in *King* v. *Phillips*, "there can be no doubt since *Bourhill* v. *Young* (1943) that the test of liability for shock is foreseeability of injury by shock." In *The Wagon Mound* (No. 1) their Lordships substituted the word "fire" for "shock" and indorsed this statement of the law. Their words could mean that a test of risk or hazard rather than precise foreseeability of damage is the appropriate one, and that the defendant is liable if the risk he has created, classified broadly in this sense, has occurred, even though the manner of its occurrence or the person whom it affects is unforeseeable.

The crux of the problem posed by the words of the Privy Council is seen in those cases in which the type of damage that occurs is foreseeable but the manner of its occurrence is not. *Hughes* v. *Lord Advocate* (1963) was such a case—

Post office workmen employed by the defendant left a manhole shelter unattended during their tea-break. Four lighted paraffin lamps were placed at the corners of the shelter. The plaintiff, a boy aged eight, took one of the lamps into the shelter to explore the manhole. He tripped over the lamp which fell into the manhole. An explosion occurred in which the plaintiff suffered severe burns. The trial judge found that though the workmen should have foreseen injury by burning to children to whom the unattended shelter and lamps were an allurement, injury by explosion, which occurred through vaporisation of the paraffin in the lamp and its subsequent ignition, was not reasonably foreseeable.

The House of Lords held the defendants liable in negligence. They had created a foreseeable risk of injury by burning, and this risk included injury by burning through explosion, which though itself unforeseeable, was sufficiently similar to the foreseeable risk created as to count as part of it. The risk is therefore defined broadly by reference to the type or types of damage which are foreseeable.

An example of the application of this principle is *Bradford* v. *Robinson Rentals Ltd.* (1967) in which the defendants ordered the plaintiff, their employee, to make a journey of some 500 miles in their van which did not possess a heater, in the exceptionally severe winter of 1963. The plaintiff suffered frostbite as a result. The plaintiff recovered damages from the defendants in negligence because the frostbite, though unlikely, was part of the general class of risk arising from unnecessary exposure to severe cold. *Hughes* v. *Lord Advocate* may be explained as representing the furthest extension of this principle without actually incorporating the risk principle as part of English law. But *Doughty* v. *Turner Manufacturing Co.* (1964) shows that the principle has limits. The defendants kept on their premises a large bath containing acid heated to a temperature of 800° Centigrade. The bath had a loose cover made of a compound of asbestos and cement. This cover was knocked carelessly into the bath by the plaintiff's fellow workman. A chemical reaction took place which caused an eruption of the acid from the bath, and the plaintiff was burned by the acid.

The eruption was found to be not reasonably foreseeable by the defendants, although some risk by splashing of the acid was foreseeable. But the plaintiff failed to recover because no splash had been created by the fall of the cover, and in any case it would be unrealistic to regard the eruption as simply a variant of the perils from splashing. The court described the eruption in Lord Reid's words in *Hughes* v. *Lord Advocate* as "the intrusion of a new and unexpected factor." Following this, in *Tremain* v. *Pike* (1969), Payne J. held that, had the defendant been negligent in keeping a rat-infested farm (which on the facts he was not) he would not have been liable to the plaintiff who contracted Weil's disease as a result, since the foreseeable perils were those of a disease through rat-bite or through eating contaminated food, and Weil's disease, which is contracted through contact with rat's urine, was not a mere variant of these. Clearly, the *Hughes* v. *Lord Advocate* reasoning will not be pushed too far.

These cases do not therefore go as far as importing a test of risk or hazard into English law, whereby the risk created by the defendant is defined in terms of the foreseeable type of damage, and the defendant is liable if that damage occurs, even though unforeseeably.

Cases where the damage is aggravated by physical peculiarities of the victim

While *Polemis* was law it was never doubted that the principle was that the tortfeasor took the victim as he found him, so that the greater amount of damage suffered by the haemophiliac or the man with an egg-shell skull was recoverable. After *The Wagon Mound*, it was arguable whether the peculiarities of the victim which were probably unforeseeable could be allowed to affect the extent of the defendant's liability. But the courts have made it clear that the rule remains unchanged.

In *Smith* v. *Leech, Brain & Co.* (1962) the Court of Appeal allowed the deceased's estate to recover damages from the defendants for his death from cancer of the lip. The lip had been in a premalignant condition and cancer broke out when the deceased received a burn from molten metal owing to negligence by the defendants.

Wieland v. *Cyril Lord Carpets* (1969) shows that the above principle extends to the case where the plaintiff's further injury is brought about by his own act, rather than the workings of the injury on his own body. In this case, the plaintiff received personal injuries in a motor accident caused by the negligence of the defendants. Because of the shakiness induced by the accident, she could not adjust to the wearing of her bi-focal glasses (which she had worn for ten years prior to the accident) and suffered further injury in a fall soon after the accident. The plaintiff recovered damages for the fall from the defendants. (*Cf.* also, *Robinson* v. *Post Office* (1974).)

It is suggested that the basis of the egg-shell skull cases is that, as explained elsewhere (p. 116), once the defendant has negligently injured the plaintiff, the issue of the defendant's liability for further injuries is a pure issue of causation to which foreseeability is not relevant. *Smith* v. *Leech, Brain & Co.*, which supports the rule on the basis that it affects measure of damages rather than remoteness of damage, provides some confirmation of the view expressed in the text, although it seems preferable to describe the issue as one of the causation rather than measure of damages. If this basis for the rule is correct, it seems essential that there must be a *completed* rather than an *incipient* tort. Failure to understand this point has caused confusion in two recent cases. In *Bradford* v. *Robinson Rentals* (*supra*, p. 108) Rees J. observed, *obiter*: "But even if there had been—and there is not—evidence that the plaintiff was abnormally susceptible to frostbite ... he would be entitled to succeed on the ground that a tortfeasor must take his victim as he finds him." But inasmuch as the defendant did not become a tortfeasor until the frostbite supervened (unless it was considered that the negligent infliction of severe cold on the plaintiff was a tort), the principle that the defendant takes the victim as he finds him does not seem applicable here. Another example of the same confusion is *Tremain* v. *Pike* (1969). In this case also the court appears to have taken the view that had there been a breach of duty proved against the defendant, the principle that the defendant took the victim as he found him would have applied. This also ignores the fact that no foreseeable damage had occurred in respect of which the defendant was a tortfeasor. Street (*Law of Torts*, p. 146) suggests that the principle that the victim is taken as the defendant finds him applies to the victim's surrounding physical circumstances, relying on *Great Lakes S.S. Co.* v. *Maple Leaf Milling Co. Ltd.* (1923). In that case, due to the defendants' negligent failure to lighter the plaintiff's ship (a breach of contract, but it is assumed the same principles apply) it ran aground. The damage was increased by the fact that it came to rest on a large submerged anchor, whose presence could not have been foreseen by the defendants. The increased amount of damage was held to be recoverable from the defendants. The difficulty with allowing the victim's surrounding physical circumstances to be taken as they are found is that this would mean *Re Polemis* itself would be decided in the same way since the presence of petrol vapour in the hold would not need to be foreseen. An alternative way of justifying the *Great Lakes* decision is by relying on the principle in *Hughes* v. *Lord Advocate*—the foreseeable risk was injury by impact and it was that which occurred; the details of the impact did not need to be foreseeable. In *Maclaren* v. *Bradstreet* (1969) the surrounding family circumstances of a tort victim which had the effect of increasing the effects of nervous shock caused by the tort did not justify the award of increased damages in respect of this shock.

Finally, it may be noted that where damage which is foreseeable has occurred, the fact that it was far greater in extent than was foreseeable does not excuse the tortfeasor (*Vacwell Engineering Co.* v. *B.D.H. Chemicals* (1971)—defendants liable for unforeseeably large explosion since they should have foreseen the possibility of an explosion).

Measure of damages

Foreseeability is not relevant to the measure of damages. Thus the fact that a defendant has to pay greater damages in loss of earnings to a millionaire than to a bank clerk is not because of the rule that the defendant takes the victim as he finds him. It is because of the principle that the plaintiff is entitled to be compensated for the financial consequences of the injury inflicted upon him by the defendant whether or not these are foreseeable. A limitation has been put upon this by the case of *Liesbosch Dredger* v. *Edison S.S.* (1933). The plaintiff's dredger was sunk by the negligence of the defendants. The plaintiffs recovered the following by way of damages: (1) the market price of a comparable replacement and the costs of getting it to the place of work; (2) financial losses incurred under the plaintiff's contract with the Patras Harbour Authority.

The latter loss was not foreseeable, but was recoverable because at that stage the only question was one of quantification of damage, not of liability. The plaintiffs also claimed for financial loss they suffered because they were unable, because of their own lack of means, to purchase a replacement dredger. This claim the House of Lords refused to allow, because the plaintiffs' impecuniosity was regarded as a new cause which freed the defendants from loss resulting from it. Since it is hard to see how a pre-existent condition can operate as a new cause, the decision seems to be one of policy. There must be some limit to the defendant's liability for the financial consequences he has inflicted upon the plaintiff. If the defendant's tort has bankrupted the plaintiff or driven him out of business, such loss is not recoverable since it is reasonable to expect the plaintiff to provide for such eventualities by adequate insurance or capital backing.

Liability for ulterior harm

Ulterior harm may be defined as harm for which a separate cause or causes intervening between the defendant's act and the plaintiff's damage is responsible. Where the cause has the effect of relieving the defendant from responsibility towards the plaintiff, it is generally called a *nova causa* (or *novus actus*) *interveniens*. But there are many cases, now to be discussed, in which the intervention of a new cause does not free the defendant from responsibility. Most of the cases concern liability for later human conduct, but there is no reason why liability should not be imposed where the later cause is a natural event. For example, if A negligently leaves B's goods uncovered in the open, he will be liable for their being spoilt through soaking in a storm of rain. The storm is foreseeable and an event against which he ought to take precautions. The first cases to be considered will be those in which a later event has intervened between the defendant's act and the infliction of any damage upon the plaintiff. In such cases liability turns upon whether the later event was one which the defendant should have foreseen and therefore taken precautions to prevent. Different considerations affect the case where the defendant's negligence has already inflicted damage upon the plaintiff and this damage is aggravated by later events. This type of case will therefore receive separate treatment.

In the first type of case liability turns upon the foreseeability of the later event. In *Stansbie* v. *Troman* (1948) the defendant, who was a painter and decorator employed to work at the plaintiff's house, was held liable for the loss by theft of the plaintiff's jewellery which was stolen when the defendant left the house unlocked for two hours. The possibility of theft from an unlocked house was one which should have occurred to the defendant. In a case such as this, the qestions of breach of duty, of remoteness of damage and of causation are the same and are all governed by foreseeability. (Hart and Honore, *Causation in the law*, pp. 179–181, describe *Stansbie* v. *Troman* as a case of occasioning rather than causing harm. Clearly, however, the court regarded the defendant's act as a cause in law of the theft.)

Cases where deliberate human conduct of the third party intervenes between the defendant's act and the plaintiff's damage

Several cases have shown that where the deliberate act of a third party is foreseeable, the defendant may be required to take care that it does not occur. Some of these cases turn upon the fact that the third party is not fully responsible for his actions, for example, *Scott* v. *Shepherd* (1773) (*supra*, p. 8) in which the people who threw on the squib were acting in the agony of the moment, and *Shiffman* v. *Venerable Order of the Hospital of St. John of Jerusalem* (1936) in which children playing in Hyde Park brought down a flag-pole insecurely erected there by the defendant, thus injuring the plaintiff, and the defendant was held liable in negligence to the plaintiff.

In *The Oropesa* (1943) the action of a ship's master in putting to sea in a lifeboat in order to discuss the possibility of salvaging his ship with those in charge of the defendant ship, who by their negligent navigation had caused a collision between the two ships, was held to be reasonable in the circumstances and therefore a foreseeable result of the collision. The personal representatives of the plaintiff who was in the lifeboat and who drowned when it capsized therefore recovered from the defendant in negligence.

In some cases the plaintiff will fail because the deliberate act of the third party is unforeseeable. In *Philco Radio* v. *Spurling Ltd.* (1949) the defendants delivered some wooden packing-cases containing highly inflammable material by mistake to the premises of the plaintiffs. The cases were ignited by the plaintiffs' employee who approached the cases with a lighted cigarette, and damage was done to the premises. The court held that since the employee's action was probably not deliberate, but was one of inadvertence or negligence, the plaintiffs should succeed. A deliberate act would in this case have been regarded as outside the risk created by the defendant.

Deliberate act by plaintiff

Rescue cases

In *Haynes* v. *Harwood* (1935) the defendant had left his cab and horses unattended in a crowded street. The horses bolted when a boy threw a stone at them. The plaintiff, a police constable, seeing the danger to women and children, managed to stop the horses but in doing so incurred serious personal injuries. He was able to recover damages from the defendant.

In order for the rescue principle to apply, it seems that three conditions must be fulfilled: (1) the rescue must be reasonably foreseeable; (2) it must be necessary; (3) it must be reasonable. These requirements tend to merge together. For example, the fact that the rescue attempt is unnecessary or unreasonable will in many cases make it not reasonably foreseeable. But it seems that cases can arise in which the rescue is both necessary and reasonable, and yet not reasonably foreseeable (for example, when the presence of the rescuer is unforeseeable).

Cutler v. *United Dairies Ltd.* (1933) shows the effect of an unnecessary rescue attempt. A horse belonging to the defendants had bolted and had run off the road into a field where the defendants' servant was attempting to pacify it. The defendants were found to be negligent in using this horse which had bolted once, if not twice before. The plaintiff went to the assistance of the servant at the servant's request and was injured by the horse. The Court of Appeal held that the plaintiff could not recover damages because he was not attempting to rescue anyone from danger; he was merely assisting the defendants' servant in pacifying the horse. The decision appears to show that a plaintiff who cannot bring himself within the requirements of the rescue principle will be treated as *volens* (*infra*, p. 131) to the risk he has incurred. There seems, however, to be a difference between a deliberate and unnecessary facing of a risk and conduct such as that of Cutler which, though not strictly within the conditions of the rescue principle, was foreseeable and may have been rendered under what the plaintiff believed to be a moral duty. A better solution in this type of case, not open to the Court of Appeal in 1933, would be a reduction of damages for contributory negligence under the Law Reform (Contributory Negligence) Act of 1945.

The question of the reasonableness of the rescue attempt has not been much explored in the English cases. The fact that it exposes the rescuer to the risk of serious physical injury clearly does not make it unreasonable as *Haynes* v. *Harwood* (1935) and *Videan* v. *British Transport Commission* (1963) (*infra*) show. Would it make any difference if the rescuer chose certain death in order to make the rescue?

In *Hyett* v. *G. W. Ry Co.* (1948) the plaintiff rescuer, while attempting to remove some drums of paraffin from railway wagons which were threatened by fire, was injured when one of the drums exploded. He succeeded in negligence against the defendants who were responsible for the fire. Clearly, therefore, even in cases of rescue of property, the facing of a considerable risk of personal injury is not unreasonable.

It is used to be thought that the rescuer's claim was in a sense parasitic upon that of the victim; that the breach of duty was towards the victim rather than the rescuer. This created problems where the person rescued had carelessly created his own predicament. In *Baker* v. *Hopkins* (1959), Barry J. thought *obiter* that even if the plight of the rescued person were self-inflicted, the rescuer could recover damages on the basis of the breach of a duty owed by the rescued person to him. The idea that the duty owed to the rescuer is independent of any duty owed to the victim derives further support from *Videan* v. *British Transport Commission* (1963). In that case the plaintiff, a stationmaster, was killed through being struck by a railway trolley negligently driven by the servant of the defendants. The plaintiff was at the time trying to rescue his infant son who was trespassing on the line. Although the defendants were not in breach of any duty towards the infant, the defendants were held liable to the father's estate because it was foreseeable that a rescue attempt might have to be made if the trolley were operated without care. The case therefore turns clearly on the breach of a duty owed to the rescuer himself.

English courts have not yet had to consider the difficult question of the liability of a rescuer whose rescue attempt fails. To penalise the rescuer for this may be undesirable as a matter of policy because it may discourage rescue attempts. Two situations need to be distinguished. The first is that in which the rescuer by his negligence makes matters worse than they would have been but for his intervention. On ordinary principles of negligence the rescuer seems liable here, although the courts may be unwilling to categorise as negligence mistakes which the rescuer may make in a situation of emergency. The second situation is that in which the rescuer by his negligence fails to achieve a rescue. On the principles established by the House of Lords in *East Suffolk River Catchment Board* v. *Kent* (1941), the rescuer would not be liable here and nothing in the remarks of the Court of Appeal in *Dutton* v. *Bognor Regis U.D.C.* distinguishing that case appears to affect the case of the rescuer. In the Canadian case of the *Ogopogo* (1971), the defendant invited two guests out in his boat. One guest fell from the boat. The defendant backed the boat towards him rather than turning it round. The other guest jumped into the water to attempt a rescue. Both guests were drowned. The court held that though the defendant as host and owner of the boat, owed a duty of care to the first guest to attempt a rescue, and to the second guest not to mismanage his attempts at rescue so as to necessitate a further rescue, the defendant was not in breach of duty here, since the backing of the boat may have been an error of judgment but in the emergency situation did not amount to negligence.

Defendant's liability where there is later negligence

There is a great deal of authority to the effect that the possibility of another person's negligence is a risk that may have to be foreseen and guarded against. The whole of the law of contributory negligence is based upon the fact that the defendant is not excused simply because the plaintiff might by proper care have avoided the risk to which the defendant had exposed him. Similarly a defendant is often not excused because of a later act of negligence by a third party as the result of which the plaintiff is injured. Thus in *Hale* v. *Hants & Dorset Motor Services* (1947) the defendant corporation negligently allowed branches of a tree to overhang the highway. The servant of the second defendants, an omnibus company, negligently drove his bus so that one of the branches struck a window of the bus and the plaintiff, a passenger in the bus, was blinded when struck in the eye by a fragment of the shattered window. Both defendants were held liable in negligence to the plaintiff.

Damage inflicted by the defendant's negligence aggravated by later events

Where the defendant by his negligence has inflicted damage on the plaintiff and the question is whether the defendant is also liable for further damage inflicted upon the plaintiff by later events, the answer is that the defendant is liable if there is a causal relationship between the damage he inflicted and that inflicted subsequently. To this causal question foreseeability is not relevant, for two reasons. First, the defendant has already been found to have committed negligence; what he should have foreseen is thus not relevant in deciding on his liability. Secondly, since foreseeability in relation to a causal question can only refer to foreseeability in the abstract and not to what is reasonably foreseeable as the result of balancing the degree of risk against the other relevant factors, liability would be too extensive since most events are foreseeable in the abstract. The answer to the question depends, therefore, upon deciding in what circumstances causal connection is maintained and in what circumstances it is interrupted. The question will be considered solely in relation to later human conduct, though similar principles no doubt apply to later natural events.

In the case of a later deliberate act, whether or not that of the plaintiff, causal connection is normally broken. In *McKew* v. *Hollande, Hannen & Cubitts* (1969), the House of Lords had to consider a case in which the plaintiff had received an injury to his leg through the negligence of the defendants, and later, because of the disability brought on by the injury, had received further injury when he fell down some steps which he was trying to descend although they did not possess a handrail. The court found that the plaintiff had acted unreasonably in attempting to descend the steps knowing of his disability and refused to allow him damages in respect of his further injury. The judgment fails to make clear whether McKew's conduct was regarded as a deliberate running of the risk or a negligent failure to realise it. This is unfortunate since if the conduct was merely negligent it is arguable that the original injury should have been regarded as causally operative in respect of the later, subject to a deduction for contributory negligence by the plaintiff. The case is clearly authority, however, for a deliberate act negativing causal connection.

On the other hand, in *Pigney* v. *Pointer's* Transport Services (1957) the plaintiff committed suicide some years after he had received an injury to his head due to the negligence of the defendants. It was found that the suicide was the result of an acute anxiety neurosis and depression brought on by the head injury. Pigney's widow succeeded in claiming damages for his death from the defendants. The difference between this case and *McKew* is that the original injury was still operating on Pigney so as to make him not entirely responsible for his actions whereas in *McKew* the original injury did not prevent McKew from taking proper care of himself. *Pigney's* case should be compared with the criminal case of *R.* v. *Blaue* (1975). The accused was convicted of manslaughter. His victim, whom he stabbed, died only because she was a Jehovah's Witness and refused a blood transfusion. The Court of Appeal held that this did not destroy causal connection between the stabbing and the death. Here again, perhaps, we have a case of an act which is not, because of the religious conviction, entirely deliberate. Greater problems arise when the later damage is inflicted by negligence. A typical example is that of tortiously inflicted injuries which are aggravated by later medical negligence. The answer to the problem is obtained by deciding whether the first cause was still operative at the time of the negligence so that a situation of danger existed even though one which could have been averted by the exercise of proper care. Thus in *The Calliope* (1970) a collision occurred between two ships, the *Calliope* and the *Carlsholm* for which the *Carlsholm* was held 45 per cent to blame. The *Calliope* was grounded and suffered damage but was refloated. On the following day, while executing a turning manoeuvre in fog which was necessary in order to recommence her original voyage, the *Calliope* grounded twice and collided with the tug which was rendering her assistance, so suffering further damage. The *Calliope* was found to be negligent in the execution of this turn. Nevertheless it was held that the original negligence of the *Carlsholm* was partially responsible for the later damage because the turning manoeuvre which the *Calliope* had had to perform as a result of the original collision was of an exceptionally difficult nature and was performed in fog. On this reasoning the solution to the case of the aggravation of injuries through medical negligence appears to be to ask whether the case was one which presented any real difficulties to the medical staff. (In the only English case to have considered this question, it was held that medical negligence interrupted causation—*Hogan* v. *Bentick Collieries* (1949), a case under the Workmen's Compensation Acts.) The *Calliope* may be compared with *S.S. Singleton Abbey* v. *S.S. Paludina* (1927). The *Paludina* was in collision with the *Singleton Abbey* due to the negligent navigation of the crew of the *Paludina*. The *Singleton Abbey*, having been cast adrift by the collision, caused another collision, in which another ship, the *Sara*, was cast adrift. Later the *Sara* again collided with the *Singleton Abbey* and was sunk. The owners of the *Paludina* were held not liable for the sinking of the *Sara* for which its own negligent navigation was entirely responsible. The effects of the original collision were spent at the time of the final collision. It was as if the *Sara* and the *Singleton Abbey* were then on a normal voyage.

Where the later damage is neither deliberately nor negligently caused, there is even less reason for finding any interruption in causal connection. The facts of *Wieland* v. *Cyril Lord Carpets* (1969) are a good illustration of this. In fact, the principle underlying the egg-shell skull cases generally appears to be that once the negligence of the defendant has caused actual physical damage to the plaintiff, he is liable for all the further damage caused by the original damage, and foreseeability is irrelevant in deciding how much damage is recoverable.

Significance of the change to foreseeability

At the time of the decision in *The Wagon Mound* (*No. 1*) it was thought that a great change had been brought about in the law of tort by the introduction of a rule for remoteness based upon foreseeability. Since then, however, it has become apparent that little has really changed. No case decided since 1961 has been decided differently than it would have been had *Polemis* been applied. The reason for this is that in the first place *Hughes* v. *Lord Advocate* has introduced a test of foreseeability which requires broad foresight of the class of risk rather than precise foreseeability of the manner in which the risk materialises. It is hoped that the attitude of the court in *Tremain* v. *Pike* will not be typical of the way in which the test in *Hughes* v. *Lord Advocate* is applied. In the second place, *The Wagon Mound* (*No. 1*) has produced no difference in the way in which the courts seek to ascribe liability for ulterior harm. Finally, the egg-shell skull principle survives unscathed, probably because, as suggested above, it raises an issue of causation to which foreseeability is not relevant.

Multiple causes and the apportionment of damage

The cases on liability for ulterior harm show that legally speaking an event may have more than one cause, and that a later act of negligence will not necessarily prevent an earlier negligent actor being held liable. In principle this would seem to give rise to problems of apportionment of the plaintiff's damage among the various tortfeasors responsible for it. In practice the idea that any tortfeasor has a right to demand an apportionment of the plaintiff's damage as between himself and his fellow tortfeasors has been of slow growth in English law. There seem to be two chief reasons for this. In the first place, something of a moral stigma attached to the commission of a tort, and therefore on grounds akin to the *ex turpi causa* principle, tortfeasors were not allowed to claim contribution from each other. With the expansion in the torts of negligence and of strict liability, this reasoning lost whatever validity it once had. Secondly, it appears that only in the present century has the problem of multiple causation been generally recognised. Where, for example, there were successive acts of negligence, the latest was normally taken as the cause of the damage.

Before discussing the introduction of the rule allowing apportionment of damage, it may be said that the problem only arises where two or more have tortiously contributed to the *same* damage, and it is impossible to allocate different parts of that damage to different persons. Where the plaintiff's damage can be separately allocated, there is no problem of apportionment. Thus if A and B simultaneously commit battery against C, it may be possible to show that A caused one injury and B another (but the harm will not be divisible if A and B have acted in the furtherance of a common design—see *infra*).

The damage may, however, not be readily divisible among the tortfeasors responsible. In a motor accident caused by the negligent driving of X and Y and in which Z, a pedestrian, suffers personal injuries, it would obviously be impossible to attribute any particular part of Z's injuries to X or Y. In such a situation X and Y are said to be separate concurrent tortfeasors (they will be referred to hereafter as concurrent tortfeasors). Each is liable for the whole of Z's injuries and Z may choose to sue either of them for his damages.

In English law a distinction is drawn between concurrent tortfeasors and joint tortfeasors. The distinction may be explained as follows. Concurrent tortfeasors are responsible for different torts producing the same damage, whereas joint tortfeasors in law commit the same tort. The most important examples of joint tortfeasors are:

(i) In cases of vicarious liability, the person held vicariously liable is a joint tortfeasor with his servant, an employer with his independent contractor.

(ii) In cases where there has been concerted action in the furtherance of a common design, those participating are joint tortfeasors. Thus conspirators are joint tortfeasors. So are the author, publisher, and printer of a defamatory work. *Brooke* v. *Bool* (1928) furnishes another illustration: the defendant landlord invited his lodger to help him look for an escape of gas by striking a match in the vicinity of the escape. The landlord and the lodger were held to be joint tortfeasors in respect of the damage caused by the ensuing explosion.

(iii) Where one person has instigated or authorised another to commit a tort, the two are joint tortfeasors. Thus the landlord who authorises his tenant to commit a nuisance is a joint tortfeasor with the tenant.

(iv) The partners in a firm are jointly and severally liable for the torts of a partner acting in the ordinary course of business of the firm. The basis of this may be vicarious liability, or community of design among the members of the partnership.

The distinction between joint and concurrent tortfeasors is not now of great importance. *Brinsmead* v. *Harrison* (1872) prevented action against joint tortfeasors after one of them had been sued to judgment and was abolished by section 6 (1)(*a*) of the Law Reform (Married Women & Tortfeasors) Act 1935 which provides that where damage is suffered by any person as a result of a tort, judgment recovered against any tortfeasor liable in respect of that damage shall not be a bar to an action against any other person who would, if sued, have been liable as a joint tortfeasor in respect of the same damage. The question has arisen recently whether judgment recovered against one joint tortfeasor in proceedings in which another joint tortfeasor is sued but against whom judgment has not been recovered prevents further action by the plaintiff against the tortfeasor against whom judgment has not been recovered. In *Bryanston Finance* v. *De Vries* (1975) the Court of Appeal, and in *Wah Tat Bank* v. *Chang Cheng Kum* (1975) the Privy Council, both held that it did not. Since the action envisaged by section 6 (1) (*a*) as being taken against the other joint tortfeasor is a purely hypothetical one, the fact that he has actually been sued does not affect his liability (*cf.* section 6 (1) (*c*) and *George Wimpey* v. *B.O.A.C.*, *infra*).

The abolition of the common law rule concerning judgment does not affect the principle that the plaintiff cannot have in the aggregate more than the amount awarded as damages to him in the first judgment whatever number of tortfeasors he proceeds against (section 6 (3)(*b*) of the 1935 Act). But a release by way of accord and satisfaction, or a release under seal given to one joint tortfeasor, releases the rest. This is not so in the case of concurrent tortfeasors. A mere covenant not to sue given to a tortfeasor of either class has no effect on the liability of the others.

The distinction between joint and concurrent tortfeasors on the one hand, and other tortfeasors remains of importance. The most important difference is that each joint or concurrent tortfeasor is liable to the plaintiff for the whole of his damage, whereas other tortfeasors are liable only for the damage they actually have caused. The effect of this rule is mitigated both by the rules of contribution discussed below, and by the fact that the plaintiff can only recover his damages once. Other obvious points of difference exist. Thus satisfaction of the plaintiff's damages by one joint or concurrent tortfeasor releases all the rest. This is not true of tortfeasors whose combined acts have produced differing damage.

Contribution

Merryweather v. *Nixan* (1799) laid down the rule that no right to contribution existed between joint tortfeasors. There was little doubt that the rule applied to concurrent tortfeasors also. At any rate, when in 1935 a right to contribution was introduced, the right was given to both joint and concurrent tortfeasors. Section 6 (1) of the Law Reform (Married Women & Tortfeasors) Act 1935 provides:

"Where damage is suffered by any person as a result of a tort ... (c) any tortfeasor liable in respect of that damage may recover contribution from any other tortfeasor who is, or would if sued have been, liable in respect of the same damage, whether as joint tortfeasor or otherwise ..."

Who may claim contribution?

Any tortfeasor liable in respect of the damage may recover contribution. This includes one actually held liable, one who would be liable if sued to judgment, and one who has settled the claim against him, whether with an admission of liability or not (*Stott* v. *West Yorkshire Road Car Co.* (1971). In the last case, despite the settlement the person must prove his own liability as well as that of the person from whom he claims contribution (*Stott's* case—for criticism of this, see Law Commission Working Paper, No. 59, on Contribution).

From whom may contribution be claimed?

The words of the section clearly contemplate that contribution may be claimed from one who has actually been sued and held liable. More difficulty exists in interpreting the words, "would if sued have been liable." The words do not indicate the time at which such hypothetical action might have been brought, and in particular whether it is to be regarded as being brought within the relevant limitation period on the cause of action. This uncertainty has led to an unfortunate conflict of decisions. In *George Wimpey & Co.* v. *B.O.A.C.* (1955) the House of Lords interpreted these words as excluding a claim for contribution against one who had actually been sued and found not liable because of the expiry of a limitation period. Two members of the House also thought, *obiter*, that the words of the Act had a temporal connotation and meant, "if sued at the time when the joint tortfeasor claims contribution." But in *Harvey* v. *O'Dell* (1958) McNair J. refused to follow this interpretation and held that the words meant, "if sued at any time," and therefore allowed a claim for contribution from one against whom a limitation period had expired but against whom no action had been brought by the victim of the tort. It is questionable whether this approach does not run counter to the actual decision in *Wimpey's* case, since if the words have no temporal connotation it seems to be irrelevant whether the tortfeasor has actually been sued or not. Nevertheless the decision in *Harvey's* case seems supportable. The injustice of allowing the right to contribution to be lost through the victim's delay in suing seems to outweigh that in allowing a person to be capable of being held liable in contribution proceedings though not in the tortious action itself. (This view receives the support of the Law Commission in its Working Paper referred to above, although reservations are expressed about the length of time which may elapse before contribution proceedings are commenced, since under section 4 (2) of the Limitation Act, 1963, the limitation period on such proceedings does not begin to run until the liability of the first defendant has been settled by judgment or settlement.)

contribution and apportionment

The words "may recover contribution" in section 6 (1) may suggest that a separate action must be brought in order to enforce the right to contribution. This is, however, not normally the case although it is a possibility. Where the plaintiff has joined as defendants in his action all possible tortfeasors, the court may apportion responsibility among them under section 6 (1) and this dispenses with the need for separate contribution proceedings. Where the plaintiff has not joined all possible tortfeasors as defendants, the defendant or defendants actually sued can issue a third-party notice against anyone from whom he is claiming relief whether by way of contribution or indemnity, under Order 16, rule 1, of the Rules of the Supreme Court. The effect of this is to make the third party a party to the plaintiff's action with the result that the court can apportion responsibility for the tort as between him and the other defendants under section 6 (1). Only therefore when the plaintiff's action is disposed of without a claim for contribution being made in the course of that action will the need to bring separate contribution proceedings arise.

Basis of apportionment

Section 6 (2) of the Act of 1935 provides: "... the amount of the contribution recoverable from any person shall be such as may be found by the court to be just and equitable having regard to the extent of that person's responsibility for the damage; and the court shall have power to exempt any person from liability to make contribution or to direct that the contribution to be recovered from any person shall amount to a complete indemnity."

Despite some early authority which suggested that the causative potency of the tortfeasor's act was the only test, it seems probable that the same two tests govern the apportionment of responsibility under this Act as govern apportionment of damages between plaintiff and defendant under the Law Reform (Contributory Negligence) Act 1945 (*infra*, p. 127). If this is true the court must take into account both the causative potency of the acts of the defendants and the degree of blameworthiness involved in their commission. That blameworthiness is also relevant appears to follow from a case such as *Jerred* v. *Roddam, Dent & Son Ltd.* (1948) in which the plaintiff complained of the same failure to act by both tortfeasors, with the difference that in the case of one the failure was negligent, but it was a non-negligent breach of statutory obligation by the other. The apportionment arrived at was 90 per cent of the plaintiff's damages against the former tortfeasor and 10 per cent against the latter.

Section 6 (2) contemplates that in some cases one tortfeasor will be entitled to a complete indemnity against the other. The chief case where an indemnity will be recoverable is that of vicarious liability. Thus a master is entitled to an indemnity from his servant for whose tort he has been held vicariously liable (*Harvey* v. *O'Dell* (*supra*)); he is also entitled to be indemnified for breach by the servant of an implied term of his contract of service to perform his duties with proper care (*Lister* v. *Romford Ice and Cold Storage Co.* (1957)). The importance of the master's right to indemnity has been minimised by the agreement among insurance companies not to have recourse to suing the servant by way of subrogation to the master's claim.

CHAPTER 9

DEFENCES TO NEGLIGENCE

CONTRIBUTORY NEGLIGENCE

Introduction

The rules of contributory negligence deal with the situation where the plaintiff has suffered damage through the negligence of the defendant, but has also contributed to that damage through his own negligence. The law on this seemingly straightforward situation was formerly full of complications, but now, because of the courts' power to apportion responsibility for the damage as between the plaintiff and defendant, generally works satisfactorily.

Before the Law Reform (Contributory Negligence) Act 1945, where the defendant successfully established contributory negligence on the part of the plaintiff, this was a complete defence to the plaintiff's action. The basis of the defence appeared to be that the plaintiff's negligence destroyed the causal link between the defendant's negligence and the damage, rather than that, where both the parties had been negligent, in the absence of a power to apportion the damage, the loss should lie where it fell. Where the defendant's negligence post-dated that of the plaintiff it could be seen effectively as the cause of the damage; in the reverse situation the plaintiff was regarded as having caused his own downfall (*cf.* the old cases *Davies* v. *Mann* (1842) with *Butterfield* v. *Forrester* (1809)).

The courts therefore applied, more or less mechanically, a rule of letting the loss fall on whichever of the plaintiff or defendant had the last opportunity of avoiding the accident.

The decisions on this so-called rule of last opportunity are no great credit to our jurisprudence. But the courts were faced with the difficulty that, in the absence of a power to apportion the damage, they were forced to take the negligence of one party as the only cause of the damage. Even so, there was no reason why the later negligence should always have been chosen. The problem was recognised in *Swadling* v. *Cooper* (1930) in which a trial judge's direction to a jury in a case involving a road accident that the question was, if both plaintiff and defendant were negligent whose negligence substantially caused the accident, was upheld by the House of Lords.

The Court of Admiralty, which had to deal with similar problems of dual responsibility in connection with collisions at sea, was not so hamstrung in its approach to the problem, because of its power to apportion damages under the Maritime Conventions Act 1911. In a famous judgment in *The Volute* (1922) Viscount Birkenhead made it clear that there was no rule of admiralty law corresponding to the rule of last opportunity. It was therefore to be expected that with the provision in 1945 of a general statutory power to apportion damages in all cases of contributory negligence, the last opportunity rule would disappear. Cases decided since then have borne out this expectation.

Law Reform (Contributory Negligence Act) 1945

Section 1 (1) provides as follows: "Where any person suffers damage as the result partly of his own fault and partly of the fault of any other person or persons, a claim in respect of that damage shall not be defeated by reason of the fault of the person suffering the damage, but the damages recoverable in respect thereof shall be reduced to such extent as the court thinks just and equitable having regard to the claimant's share in the responsibility for the damage."

Fault of the plaintiff

In order that the power of apportionment be exercised in his favour, the defendant must show both that the plaintiff was at fault and that this fault contributed to his damage. "Fault" is defined by section 4 of the Act to mean negligence, breach of statutory duty or other act or omission which gives rise to a liability in tort, or which would, apart from the Act, give rise to the defence of contributory negligence. Although, therefore, it is possible that the plaintiff's contributory negligence may consist in a tort or breach of a duty of care owed to someone else, it is clear that this is not necessary, and that it may consist simply in a failure to look after his own safety. For example, in *Davies* v. *Swan Motor Co. Ltd.* (1949) the plaintiff was held to be contributorily negligent in that he rode on the back of a dust lorry contrary to his employer's instruction and thus unnecessarily exposing himself to danger.

The defendant must also show that the plaintiff's fault contributed to the damage he suffered. In the first place, *dicta* in *Jones* v. *Livox Quarries* (1952) suggest that the present rules of remoteness of damage in tort that the plaintiff's damage must be a foreseeable consequence of the defendant's negligence, applies also in determining whether the plaintiff's damage is contributed to by his own fault. For example, Singleton L.J. thought that there would be no reduction of damages where the plaintiff negligently sat on an unsafe wall, and the defendant negligently drove into the wall and injured the plaintiff. This view appears correct.

Apart from being within the risk of the plaintiff's negligence, the defendant must also show that the plaintiff's damage is *caused* by that negligence. With the court's power to apportion damages, there has been a great deal of simplification of the causal problems connected with contributory negligence. The courts are now able to recognise that an event may have more than one cause, and by their apportionment to reflect the comparative importance of each cause. Thus in *Davies* v. *Swan Motor Co.* (*supra*) the plaintiff was injured while riding on the back of a dust lorry in an accident caused by the combined negligence of the driver of the lorry and the driver of a bus. Liability was apportioned among the two defendants, the employers of the bus driver and the lorry driver (under section 6 (1) of the Law Reform (Married Women & Tortfeasors) Act 1935) and the plaintiff who was found to be contributorily negligent in riding where he did.

Furthermore, several cases have made it plain that, because the negligence of either party occurred later than the other, this does not excuse the earlier negligent person. Thus, in one case, *Henley* v. *Cameron* (1949), the defendant left his car without lights on the highway at night. The plaintiff's husband, driving a motor-cycle carelessly collided with the car and was killed. The plaintiff recovered damages on behalf of his estate subject to a reduction for his contributory negligence. It is now clear, therefore, that there is no such thing as a rule of last opportunity. Of course it is still possible for a court to regard the negligence of one party as so pre-eminently the cause of the damage, that the other, despite being negligent, is totally excused. Furthermore, this situation seems most likely to arise where a clear margin of time exists between the two acts of negligence. But whether this is so depends upon the normal principles of causation and remoteness of damage, already outlined, not on a rule which always takes the last act of negligence as the sole cause.

Thus, in *Rushton* v. *Turner Bros. Asbestos Co.* (1960), the defendants, in breach of their statutory duty under section 14 (1) of the Factories Act 1937, failed to fence a dangerous part of their machinery. The plaintiff attempted to clean the machine while it was in motion by inserting his hand into it despite instructions by the defendants never to clean the machine while it was in motion. It was held that the plaintiff was solely responsible for his own injuries.

Fault of the defendant

Section 4 of the Act of 1945, in so far as it refers to the fault of the defendant, requires him to have committed negligence, breach of statutory duty, or other act or omission which gives rise to a liability in tort. The latter words clearly permit the power of apportionment in the case of all torts. But it is very unlikely that an apportionment will ever be made when the tort is committed intentionally, although the Act has been applied in the case of conversion of a cheque—*Lumsden* v. *London Trustee Savings Bank* (1971). In that case, however, the defendant was not an intentional converter. It also seems likely that the number of factual situations in which contributory negligence is operative in the torts of strict liability and nuisance will be limited.

Basis of apportionment

The plaintiff's damages will be reduced "to such extent as the court thinks just and equitable, having regard to the plaintiff's share in the responsibility for the damage." It is now settled that the courts apply two tests in deciding the extent of the reduction of damages the plaintiff must suffer. They must assess (i) the causative potency of the acts of the plaintiff and defendant; (ii) the degree of blameworthiness to be attached to these acts (*per* Lord Reid in *Stapley* v. *Gypsum Mines* (1953)). Degree of blameworthiness appears to mean, at least as far as negligence is concerned, degree of departure from the requisite standard of care rather than degree of moral blameworthiness. Although the two tests have been criticised (the causative potency test was criticised by Glanville Williams (1954) 17 M.L.R. 66, at p. 69, on the ground that causation itself was difficult enough, and that degrees of causation would be a nightmare), they seem justifiable on the ground that in some torts there is no element of blameworthiness so that no other basis of assessment than causative potency exists; also that it seems sensible to assess the causative force of factors such as, for example, dangerous machinery, independently of the degree of blameworthiness in the operation of such machinery. But very few cases have produced a conflict in the operation of the two tests.

One such case was *Cavanagh* v. *London Transport Executive* (1956). The plaintiff was injured by a bus negligently driven by the defendants' employee. The plaintiff was contributorily negligent. Devlin J. found that on the causative potency test the plaintiff should recover half his damages, but found the bus driver only 20 per cent blameworthy on the second test. He therefore compromised by holding the defendants $33\frac{1}{3}$ per cent responsible for the plaintiff's damages.

The mathematics of apportionment are by no means difficult, typical reductions being one-fifth, one-third, one-half and three-quarters. It is unusual for a court to find a plaintiff less than 10 per cent responsible for his damage, nor more than 90 per cent. But in *Laszczyk* v. *National Coal Board* (1954) where the plaintiff's contributory negligence consisted in a breach of statutory duty binding on himself and committed under instructions from a superior, his damages were reduced by 5 per cent.

Particular cases of contributory negligence

(1) *Workmen*

In *Staveley Iron and Chemical Co.* v. *Jones* (1965) it was suggested by Lord Tucker that in cases of liability for breach of statutory duty not every "risky act due to familiarity with the work or some inattention due to noise or strain" amounted to contributory negligence. The suggestion was concurred in by Lord Reid. Lord Tucker thought that this applied even if the particular risky act might involve the employer in liability to third parties. It is difficult to say whether the same doctrine applies in the case of actions for common negligence by the workman. There appears no reason to differentiate such actions and some of the statements in the *Staveley* case appear to support the application of the doctrine.

(2) *Children*

It has already been pointed out (*supra*, p. 95) that a lower standard of care is expected of children than adults and that this applies to both negligence and contributory negligence.

(3) *Agony of the moment*

Where the plaintiff has been put into a position of peril by the defendant's negligence, compelling him to choose one of two or more risky alternatives, he is not guilty of contributory negligence if his choice turns out to be a mistaken one.

Thus, in *Jones* v. *Boyce* (1816), the plaintiff, a passenger in a coach owned and driven by the defendant, reasonably believed that the coach was about to overturn through the defendant's negligent driving. The plaintiff jumped off the coach, breaking his leg. The coach did not overturn, but the plaintiff was found not to be contributorily negligent. The requirement for the operation of this principle is often stated to be that the plaintiff must have acted in the agony of the moment. But there seems to be no reason why it should not apply also where the plaintiff has time to make a calculated decision. Where this is the case, however, the court is probably less likely to acquit the plaintiff of contributory negligence if it considers that his reaction to the situation is unreasonable.

(4) *Contributory negligence by rescuer*

Where the act of rescue does not comply with the conditions laid down (*supra*, p. 113) for the success of actions by rescuers, it seems to be the law that the rescuer's action will totally fail, rather than that he will be regarded as contributorily negligent and suffer reduction of his damages. The rule is perhaps over-harsh on rescuers. It also seems clear that a rescuer whose act of rescue is reasonable but who suffers injury in the course of it through his own negligence may have his damages reduced for contributory negligence. Authority is lacking on this point, but in *Sayers* v. *Harlow U.D.C.* (1958) (*supra*, p. 15) the plaintiff had her damages reduced by a quarter because, though it was reasonable to attempt to extricate herself from her predicament, she was negligent in the course of attempting to do so.

Where the rescuer has acted in the agony of the moment, it seems that he may recover damages although otherwise his act of rescue would have been unreasonable. In *Brandon* v. *Osborne, Garret & Co.* (1924) the plaintiff thinking that a pane of glass which fell from above through the negligence of the defendants was falling on her husband tried to pull him out of the way and in doing so injured her leg. The court held that she could recover damages for this from the defendants because she had acted instinctively on the spur of the moment. The court did not consider whether her rescue attempt was reasonably necessary or reasonable, not surprisingly since at that time the rescue principle had not been formulated. They treated the plaintiff's action as a reflex one produced by a situation of imminent peril. It is not yet clear how "agony of the moment" would affect a genuine rescue case. The most likely solution is that where the rescue attempt was either not reasonably necessary or the manner of it was unreasonable, the rescuer, if he acted in the agony of the moment, would suffer a reduction of damages for contributory negligence but would not fail altogether.

(5) *Seat belts, crash helmets*

The courts have been much troubled in recent years over the question whether failure to wear a seat belt or crash helmet is contributory negligence in respect of damage attributable to it. Such behaviour clearly operates, generally, only as a failure to mitigate damage some of which would have occurred anyway. The Court of Appeal, in the less controversial case of the crash helmet, held in *O'Connell* v. *Jackson* (1971) that failure to wear it amounted to contributory negligence so that the increased damage suffered by the plaintiff through his failure to wear the helmet must be apportioned between plaintiff and defendant. On the question of seat belts, there was much variance among lower courts but the Court of Appeal has now decided in *Froom* v. *Butcher* (1975) that failure to wear a seat belt amounts to contributory negligence. Lord Denning suggested that where the wearing of the seat belt would have averted all injury the deduction should be in the region of 25 per cent. Where it would have prevented some injury but not all, it should be in the region of 15 per cent (*i.e.* of the total injury).

Neither in *O'Connell* v. *Jackson* nor in *Froom* v. *Butcher* was the question of law considered whether negligence which merely has the effect of failing to mitigate damage which the plaintiff would in any case have suffered amounted to contributory negligence at common law (the Act did not increase the scope of what is to be regarded as contributory negligence—section 4). The probability is that it did not (see J C. Hicks, (1974) 37 M.L.R. 308).

Imputed contributory negligence

Under a largely discredited common law doctrine, the contributory negligence of one person might be imputed to another so as to constitute contributory negligence on the part of that other. Several decisions have whittled away the doctrine, so that now the only important case of it is that the negligence of a servant acting in the course of his employment is imputed to his master. But the negligence of a carrier is not imputed to his passenger, that of an adult is not imputed to a child of whom he is in charge, and that of an independent contractor is not imputed to his employer.

It is not easy to see why the rule should survive in the case of master and servant. It cannot be explained on the ground of the master's vicarious liability for the negligence of his servant committed in the course of his employment, since the basis of policy underlying the doctrine of vicarious liability is that the servant's liability is transferred to a financially solvent defendant, whereas imputed negligence affects the case where the employer is the injured party, and there is no reason of policy requiring financially solvent plaintiffs to meet part of their own loss out of their own pockets. By an unwarranted extension of the doctrine, it applies also in those cases where the owner of a car is vicariously liable for the negligence of the person driving the car (*infra*, p. 229). Thus, in *Lampert* v. *Eastern National Omnibus Co.* (1954), it was held that the plaintiff who had delegated the driving of a car which she owned to her husband was contributorily negligent as to the amount of his negligence in an accident caused also by the negligent driving of the defent. This is less serious now that the liability of the person driving the car towards passengers is required to be covered by insurance under section 145 (3)(*a*) of the Road Traffic Act 1972.

VOLENTI NON FIT INJURIA

Introduction

The defence of *volenti non fit injuria* was of importance during the nineteenth century, when it was confined within less narrow limits than it is today. In particular it was used to defeat actions by workmen who had suffered injuries in the course of their employment as the result of their employer's negligence; it was enough to establish the defence that the workmen knew of the negligence and had remained in his employment. This doctrine was removed by *Smith* v. *Baker* (*infra*, p. 134) and this century has seen a further narrowing down of the defence. It is, however, still often unpredictable whether the defence applies in a given case. The exact boundaries between it and contributory negligence have not yet been drawn by the courts. As a matter of law, the latter defence requires an unreasonable failure by the plaintiff to look after his own safety, whereas *volenti* requires the plaintiff to be willing to run the risk of being injured by the defendant's negligence. But the application of this distinction to concrete factual situations can produce and has produced uncertainty. This is made more serious by the fact that whereas the plaintiff may suffer only a reduction of his damages for his contributory negligence, *volenti* has the effect of totally defeating the plaintiff's claim.

Volenti applies to the unintentional torts

The basis of the defences of consent and of *volenti non fit injuria* is the same—the plaintiff has in effect consented to his own injury. But the defence is normally called consent where the plaintiff has consented to the commission of an actual tort against himself, for example, the licensing of a battery by one who agrees to have a haircut. The defence is called *volenti non fit injuria* where the plaintiff consents to tortious behaviour which may injure him in the future. This distinction means in effect that the defence of consent is confined to the intentional torts, since only in these torts can there be certainty that the tort will be committed. *Volenti* is confined to torts of negligence and strict liability, since in such cases an actual tort is a risk rather than a certainty. Both consent and *volenti non fit injuria* are, however, derived from the same general principle. The rules determining the effect of consent given by minors, and the effect of fraud and duress on consent, will therefore apply also to *volenti.*

Limits of the defence

Recent authority would make *volenti* a defence only in very exceptional circumstances.

In *Woolridge* v. *Summer* (1963) the plaintiff, a professional photographer, who was standing inside a show-jumping arena, was injured when a horse ridden by the defendant galloped off the course and crashed into him. The trial judgment found that there was an error of judgment on the defendant's part.

The plaintiff's action failed because the error of judgment was found not to amount to a breach by the defendant of his duty of care because an error of judgment on the part of a professional sportsman who was concentrating on the game and doing his best to win did not amount to a breach of the sportsman's duty of care, whether the person injured was another participant or a spectator. This was not because of *volenti non fit injuria*, but because those present at the game or sport were deemed to run the risk of dangers incidental to it. Diplock L.J. went so far as to say that "the maxim (*i.e. volenti non fit injuria*) in the absence of express contract, has no application to negligence simpliciter where the duty of care is based solely on proximity or 'neighbourship' in the Atkinian sense." On this view it seems that the court determines, as part of the decision whether the defendant is in breach of duty, whether the plaintiff ought to take the risk of the defendant's conduct. This approach provides the best explanation of a case such as *Murray* v. *Harringay Arena* (1951), sometimes regarded as turning on *volenti*. In that case, the plaintiff, a boy aged six, was taken by his father to watch a game of ice-hockey at the defendants' arena. He was struck in the eye by a puck hit by one of the players. No protective netting was provided around the rink. The failure of the plaintiff's action in negligence against the occupiers of the rink seems best understood as turning on the fact that no breach of duty had been committed by the defendants, since all spectators were deemed to accept the risk of watching without a protective netting (the provision of which would have interfered with vision) rather than on *volenti non fit injuria* which could hardly have been established by the consent of a six-year-old. However, *I.C.I.* v. *Shatwell* (*infra*) shows that *volenti non fit injuria* still survives in a case of negligence simpliciter, and the extent of the doctrine laid down by *Woolridge* v. *Sumner* is uncertain.

Apart from these doubts about the present status of the defence, there are also indications that it will be confined by the courts within narrow limits. In *Woolridge* v. *Sumner* Diplock L.J. also said: "The consent that is relevant is not consent to the risk of injury but consent to the lack of reasonable care that may produce that risk and requires on the part of the plaintiff at the time at which he gave his consent full knowledge of the nature and extent of the risk that he ran." He went on to express doubts whether consent preceding the act of negligence could ever be effective, since in such a case the plaintiff does not know in full the nature and extent of the risk.

It is clear that by "act of negligence" Diplock L.J. did not mean the moment of infliction of damage, since this would reduce the scope of *volenti* to infinitesimal proportions. The plaintiff's consent must be given therefore at a time when he knows that the defendant is acting negligently in such a way tht he (the plaintiff) is likely to suffer damage. *Dann* v. *Hamilton* (1939) shows how difficult it may be to establish this. The plaintiff was a passenger in a car driven by the defendant. She knew when getting into the car that the defendant was very drunk. She found during the course of the journey that he was driving very badly, but although she had several opportunities to leave the car, she remained and received injuries in an accident caused by the defendant's negligence. The defence of *volenti non fit injuria* failed. It seems hard to imagine a clearer case where the consent was given to the negligent driving rather than to the risk of being injured. Even if the plaintiff was not *volens* at the time she entered the car she surely became so during the course of the journey. This narrow construction of *volenti* does mean, however, that the more equitable solution can be imposed, *viz.* a reduction of damages because of the plaintiff's contributory negligence (not open to the court in *Dann* v. *Hamilton*, but applied in a similar situation in *Dawrant* v. *Nutt* (1961)—the courts no longer need to consider *volenti* as a defence on facts such as those of *Dann* v. *Hamilton* since section 148 (3) of the Road Traffic Act 1972 prevents the driver of a car from relying on it against his passenger).

I.C.I. v. *Shatwell* (1965) shows that despite these limitations upon *volenti*, it may still be difficult to distinguish it from contributory negligence. The plaintiff and his brother agreed to disregard their employers' instructions in testing some detonators without taking precautions. As a result of doing this, the plaintiff was injured by an explosion. He sued his employers on the ground that they were vicariously liable for his brother's negligence. The House of Lords held that the defence of *volenti non fit injuria* applied, reversing the decision of the Court of Appeal which had allowed the action subject to a reduction of half the plaintiff's damages for his contributory negligence. The case is clearly a stronger one than *Dann* v. *Hamilton* because there was here a common agreement between the plaintiff and his brother to act negligently. Other cases have shown the survival of the defence despite what was said in *Woolridge* v. *Sumner*. In *Simms* v. *Leigh Rugby Football Club* (1969) it was held that a rugby league player had willingly accepted the risk of a wall around the pitch with which he had collided during play so that he had no action against the club as occupiers of the ground for breach of their common duty of care (*infra*, p. 143). In *Nettleship* v. *Weston* (1971) a driving instructor who had asked whether his pupil was comprehensively insured was found by this inquiry not to be *volens* to negligence shown by her during a lesson. Lord Denning appeared to share the view of Diplock L.J. that nothing short of actual agreement would suffice for the defence to apply, but the other members of the Court of Appeal appeared satisfied that the defence may have been available but for the question.

Voluntary act of plaintiff

The plaintiff's consent must be freely given. So a workman who through economic pressures chooses to stay in his employment knowing of a danger created by his employer's negligence does not consent to that negligence (*Smith* v. *Baker & Sons* (1891); *Bowater* v. *Rowley Regis Corporation* (1944)). Equally one who chooses to face a danger in order to exercise a right is not *volens* (right of access to highway—*Clayards* v. *Dethick and Davis* (1848)—the defence in the case was contributory negligence but it seems clear that *volenti* would also have failed). However, it seems clear that an unreasonable insistence on exercising a right could be contributory negligence. In the *Clayards* case itself, there was no alternative route by which the plaintiff could take his horse on to the highway, and as a cabman he needed the horse for the purposes of his trade.

Agreement between Plaintiff and Defendant

Where the plaintiff has contracted with the defendant to exempt him from tortious liability, the defence to an action of negligence is the contract itself which prevents liability arising rather than *volenti non fit injuria*. Such contractual exemption of tortious liability is generally possible although there are a number of important exceptions. For example, an employer cannot contract out of his vicarious liability in tort towards his employers (section 1 (3), Law Reform (Personal Injuries) Act 1948). A driver of a motor vehicle cannot contract out of liability towards his passengers (section 148 (3), Road Traffic Act 1972). There are also exceptions in the case of carriage of persons by road in public vehicles, by rail and by air.

Where no contract but a consensual relationship exists, an agreement that the defendant should not be liable in tort may be effective but here the basis of the defence is *volenti non fit injuria*. In *Buckpitt*

v. *Oates* (1968) the plaintiff, a minor, travelled in a car driven by a defendant, another minor. The defendant drew the plaintiff's attention to a notice displayed in the car excluding his liability to passengers for negligent driving. This notice was held to give the defendant a defence to the plaintiff's action for injuries caused by the defendant's negligent driving, not on the ground of contract, since the plaintiff could not make a binding contract, but because of *volenti non fit injuria*. The case shows that at least where such a consensual relationship exists between plaintiff and defendant, the plaintiff's consent may license in advance a subsequent act of negligence by the defendant. *Buckpitt* v. *Oates* has been followed in *Bennett* v. *Tugwell* (1971) and *Birch* v. *Thomas* (1972). In the latter case the Court of Appeal reached the surprising conclusion that a statement by the defendant to the plaintiff that he was not insured against passenger liability must be construed as a warning that the defendant was excluding his liability in tort. The plaintiff by travelling in the car thereby agreed to this exclusion. The practical effect of these decisions has disappeared now that insurance against liability to passengers is compulsory, and now that a driver cannot contract out of such liability.

In order to find that the plaintiff has consented to the terms of an exclusionary notice such as that in the above cases, it must be clear that he had a choice in the matter. In *Burnett* v. *British Waterways Board* (1972), the plaintiff, a lighterman, had an obligation under his contract of employment to enter the defendants' dock. It was held that he did not consent to run the risk of negligence by the defendants' servants despite the existence of an exclusionary notice to that effect at the entry to the dock (see also, *infra*, p. 150).

CHAPTER 10

PROOF OF NEGLIGENCE

Judge and jury

It was at one time important to differentiate between the functions of judge and jury in the trials of civil actions for negligence. Appellate courts, while willing to overrule the judges' decisions on points of law would seldom disturb the findings of the jury unless they were completely unreasonable having regard to the evidence in the case. This was a quite serious limitation upon the function of the appellate court, since juries were not confined to determining the actual facts of the case, but also had to perform the evaluation of the defendant's conduct (in the light of the judge's direction to them about what standard was demanded of the defendant) required in order to decide whether he was negligent. But with the virtual disappearance of the jury in actions of negligence, it is no longer of much importance to attempt to distinguish "jury questions" from those which the judge has to decide. The judge sitting alone will decide all the issues in the case, the actual facts, the inferences to be drawn from those facts, and matters of law, such as the existence of a duty of care, the standard of care required by the defendant in discharging that duty, and questions of remoteness of damage. Furthermore, the appellate court will not regard itself as precluded from reviewing decisions of the trial judge on matters which were formerly left exclusively to the jury, for example, the decision whether the defendant has acted reasonably, and the award of damages in the action, though the appelate court will invariably accept the judge's finding on the actual facts of the case rather than inferences to be drawn from those facts. The differentiation in function between judge and jury remains in those cases where the action is heard before a jury, and is also relevant in the case of appeals from the County Court to the Court of Appeal which lie only on points of law if the action is for £200 or more. In both these cases the appellate court will accept the jury's findings both of fact and of the inferences to be drawn from them unless satisfied that the latter are wholly unreasonable.

No evidence of negligence

It is a matter of law whether there is sufficient evidence of negligence on which a judge might decide that the defendant was negligent. Accordingly an appellate court may reverse a judge's decision that there was, or was not, sufficient evidence of negligence to be left to the jury. The decision that there is no evidence of negligence may be reached either because the facts proved by the plaintiff do not tend to support his allegation of negligence against the defendant, or because he has given insufficient evidence to be left to a jury of facts which if proved would clearly establish negligence on the defendant's part. An example of the former situation is the case where the facts proved by the plaintiff are equally consistent with negligence or no negligence by the defendant. Thus, in *Hammack* v. *White* (1862), the defendant was riding a horse he had purchased the previous day in a busy street. The horse for no apparent reason became restive, and, despite the defendant's efforts to control it, ran upon the pavement and killed the plaintiff's husband. There was held to be no evidence of negligence, since the facts proved might have pointed to a negligent failure to control the horse by the defendant, but were equally consistent with no negligence at all by him.

A different situation exists where the plaintiff has given sufficient evidence to be left to a jury of facts which if proved would establish negligence by the defendant. Here the trial court's decision as to whether the plaintiff's evidence is sufficient proof of these facts is not a matter of law and its verdict will not be disturbed by an appellate court unless it is clearly unreasonable. Equally conflicts of evidence as to such facts must be resolved by the trial court.

Burden of proof

The legal burden of proving negligence rests upon the plaintiff. He must show, in accordance with the general rule for civil trials, that on the balance of probabilities the defendant was negligent and that this negligence caused the plaintiff injury. The burden of proving the facts establishing both breach of duty and causation thus rests on the plaintiff.

It used to be thought that the plaintiff who had established a prima facie case of negligence might still fail, even if the defendant provided no explanation. In *Henderson* v. *H. E. Jenkins & Sons* (1970), however, Lord Pearson said in the House of Lords, "But if in the course of the trial, there is proved a set of facts which raises a prima facie inference that the accident was caused by negligence on the part of the defendants, the issue will be decided in the plaintiff's favour, unless the defendants by their evidence provide some answer which is adequate to displace the prima facie inference." The defendant achieves this by satisfying the so-called evidential burden of proof. He must show that the accident was at least as likely as not to have occurred not through his negligence. This is enough for him to succeed since the legal burden of proving that on the balance of probabilities the defendant was negligent rests on the plaintiff.

Res ipsa loquitur

The effect of this rule of evidence is to allow the plaintiff to treat the actual facts of the case as evidence of the defendant's negligence —the facts speak for themselves. The rule is an important concession to plaintiffs since it recognises the difficulty that exists in the case of many accidents of furnishing direct evidence that they were the result of negligence. In order that the rule should operate three conditions are necessary: (1) the plaintiff's injury must be such as does not in the ordinary course of things happen in the absence of negligence; (2) the facts proved must point to negligence by the defendant; (3) the court must not have facts before it which enable it to make up its mind on the issue of negligence independently of *res ipsa loquitur*. Whether the rule applies to the case before it is a question of law for the judge to decide.

(1) *The plaintiff's injury is one that would not in the ordinary course of things have happened without negligence*

The rule has been applied to the case of objects falling from upper storeys of buildings on to the highway below (for example, in *Byrne* v. *Boadle* (1863), flour bags falling from the upper window of the defendant's building). Numerous cases have established the applicability of the rule to motor vehicles going out of contol (for example, *Laurie* v. *Raglan Building Co. Ltd.* (1942)—a lorry driven at ten m.p.h. skidded and mounted the pavement, killing the plaintiff's husband) and it has been applied to stones found in buns (*Chaproniere* v. *Mason* (1905)), to sulphites found in underpants (*Grant* v. *Australian Knitting Mills Ltd.* (1933)) and to the effects of a surgical operation upon the plaintiff (*Cassidy* v. *Minister of Health* (1951)), disposing of doubts whether *res ipsa loquitur* applied in medical cases.

(2) *Facts proved must point to negligence by the defendant*

If facts proved merely point to negligence by one of a number of persons of whom the defendant is one, this is insufficient (for qualifications upon this when negligence is proved to be committed by one of the defendant's servants or independent contractors, see *infra*, p. 222). The second requirement is sometimes stated to be that the "*res*" must be under the defendant's control. So in *Easson* v. *L. & N.E. Ry. Co.* (1944) the fact that a door of the defendants' train fell open when the train, an express, was in between stations, did not raise a presumption that the defendants' servants had failed to close it on leaving its last stop. But in *Gee* v. *Metropolitan Ry. Co.* (1873) when the train door fell open shortly after the train had left a station, it was held that *res ipsa loquitur* applied. In *Lloyde* v. *West Midlands Gas Board* (1971) the members of the Court of Appeal appeared to agree that exclusive control by the defendant is not necessary to establish *res ipsa loquitur*. The plaintiff would, however, have to establish the improbability of outside interference in order that the doctrine should apply.

The rule is qualified to some extent in the case of collisions between motor vehicles. Where a collision occurs between two such vehicles and there is nothing in the evidence on which the court can make up its mind as to which driver was to blame, or as to the proportions in which each driver was to blame, then the court will hold each driver equally responsible. This result was arrived at in *Bray* v. *Palmer* (1953) (head-on collision near centre of road) and *France* v. *Parkinson* (1954) (collision on cross-roads of equal status). This is in fact a case of *res ipsa loquitur* where the fact establish a balance of probability of two people sharing equally in the responsibility for the damge.

(3) *Facts must not be present before the court which enable it to make up its mind on the issue of negligence independently of res ipsa loquitur*

Barkway v. *South Wales Transport* (1950) established that where actual evidence is given of the defendant's negligence, *res ipsa loquitur* can no longer apply (evidence of negligent system of tyre inspection excluded *res ipsa loquitur* in case where tyre of defendant's bus had burst causing the bus to go out of control).

Effect of *res ipsa loquitur*

It appears that the applicability of the rule *res ipsa loquitur* might have one of three possible effects, according to the rules of evidence (see Cross, *Law of Evidence*, fourth edition, p. 131). First, it might be relevant evidence of the defendant's negligence, sufficient to be left to a jury. On this view, the plaintiff might still fail, even if the defendant failed to provide an explanation of the accident consistent with lack of negligence on his part. This effect is, however, seemingly impossible since *Henderson* v. *Jenkins* (*supra*) which contemplates that once a prima facie case of negligence exists, the defendant must fail unless he provides some explanation consistent with no negligence on his part. Whether the reasoning of the House of Lords in that case extends to *res ipsa loquitur* is however uncertain. Secondly, the effect might be that the defendant has the evidential burden of providing an explanation for the accident which is at least as consistent with no negligence as with negligence on his part. If he fails to do this, the plaintiff succeeds. Thirdly, the effect might be that the defendant must satisfy the court that on the balance of probabilities he was not negligent. The third possibility appears anomalous. For one thing, it would mean that, once *res ipsa loquitur* applies, the legal burden of proof shifts to the defendant, and would make necessary a qualification upon the statement that the legal burden rested on the plaintiff throughout the trial. There is also the point that to treat the effect of *res ipsa loquitur* in this way would give the plaintiff relying on *res ipsa loquitur* an advantage over one relying on direct evidence of negligence, since it is clear that there is no transference of the legal burden of proof when such a person has made out a prima facie case of negligence. In view of this it is perhaps surprising that the English courts have tended to speak in favour of the third possible effect of *res ipsa loquitur* as the correct one. So in *Moore* v. *Fox & Sons* (1956) the Court of Appeal approved *obiter* remarks of Asquith L.J. (also speaking *obiter*) in *Barkway's* case, to the effect that once *res ipsa loquitur* applies, the defendant must prove on the balance of probabilities either a specific cause of the accident not connoting negligence on his part, or that he took all reasonable care. It is suggested that the effect of *res ipsa loquitur* may differ from case to case. In some cases it may not create a sufficiently strong presumption of negligence for the court to hold that the defendant must fail in the absence of an explanation. In other cases the presumption may be stronger so that the court will hold for the defendant unless he provides an explanation. But it seems against principle to make the defendant prove his case on the balance of probabilities.

Cases where the defendant relies on showing that he took all reasonable care create some difficulty. In *Walsh* v. *Holst & Co.* (1958) the defendants were subcontractors engaged in the process of making brick apertures for windows in buildings. It was their duty to ensure that bricks dislodged in the process of breaking them out from the wall should not fall on the highway beneath the building. The plaintiff was injured by the fall of a brick from the building and the court held that *res ipsa loquitur* applied but it found that the defendants' inspection system showed them to have taken reasonable care and that the fall of the brick must have been caused by something other than their negligence. There seems to be force in the dissenting judgment of Morris L.J. who considered that the fall of the brick could only have been explained by deficiencies in the precautions the defendants took or in the operation of the system by their servants.

Res ipsa loquitur and causation

The plaintiff in an action of negligence must prove not only that the defendant was negligent but also the existence of a causal connection between that negligence and the damage he suffered. Thus, in *Wakelin* v. *L. & S.W. Ry. Co.* (1886), the plaintiff's husband was killed by the defendants' train which was negligent in failing to whistle. But as no evidence was given of the way in which the accident occurred, no causal connection could be established between the negligence and the death and the action failed. As it appears that the factual inference allowed by *res ipsa loquitur* is only as to the defendant's negligence and not as to causal connection between the negligence and the plaintiff's damage, it cannot be used to prove such causal connection. But in certain cases where causal connection is very likely the plaintiff is allowed to succeed even though he cannot prove the exact way in which his accident occurred (see, for example, *Thurogood* v. *Van den Burghs and Jurgens Ltd.* (1951), and *Allen* v. *Aeroplane and Motor Aluminium Castings* (1965)—do not these decisions ignore possible contributory negligence by the plaintiff? The discussion in an earlier chapter of *Cook* v. *Lewis* and *McGhee* v. *National Coal Board* (pp. 102–3) is also relevant to the question of proof of causation).

Section 11 of the Civil Evidence Act 1968

The Civil Evidence Act 1968 removed the rule of the common law that a conviction could not be used as evidence in civil proceedings. Section 11 allows the conviction to be used as evidence of the facts which constituted the offence, although allowing the defendant to controvert such evidence by evidence of his own (*cf. Stupple* v. *Royal Insurance Co.* (1971) for the nature of the evidential burden which this casts on the defendant). A conviction for careless or dangerous driving may now, therefore, be used as evidence of negligence in a civil court.

CHAPTER 11

LIABILITY FOR PREMISES

LIABILITY for defective premises (the term includes land itself) is in the process of being assimilated to liability in negligence. But it justifies separate treatment because to some extent special rules still apply to it. In particular the common law distinguished the liability of the occupier towards those injured when on his premises from those who were injured when outside the premises. The latter could if they could prove injury from a dangerous condition in the premises, sue in nuisance or negligence. The former made use of the special rules of occupiers' liability. Whatever the logic of the distinction, it has been preserved because the Occupiers' Liability Act of 1957 has rendered the obligations of the occupier towards his visitors statutory while leaving untouched his obligations to those outside his premises. But as the Act has gone a long way towards making the liability of the occupier turn entirely on his negligence the divergence is now no longer very marked.

Something must be said about the law before the Act before considering the rules introduced by it.

PRE-1957 LAW

The old law recognised five different classes of entrant: (1) the invitee; (2) the licensee; (3) the person entering under a contract with the occupier; (4) the person entering as of right; (5) trespassers and others.

The invitee was a person who was both permitted to enter and whose entry was in the interests of the occupier, for example, a customer entering a shop. The licensee was one merely permitted to be on the land, for example, a person permitted to take a short-cut over the occupier's land. The importance of the distinction was that more onerous obligations were owed to the invitee than to the licensee, to whom the occupier's only obligation was to warn of concealed dangers of which the occupier was aware. Criticism of the distinction between invitee and licensee, and of the injustices it led to, in particular by the Law Reform Committee in 1954, was the chief reason for the passing of the Occupiers' Liability Act in 1957.

The person entering under contract with the occupier might

himself be in contractual relationship with the occupier, or might be permitted to enter under the terms of the occupier's contract with another. In the former case the occupier's duties depended on the terms of the contract, and in the absence of an express term, the courts would imply a term that the premises were to be reasonably safe for the purposes for which entry was made. The latter type of entrant was treated as a licensee of the occupier.

Various persons have a right to enter premises, without obtaining the permission of the occupier. For example, factory inspectors, Gas and Electricity Board officials, and policemen acting under a search warrant or in the course of effecting an arrest have such a right, whether under statute or at common law. Private individuals may also in some situations enter land without committing trespass, for example, in order to recapt a chattel on that land, or to abate a nuisance. A private individual may also enter land in the exercise of a public or private right of way. The duty owed to the person entering as of right was probably the same as that owed to the invitee, although in the case of an entrant under a public or private right of way, the only duty appeared to be not to commit acts of misfeasance rendering the right of way dangerous.

The fifth type of entrant is the person who enters without permission of the occupier and not in exercise of a right conferred by law. The trespasser is by far the most important case, but there are others. For example, a person thrown on to the land by another person is not a trespasser but comes within this category. Also section 1 (4) of the Occupiers' Liability Act 1957 has added the case of the person who enters under an access agreement or order under the National Parks and Access to the Countryside Act 1949. The Act of 1957 has not affected the occupier's duty to trespassers and other entrants of this type. Their rights will be considered later in this chapter.

Occupiers' Liability Act 1957; the Common Duty of Care

The distinction between invitees and licensees has now been abolished by the Occupiers' Liability Act 1957. The occupier now owes the same duty, the "common duty of care," to all his lawful visitors, defined by the Act as comprising those persons who would at common law be treated as his licensees or invitees (this result is achieved by sections 1 (1), 1 (2) and 2 (1) in combination). The common duty of care is defined by section 2 (2) as a duty to take such care as in all the circumstances of the case is reasonable to see that the visitor will be reasonably safe in using the premises for the purposes for which he is invited or permitted by the occupier to be there. The Act has therefore created a tort of statutory negligence to replace the special rules which an occupier owed to his invitees and licensees at common law. It seems to be the effect of section 2 (6) of the Act that all persons entering as of right are to be treated as if they are licensees and are therefore owed the common duty of care. *Greenhalgh* v. *British Railways Board* (1969), however, shows this view to be fallacious. Section 2 (6), treats the entrant as of right as a licensee only "for the purposes of this section," and section 2 is concerned with the definition of the content of the common duty of care, rather than the persons to whom it is owed. It does not therefore extend the class of entrants as of right who are to be treated as licensees to those entrants who would not be treated as licensees at common law. In the case of the entrant under a public right of way, for example, the occupier merely had a duty not to commit acts of misfeasance rendering the right of way dangerous (a less onerous duty than that owed to licensees), and it was held in *Greenhalgh* that this rule had survived the Act. The same reasoning would apply in the case of an entrant under a private right of way.

Section 1 (3)(*b*) appears to be intended to preserve the common law position relating to liability for damage to property. In so far as such damage could be claimed at common law, it is now possible to claim it in an action for breach of the common duty of care. The Act expressly envisages that the property damaged need not be that of a visitor. No doubt such property must lawfully be on the premises. The common law rule whereby the occupier was not liable for loss of property, for example by theft, on the premises, remains unaffected by the Act (*Tinsley* v. *Dudley* (1951). *Cf.* the comparable rule in the case of the employer in *Deyong* v. *Sherburn* (1946)). There may be liability where the property is bailed to the occupier or the occupier is an innkeeper. The basis of the rule in *Tinsley* v. *Dudley* is not clear. It may be that the occupier is never liable for loss of property or it may be that, although there is generally no duty to safeguard property on the premises, special circumstances may place the occupier under such a duty (for example, frequent thefts on the premises or a structural defect in the premises likely to cause loss of property).

Activity duty

The pre-1957 law distinguished between the occupier's duty in respect of the static condition of his premises (occupancy duty) and his duty in respect of his activities carried out on those premises (activity duty). In particular, the distinction between invitee and licensee was not relevant in the case of the latter, the occupier's liability being governed by principles of ordinary negligence (*Slater* v. *Clay, Cross & Co.* (1956)). With the removal of the distinction between invitees and licensees by the Act of 1957, it is now hardly necessary to distinguish the two duties. The Act, however, unfortunately fails to make the fate of the activity duty clear. It may continue to exist at common law, unaffected by the Act's provisions; or it may have become statutory. The answer depends upon the interpretation given to section 1 (1) and 1 (2) of the Act. Subsection (1) states that the rules made by the two following subsections shall have effect in place of the common law duties of the occupier regarding the state of his premises *or things done or omitted to be done on them*, but section 1 (2) states that the rules so enacted shall regulate the nature of the duty imposed by law in consequence of a person's occupation or control of premises. Since the activity duty is hardly imposed in consequence of a person's occupation or control of premises, the bizarre result of the Act might be that it has abolished the activity duty without replacing it. For this reason, it seems better to confine the ambit of section 1 (1) to "things done" on the premises which affect their static condition, thus allowing the activity duty to survive outside the Act.

Conditions for the application of the Act; "occupier"; "premises"

The defendant must under section 1 (2) be in occupation or control of the premises in order that the statutory obligation be demanded of him. As it is clear that no legal or equitable interest in the premises is necessary to satisfy the requirements of the statute, the circumstances of each case will have to be considered to decide whether such occupation or control exists.

In *Wheat* v. *Lacon & Co.* (1966) the plaintiff, a guest staying in a public house owned by the defendants, was killed in a fall from a defective staircase, the staircase being in the part of the public house which was occupied as his private living-quarters by the defendant's manager. The court decided that the brewery retained sufficient control over the premises to be in occupation within the meaning of section 1 (2), although it was held that the manager, also a defendant, was also an occupier.

The case makes it clear, therefore, that exclusive occupation of the premises, such as is necessary to maintain an action of trespass, is not required. Equally there can be more than one "occupier" of the premises at a given time. It has also been decided that a person does not necessarily lose occupation or control by having an independent contractor do work on the premises. But it may be that the contractor is also an occupier. Thus, in *Hartwell* v. *Grayson Docks Ltd.* (1947), it was held that a contractor converting a ship into a troopship in dry dock was an occupier of the ship. This is clearly not inconsistent with occupation by the shipowner.

"Premises" included at common law not only land and buildings on the land, but also other erections and structures on the land, such as electricity pylons, diving-boards and grandstands. Movables such as ladders, ships and aeroplanes were also included provided they were occupied by the defendant, and provided the plaintiff's injury resulted from some structural defect in them. If, for example, a ladder is lent by A to B, and B suffers injury because of a defect in the ladder, A's liability is governed by the principles of liability for chattels, since he no longer occupies the ladder. And negligent operation of any locomotive was governed by ordinary negligence, not occupier's liability. These rules are preserved by section 1 (3)(*a*) of the Act —the rules of the Act regulate the obligations of a person occupying or having control of any "fixed or movable structure, including any vessel, vehicle or aircraft," "in like manner and to the like extent" as the common law rules of occupiers' liability regulated the liability of persons occupying such structures.

Special Provisions about the Common Duty of Care

It is clear that most cases on occupiers' liability will turn on questions of negligence indistinguishable from negligence at common law. There are, however, certain provisions in the Occupiers' Liability Act about the nature of the common duty of care, its discharge, and the defences available to an action for breach of it, which need to be specially considered. Section 2 (3) provides that the circumstances relevant for the purpose of deciding whether the occupier has committed a breach of his duty of care, include the degree of care, and of want of care, which would ordinarily be looked for in a visitor, so that in proper cases (a) an occupier must be prepared for children to be less careful than adults; and (b) an occupier may expect that a person, in the exercise of his calling, will appreciate and guard against any special risks ordinarily incidental to it, so far as the occupier leaves him to free to do so.

Duty towards children

The first problem concerns the occupier's liability towards children who are lawfully present on his land. He must not have on his land objects that are dangerous but are also an allurement or invitation to them. Thus, in *Glasgow Corporation* v. *Taylor* (1922), the plaintiff, a child aged seven, died through eating some poisonous berries which he picked from a tree in the defendants' public gardens. The defendants were held liable despite the commission by the plaintiff of an otherwise trespassory act in picking the berries. The allurement therefore appears both to have nullified the trespass and established liability on the defendant's part. The concept of an allurement involves the idea of "concealment and surprise, of an appearance of safety under circumstances cloaking a reality of damage" (*per* Hamilton L.J. in *Latham* v. *Johnson and Nephew Ltd.* (1913)). Thus in that case a child who was injured while playing with a heap of stones on the defendants' land was held to have no remedy against the defendants. Equally, in *Perry* v. *Wrigley Ltd.* (1955), a hole in the ground into which a child fell was held to be no allurement to a child who was injured by falling into the hole. It is perhaps questionable whether this emphasis on the concealment of the danger is desirable. The obviousness of the danger may increase its attractions to a child. This seems to be recognised by *Gough* v. *National Coal Board* in which slow-moving railway trucks were held to be an allurement and also in *Holdman* v. *Hamlyn* (1943) in which the same was held of a threshing machine.

The question whether there is an allurement on the land is also relevant to the question whether the child is a trespasser or licensee on the land. This is discussed below at page 153.

Very young children

To the very young child, almost anything can be dangerous. Furthermore, the obviousness of the danger will not prevent the child from encountering it. It might be expected therefore that the law would differentiate between the occupier's duty to the young and to the very young child. This was confirmed in *Phipps* v. *Rochester Corpn.* (1955)—

The plaintiff, aged five, and his sister, aged seven, were licensees on the defendants' land. There was a trench on the land, nine feet deep by two-and-a-half feet wide. The plaintiff fell into this and broke his leg. The defendants were held not liable because they could not anticipate that a child of this age would not be accompanied by a responsible person and so had not broken their duty of care.

There is a lack of precision about the nature of the occupier's duty towards very young children. In particular these questions may be asked:

(1) At what age does the very young child become a young child?

(2) Is the age of the child alone relevant in determining whether the occupier can expect him to be accompanied by a responsible person? The answer seems to be probably not, since the judgment of Devlin J. in the above case takes into account the fact that the land in question was not a playground in a slum area, where the presence of unaccompanied very young children could be foreseen.

(3) In what circumstances does the occupier break his duty to very young children? Clearly the occupier is liable to the very young

child injured when the accompanying person himself would not, without negligence, have foreseen the danger. It also seems incorrect to assume that where there is negligence by the occupier, he is entitled to rely on the responsible person protecting the very young child from the danger, and is not liable if by negligence of that person, the child suffers injury. It has been pointed out in an earlier chapter that a later act of negligence does not necessarily break the chain of causation between the earlier negligence and the plaintiff's damage. But in *O'Connor* v. *British Transport Commission*, the plaintiff, a child of three, opened a train door while the train was moving, and was killed through falling out of the train. The child was accompanied by its mother but she was not with the child at the relevant time. It was argued on the plaintiff's behalf that the defendants should not have allowed the door to be unlocked in such a way that it could be opened by a small child, but the court held that it was the primary responsibility of the child's mother to prevent accidents of this kind. It is arguable that the correct solution should have been an apportionment of liability as between the defendants and the mother. The distinction between this situation and that in the *Phipps* case is that in O'Connor the danger was one which was not obvious to an accompanying adult. In these circumstances the occupier ought not to be totally exonerated simply because the accident would not have occurred had the adult shown proper care.

(4) Who is a responsible person for the purposes of the rule? *Coates* v. *Rawtenstall B.C.* (1937) regarded a child of fourteen as sufficiently responsible, and this seems reasonable.

Risks incidental to calling

Section 2 (3) (*b*) was judicially considered in *Roles* v. *Nathan* (1963)—

The plaintiffs, two chimney-sweeps, were employed by the defendants to block up holes in the flues of a heating-system which employed coke. They attempted to block up one of the holes while the coke-fire was lit, despite a warning against this by their employer's agent. Both were killed by the escape of carbon monoxide gas. One of the grounds for the Court of Appeal's decision in favour of the defendants was that this was a risk incidental to their calling which they appreciated and should have guarded against.

***Volenti non fit injuria*; contributory negligence; warning**

The defence of *volenti non fit injuria* is expressly provided for by section 2 (5) of the Act. Where the visitor has entered the premises with knowledge of the danger it seems clear that this in itself does not make him *volens* in respect of it. But in such a case the occupier may rely on a special defence provided by section 2 (4) of the Act. Under this section, a warning of the danger given by the occupier to the visitor, although not automatically absolving the occupier for liability, has this effect if in all the circumstances it is enough to enable the visitor to be reasonably safe. The subsection appears to have reversed the common law rule in *London Graving Dock* v. *Horton* (1951) in which it was held that a warning given by an occupier of a particular danger discharged his duty towards the person to whom the warning is given, even though the warning was not enough to ensure that that person was reasonably safe. The subsection was applied in *Roles* v. *Nathan* (*supra*, p. 148) in which an additional ground for the decision was that the warning given to the plaintiffs by the occupiers' agent was enough to have enabled them to have been safe.

It seems that the effect of knowledge of the danger by the visitor can have one of three effects:

1. It may give rise to the defence of *volenti non fit injuria*, if the court finds a willingness by the visitor to run the risk of the occupier's negligence.

2. Where the knowledge is the result of the occupier's warning, section 2 (4) contemplates that this in itself may be a sufficient discharge of the occupier's duty of care.

3. The Act leaves open the question what is the position when the visitor has knowledge of the danger gained otherwise than through the warning of the occupier. If such knowledge is enough to make the visitor reasonably safe, he should, it seems, be treated no more favourably than one who is in a similar position as the result of the occupier's warning and should therefore recover no damages from the occuper if he receives injury. (This reasoning receives support from O'Connor J. speaking *obiter* in *Bunker* v. *Charles Brand* (1969).) The legal formulation of this result will, however, differ. There is no doubt that the occupier, unless he is relying on the visitor's knowledge of the danger, is in breach of his duty of care to him. The visitor's knowledge of the danger may therefore go to establish either that he willingly accepted the risk so that a defence arises under section 2 (5) of the Act, or that he was contributorily negligent thus justifying a reduction of damages under section 2 (3) of the Act. In order to achieve the result mentioned above the contributory negligence should be assessed at 100 per cent. If the visitor's knowledge is not sufficient to make him reasonably safe, it may still go towards establishing that he willingly ran the risk, or that he was contributorily negligent (though here the occupier's breach would also be causative and the result would be an apportionment of damage under the 1945 Act—this was the actual decision in

Bunker v. *Charles Brand*).

Exclusion of liability by the occupier

Section 2 (1) of the Occupers' Liability Act provides that the occupier owes the common duty of care to all his visitors, "except in so far as he is free to and does extend, restrict, modify or exclude his duty . . . by agreement or otherwise."

Clearly no objection can be made to the occupier contracting out of the common duty of care by agreement with the visitor. But the words "or otherwise" contemplate other methods of exclusion, in particular, the display of a notice of exclusion on the premises. The occupier is allowed to exclude his liability only "in so far as he is free to." If, as seems likely, the words mean, free to exclude at common law, the section appears to adopt the common law position as laid down in *Ashdown* v. *Williams and Sons* (1957). In that case the plaintiff, a licensee on the defendants' land, was injured by the negligent shunting of a railway truck driven by a servant of the defendants, the occupiers. The Court of Appeal held the defendants not liable because the notice displayed on their land to the effect that persons entering the land did so at their own risk, had been sufficiently brought to the plaintiff's attention and she was bound by its terms.

The juridical basis of the occupier's power to exclude his liability under the Act is a difficult question. In *White* v. *Blackmore* (1973), in which a majority of the Court of Appeal held that the defendant occupiers had effectively excluded their liability towards the plaintiff by displaying an exclusionary notice at the entrance to their premises, it was treated by the court as turning on whether the exclusionary term formed part of the plaintiff's licence to enter the premises. The "licence" theory has its problems. How can the occupier exclude liability towards the trespasser who enters without licence? Exclusion would also seem to be ineffective in the case of the entrant as of right who also needs no licence to enter. An alternative theory is that the defence of *volenti non fit injuria* may be available against one who enters knowing of the occupier's exclusion of liability (*cf. supra*, p. 135). This also has difficulties. It may be difficult, particularly in the case of a trespasser, to establish knowledge of the exclusionary notice, and it seems wrong to regard constructive notice as sufficient in the case of *volenti*. *Volenti* would also not be available where the entrant is under a duty to enter (*cf. Burnett* v. *British Waterways Board*, *supra*, p. 135). It would thus not be available against many entrants as of right (for example, factory inspectors).

Apart from these special cases, however, there is nothing to prevent the occupier excluding his liability towards his visitors. This seems unfortunate. In *White* v. *Blackmore*, Lord Denning dissented on the ground that it was impossible at common law for the occupier to exclude his liability towards an invitee (as the plaintiff was in that case. The plaintiff in *Ashdown* v. *Samuel Williams* was a licensee). The other members of the court refused to accept this distinction and it is open to the objection that it would revive the distinction between invitee and licensee, the removal of which was one of the reasons for the 1957 Act. It is probable that only legislative intervention can tackle the problem of widespread exclusion of liability by occupiers.

Liability for independent contractor

Section 2 (4) (*b*) has settled a question which caused uncertainty at common law, by allowing, subject to certain conditions, the occupier to discharge his duty of care by delegating its performance to an independent contractor. The section provides that the occupier is not to be treated without more as answerable for the danger if in all the circumstances he has acted reasonably in entrusting the work to an independent contractor and has taken such steps (if any) as he reasonably ought in order to satisfy himself that the contractor was competent and that the work had been properly done.

The subsection has confirmed the decision in *Haseldine* v. *Daw and Sons Ltd.* (1941) in which the defendant occupier was held not liable to the plaintiff his licensee who had been injured through the fall of a lift negligently repaired by a third party, the occupier's independent contractor. It appears not to have affected *Woodward* v. *Mayor of Hastings* (1945) which held that the clearing of snow from a school steps was not a task which involved technical knowledge and was therefore not reasonably delegated to an independent contractor.

Liability to contractual visitor

Section 5 (1) regulates the occupier's duty to one who enters under contract with him. Section 3 (1) regulates the liability of the occupier to those whom he is bound by contract to permit to enter, but who are not under contract with him.

Liability to contracting party

Clearly if there is an express term in the contract regulating the occupier's liability to the other party, this will be conclusive. In the absence of such a term, section 5 (1) implies a term that the occupier's duty is to be the common duty of care. Liability whether under an express or implied term is contractual rather than tortious, and can therefore be excluded only by subsequent variation of the contract with the agreement of the other contracting party—unilateral notice of exclusion of liability given by one contracting party to the other is not sufficient.

Liability to persons permitted to enter under contract with occupier

Since persons entering under the terms of a contract with the occupier formerly came within the class of licensees, they are now his visitors within the meaning of the Act of 1957, and are therefore owed the statutory common duty of care by the occupier. But section 3 (1) reinforces this by providing that the occupier cannot restrict the duty of care he owes to such visitors by a provision in the contract, and also that if in the contract he has undertaken obligations going beyond the common duty of care, the duty of care he owes to them "shall include the duty to perform his obligations under the contract." Section 3 (4) makes it clear that a lease is within the provisions of section 3 (1). This means that a landlord, who will normally retain occupation and control of common staircases, passage-ways and lifts in such demised premises as a block of flats, owes the visitor of his tenant the common duty of care and cannot contract out of his by provision in the lease. This is a twofold improvement on the former law, since the duty he formerly owed was that towards licensees, and he could expressly exclude this by provision in the lease.

A further question remains, whether the landlord can exclude his liability to persons entering the premises under contract by exhibiting a notice to this effect on the premises. Clearly the policy arguments which found the exclusion of the visitor's rights by provision in the contract undesirable, on the ground that the visitor would lose his rights without his knowledge, do not apply to an exclusionary notice. Further there seems no reason why the entrant under contract should be in a better position than other visitors. Both Street and Winfield, however, take the view that exclusion by notice is impossible (Street, p. 190; Winfield, p. 186). Street's arguments are: (1) The words "shall include" in section 3 (1) are mandatory, and cannot be evaded by the occupier by any means. But these words appear to make mandatory the inclusion of further contractual obligations going beyond the common duty of care. They do not appear to rule out exclusion of liability under the duty as eventually constituted. (2) A notice given subsequent to the execution of a contract is not sufficient to vary its terms. But this may be answered on the ground that the duty of care owed under section 3 (1) does not rest upon contract, although it may include contractual obligations, and may therefore be excluded by notice. On the whole it seems that the view of Payne (21 M.L.R. 369) that the occupier may by exhibiting a notice exclude the duty under section 3 (1) is probably correct.

Occupier's Liability towards the Trespasser

Liability towards the trespasser is still governed by the rules of common law unaffected by the Occupiers' Liability Act 1957. In the first place, it is necessary to consider what is meant by trespasser. It may be noted that one permitted to enter may exceed the terms of that permission by trespassing on another part of the premises (for example, *Lee* v. *Luper* (1936)—licensee in hotel trespassed by going through door marked "private"). It is vital to distinguish the trespasser from the implied licensee, since express permission of the occupier is not the only way to establish a licence to enter. Two cases on children illustrate the fine lines that are drawn in this area of the law.

In *Cooke* v. *M.G.W. Ry. of Ireland* (1909), the plaintiff was a child of four who was injured while playing with his companions on a turntable on the defendants' railway premises. The turntable was kept unlocked and was close to a public road. The defendants' servants knew that children were in the habit of entering the premises from the road for the purposes of playing on the turntable, but they took no precautions to exclude the children or lock the turntable. It was held that the plaintiff was a licensee, and that the defendants were liable for his injuries. The case may be compared with *Edwards* v. *Railway Executive* (1952). The plaintiff was a boy aged nine who made his way through a fence between the public recreation ground and a railway embankment to fetch a ball on the other side of the railway line. He was injured by a passing train. For several years children had broken through the fence and used the slope of the embankment for purposes of tobogganing. The defendants had always repaired the fence when as a result of the children's activity it was found to be in need of repair, and there was no evidence that it was in disrepair at the date of the accident. It was held that as the plaintiff was a trespasser the defendants owed him no duty of care.

The latter case can be distinguished from the former in two respects: (1) In *Edwards'* case, even if the allurement of the embankment had imported a licence to go on the embankment, it would not extend to crossing the railway line. In the *Cooke* case, the allurement actually caused the accident. (2) The defendants in the latter case had not passively acquiesced in the acts of trespass as had the defendants in the *Cooke* case. They had repaired the fence although it appeared to be inadequate to keep out children. These differences are clearly not very considerable. The occupier is under no obligation to make his land child-proof even when there is an intrinsically dangerous operation on the land such as the running of trains.

It seems likely that courts will be less willing to find that a person is an implied licensee in view of the decision in *Herrington* v. *British Railways Board* (1972) which considerably extended the occupier's duty towards trespassers.

Liability towards the trespasser

The law on this matter has recently undergone a transformation. Until 1972 the occupier was liable to the trespasser only for intentionally injuring him or for acting in reckless disregard of his presence on the land. This state of the law, imposed by the House of Lords in *Addie & Sons* v. *Dumbreck* (1929) was unchangeable by judicial decision until the House of Lords in 1966 announced its capacity to review its own decisions. In *Herrington* v. *British Railways Board* (1972) the action was brought by a child trespasser who had been electrocuted and severely injured by a live rail on land occupied by the defendants. There was evidence that the fence guarding the line on the side from which the plaintiff had entered was in a state of disrepair and had been trampled down, and that a short cut led over the line to a park on the other side. The House of Lords, in affirming the decision of the Court of Appeal that the defendants were liable, did so on the ground that the rule that an occupier is liable to a trespasser only for intentionally or recklessly injuring him is an inadequate one in the light of present social conditions. As a substitute the House of Lords used a test of humanity. Had the defendant done all that a humane person would have done for the safety of the trespasser. In view of the high degree of danger, the likelihood of trespass and the ease with which, granted their financial resources, the defendants could have maintained the fence in repair, the defendants had not shown due humanity in this case. How does the duty of humanity differ from the duty of care? In the first place it will allow the courts to do that which Viscount Radcliffe said was impossible in *Commissioner for Railways* v. *Quinlan* (1964). He said that the law relating to liability to trespassers had to be a comprehensive formulation. Distinctions could not be drawn between different types of occupier and different types of trespaser. This "all or nothing" approach has now been abandoned by the House of Lords. For example, the financial resources of the occupier will be particularly relevant in deciding whether he has acted humanely, a fact which weighed against the defendants in the case itself. So also will the type of "fault" alleged to have been committed.

In particular an occupier could hardly plead a lack of financial resources where he is alleged to have carried out carelessly activities on his land. His financial resources are, however, clearly relevant to the question what should be required of him in remedying a static condition of his premises. Distinctions will also be drawn according to the character of the entrant. More humanity must be accorded to the child trespasser, less, if any, towards the burglar. Finally the degree of likelihood of the trespasser's presence on the land appears not to be governed by ordinary principles of foreseeability. In *Herrington* the House of Lords spoke of substantial probability of the trespasser's presence as the requirement, but in *Southern Portland Cement* v. *Cooper* (1974) the Privy Council (applying law that was "substantially in line" with *Herrington*) found an occupier liable to a trespasser of whose presence on the land there was no substantial probability. Whether or not this is correct, it seems probable that something more than mere foreseeability of presence is required in the case of the trespasser.

The workings of the law laid down in *Herrington* can be seen in *Pannett* v. *P. McGuiness & Co.* (1972). Demolition contractors were occupiers of a site in a busy urban area where large numbers of children were to be expected. At the completion of demolition it became necessary to burn a quantity of rubbish on the site. The defendants realised that this activity would be an attraction to children and so employed three workmen to keep children away. The latter had chased children, including the plaintiff, a child of five, away on several occasions. One afternoon the three men absented themselves from the site at a time when a fire was burning and during this period the plaintiff entered the site and was burned. The Court of Appeal, in holding the defendants liable stressed the hazardous nature of the activity and its attraction to children together with the substantial likelihood of trespass. In these circumstances the occupier's duty went beyond merely chasing the children away and the defendants were therefore vicariously liable for the default of their men in absenting themselves from the site.

Liability of Non-occupier in Respect of Premises

Vendor: lessor of premises

At common law the vendor or lessor of premises was not liable for damage caused by the defective state of the premises. This was true even where the vendor or lessor was also the builder of the premises (*Otto* v. *Bolton and Norris* (1936)) although in *Dutton* v. *Bognor Regis U.D.C.* (1972) the opinion was expressed in the judgments of the Court of Appeal that the vendor/builder was liable at common law. It was also true where the dangerous condition of the premises arose from a negligent act committed prior to the disposal of the premises (held in the case of the lessor by *Travers* v. *Gloucester Corporation* (1947)). The difficulty felt by the courts of separating the obligations of private vendors of houses from those of builder/vendors and builder/lessors has now been dealt with by two provisions of the Defective Premises Act 1972. Section 1 imposes a duty on builders to build in a workmanlike and professional manner. The duty is not limited to builders but extends to other persons such as architects who take on work in connection with the building. The duty is owed only to the person ordering the work and persons later acquiring an interest in the dwelling (the limitation period begins to run on completion of the building). It is therefore contractual rather than tortious in character and is the less important because section 2 of the Act exempts from the operation of section 1 approved schemes of purchaser protection such as the National House Building Council scheme. Section 3 (1) is more important. It provides that where work of construction, repair, maintenance demolition or any other work is done on or in relation to premises, any duty of care owed, because of the doing of the work, to persons who might reasonably be expected to be affected by the defects in the state of the premises created by the doing of the work shall not be abated by the subsequent disposal of the premises by the person who owed the duty. Since disposal includes letting, the immunity of both the vendor/builder and the lessee/builder from liability in tort for defects in the state of the premises is thus removed.

In the case of the lessor of premises, the combined effect of section 4 (1), (2) and (4) of the Defective Premises Act is to make the lessor liable in respect of defects in the state of the premises to "persons who might reasonably be expected to be affected by" such defects, for personal injury or damage to their property, provided the lessor has an obligation under the tenancy agreement to keep the premises in repair, or has under the tenancy agreement an express or implied right to enter and do repairs, and provided the lessor knows or ought to know of the defect needing repair. Section 4 (1) of the Occupiers' Liability Act, 1957, is expressly repealed. The new obligation goes further than section 4 (1) of the 1957 Act in that it may be owed to trespassers, it covers cases where a lessor has a mere right to enter and do repairs, and notice of the need for repair by the lessee to the lessor is unnecessary. Under section 4 (5) of the Defective Premises Act 1972, statutory obligations to repair premises imposed upon lessors (for example, that arising under section 32 of the Housing Act 1961) are to be treated as being imposed by the tenancy agreement. Where the lessor has a mere right to enter and do repairs, and the obligation to repair is imposed on the lessee by the tenancy agreement, the lessor will not be liable to the lessee if the latter is injured because of defects in the premises due to want of repair.

Certain gaps still remain. If the premises which have been let have fallen into a state of disrepair prior to the let, the lessor is not liable for damage caused by defects in the premises unless he has an obligation to repair under the tenancy agreement, or has a statutory obligation to repair, or has a right to enter and do repairs. A lessor who actually enters and does repairs after the commencement of the lease is liable for damage caused by defective repair. His liability is based on ordinary principles of negligence from which in this instance there is no reason to exempt him (*cf. A. C. Billings & Sons* v. *Riden* (1958) in which the House of Lords recognised that persons who do work on premises are liable for negligence to those foreseeably present on the premises). It is not yet clear whether the reasoning in *Billings* v. *Riden* extends to the negligent installation of a defective chattel not dangerous in itself, thus overruling the Court of Appeal decision in *Ball* v. *L.C.C.* (1949) which held that the lessor was liable only if he knew of the defect in the chattel.

One special common law rule is unaffected by the Act. If through the dangerous state of the lessor's premises, persons present on the lessee's premises suffer injury or damage to property, the lessor is liable if through his negligence he has allowed the dangerous condition to arise. Thus in *Cunard* v. *Antifyre* (1933) some defective roofing and guttering forming part of the premises retained by the defendant lessor fell on to premises let by him to the plaintiff and his wife. The wife received personal injuries and recovered damages from the defendant in negligence (followed in *Taylor* v. *Liverpool Corporation* (1939)). *Cheater* v. *Cater* (1918) in which the defendant lessor was held not liable when the plaintiff lessee's mare died from eating the poisonous leaves of the defendant's yew trees, which overhung the plaintiff's premises, seems out of line.

Liability of the non-occupier towards the trespasser

Several cases had established that a non-occupier did not have the same exemption from liability in negligence towards the trespasser as did the occupier. In *Buckland* v. *Guildford Gas, Light and Coke Co.* (1949, a non-occupier was held liable in circumstances where there was no reckless disregard of the trespassers presence on the defendant's part. How the courts view the liability of a non-occupier towards the trespasser after *British Railways Board* v. *Herrington* remains to be seen.

Chapter 12

LIABILITY FOR CHATTELS

THE whole subject of liability for chattels needs to be considered in the light of the judgments of the majority in *Donoghue* v. *Stevenson* (*supra*, p. 66). The narrow ratio of that case is concerned with the question of the liability of the manufacturer of the chattel. The wide ratio, applicable to persons other than the manufacturer, may be used in the case of anyone who has been negligent in connection with a chattel. But it is too early to state that the topic of liability for defective chattels, whether that of the manufacturer or of some other person, is simply an application of the general principles of negligence to a specific field. Some anomalous exceptions to these general principles may still exist.

Liability of Persons other than the Manufacturer

In considering liability for negligence in relation to chattels, it may be noted that this phrase may cover a number of factual situations. The negligence may be that of the person who has manufactured or produced the goods, or of one who for reward has done repair work on the goods, or of a person who has merely transmitted the chattel to another person, for example, the seller, bailor, donor or lender of the chattel. It seems that the standard of care to be expected of a defendant will vary according to what he has done in relation to the chattel. The manufacturer and the repairer are expected to ensure that the chattel when it leaves their possession is reasonably safe (they both are covered by the narrow rule in *Donoghue* v. *Stevenson*). The seller and other transmitters are subject to no such onerous duties. In general, they appear to have no duty to inspect the goods they are selling (although a dealer in second-hand cars is expected to inspect them to ensure their safety before sale—*Andrews* v. *Hopkinson* (1957)). Their liability would therefore appear to be limited to failure to notice patent defects in the chattel, and allowing a defect in the chattel to arise by negligently failing to look after it, In the case of the person who transfers a chattel to another purely for that other's benefit, for example, by way of gift or gratuitous loan, there is nineteenth-century authority (for instance, *Gautret* v. *Egerton* (1867)) that the transferor was not liable for a defect in the chattel unless he actually knew of the defect and had failed to warn the transferee of it. But it seems doubtful whether the principle of this case has survived *Donoghue* v. *Stevenson.* It seems that the gratuitous transferor should be judged by the same standard as other transmitters of a chattel. He should therefore be liable if he has failed to notice obvious defects in the chattel, or where by neglect he has allowed the chattel to become defective.

Dangerous Chattels

The law in relation to liability for negligence in respect of chattels has been confused by the distinction drawn between the dangerous and the non-dangerous chattel. The distinction has received judicial criticism (for example, by Scrutton L.J. who did not "understand the difference between a thing dangerous in itself, as poison, and a thing not dangerous as a class, but by negligent construction dangerous as a particular thing. The latter if anything, seems the more dangerous of the two; it is a wolf in sheep's clothing rather than an obvious wolf" (*Hodge and Sons* v. *Anglo-American Oil Co.* (1922)).

The effect of the distinction in cases where it applies is that liability in the case of the dangerous chattel is based on ordinary negligence, whereas, in the case of the non-dangerous chattel, it is based upon knowledge by the defendant of a defect in the chattel. Although in several cases since *Donoghue* v. *Stevenson* (1932) the defendant has escaped liability on the ground that the chattel was non-dangerous and there was no question of the narrow rule in that case applying (for example, *Ball* v. *London County Council* (1949)—defendant landlords not liable for negligent installation of defective boiler which exploded and injured plaintiff on ground that boiler was not dangerous chattel and landlords did not know of defects in it), in others it has been ignored (for example, in the cases on liability of parents for son's use of a gun—*Donaldson* v. *McNiven* (1952); *Newton* v. *Edgerley* (1959)). The present-day position is therefore one of uncertainty whether the distinction survives, and if so in what cases it applies. In view of the arbitrary nature of the distinction and its unjust consequences, it seems time that the defendant's standard of care was assessed according to the capacity for doing harm of the particular chattel in the particular situation, and not of the class of chattel in the abstract.

Liability of the Manufacturer of a Chattel

Lord Atkin expressed the narrow ratio of *Donoghue* v. *Stevenson* as follows: "A manufacturer of products, which he sells in such a form that he intends them to reach the ultimate consumer in the form in which they left him with no reasonable possibility of intermediate examination and with the knowledge that the absence of reasonable care in the preparation or putting up of the products will result in injury to the consumer's life or property, owes a duty to the consumer to take that reasonable care."

The liability of the manufacturer is best treated by considering this formulation in sections.

"Manufacturer"

The rule has been extended to persons other than the manufacturer who do work on chattels, e.g. repairers (*Stennett* v. *Hancock* (1939)). It seems that it will not apply to the mere retailer of goods although an exception was recognised in the case of the dealer in second-hand cars who was held in *Andrews* v. *Hopkinson* (*supra*, p. 159) to have a duty to inspect such cars before selling them. This decision is justifiable both because of the public interest in keeping defective vehicles off the road, and because there will normally be no question of manufacturer's liability in relation to such vehicles. It has been suggested above that the retailer of goods is liable for defects which should be obvious to himself, and for allowing the goods to become defective while in his care. It may be thought that the law should go further than this and make the retailer take some steps to ensure that the goods are safe, at least by buying them from what he considers to be a reputable source. Such a duty has been imposed on the distributor of goods. Thus, in *Watson* v. *Buckley, Osborn, Garret & Co.* (1940), the defendants supplied a hair dye which was used on the plaintiff's hair by a hairdresser. The dye contained excessive acid and the plaintiff caught dermatitis as a result. The defendants were held liable because though they had advertised the dye for its safety, they had bought from a manufacturer who was unknown to them, and had failed to carry out a simple test which would have ascertained the quantity of acid in the dye. The case probably turns on its own special facts, but it seems that a general duty on distributors to take reasonable steps to ensure the safety of the goods would be an acceptable extension of it.

"Products which he sells in such a form, etc."

The words "in such a form" do not mean that the goods must reach the consumer in the same container in which they left the manufacturer. They mean that the manufacturer contemplates nothing of substance being done to the goods after they leave him.

"Possibility of intermediate examination"

It is now clear that the mere possibility of intermediate examination of the goods after they have left the manufacturer is not enough; it must also be a reasonable expectation of the manufacturer. Thus, in *Grant* v. *Australian Knitting Mills Ltd.* (1936) (*infra*, p. 138) the defendants argued that the underpants should have been washed before use. Lord Wright dismissed this by saying: "It was not contemplated that they should first be washed." Where the manufacturer reasonably contemplates intermediate examination, it seems that he is totally absolved if such examination does not take place, even though through negligent manufacture of defect exists in the goods as in *Kubach* v. *Hollands* (1937) in which the defendants had been supplied with a mislabelled and, in the circumstances, highly dangerous chemical which had been accompanied by an invoice stating that the chemical must be tested before use; (*quaere*, the effect of a negligent examination which fails to reveal the defect). In these cases it appears that in accordance with principles already discussed on page 118, there should be an apportionment here between the manufacturer and the person responsible for the later negligence.

A different problem arises where the examination has been successful in revealing the defect in the goods. Here it seems that, on causal principles, the manufacturer ought to be excused since to use the goods (or to pass them on) after discovering the defect seems a clear *novus actus*. So in *Taylor* v. *Rover Car Co.* (1966), where the plaintiff's foreman discovered a defect in a hammer manufactured by the defendants but continued to allow it to be used, the plaintiff's employers were liable to him but the defendants were not. (To similar effect is *Farr* v. *Butters Bros. & Co.* (1932) in which the plaintiff himself discovered defects in the parts of a crane manufactured by the defendants, but nevertheless attempted to assemble it and was killed as a result.) But knowledge of the defect by the plaintiff does not help the manufacturer where there is no safe way of dealing with the chattel, but it is necessary to do so (as in *Denny* v. *Supplies & Transport Co.* (1950)—plaintiff had to unload badly stowed timber as part of his employment. Although he realised the danger he recovered in full for the injuries he suffered from the defendants who had stowed the timber, because no safe way of unloading the timber existed).

"Ultimate consumer"

These words received an extremely liberal interpretation by the court in *Stennet* v. *Hancock and Peters* (1939) in which it was held that a pedestrian could recover damages from the defendants who were repairers of a lorry. Due to the defendants' negligence in the course of repair the flange of the lorry came apart from the lorry while it was being driven, and struck and injured the plaintiff. In view of this decision, it may be that anyone foreseeably injured because of the defect in the chattel is a consumer within the meaning of the rule.

Proof of manufacturer's negligence

Proof of negligence by the manufacturer or someone employed by him would clearly be difficult if the plaintiff had to show negligence by a particular person. But *Grant* v. *Australian Knitting Mills* (1936) shows that the law does not require this. In that case the plaintiff had caught dermatitis from underpants which he had bought and which were manufactured by the defendants. The cause of the dermatitis was the presence of excess sulphites in the underpants. The court found that the defect itself raised an inference of negligence by someone in the manufacturer's employ and the onus therefore lay upon him to show that this was not the case. The case is in fact one of *res ipsa loquitur* (*supra*, p. 139). The manufacturer can rebut the inference either by showing that the defect was caused by something other than his negligence or by showing that he took all reasonable care. Thus in *Daniels and Daniels* v. *White and Sons Ltd.* (1938) the manufacturers of lemonade which contained carbolic acid were excused on proof that their method of filling and cleaning the bottles was foolproof. But it seems that the courts should not too readily excuse manufacturers on the basis of their watertight system of precautions, since the possibility of human error and human mischief on the part of their servants (for both of which the manufacturer is vicariously responsible) must be taken into account. Where the clear likelihood is of wrongdoing by those employed by the manufacturer, the plaintiff should succeed (in *Grant* v. *Australian Knitting Mills*, the defendants showed that they had manufactured 4,737,600 pairs of underpants without complaint, but were still held liable).

CHAPTER 13

EMPLOYER'S LIABILITY TOWARDS HIS EMPLOYEES

Introduction

It is now necessary to consider the duties which the employer owes at common law towards the persons he employs. The employer's common law duties are now considerably supplemented by the vast number of statutory duties which are imposed upon employers for the protection of workmen, particularly in the industrial field. But a detailed account of these duties is beyond the scope of this book, and the general topic of breach of statutory duty is postponed to a later chapter.

The common law duties of the employer towards his workmen co-exist with the employer's vicarious liability for the torts of his workmen committed in the course of their employment against their fellow workmen so as normally to ensure the employer is liable where an employee has been injured through negligence at the place of work. At one time this was not so, because under the doctrine of common employment an employer was not vicariously liable for the negligence of one workman committed in the course of his employment and injuring his fellow. The rule of common employment was abolished in 1948, but it has left its traces in the law. Thus, it could be by-passed if the employer was shown to be in breach of a personal duty owed to the workman. So, a workman injured by the negligence of another workman could succeed against an employer for the latter's negligence in choosing that workman. The necessity of placing emphasis upon the employer's personal duties rather than on his vicarious liability no doubt explains the completeness of formulation of such duties and the tendency to regard them as a separate branch of negligence rather than as an example of a duty of care based upon Atkinian proximity. The absence of vicarious liability no doubt also accounts for the personal duties of the employer being construed as non-delegable—they could not be performed through the medium of his servants or independent contractors, no matter how reasonable such delegation might be. The concept of non-delegability has survived the abolition of the doctrine of common employment.

As far as his personal duties are concerned, the employer's duty is only to take reasonable care for the safety of his workmen. There is no question of his being subject to strict liability at common law, although he may be subject to strict duties imposed by statute.

Although the employer clearly has a general duty to take reasonable care for the safety of his workmen, it is customary both in decided cases and in works of reference to make a tripartite division of such duty. On the basis of this division the employer must provide (1) competent staff; (2) proper plant and premises; (3) a safe system of work. These individual duties must now be examined.

Competent staff

The importance of this duty has considerably lessened with the abolition of the doctrine of common employment, since it will normally be possible to rely on the vicarious rather than the personal liability of the employer where the plaintiff has been injured by the negligence of a fellow workman. The duty, however, came to the assistance of the plaintiff in *Hudson* v. *Ridge Manufacturing Co.* (1957). The plaintiff was injured in the course of horseplay committed against him by a fellow workman. The latter was known to be addicted to such behaviour and had several times been reprimanded for it. The employer was held to be in breach of his personal duty to the plaintiff to provide competent staff. It seems that in this case the employer would not have been held vicariously liable for the workman's negligence, which was not committed in the course of his employment.

Proper plant and premises

The employer's common law duty is to take reasonable care to provide proper tools, machinery, working places and premises generally, and to maintain them as such. The duty in respect of equipment has now been statutorily strengthened. *Davie* v. *New Merton Board Mills Ltd.* (1959) had held that the employer's duty to provide proper equipment is satisfied by the purchase of such equipment from a reputable source. So in that case where the plaintiff suffered injury through the use of a tool which had a defect in it because of the negligence of its manufacturer, it was held that the plaintiff's employer was not liable to him since he had purchased the tool from reputable suppliers who themselves had purchased from reputable manufacturers. The law as a consequence of this decision was hard for the workman who received injury in this way and was unable to discover the manufacturer's identity or found the manufacturer not worth suing. Accordingly the Employer's Liability (Defective Equipment) Act 1969 makes the employer liable to the workman where the latter has suffered personal injury in the course of his employment in consequence of a defect in equipment provided by the employer for the purposes of his business, provided that the fault is attributable wholly or partly to the fault of a third party whether the latter is identified or not. The Act thus imposes strict liability upon the employer but only if the workman can prove the defect was due to the fault of a third party. In view of the acceptance in principle of strict liability and the difficulty often involved in establishing fault, it is hard to see why the Act did not go further and make the employer liable for all defects in equipment which cause injury to his employers.

Safe system of work

The distinction between an unsafe system and dangers caused by "isolated and day-to-day acts of the servant of which the master is not presumed to be aware and which he cannot guard against" appears to be one of degree, and is today of vastly reduced importance now that the master is liable for casual acts of negligence committed by a servant against another servant in the course of operating an otherwise safe system of work. It is established that an unsafe system of work may exist in an operation which is to be performed once and for all and may never again arise. *General Cleaning Contractors* v. *Christmas* (1953) is an example of employer's liability for an unsafe system of work. The defendants required their workmen who were window cleaners to work on a narrow sill twenty-seven feet above the ground without instructing them to keep one section of the window open or providing any appliance to enable this to be done. They were held liable to the plaintiff who fell and was injured when the sash of a window fell on his fingers compelling him to release his hold on the other sash.

Delegability of the duty

The personal nature of the employer's duties has led to some doubt whether, if ever, they can be delegated to a third party. It is clear that delegation of the employer's personal duties to his servant is not a discharge of these duties (*Wilsons and Clyde Coal Co. Ltd.* v. *English* (1938)). Thus the employer's duty to prove a safe system of work cannot be delegated to a servant, however competent and however high his position, and the employer is liable even if the servant is not personally negligent in bringing about the unsafe system. (It must of course be shown that it would have been negligent of the employer himself to operate such a system.) It is clear therefore that the employer's duty, though expressed as only one to take reasonable care, may in certain cases involve him in liability when he is not personally at fault if he acted reasonably in delegating. This is *a fortiori* the case if delegation to an independent contractor is also not permissible since many of the duties of an employer are not only reasonably but also necessarily delegated to an outside agent. At one time it was thought that the employer was liable in every case for the fault of an independent contractor, but *Davie* v. *New Merton Board Mills Ltd.* (*supra*) shows this may not be the case. The reasons for the decision of the House of Lords in that case were two: (1) purchase of the tool from a third party was not delegation to an independent contractor; (2) the employer's duty was to provide, not to manufacture proper equipment and this duty was satisfied by purchasing the equipment from a reputable source. The latter reason opens up the possibility of vicarious performance of certain of the employer's duties through a competent contractor being permissible but it is difficult to say whether this would extend from cases of purchase of equipment (now in any case covered by the 1969 Act) to other contracts (for example the building of factory premises on the employer's land. In *Sumner* v. *William Henderson & Sons* (1964) it was held that an employer was liable for the negligence of any of a number of independent contractors employed to instal an electric cable, purchased by the employer, in his factory, but not liable if the negligence was in the manufacture of the cable).

Duty one of reasonable care

It must always be remembered that the employer's duty in respect of his workmen's safety is not an absolute duty. It is discharged by the exercise of reasonable care on the employer's part, and the question whether he has committed a breach of duty is decided in exactly the same way as it is in actions of negligence generally.

Extent of employer's duties

Some of the employer's duties are self-limiting, for example, the duty to provide proper plant and premises and the duty to provide a safe system of work. But it may be doubted how far the duty to provide proper equipment extends. If the workman takes home a defective tool and is injured in using it, can he sue the employer? There may be a limitation that the plaintiff must be acting in the course of his employment, but this is not so in the analogous tort of breach of statutory duty (*infra*, p. 215). No doubt a line must be drawn which would probably rule out liability in the above example, but it seems difficult to formulate a test other than that the injury must have some reasonable connection with the performance of the plaintiff's duties.

Employees are not the only persons who may be present on the premises of an employer. There may, for example, be persons present employed by the employer's independent contractor or self-employed persons. The nature of the employer's duty to such persons is by no means clear. There is clearly no liability *qua* employer, but there may be liability *qua* occupier or under ordinary principles of negligence. What is not clear is to what extent the employer must take positive action to ensure the safety of such persons, as he must in the case of his own employees. In the analogous tort of breach of statutory duty, persons other than employees have generally been held to be unable to sue the employer for breach of factory safety legislation (*infra*, p. 214). The Health and Safety at Work Act 1974, has introduced a duty (section 3 (1) on the employer to take reasonable care for the health or safety of such persons, but civil liability for breach of this duty is expressly excluded.

CHAPTER 14

TORTS OF STRICT LIABILITY—INTRODUCTORY

STRICT liability is liability which arises without fault—*i.e.* the defendant need have acted neither intentionally nor negligently. The instances of strict liability in the English law of tort are of a somewhat unconnected nature. Although it might be possible to deduce a principle of strict liability for carrying on an ultrahazardous activity under the rule in *Rylands* v. *Fletcher* (1868) and liability for animals, the courts have refused to recognise any such general principle (*cf. Read* v. *Lyons & Co.*, *infra*, p. 191). The strict liability involved in breach of statutory duty depends upon interpretation of the relevant statute. Vicarious strict liability is justified by its provision of a financially responsible person as a defendant. In nuisance and liability for fire, there appear now to be only vestigial traces of original strict liability. It must be remembered, also, that other torts not regarded as torts of strict liability, may operate as such. Conversion and defamation are examples of this.

The Law Commission has recently expressed citicism of the difficulty and uncertainty of the present rules concerning strict liability, but has recommended no change in the law because the question of survival of the present forms of strict liability was part of the larger question, to what extent there should be strict liability generally in cases of personal injury, and this question the Commission was precluded by its terms of reference from examining (Law Commission Report No. 32, 1970, "Civil Liability for Dangerous Things and Activities"). The Royal Commission on Compensation for Personal Injury (the Pearson Commission) has wider terms of reference. It has been appointed to consider to what extent, in what circumstances and by what means compensation should be payable in respect of death or personal injury (including ante-natal injury) suffered by any person:

(*a*) in the course of employment;

(*b*) through the use of a motor-vehicle or other means of transport;

(*c*) through the manufacture, supply or use of goods or services;

(*d*) on premises belonging to or occupied by another;

(*e*) otherwise through the act or omission of another where compensation under the present law is recoverable only on proof of fault or under the rules of strict liability, all this having regard to the cost and other implications of the arrangements for the recovery of compensation, whether by way of compulsory insurance or otherwise.

It is confidently expected that one result of the commission's deliberations will be a recommendation that the necessity for proving fault which generally applies where the plaintiff is claiming damages for personal injury will be relaxed, although whether it will be replaced by a greater measure of strict liability in tort or by a state-run insurance scheme against accidents causing personal injury is anyone's guess. A further result may be a rationalisation of the somewhat heterogeneous cases of strict liability which already exist in English law and which will be described in the following pages. Finally, it may be noted that in certain special situations, strict liability has been created by statute, namely by the Nuclear Installations Act 1965, the Merchant Shipping (Oil Pollution) Act 1971 and the Control of Pollution Act 1974. Details of these Acts are beyond the scope of this book.

CHAPTER 15

NUISANCE

MUCH of the confusion that centres round the word "nuisance" in the law of tort is caused by the fact that the term covers two concepts, those of private and public nuisance, which, while not totally dissimilar, are not too closely related. In private nuisance the central idea is that of invasion of land: the defendant causes the entry into the plaintiff's land of such things as noise, smell, vibrations, water or chattels. In the words of Lord Macmillan in *Read* v. *Lyons & Co.* ((1947)—spoken of *Rylands* v. *Fletcher*, but true also of private nuisance), the tort "derives from a conception of mutual duties of adjoining or neighbouring landowners," (this does not mean that the nuisance must always emanate from the defendant's land —it may emanate from land belonging to another, from the highway, or presumably, from the airspace above or adjoining the plaintiff's land—*cf. Lyons* v. *Wilkins* (1899)—watching and besetting the plaintiff's premises (presumably from the highway) in the course of picketing held to be a private nuisance; *cf.* also *Hubbard* v. *Pitt* (1975)). Public nuisance derives from the criminal law, its place in the law of tort depending upon the fact that a member of the public who can prove that he has suffered special damage from the defendant's commission of the common law crime of public nuisance may sue the defendant in tort. It does not require the invasion of private land, but the annoyance of the public by such acts as the obstruction of the highway, the pollution of the public water supply, and the keeping of a common gaming-house. The generic concept underlying both forms of nuisance, which may be expressed by saying that the defendant must have acted to the annoyance of another person or persons, is so broad as to be valueless.

The difference in origin of the two torts explains certain differences between them. For instance, the inability to sue in private nuisance for personal injury is explained because that tort protects exclusively the plaintiff's interest in his land; the same limitation does not exist in public nuisance. Generally speaking, however, the courts appear to assume that the two aspects of nuisance are governed by similar rules.

PRIVATE NUISANCE

One requirement of the tort of private nuisance, mentioned already, is that the defendant's act must interfere with the defendant's use and enjoyment of his land. This in itself is not enough to constitute private nuisance—the interference must also be unreasonable. What is an unreasonable interference is often a difficult question to decide, and one in which matters of law and fact are involved. Besides this, private nuisance, being derived from the action on the case, has the attribute that it lies only for an indirect interference.

The type of interference required by the tort of private nuisance may be either actual damage to the plaintiff's land or property thereon, or an interference with the enjoyment of such land not accompanied by any actual damage, or both.

The use interfered with by private nuisance may be the normal one of residing on the land and putting it to domestic use, but it is possible for other types of use to be protected, for example, agricultural, commercial or industrial use. The interference may be caused by a variety of different types of invasion: by vibrations, flooding, electricity, fire, smell, noise, dust, and sewage. Even an offensive sight has been held to be an actionable nuisance. Thus, in *Thompson-Schwab* v. *Costaki* (1956), the defendants were prostitutes who used premises adjoining the plaintiff's for the purposes of prostitution. The plaintiff sued them successfully in nuisance.

There is, however, no right to a particular view from one's house, provided that the defendant does not replace this with such an eyesore that this is in itself a nuisance. Equally, nuisance does not protect a monopoly of view of what takes place within one's land. Thus, in *Victoria Park Racing Co.* v. *Taylor* (1937) (an Australian case which would probably be followed in this country), the defendant, by broadcasting commentaries of racing held on the plaintiff's premises, which he was able to view from an adjoining building, did not commit nuisance. Privacy may be protected by the tort of nuisance, but only where in infringing it the defendant has also substantially interfered with the plaintiff's enjoyment of his land.

Private nuisance and other torts

Nuisance has to be distinguished from other torts, with some of which it may overlap. The difference between nuisance and trespass to land is the difference between indirect and direct interference with the plaintiff's land: there is no possibility of an overlap between these two torts. On the other hand, nuisance and *Rylands* v. *Fletcher* (1968) are often available on the same set of facts. The differences between the two are dealt with in the chapter on *Rylands* v. *Fletcher*.

The greatest difficulty is experienced in distinguishing between the torts of nuisance and negligence. Clearly negligence is much wider than nuisance, in the sense that the interests which it protects are not limited to the use and enjoyment of land. Apart from this the following differences exist between the two torts:

(i) In negligence, the plaintiff must establish that the defendant was under a legal duty to take care. In nuisance, there is usually no difficulty in showing that the defendant had a duty not to interfere unreasonably with the plaintiff's enjoyment of his land. Where, however, the nuisance arises by omission to act, the plaintiff must normally show that the defendant was under a duty to act carefully (*infra*, p. 180).

(ii) Nuisance may be committed intentionally, or, perhaps, without negligence (*infra*, p. 177). It is certain that in nuisance, negligence does not have to be *proved* by the plaintiff, though it may be relevant to show the unreasonableness of the interference.

(iii) It seems unlikely that mere interference with the enjoyment of land would be sufficient to constitute damage for the purpose of an action in negligence.

(iv) In nuisance, the question whether there has been an unreasonable interference must be determined both in the light of the defendant's conduct and of the seriousness of the interference suffered by the plaintiff. In negligence, any damage, however small, is always sufficient to support the action, although the triviality of the anticipated damage may be a factor in the court's decision that the defendant did not need to take precautions against the risk of its occurrence.

Unreasonableness

Interference with the enjoyment by the plaintiff of his land is not, as such, actionable. The plaintiff must show that such interference is unreasonable. The question of unreasonableness in nuisance is Janus-like: the court must consider *both* the conduct of the defendant in creating the interference *and* the effect that such interference has upon the victim, the plaintiff. These factors are not considered in isolation from each other. Thus the fact that the defendant has acted carelessly or maliciously may tip the scales in favour of showing an unreasonable interference. Equally, however carefully the defendant may have acted, if it is proved that the interference is sufficiently unreasonable, he will be liable in nuisance. Besides this, the court may take into account factors external to the parties, such as the locality in which the alleged nuisance takes place and the public interest in whether the defendant should be restrained from carrying out the activity. In the light of these factors, the court must then ask itself the question that is central in all nuisance actions, "Is it reasonable that the plaintiff should have to put up with this interference?"

Conduct of defendant

In some cases, the mental state of the defendant may make his conduct nuisance, although, had that mental state been different, nuisance would not have been committed. Where, for example, he is actuated by spite or malice toward the plaintiff, nuisance may be committed for that reason. Thus, in *Christie* v. *Davey* (1893), the plaintiff was a music teacher who held lessons in her house. The defendant, a neighbour, made a variety of noises during these lessons, solely, as the court found, for the purpose of annoying the plaintiff. The defendant was held liable in nuisance. And, in *Hollywood Silver Fox Farm Ltd.* v. *Emmett* (1936), the defendant caused his son to discharge guns on his land for the purpose of interfering with the breeding of the plaintiff's silver foxes. The defendant was held liable in nuisance.

It may be that the court would have found, in each case, that the interference was unreasonable also by reason of the annoyance to which it subjected the plaintiff. The nature of the defendant's conduct, however, made it possible to regard his action as unreasonable without reference to the degree to which it interfered with the plaintiff's enjoyment of his land. The two cases are not inconsistent with the earlier decision in *Bradford Corpn.* v. *Pickles* (1895). The right to appropriate water from an underground stream is not, like the right to make a noise on one's land, a right limited by the requirements of reasonableness. It is an absolute right, and the fact that it was exercised maliciously could not make it a nuisance.

Another factor which may go towards rendering the defendant's conduct unreasonable is that he has not taken reasonable care to prevent the interference of which the plaintiff complains. If a factory emits smell or noise which could be circumvented by some reasonable outlay or trifling precaution by the defendant, this might well determine the court's mind that the interference caused by the smell or noise is unreasonable. On the other hand, the fact that the defendant has taken all reasonable care to prevent the nuisance arising will not necessarily exclude liability. Whether this makes private nuisance a tort of strict liability is discussed below (p. 177).

Where the defendant is carrying out an activity which has public utility and has taken all reasonable care to prevent a nuisance arising, it is a moot point whether the utility of his activity is relevant in deciding on his liability in nuisance. It may be that in such a case, a greater degree of interference is justifiable than where the defendant's activity has no utility. The point awaits authoritative resolution (*cf. Munro* v. *Southern Dairies* (1955); *Bellew* v. *Cement Co.* (1948)). It is certain that where a sufficient degree of interference has been reached, nuisance will be established whatever the utility of the defendant's conduct.

Another factor which may influence the court is the temporary nature of the disturbance. In the case, for example, of demolition or construction work on buildings, what might appear an intolerable interference with the plaintiff's enjoyment of his land if committed in perpetuity may be justifiable on the ground that the plaintiff need only suffer it for a short time. The defendant must not however abuse the position and must take reasonable steps to safeguard the plaintiff from unnecessary interference. Thus in *Andreae* v. *Selfridge & Co. Ltd.* (1938), the plaintiff, a hotel owner, recovered damages from the defendants who in the course of demolition operations carried out by them had subjected the plaintiff's premises to an unnecessary amount of noise and dust.

Seriousness of the interference

In *Walter* v. *Selfe* (1851) Knight Bruce V.C. stated the test to be whether the interference was an "inconvenience materially interfering with the ordinary comfort physically of human existence, not merely according to elegant or dainty modes and habits of living, but according to plain and sober and simple notions among the English people." Thus stated it is clear that questions of degree must be resolved in order to decide whether the interference was sufficiently serious. The reports are full of examples of courts' decisions on the seriousness of the interference but as in each case the question is one of degree, these cases will not be examined here (a good example is *Halsey* v. *Esso Petroleum Co. Ltd.* (1961), in which Veale J. found proved against the defendants private nuisances by noise, smell and invasion of acid smuts).

An unresolved question is whether the degree of interference is taken into account where the plaintiff has suffered damage to his property (*contra*, Clerk & Lindsell, 1394; *pro*, Street, p. 226). Such slight authority as there is supports Street (in *Halsey's* case Veale J. appeared to assess degree in the case of the damage caused by acid smuts; and in the Scottish case of *Watt* v. *Jamieson* (1954) the court found an insufficient interference where the defender had, by discharging a considerable amount of water periodically from his house through a gable common to his property and to that of the pursuer caused damage to the walls of the pursuer's house). Against this the exclusion of locality as a factor where the interference consists in damage to property justifies the opinion that degree is far less important where actual damage occurs. The justification for its having to be assessed at all may be that in every case of nuisance interference with the *enjoyment* of land must be established. Trivial damage not sufficient to support an action in nuisance is no doubt recoverable in negligence, in which as we have seen the degree of damage is irrelevant.

Locality of nuisance

In *St. Helens Smelting Co.* v. *Tipping* (1865) the plaintiff complained of a nuisance by fumes from the defendants' factory which had caused damage to his shrubs. The defendants argued that, since the locality in question was an industrial one, the plaintiff must put up with the invasion of industrial fumes into his land. The court held, however, that though locality was an important consideration where the alleged nuisance took the form of interference with the occupier's comfort and enjoyment of his land, it was irrelevant where physical damage to property had been occasioned. In the case of this factor, therefore, the distinction between physical damage to property and mere interference with the enjoyment of property is vital. An example of locality influencing the decision that the defendant's act was a nuisance is *Sturges* v. *Bridgman* (1879). In this case the plaintiff was a physician whose use of his consulting room at the foot of his garden was interfered with by noise from the defendant's machinery which he used in his business of confectioner. The court found that the interference was unreasonable in view of the fact that the area was one in which numerous medical practitioners had their consulting rooms.

The distinction between physical damage to property and interference with enjoyment

As we saw above, where the plaintiff can establish actual damage to his land or other property, it may be that he is not required to do more in order to show a sufficient degree of interference for nuisance. It is certain, also, that the locality of the alleged nuisance is then irrelevant. It therefore becomes important to distinguish between what is actual damage for the purposes of the tort and what is a mere interference with the enjoyment of land. This distinction, though easy to state and to appreciate, is not without difficulties. In the first place, the courts insist on visible change in the property and require such change to be palpable to the ordinary observer. Scientific evidence of the damage is therefore excluded, presumably on the ground that if the plaintiff's damage can only be detected by scientists the damage is not sufficiently substantial. But may not such serious damage as the undermining of the foundations of the plaintiff's house be only capable of being established by scientific evidence?

Damage to property includes damage to the land itself, to buildings on the land, to plants and shrubs and to chattels on the land (*Halsey* v. *Esso Petroleum Co. Ltd.* (1961)). It appears to exclude financial damage such as loss of the plaintiff's business profits, or depreciation in the value of his land. In the case of the latter this is not surprising. If this were allowed to rank as damage to property, for the purpose of the rule, the distinction would lose most of its foundation, since in few cases in which there is a substantial interference with the comforts of the occupier will his property retain its value.

In some cases it may be uncertain whether the nuisance is of the "physical damage" or "interference with enjoyment" type. Nuisance by dust, which is arguably within either category, appears to be treated by the courts as a mere interference with enjoyment (in *Andreae* v. *Selfridge*, locality was considered a relevant factor in such a nuisance, but this would not have been so, had the court found damage to property).

Unusually sensitive plaintiffs

Where the plaintiff has put his land to some special use, nuisance will not lie for interference with such use, if it is shown that the amount of protection required goes beyond that required by persons generally. So, in *Robinson* v. *Kilvert* (1889) it was held that nuisance was not available where heat rising from the defendant's flat damaged brown paper manufactured by the plaintiff on his premises. There was no allegation that the heat was excessive, and the process of manufacture was exceptionally sensitive to heat (but n.b. that locality might operate to make such use "normal" rather than special). Opinions clearly may differ as to what is a special use. In *Bridlington Relay Ltd.* v. *Yorkshire Electricity Board* (1965) the court said *obiter* that the reception of television by the private householder was a special use of land. In the same case it was doubted *obiter* whether nuisance would ever lie for interference with a purely recreational use of land. Both opinions are clearly debatable.

Once nuisance has been established, the plaintiff can recover for interference with a special use, even where such use is not foreseeable (because the victim is taken as the defendant finds him—*cf. McKinnon Industries Ltd.* v. *Walker* (1951)—damage to hypersensitive orchids recoverable).

Damage

It is often said that nuisance is actionable only upon proof of damage. This appears to be a misconception. Only where the only way of establishing a nuisance is by showing actual damage to land or property (*i.e.* in a case where no other interference is experienced) will it be necessary to prove such damage. Cases on projections show that it is not necessary to prove actual damage in order to be able to succeed in nuisance. Thus in *Lemmon* v. *Webb* (1895) boughs of trees on the defendant's land which projected over the plaintiff's land were held to be a nuisance which the plaintiff was entitled to abate. The plaintiff did not need to show actual damage to establish the nuisance. In *Fay* v. *Prentice* (1845) the court found a nuisance proved in respect of a cornice which projected from the defendant's land over the plaintiff's. Even though the plaintiff could show actual damage (such as the discharge of rain-water on to his land from the cornice), the court thought that general damage could be presumed from the mere erection of the nuisance. In other words, where there is a sufficient degree of interference with the plaintiff's use and enjoyment of his land, damage will be presumed and actual damage does not have to be proved.

The plaintiff in private nuisance does not appear to be able to recover for his personal injuries. The explanation generally given for this, that private nuisance protects only the plaintiff's interest in the enjoyment of his land, does not seem adequate in a case where there is an interference with enjoyment leading to personal injury (where, for example, fumes cause physical illness). Certainly damage to chattels is recoverable in private nuisance, not only where there is a sufficient degree of interference to constitute nuisance apart from the damage to chattels (*Halsey* v. *Esso Petroleum Co.* (1961)), but also where there is an isolated escape producing damage to chattels (*British Celanese* v. *A. H. Hunt* (1969)). If the analogy between personal injury and damage to chattels is correct, the latter case would suggest that personal injury, even where produced by an isolated escape which gives rise to no other interference is actionable in nuisance.

Strict liability in nuisance

Differences between the torts of nuisance and negligence have already been noted. In this section, the question will be examined when, if ever, private nuisance operates as a tort of strict liability. Nuisance differs from negligence in that most nuisances are of a continuing nature whereas the damage complained of in negligence generally occurs once and for all. This fact means that in the majority of nuisance actions the defendant either knows of the nuisance (in which case he may be regarded as intending it) or should be aware of it (in which case he is negligent). There appears to be no authority to indicate whether the plaintiff may recover damages in respect of interference from a continuing nuisance for the period during which the defendant neither knew nor ought to have known of the interference. In the case of the continuing nuisance created by the defendant, the possibility of strict liability seems therefore remote.

Two other situations may give rise to the possibility of strict liability. The first is the case of the non-continuing nuisance, or nuisance caused by the isolated escape. It is settled that an action in nuisance will lie for such an escape provided the escape is the result of a state of affairs of some permanency on the defendant's land (for example, defective electric wiring causing an escape of fire (*Spicer* Smee (1946)). In *Kiddle* v. *City Business Properties* (*infra*, p. 183), the court assumed that liability for such an escape was strict, though this was *obiter*, the action failing because of the plaintiff's consent. Despite this decision, in those cases in which liability has been imposed for an isolated escape, the defendant has been negligent (*Midwood* v. *Manchester Corporation* (1905); *Spicer* v. *Smee* (1946); *Castle* v. *St. Augustine's Links* (1939); *British Celanese* v. *A. H. Hunt* (1969)).

The second situation in which strict liability is possible is that in which the defendant is held liable for a nuisance created by another. No case, however, points unequivocally to strict liability for such nuisance and the effect of the House of Lords decision in *Sedleigh-Denfield* v. *O'Callaghan* (1940) appears to be that negligence on the defendant's part is necessary.

One clear instance of strict liability in nuisance is provided by the rule in *Wringe* v. *Cohen* (1940) discussed below, at page 182. It seems likely, however, that this form of liability is in public nuisance only, and is based on the necessity of protecting users of the highway from the dangers from unsafe constructions near the highway.

The authority mainly relied on for regarding nuisance as a tort of strict liability, *Rapier* v. *London Tramways Company* (1893), does not carry the point. In that case the plaintiff complained of a nuisance by smell caused by overcrowding of horses in the defendants' stables. The court rejected the defendants' plea that they took all possible precautions. "If they cannot have 200 horses together, even where they take proper precautions, without committing a nuisance, all I can say is, they cannot have so many horses together" (*per* Lindley C.J.). In other words, given the existence of a sufficiently serious interference by smell, it was beside the point that the defendants might have done everything possible to prevent it.

Who can sue in nuisance?

The plaintiff in nuisance must, with rare exceptions (see *Newcastle-under-Lyme Corporation* v. *Wolstanton Ltd.* (1947)), show that he was in occupation of land affected by the nuisance under some legal or equitable title. So the tenant of land may sue in nuisance, but his wife and children resident with him are excluded. Similar considerations no doubt will determine the ability of a licensee with exclusive occupation to sue as were indicated in connection with trespass to land (*supra*, p. 44). A reversioner may sue if he can show that his interest in the land has been affected (where, for example, the nuisance has caused permanent damage to the land).

Who can be sued in nuisance?

Responsibility for the nuisance is not limited to the person who actually creates the nuisance. In numerous situations an occupier of land may be responsible for a nuisance created on that land by someone else.

Creation; authorisation of nuisance

The person who creates a nuisance on land is liable although he may have given up occupation of the land, and cannot enter it in order to remove the nuisance. It is, however, an unsettled question whether the creator must have been in occupation or control of the land at the time of the creation. A dictum of Devlin J. in *Southport Corporation* v. *Esso Petroleum Co. Ltd.* (1953) supports the view that a nuisance can be created by a licensee or even a trespasser. In principle this seems correct.

The person who authorises the commission of a nuisance by another is also liable for creating that nuisance. Where a landlord let a field, knowing it was to be used as a lime quarry, he was held liable for authorising the nuisance created by working the quarry, since it was clear that such working would inevitably create a nuisance (*Harris* v. *James* (1876)).

The principle of this case has been extended to the situation where it is foreseeable that acts of nuisance may be committed by other persons on one's land. In *Att.-Gen* v. *Stone* (1895), the landowner was held liable in nuisance where he had permitted gypsies to camp on his land, and create a nuisance there. On the other hand, where a local authority let property to a family which was known by the authority to be a "problem" family, it was held that the authority was not liable for nuisances in respect of physical damage and noise committed by the family, since the tenancy agreement expressly prohibited the commission of a nuisance by the tenant, and the authority could therefore not be said to have authorised the nuisance (*Smith* v. *Scott* (1972)).

Can nuisance be created by a failure to act?

At one time the courts refused to hold a person liable for a condition arising naturally on his land. For example, in *Giles* v. *Walker* (1890) the defendant was held not liable in nuisance or negligence for the spread of thistles from his land to that of the plaintiff. In *Pontardawe Rural District Council* v. *Moore-Gwyn* (1929) the defendant was held not liable in nuisance for a fall of rock from his land to that of the plaintiff, the fall being due to weathering of the rock. The rule has been applied in numerous cases concerning animals, for example *Stearn* v. *Prentice Bros. Ltd.* (1919) (rats attracted to defendant's land on which he manufactured bone manure—not nuisance when they spread to land of plaintiff), and *Seligman* v. *Docker* (1949) (pheasants bred in large numbers on the defendant's land and spread to land of the plaintiff). The issue has been further perplexed by the courts' failure to distinguish between a plea by the defendant that the thing came naturally to his land and one that he caused it to arise by natural use of his land. The latter plea is a defence to an action based on *Rylands* v. *Fletcher* but appears to have no relevance in an action of nuisance. Yet it was the reason given by the court for the decision in *Pontardawe Rural District Council* v. *Moore-Gwyn*, above, and it has also been used to explain cases where the defendant in conducting mining operations on his land has caused flood water to enter the land of the plaintiff (for example, *Smith* v. *Kenrick* (1849)).

It now appears true to say that the courts have shaken off these earlier cases to the extent that it is no longer possible for a defendant to argue that he cannot be held liable for the spread of something which came naturally to his land. In several cases the courts have held that a defendant is under a duty to act to prevent the thing escaping. Thus an occupier is now liable for damage caused by the fall of trees, whether planted or self-sown, and whether through the fall of branches (*Noble* v. *Harrison* (1926), where the defendant escaped liability because he was not negligent) or through the encroachment of roots (*Davey* v. *Harrow Corporation* (1958)). The occupier of land has also been held liable for failure to prevent the spread of a fire from his land to that of his neighbour, the fire having been begun by the ignition of a tree on the land by lightning (*Goldman* v. *Hargrave* (1967)).

In these cases liability in nuisance appears to be indistinguisable from liability in negligence, even to the extent that the court must find that the defendant is under a duty to take careful action to deal with the nuisance. But in assessing the standard of care required of the defendant the court takes into account the fact that the nuisance arose spontaneously on his land without the defendant's volition. Thus the requisite standard of care does not require him to go to considerable expense in order to remove the nuisance (*per* Lord Wilberforce in *Goldman* v. *Hargrave*, distinguishing earlier cases of *Pontardawe Rural District Council* v. *Moore-Gwyn*, above, where it would have cost the occupier £300 to ensure the safety of the rocks). On the other hand, in *Goldman* v. *Hargrave* the defendant was held liable because the fire could easily have been extinguished at an early stage by the use of water at trivial expense by the defendant. *Goldman* v. *Hargrave* has been followed to its logical conclusion in New Zealand where the New Zealand Supreme Court in *French* v. *Auckland City Corporation* (1974) refused to follow *Giles* v. *Walker* and held the defendant liable in nuisance for allowing his land to become overrun by thistles which spread to the land of the plaintiff.

In the case of nuisances arising from a failure to repair premises, there may clearly be liability on the occupier's part if this is the result of negligence on his part. Liability for such failure may also be strict under principles to be discussed later at page 182, if the premises adjoin the highway. Special rules regulate the liability of landlord and tenant for such failure to repair (*infra*, p. 182).

Vicarious liability

The employer is liable for nuisances created by his servant or independent contractor on principles discussed below (pp. 220–230).

Personal liability for nuisance created by another

It now appears true to say, in general, that an occupier of land is not liable for a nuisance created by another on that land, in the absence of negligence on the occupier's part. Thus the occupier has been held liable for nuisance created by a trespasser on his land, because through the negligence of his servants he was not aware of the existence of the nuisance (*Sedleigh-Denfield* v. *O'Callaghan* (1940)). He is liable in similar circumstances for a nuisance created by his predecessor in title. In *St. Anne's Well Brewery Co.* v. *Roberts* (1929) the defendant, an occupier of land, was held not liable for a nuisance created on the premises by a previous occupier, because he neither knew nor ought to have known of the existence of the nuisance.

Landlord and tenant

Special rules apply to this case. The question to be answered here is to what extent the landlord, and to what extent the tenant are liable to third parties for nuisance caused by the state of the premises. The question of the landlord's liability towards the tenant for defects in the state of the premises is considered elsewhere. Difficulties arise in this connection because the normal obligations of landlord and tenant towards third parties can be modified by the obligations which each has undertaken under the lease. The landlord is liable in these circumstances.

(i) He is liable in nuisance to a third party if he knew or ought to have known of the nuisance at the commencement of the letting (*Brew Brothers Ltd.* v. *Snax* (*Ross*) *Ltd.* (1970)—this case shows also that the landlord is not excused where he has taken a repairing covenant from the tenant, otherwise he could defeat his obligations by letting to a man of straw).
of premises adjoining the highway, where he has covenanted to repair (*Wringe* v. *Cohen* (1940)), or has reserved the right to enter and do repairs (*Wilchick* v. *Marks and Silverstone* (1943)), or if a right on the part of the landlord to enter and do repairs can be implied as it can in a weekly tenancy (*Mint* v. *Good* (1951)). This liability may be limited to public nuisance (see discussion below, p. 187). The rule in *Wringe* v. *Cohen* can no doubt be extended to breach of the landlord's obligation to repair under the Housing Act 1961.

(iii) Where the rule in *Wringe* v. *Cohen* does not apply, the landlord is liable for nuisance arising from lack of repair where he has covenanted to repair, although liability in such a case does not appear to be strict (*Payne* v. *Rogers* (1794)).

(iv) If he has authorised the commission of a nuisance by the tenant (*supra*, p. 179), the landlord is liable for it.

The tenant as occupier is liable for creating the nuisance, whether this is by an act of misfeasance on his part, or through an omission, for example, a failure to repair. In accordance with principles already discussed, the tenant is liable for non-feasance only if he has been negligent, unless his liability is under the rule in *Wringe* v. *Cohen*, above. Where the tenant is liable he is not excused by the fact that the landlord is also liable, because, for example, he has covenanted to repair. This rule is clearly necessary because the landlord may not be available to do the repairs.

Defences to private nuisance

Prescription

The right to commit a nuisance may be acquired by prescription, that is, by twenty years' exercise of the acts constituting the nuisance, provided that this exercise is *nec vi*, *nec clam*, *nec precario* the owner of the servient estate (neither done violently, nor secretly, nor by his permission). The content of the nuisance must be capable of existing as an easement. Whether it does or not is a question that the law of real property decides. It was stated *obiter* in *Sturges* v. *Bridgman* (1879) that the right to cause vibrations could be acquired by prescription, but this is open to doubt (and see Megarry and Wade, *Law of Real Property*, 4th ed., p. 880, where the case is criticised).

Conduct of the plaintiff

It is no defence that the plaintiff acquired the land with knowledge of the nuisance existing there, *i.e.* that he "came to the nuisance." Equally, as *Sturges* v. *Bridgman* illustrates, the fact that the nuisance only arises because the plaintiff has put his land to some particular use is not a defence, provided that this is not a special use which nuisance would not protect. Once the nuisance has been established, the normal duty in tort to take reasonable steps to mitigate damage no doubt applies. Could this be used to inhibit a person from putting his land to an otherwise reasonable use? The question was put in argument by Jenkins L.J. in *Davey* v. *Harrow Corporation* (*supra*, p. 180) whether he who sees encroaching roots on his land can build a house and wait for it to fall. It seems likely that the duty to mitigate operates to prevent this use of the plaintiff's land.

Consent may be a defence to nuisance. In *Kiddle* v. *City Business Properties Ltd.* (1942) it was held that the tenant of part of premises consents to run the risk of nuisances due to the condition of the premises retained by the landlord provided there is no negligence on the part of the latter; so in that case the plaintiff tenant could not succeed in nuisance when the landlord's gutter became flooded and water poured into the plaintiff's premises, damaging his stock.

Contributory negligence on the part of the plaintiff is an unlikely factor in private nuisance where the wrong complained of is an interference by the defendant with the plaintiff's enjoyment of his land. It is not contributory negligence on the plaintiff's part to "come to the nuisance," nor to put his land to the use with which the nuisance interferes. Where the nuisance consists of an isolated escape, contributory negligence of the plaintiff may well be relevant, since liability here is essentially one for negligence.

Statutory authority

Statutory authority is a defence where the statute imposes an obligation upon the defendant to act, the inevitable result of such action being to create a nuisance (even though the statute expressly preserves liability in nuisance). Where, however, the nuisance is created by negligence on the defendant's part, statutory authority is no defence to an action of nuisance, and the defendant has the onus of showing that he took due care (*Manchester Corporation* v. *Farnworth* (1930)). Where the statute is merely permissive rather than mandatory, it again is the law that statutory authority is a defence if the creation of the nuisance is the inevitable result of carrying out, without negligence, the statutory permission. In such a case, if the statute expressly preserves liability in nuisance, it appears to be the law that there can be liability in nuisance even without negligence provided the creation of the nuisance is not the inevitable result of carrying out the statutory power.

Fires Prevention (Metropolis) Act 1774

The effect of this statute upon actions in nuisance will be considered in a later chapter.

Remoteness of damage in nuisance

In *The Wagon Mound* (No. 2) (1966) (*supra*) the Privy Council held that, in order to establish public nuisance, the plaintiff must show that the infringement of which he complains is a foreseeable consequence of the defendant's act. There seems little reason to doubt that the foreseeability test for deciding questions of remoteness of damage will apply also in private nuisance.

Remedies

Damages

The plaintiff is entitled to compensation for the damage he has suffered as a result of the nuisance. Thus he may recover for physical damage to his property, for depreciation in the value of his property, and for business loss resulting from the nuisance. In the case of the latter, the plaintiff may not recover the whole amount of the loss if the court considers that some loss would have been suffered even though no actionable nuisance had been committed. Thus in *Andreae* v. *Selfridge & Co. Ltd.* (1938) (*supra*), the court quantified the loss of custom which might have been expected had the defendant's interference been reasonable, and this amount was deducted from the total damages. The reasoning of this case would also seem to apply to depreciation of the plaintiff's land.

Where the nuisance is a continuing one, the award of damages in an action for the nuisance does not bar subsequent actions, since a cause of action in respect of the nuisance arises from day to day so long as it persists. It is otherwise when the nuisance is complete; then all the damages the plaintiff claims must be obtained in one action.

Injunction

It is common for the plaintiff in nuisance to ask for an injunction against further continuance of the nuisance by the defendant. This may be combined with a claim for damages. The injunction is a discretionary remedy and in some cases of actionable nuisance may be refused by the court (see, for example, *Att.-Gen.* v. *Sheffield Gas Consumers* (1853) where an injunction was refused on the ground that the nuisance would only be repeated at long intervals and would on the occasion of each repetition be of short duration). The court may grant a *quia timet* injunction in cases where no nuisance has actually been committed by the defendant, but the commission of one by him in the future is reasonably apprehended by the plaintiff. The court may grant damages in lieu of a *quia timet* injunction by virtue of their jurisdiction under Lord Cairns' Act 1858, though this leads to the startling result that one who has suffered no tort may recover damages (*Leeds Industrial Co-operative* v. *Slack* (1929)).

Public Nuisance

A public nuisance is, in the words of Romer L.J. in *Att.-Gen.* v. *P.Y.A. Quarries* (1957), "any nuisance 'which materially affects the reasonable comfort and convenience of life of a class of Her Majesty's subjects.' The sphere of the nuisance may be described generally as the 'neighbourhood'; but the question whether the local community within that sphere comprises a sufficient number of persons to constitute a class of the public is a question of fact in each case." This definition makes it clear that no absolute line can be drawn between public and private nuisance so that overlapping between the two may exist. So, in the above case, a nuisance by the quarrying operations of the defendants which caused vibrations and dust to affect houses in the vicinity was held to be a public nuisance; clearly on the facts the individual householders could have sued in private nuisance. In fact an action is public nuisance by a private individual would not have succeeded on these facts (the actual action was brought by the Attorney-General—see below), because of the rule that the plaintiff in public nuisance must show damage to himself greater than that suffered by the public generally. Public nuisance is a common law crime, and is also restrainable at the instance of the Attorney-General by a civil proceeding known as a relator action. Apart from this there is the rule that one who suffers special damage as the result of the nuisance may sue in tort.

Basis of liability

The basis of liability in tort for public nuisance remains in doubt. In *The Wagon Mound* (No. 2) (*supra*, p. 92), the Privy Council found that, although the charterers committed the crime of public nuisance by discharging the oil into the harbour, their liability in tort depended upon whether they should have foreseen the risk of fire. Further, although Lord Reid appeared to regard the question of liability as turning on whether the fire was a foreseeable consequence of the nuisance, in deciding this question he took into account all the factors relevant to deciding whether a person has committed a breach of a duty of care (*supra*, pp. 90–91). On this approach, it seems that the "wrongfulness" of the conduct involved in committing a public nuisance is irrelevant to the question of liability in the tort, and that in order to succeed the plaintiff must prove that the requirements of the tort of negligence are fulfilled.

In *Dymond* v. *Pearce* (1972) the Court of Appeal considered the liability in public nuisance of the defendant who had parked his lorry for several hours on one side of a dual carriageway. The plaintiff, a passenger on a motorcycle, had been injured when the motorcycle was driven into the back of the lorry. The lorry had been properly lighted and the street lighting was excellent. The Court of Appeal concluded that, although the defendant had committed a public nuisance through obstructing the highway by parking his lorry on it, he was not liable in tort to the plaintiff since the accident which occurred was not a foreseeable result of the nuisance but was due entirely to the fault of the driver of the motorcycle. The issue was treated by the Court of Appeal as one of causation, a different approach from that of the Privy Council in *The Wagon Mound* (No. 2) in which liability in public nuisance seems to be treated as identical with negligence, so that breach of a duty of care must first be established. Since the issue of causation was regarded as turning on foreseeability of danger arising from the nuisance, the practical difference between these approaches may be minimal. Two members of the Court of Appeal, however, thought that cases might occur in which it was possible to establish causal connection between the nuisance and later damage even where such damage was not a foreseeable result of the nuisance, so that the theoretical possibility of public nuisance operating as a tort of strict liability remains (though the tentative examples given by Sachs L.J. of supervening fog and unexplained rear light failure appear to be cases where the risk though slight is foreseeable).

Special cases of public nuisance

(1) *Buildings and projections on or over the highway*

The classic type of public nuisance is interference with the public right of passage along the highway, for example, by obstructing it, or by rendering passage unsafe by erecting dangerous structures on or near the highway. In *Wringe* v. *Cohen* (1940) the Court of Appeal held that "if owing to want of repair, premises on a highway become dangerous and therefore a nuisance, and a passer-by suffers damage by their collapse, the occupier, or the owner if he has undertaken the duty of repair, is answerable whether he knew or ought to have known of the danger or not." The defendant landlord was therefore held liable for the collapse of the demised premises, which he had covenanted to repair, on to the plaintiff's premises. It seems fairly certain that the ratio is limited to public nuisance, and that where there is no element of danger to the highway the decision does not apply. The strict liability laid down by the case is of a somewhat special kind, since it only applies where the danger arises through want of repair, not through some secret, unobservable process of nature, nor through the act of a trespasser (*Cushing* v. *Walker & Son Ltd.* (1941)—enemy action caused tile to fall from roof). Liability is strict, therefore, only where the need for repair accrues faster than a reasonable man would appreciate. It would follow logically from *Wringe* v. *Cohen* that the same strict liability should exist in respect of defects arising from want of repair in artificial constructions projecting over the highway, and *Tarry* v. *Ashton* (1876), although the ratio of this case is disputed, appears to impose such liability on the occupier of the house to which the construction is attached. In the case of projecting trees, however, there is no liability for the fall of the tree in the absence of negligence, whether the trees are planted by the defendant, by a predecessor in title, or are self-sown (see *Noble* v. *Harrison* (1926); *Caminer* v. *Northern and London Investment Trust* (1951); *British Road Services* v. *Slater* (1964)).

(2) *Failure to maintain highway by highway authority*

At common law a highway authority was liable only for its acts of misfeasance in relation to the highway. Such liability might be in negligence, nuisance or breach of statutory duty. The Highways (Miscellaneous Provisions) Act 1961 makes the highway authority liable also for its failure to maintain the highway so that it becomes dangerous for traffic, subject to the defence that the authority took reasonable care (five statutory criteria are provided by section 1 (3) for deciding whether such care has been shown). The Act applies whether the action is brought for negligence, nuisance, or breach of statutory duty. In the case of a failure to repair the highway, action lies for breach of the absolute statutory obligation in section 44 of the Highways Act 1959 to maintain the highway—*Griffiths* v. *Liverpool Corporation* (1967).

The Act has the effect of placing the onus of showing that it took reasonable care on the authority, provided that the plaintiff can establish that the highway was dangerous to traffic through a failure to maintain it. In *Griffiths* v. *Liverpool Corporation* (1967), a majority of the Court of Appeal held that, if the authority could not show that it took reasonable care, it was not excused by proving that the damage would have occurred even had they shown such care (but Diplock L.J. expressed the opinion that the common law defence of inevitable accident might here be available—it was not available in the case itself because on the evidence it was a matter for speculation whether had due care been shown by the authority the plaintiff's injury would have been averted). An unresolved question is whether the Act applies to acts of misfeasance by the highway authority. The advantage of applying one rather than two bodies of law to cases concerning the liability of highway authorities ought, it seems, to outweigh the necessity of interpreting the words "failure to maintain" in a strained fashion in order to do so.

Special damage

The plaintiff must show special damage over and above that which is suffered by the public as a result of the nuisance. This may take the form of personal injury, damage to property, or loss of business profits. It seems that special damage includes inconvenience provided this is greater than is suffered generally. So the plaintiff may recover for being delayed at a level-crossing (*Boyd* v. *G.N. Ry. Co.* (1895)—an Irish case) or for loss of sleep caused by vehicular noise (*Halsey* v. *Esso Petroleum Co. Ltd.* (1961)). The overall limit on the recovery of damage is that it must be a foreseeable consequence of the nuisance (*The Wagon Mound* (No. 2)).

Where nuisance to the highway is complained of, the special damage complained of by the plaintiff does not have to be sustained in his capacity as user of the highway. If, for example, the nuisance consists of an obstruction of the highway, the plaintiff may recover loss of profits due to the interference with the access of the public to his shop (*Wilkes* v. *Hungerford Market Co.* (1835)).

But where the plaintiff suffers personal injury, he must show that he suffered it on the highway or in the course of a slight deviation from it (*Jacobs* v. *L.C.C.* (1950)—plaintiff injured by falling over projection on forecourt of shop not forming part of the public footpath had no action in nuisance).

Relationship with private nuisance

Differences between the two forms of nuisance do exist. Thus prescription is no defence to an action based on public nuisance. In public nuisance it is possible to claim for personal injury. But the rules applicable to the two torts are generally speaking treated by the courts as similar, if not identical. The rules concerning liability for the nuisance, for example, do not appear to discriminate between public and private nuisance.

Statutory nuisances

The above account does not exhaust the rights of the citizen to complain of a nuisance. Various nuisances have been created by statute under which the individual may bring a complaint, though this is not quite the same thing as bring a civil action for damages. Statutes deserving particular mention are the Public Health Act 1936, Part 31 (*cf. Coventry City Council* v. *Cartwright* (1975); *Salford City Council* v. *McNally* (1975), the Clean Air Act 1956 and the Noise Abatement Act 1960).

CHAPTER 16

THE RULE IN RYLANDS v. FLETCHER

The decision in Rylands v. Fletcher

The facts in *Rylands* v. *Fletcher* (1868) were as follows: the defendant, a millowner, employed independent contractors to build a reservoir on his land for the purpose of supplying water for his mill. In the course of making excavations upon the defendant's land, the contractors came upon some disused mine-shafts which, unknown to them, connected with mines underneath adjoining land. The plaintiff had taken a lease of this land in order to work the mines. The contractors negligently failed to seal up these shafts and when the reservoir was filled with water, the mines were flooded.

The case came upon appeal to the Court of Exchequer Chamber, where the plaintiff succeeded, and this decision was upheld by the House of Lords. The ground for the Exchequer Chamber's decision is contained in this extract from the judgment of the court, delivered by Blackburn J.: "We think that the true rule of law is, that the person who for his own purposes brings on his lands and collects and keeps there anything likely to do mischief if it escapes, must keep it in at his peril, and if he does not do so is prima facie answerable for all the damage which is the natural consequence of its escape."

This sentence makes it clear that the defendant's liability was personal, not a mere vicarious liability for the negligence of his independent contractor, and that such liability was strict.

In the House of Lords, a qualification was put by Lord Cairns upon this statement of the rule by Blackburn J. to the effect that the defendant was only liable if he brought the thing on his land in the course of non-natural use of the land. This qualification has been accepted by later cases as an essential part of the rule.

The importance of Rylands v. Fletcher

At the time of the decision *Rylands* v. *Fletcher* did not appear to lay down new law. In the course of his judgment, Blackburn J. drew analogies from recognised cases of cattle trespass and nuisance to justify his decision. Thus he compared the plaintiff's case to that of the person whose grass or corn was eaten by escaping cattle of his neighbour, or whose land was invaded by smells from his neighbour's alkali works or filth from his privy. He stressed that the defendant was liable for the escape of the thing even in the absence of any personal fault on his part but there is nothing to suggest that he thought there was anything new about this; such strict liability existed also in the examples which he gave of cattle trespass and nuisance. What was important at the time about the decision in *Rylands* v. *Fletcher* was that a comprehensive rule was laid down governing the incidence of strict liability in the case of the escape of dangerous things from a man's land. This rule was accepted by the courts and applied by them in numerous cases following *Rylands* v. *Fletcher*, but it still remained doubtful whether the rule was merely a special branch of the law of nuisance or whether it established a separate tort. Now that the courts are moving away from the conception of nuisance as a tort of strict liability, it seems that a real difference may exist between it and *Rylands* v. *Fletcher*. The difference may be summed up by saying, that whereas in nuisance the defendant is only liable if as the result of a state of things he has created on his land an escape of something on to the plaintiff's land is foreseeable, in *Rylands* v. *Fletcher*, the defendant is liable even if the escape of the thing which he has brought on his land is totally unforeseeable.

At one time it was thought that the decision in *Rylands* v. *Fletcher* might have introduced into English law a general principle of strict liability for the carrying on of dangerous activites. In *Read* v. *J. Lyons & Co.* it was necessary to examine the question whether such a principle had been established. The defendants operated a munitions factory as agents of the Ministry of Supply. The plaintiff was an inspector appointed by the Ministry. In the course of her duties she was in the shell-filling shop in the factory when an explosion occurred in the shop causing her serious injuries. She based her claim against the defendants on *Rylands* v. *Fletcher*, making no assertion that the defendants had been negligent. The House of Lords held that she could not succeed under *Rylands* v. *Fletcher* because her injuries had been suffered *on the premises of the defendants*; the explosives had not escaped within the meaning of the rule. The case is important because it shows that the courts treat the rule in *Rylands* v. *Fletcher* like a statute, and have applied to it the literal rather than the mischief rule of statutory interpretation.

Requirements of the rule in Rylands v. Fletcher

(1) *The defendant must bring the thing on his land; he must do this for his own purposes*

The first point to note is that the defendant need not own the land on to which he has brought the thing. A temporary occupier of land such as a lessee, or a person physically present on land but not in legal occupation of it such as a licensee, is equally within the scope of the rule (*Rainham Chemical Works Ltd.* v. *Belvedere Fish Guano Co.* (1921)) and in *Charing Cross Electricity Supply Co.* v. *Hydraulic Power Co.* (1914) the rule was applied to one who had a statutory right to lay electric cables under the highway. It has been decided that where the thing is brought on to the land by a licensee, the licensor is also liable under *Rylands* v. *Fletcher* at least where it is brought there for his purposes (*Rainham case*, *supra*). Whether this would be extended to an owner of land out of occupation is uncertain.

The requirement that the thing must be brought on the land for the purposes of the defendant does not mean that it must benefit the the defendant, according to *Smeaton* v. *Ilford Corporation* (1954), where it was stated *obiter* that a local authority which was under a statutory duty to collect sewage, collected it for its own purposes within the rule in *Rylands* v. *Fletcher*. On the other hand in *Dunne* v. *North Western Gas Board* (1964) it was doubted *obiter* whether the defendant Board which was under a statutory duty to supply gas collected it for its own purposes within the meaning of the rule. Doubtless a gratuitous depositee of the thing would be within the rule.

Where the thing is naturally present on the land of the defendant, he cannot be liable for its escape under *Rylands* v. *Fletcher*. The escape of such things as weeds, vermin, rocks, and flood-water is thus normally outside the scope of the rule (*Giles* v. *Walker* (1890); *Stearn* v. *Prentice Brothers Ltd.* (1919); *Pontardawe Rural district Council* v. *Moore-Gwyn* (1929); *Whalley* v. *Lancashire and Yorkshire Ry. Co.* (1884)). Recent decisions, however, have established the possibility of an action in nuisance in such circumstances (*Davey* v. *Harrow Corporation* (1958); *Goodman* v. *Hargrave* (1967)).

(2) *The thing must be likely to do mischief if it escapes*

The rule does not require that the thing should be both likely to escape, and likely to do mischief on escaping. If this were the rule there would be little difference between *Rylands* v. *Fletcher* and negligence. Furthermore, the *Rylands* v. *Fletcher* "thing" need not be a thing dangerous in itself. The most harmless object may cause damage on escape from a man's land. The rule has been applied to a large class of objects including gas, electricity, explosives, the poisonous leaves of a tree, a flag pole, a revolving chair at a fair ground, and acid smuts from a factory (*Batcheller* v. *Tunbridge Wells Gas Co.* (1901); *National Telephone Co.* v. *Baker* (1893); *Rainham Chemical Works Ltd.* v. *Belvedere Fish Guano Co. Ltd.*

(1921); *Crowhurst* v. *Amersham Burial Board* (1878); *Shiffman* v. *Order of St. John* (1936); *Hale* v. *Jennings Bros.* (1938); *Halsey* v. *Esso Petroleum Co. Ltd.* (1961)). The courts have established the sensible rule that the thing brought on the land need not be the thing which escapes. Thus a defendant who kept a motor-car in his garage with petrol in the tank was held liable for a fire which spread from the tank (*Musgrove* v. *Pandelis* (1919)). The rule has even been applied to human beings. In *Att.-Gen.* v. *Corke* (1933) a landowner who permitted caravan dwellers to camp on his land was held liable when they committed insanitary acts on neighbouring property (but ought liability to be strict here, bearing in mind that there is no lawful way to prevent human beings escaping? Inasmuch as the plaintiff was complaining of an unreasonable use by the defendant of his land in allowing on it persons who were foreseeably likely to trespass on neigbouring land, the case seems more correctly regarded as one of nuisance rather than *Rylands* v. *Fletcher*—*cf. Att.-Gen.* v. *Stone*, *supra*, p. 179).

(3) *The defendant's use of the land must be non-natural*

Non-natural use of land was explained by the Privy Council in *Rickards* v. *Lothian* (1913) as follows: "it must be some special use bringing with it increased danger to others, and must not merely be the ordinary use of the land or such a use as is proper for the general benefit of the community."

Ordinary use cannot simply be equated with domestic or agricultural use; the working of mines is a natural use of land (*Rouse* v. *Gravelworks Ltd.* (1940)). Most domestic and agricultural uses of land are in fact outside the rule, for instance, the planting of trees (*Noble* v. *Harrison* (1926); but the planting of a poisonous tree is a non-natural use; *Crowhurst* v. *Amersham Burial Board* (1878)). The lighting of a household fire (*Sochaki* v. *Sas* (1947)), the installation of water pipes for a water closet (*Rickards* v. *Lothian* (*supra*)), the wiring of a building for the supply of electric light (*Collingwood* v. *Home and Colonial Stores Ltd.* (1936)) are examples of natural use.

Non-natural use of land is constituted by such activities as the storage on the land in bulk of water, gas or electricity and the collection of sewage by a local authority (*Smeaton* v. *Ilford Corporation* (1954)). It is arguable that all the above examples should be saved by the second part of the Privy Council's definition as being for the general benefit of the community. The opinion of certain members of the House of Lords (*e.g.* Viscount Simon in *Read* v. *Lyons* (1947)) that running a munitions factory in wartime was a natural use of land may be supported on this ground although this was not the reason advanced in the judgments. This is supported by the judgment of Lawton J. in *British Celanese* v. *A. H. Hunt* (1969) in which he held that the benefit derived by the community from the defendant's business of manufacturing electrical components made the use of land for this purpose and the storing of strips of metal foil thereon a natural use of the land. If this case is followed it seems to mean that the rule in *Rylands* v. *Fletcher* can only be applied in exceptional circumstances.

(4) *The thing must escape*

This requirement has already been illustrated by *Read* v. *Lyons*.

Status of the plaintiff; type of damage recoverable

In the judgment of Blackburn J. in *Rylands* v. *Fletcher*, there was no requirement that the thing should escape on to land in which the plaintiff had an interest. However, in *Read* v. *Lyons* (1947) the opinion was expressed by Lord MacMillan that the doctrine of *Rylands* v. *Fletcher* "derives from a conception of mutual duties of adjoining or neighbouring landowners." In *British Celanese* v. *A. H. Hunt*, however, Lawton J. refused to limit the rule in this way, holding that there is liability provided there is an escape from a place over which the defendant has occupation or control to a place which is outside his occupation or control. So, in that case, liability would have existed for the escape of strips of metal foil from the defendants' land which caused a power failure and consequent damage to machinery in the plaintiff's factory by being blown on to a power station owned and operated by a third party (but for the fact that there was natural use).

This divergence of opinion also affects the question of what damage is recoverable. If Lord Macmillan's view is correct, only damage to land occupied by the plaintiff and his chattels on that land is recoverable, by analogy with nuisance, *supra*, p. 177). On the view that the plaintiff need not be an adjoining landowner, it appears that every type of damage is recoverable provided it is not too remote. There is a certain amount of authority suggesting that the latter view is correct. Thus successful actions have been brought under *Rylands* v. *Fletcher* for personal injuries, both where the plaintiff had an interest in the land on to which there was an escape (*Hale* v. *Jennings Brothers* (1938)) and where he had no such interest (*Shiffman* v. *Order of St. John* (1936)). It is suggested that the basis of the cause of action under *Rylands* v. *Fletcher* is not the defendant's interference with the plaintiff's enjoyment of his land, but the fact that the plaintiff has suffered damage as the result of an escape of a noxious thing from the defendant's land.

It seems probable that the damage recoverable under the rule is limited to damage to person or property (*Cattle* v. *Stockton Waterworks Co.* (1875) in which it was held that purely pecuniary loss was not recoverable).

There must be proof of actual damage. This appears to mean actual physical damage to property (or possibly person), and to exclude a mere interference with the plaintiff's enjoyment of his land, such as would ground an action in nuisance. However in *Eastern & S.A. Telegraph Co.* v. *Cape Town Tramways Co.* (1902) such an interference was thought to be actionable in *Rylands* v. *Fletcher*, although the plaintiff's action failed because his use of the land was abnormal (*i.e.* receipt through a submarine cable of telegraphic messages, with which electricity from the defendants interfered). Where physical damage to the plaintiff's property is sustained only because of its weak condition, this appears to be recoverable (held *obiter* in *Hoare* v. *McAlpine* (1923)—no defence that damage to plaintiff's hotel through vibrations occurred because of its allegedly unstable condition).

Defences to Rylands v. Fletcher

(1) *Act of God*

The basis of this defence, and of act of a stranger, is that the defendant ought not to be held responsible for an escape which is caused by something beyond his control. They show that the obligation of the occupier is not an absolute one. Act of God has been defined as an operation of nature "which no human foresight can provide against, and of which human prudence is not bound to recognise the possibility." (*Tennent* v. *Earl of Glasgow* (1864)). The definition of act of God in terms of human foresight tends to assimilate *Rylands* v. *Fletcher* with negligence and this has been criticised (Goodhart, *Current Legal Problems* (1951) 177). However, not every event which is not reasonably foreseeable may constitute an act of God since the requirement is that the event be one against which no human foresight can provide. The defence was successful in *Nichols* v. *Marsland* (1876) where an extraordinary rainfall caused flooding from some artificial lakes on the defendant's land. It was rejected in very similar circumstances by the House of Lords in a Scottish case, *Greenock Corporation* v. *Caledonian Ry. Co.* (1917), on the ground that rainfall, however heavy, is not sufficiently unprecedented to be an act of God.

(2) *Act of a stranger*

If the escape is caused by the unforeseeable act of a stranger, and not by such persons as the occupier's servants, independent contractors, members of his family and possibly guests, this is a defence to *Rylands* v. *Fletcher*. Thus, where the plaintiff's premises were flooded because an unidentified person had turned on a water tap in the defendant's premises there was no liability under the rule (*Rickards* v. *Lothian* (1913)). Where the act of the stranger, whether it is deliberate or negligent, is foreseeable, there is liability under *Rylands* v. *Fletcher*, although here it will normally co-exist with negligence (*Perry* v. *Kendricks Transport Ltd.* (1956); *Hale* v. *Jennings Brothers* (1938)). In relation to the defence of act of a stranger, there seems greater force in Goodhart's criticism that its effect is to assimilate *Rylands* v. *Fletcher* with negligence. Even so, there may be a difference since it may be that the burden of establishing that the stranger's act was unforeseeable rests on the defendant, but the matter is unclear (in *North Western Utilities* v. *London Guarantee & Accident Co.* (1936), the Privy Council appeared to assume that the defendant must prove both that the escape was due to the act of a stranger and that this act was unforeseeable. In *Perry* v. *Kendricks Transport* (1956) the Court of Appeal regarded the burden of proof as resting on the plaintiff to prove that it was foreseeable).

(3) *Contributory negligence*

This will no doubt constitute a defence in a suitable case, though no actual authority exists.

(4) *Statutory authority*

Where a contractor or public body is carrying out under statutory authority an undertaking that would normally attract the operation of the rule in *Rylands* v. *Fletcher*, for example, the provision of a gas, water or electricity supply, it is a question of statutory interpretation whether the rule in *Rylands* v. *Fletcher* applies to the activity (*Green* v. *Chelsea Waterworks Co.* (1894)). Where the statute does not mention the rule in *Rylands* v. *Fletcher*, the rule appears to be that if the activity is carried out under a statutory *duty* as opposed to a power, *Rylands* v. *Fletcher* is excluded (*Dunne* v. *North Western Gas Board* (1964)), and this rule applies even if, as in *Dunne's* case, the statute expressly preserves liability in nuisance. Where the activity is carried on under a statutory *power*, *Rylands* v. *Fletcher* is available, at least where the statute expressly preserves liability in nuisance (*Charing Cross* case, *supra*) and even though the activity does not exceed the terms of the power and there is no negligence. The effect of *Dunne* v. *North Western Gas Board* is to place outside the operation of the rule in *Rylands* v. *Fletcher* nationalised industries such as the various Area Gas and Electricity Boards, to whose activities the type of liability embodied in *Rylands* v. *Fletcher* would seem particularly appropriate. Thus, in *Pearson* v. *North Western Gas Board*, (1968), the plaintiff who suffered serious personal injuries and lost her husband and home as the result of an explosion which occurred underneath her house following an escape of gas from the defendants' gas main, was unable to recover in *Rylands* v. *Fletcher* because the defendants were under a statutory duty to supply the gas.

(5) *Consent of plaintiff*

Where there is an express consent by the plaintiff to the defendant's bringing the thing on his land, this will be a good defence to an action under *Rylands* v. *Fletcher* (*Att.-Gen.* v. *Cory Brothers & Co.* (1921)). It is more normal for the plaintiff's consent to be implied from his conduct. The cases on implied consent fall into two categories. The first category is where the relationship of landlord and tenant exists between the defendant and the plaintiff. The tenant is deemed to consent to anything kept by the landlord on his premises at the time of the tenant's taking the lease. Thus a tenant of a shop in the defendant's theatre could not complain when his shop was flooded because of the freezing-up of a sprinkler system which the defendants had installed in their theatre to prevent fire (*Peters* v. *Prince of Wales Theatre Ltd.* (1943)).

The second category is where the plaintiff and defendant are occupants of different parts of the same building, there being no relationship of tenant and landlord between them, and something kept on the defendant's premises escapes into the premises of the plaintiff. Most of the cases concern the escape of water from premises on the upper storey to those on the lower. These cases have decided that the lower occupant cannot complain of such an escape (*Ross* v. *Fedden* (1872); *Anderson* v. *Oppenheimer* (1880)). The reason for this appears to be the same as in the case where the parties are landlord and tenant, namely, that the plaintiff must take the condition of the defendant's premises as he finds them at the time of taking occupation of his own premises, provided there is nothing unusually dangerous about their condition. This explanation involves the anomaly that consent is implied merely because the plaintiff has come to the nuisance. An alternative explanation, that the plaintiff consents to the presence on the defendant's premises of something from which he also obtains benefit, for example, a common water supply, is, however, insufficient to explain those cases where the plaintiff has failed to recover even though the element of benefit to himself is lacking (see *e.g. Ross* v. *Fedden* (*supra*), where the presence of water in the building did not benefit the plaintiff).

Remoteness of damage

The rule as to remoteness of damage in *Rylands* v. *Fletcher* has never been authoritatively settled. Blackburn J. spoke of liability for the "natural consequences" of the escape, which may suggest a similar rule to that laid down for negligence in *The Wagon Mound (No. 1)*. On the other hand, it appeared to be assumed before the latter case that the Polemis rule of direct consequences would apply to *Rylands* v. *Fletcher* and the Privy Council in *The Wagon Mound (No. 1)* expressly excluded from the width of their remarks concerning remoteness the rule in *Rylands* v. *Fletcher*. It may be, therefore, that the direct consequences rule survives in relation to this tort.

Rylands v. Fletcher and other torts

In many cases *Rylands* v. *Fletcher* overlaps with other torts, especially nuisance and negligence. The differences between *Rylands* v. *Fletcher* and negligence are fairly obvious but it is quite common for both to be committed in a given case. Furthermore, where the success of an action under *Rylands* v. *Fletcher* depends upon whether the event causing the escape could be foreseen, as is the case if the defendant claims the escape was caused by act of God or of a stranger, the two torts are identical apart from the requirement of non-natural use in *Rylands* v. *Fletcher*, and the fact that in *Rylands* v. *Fletcher* the burden of proving the unforeseeability of the escape may rest on the defendant.

The similarity between private nuisance and *Rylands* v. *Fletcher* has already been mentioned. Of course private nuisance can be committed in circumstances quite remote from *Rylands* v. *Fletcher*. Thus in many cases of nuisance there is no question of the defendant's bringing something on to his land. Where the case does concern the escape of something brought by the defendant on his land, the following are the more important differences between *Rylands* v. *Fletcher* and nuisance:

1. It is unlikely that *Rylands* v. *Fletcher* extends to the escape of intangibles such as noise. *Hoare & Co.* v. *McAlpine* (1923), in which liability was imposed for the escape of vibrations, has received criticism.

2. In *Rylands* v. *Fletcher* the defendant is liable if he has brought the thing on the land in the course of non-natural use. In nuisance the requirement is that the defendant should have used the land unreasonably.

3. In *Rylands* v. *Fletcher* there is always liability for an escape

caused by an independent contractor. In nuisance, liability is not invariably imposed for the acts of an independent contractor.

4. Other differences have already been mentioned. In *Rylands* v. *Fletcher* liability is strict and there is liability even for an unforeseeable escape. In nuisance it is probable that an unforeseeable escape is not actionable. *Rylands* v. *Fletcher* probably does not share the characteristics of private nuisance that the plaintiff must have an interest in land and that he cannot recover for personal injuries.

Status of Rylands v. Fletcher today

Rylands v. *Fletcher* is now recognised as a tort in itself, independent of, though resembling, nuisance. At one time it was thought that it might form the basis for the incorporation of a greater measure of strict liability into English law, either in the form of liability for hazardous activities, or in the form of enterprise liability. Neither of these developments has taken place. Instead by a series of restrictive decisions, in particular the establishment of the defences of act of God, act of a stranger and statutory authority, the rule itself has become diminished in scope. Whether the rule in *Rylands* v. *Fletcher* should continue to survive in its present form will no doubt be a question which the Pearson Committee will consider.

Chapter 17

LIABILITY FOR THE ESCAPE OF FIRE

In so far as there are any special principles applicable to liability for damage caused by fire, it is because of the former existence of a particular form of the action on the case by which a person was liable for the keeping of a fire on his land which spread to and caused damage on that of his neighbour. It is a disputed question whether liability was strict. In any event, the occupier was liable for the acts of members of his own household and of his servants, agents and guests (*Beaulieu* v. *Finglam* (1401)). In 1774 the Fires Prevention (Metropolis) Act afforded a protection to the occupier on whose land a fire "shall accidentally begin." The courts have given to this Act the interpretation that, unless there is intention or negligence in causing the fire to spread or the constituent requirements of a tort of strict liability are present, the occupier is not liable.

Negligence

Filliter v. *Phippard* (1847) decided that the Act of 1774 was no defence when the fire began through the defendant's negligence. Furthermore, the fact that the fire began accidentally and is allowed to spread through negligence does not make the statutory defence available (*Musgrove* v. *Pandelis* (1919)). In *Sochaki* v. *Sas* (1947) it was held that where a lodger left a fire in his room unattended and without a fire guard for a few hours, and the fire spread, *res ipsa loquitur* did not apply to prove his negligence. This case makes it clear that negligence must be proved even where the fire is intentionally lit, even though this appears to contradict the wording of the 1774 Act. The occupier is liable also for the negligence of his servant or independent contractor. The liability for the latter's negligence can no doubt be explained by the normal principles of the employer's liability for his contractor's actions (*infra*, p. 227) but in *Balfour* v. *Barty-King* (1957) was treated as a survival of the occupier's liability under the former action on the case.

Strict liability

There is liability where the conditions of liability under the rule in *Rylands* v. *Fletcher* are present and the Fires Prevention (Metropolis) Act will not provide a defence. In *Musgrove* v. *Pandelis* (1919) the defendant was held liable for a fire which began in the carburettor of his car and spread to the plaintiff's premises, since the car was a *Rylands* v. *Fletcher* "object," and the keeping of a car in a garage was a non-natural use of land. The former finding seems artificial, the latter questionable. The approach in *Mason* v. *Levy Auto Parts* seems preferable. In that case the judge, in considering whether wooden stacking cases on the defendant's land were objects within the rule in *Rylands* v. *Fletcher*, thought that the correct test was whether they were likely to catch fire, and the fire spread to the plaintiff's land.

Other torts which may involve strict liability, for example, nuisance and breach of statutory duty, may be committed by means of fire. The existence of the form of strict liability embodies in the former action on the case has received recent confirmation in *H. & N. Emanuel* v. *G.L.C.* (1971). The defendants, the G.L.C., were held liable for a fire which spread from land they occupied to the premises of the plaintiff and caused damage there. The fire had been started by a contractor employed by the Ministry of Works which by the permission of the defendants had engaged him to clear the defendants' site of some houses. The fire had spread through the contractor's negligence. All three members of the Court of Appeal found the defendants liable under the *Beaulieu* v. *Finglam* principle, since the contractor was not a "stranger," and the defendants were therefore liable for his negligence, Lord Denning M.R. thought that the Ministry of Works contractor was not a stranger, because the occupier should have anticipated that he would light a fire, and so had a duty to control him. This seems to involve reviving the old rule, under which liability may have been strict, and applying it in such a way that it is virtually equivalent to negligence.

Chapter 18

LIABILITY FOR ANIMALS

Introdction

It is important to note that a person may be liable for the acts of his animals under the ordinary principles of torts not specifically associated with animals. Thus he may commit nuisance by keeping a noisy dog, or negligence by carelessly allowing his dog which he knows to be dangerous to mankind to escape and injure another person. The principles upon which a person will be held liable in negligence for the acts of his animals will be considered later in this chapter. First, however, it is necessary to consider those torts which are exclusively concerned with the acts of the defendant's animals, in particular, the common law torts of *scienter* liability and cattle-trespass. Both these torts embody a form of strict liability, but the reasons for the imposition of strict liability appear to differ. In the case of *scienter* liability, strict liability is imposed because the defendant has created a special risk by keeping a dangerous animal. In the case of cattle-trespass, strict liability is part of the give and take of an agricultural community in which each farmer expects to pay for the damage caused by his trespassing cattle irrespective of fault on his part. Both these torts had considerable obscurities attached to them and for this reason the law relating to liability for animals (including liability for negligence) was the subject of review by the Law Commission, the result of which was the Animals Act 1971, which came into force on October 1, 1971. Some understanding of the previous law is necessary in order that the legislative purpose behind this enactment be understood, and accordingly the pre-1971 rules relating to liability for animals will be described in outline.

Strict Liability at Common Law

The law previous to the Animals Act concerning strict liability for dangerous animals can be summed up in this way:

(i) A distinction was drawn between dangerous animals (*ferae naturae*) and harmless animals (*mansuetae naturae*). The former were animals belonging to a species regarded as in itself dangerous to mankind. The basis for classifying the the species as *ferae naturae* was that its members had the propensity of attacking human beings. Examples of species actually held to be dangerous are the bear, elephant, zebra, leopard, and particular species of monkey. Animals which merely had the propensity to damage property (Colorado beetle, locust) were thus not *ferae naturae*. Nor it seems were animals dangerous to man through being likely to spread disease rather than through attacking him. The extent of the species' domestication, even outside the United Kingdom, was relevant evidence, along with the general characteristics of the species, as to whether it was *ferae naturae* (*McQuaker* v. *Goddard* (1940)—camel held to be *mansuetae naturae*). Once an animal was regarded as *ferae naturae*, however, it did not matter that in certain parts of the world it had been domesticated (*Behrens* v. *Bertram Mills Circus Ltd.* (1957)—Indian elephant held to be *ferae*). The keeper of an animals *ferae naturae* was strictly liable for damage done by it when acting in accordance with its dangerous characteristics.

All other animals, whether domesticated such as cattle and sheep, or wild such as rabbits were *mansuetae naturae*. In the case of an animal *mansuetae naturae*, the keeper was strictly liable for damage done by it if he knew that the particular animal had a propensity to attack human beings or other animals, and the animal acted in accordance with this propensity in causing damage. In the case of both types of animal, liability was enforced by the *scienter* action (*i.e.* the animal was kept by the defendant knowing of its dangerous nature) but only in the case of the animal *mansuetae naturae* was proof of *scienter* required.

(ii) In order to prove the *scienter*, the plaintiff had to prove that the particular animal had either attacked or shown a tendency to attack human beings or other animals, and that the defendant knew this. Proof that the animal had acted in accordance with a characteristic normally found in animals of that species was not enough (no liability for cat killing pigeons—*Buckle* v. *Holmes* (1926); nor for fillies committing playful attack on the plaintiff—*Fitzgerald* v. *Cooke Bourne* (*Farms*) (1964)). Proof of knowledge of the heightened aggressive tendencies of Alsatian dogs rather than dogs generally, or of bulls rather than cattle was equally insufficient. There was, however, some authority that knowledge of occasional characteristic aggressiveness by a particular species was enough (attack by bitch with pups—*Barnes* v. *Lucille Ltd.* (1907); by butting ram—*Jackson* v. *Smithson* (1846)).

(iii) The animal whether *ferae* or *mansuetae* had to be acting in accordance with the characteristic which led to its being regarded as dangerous in order to render its keeper liable; otherwise the damage was too remote. *Behrens* v. *Bertram Mills Circus* (*supra*) showed that the risk created by an animal *ferae naturae* would not be defined narrowly (personal injuries inflicted by stampeding elephants recoverable even though they acted in fright). Further, provided the animal manifested its own dangerous tendency, any damage not excluded by the rules of remoteness was recoverable (for example damage to property inflicted by a dangerous bull attacking human beings; or personal injury inflicted by a dog on the owner of another animal while attacking that animal in accordance with its known tendency (*cf. Whycherley* v. *Grave* (1967)). The rule might still operate restrictively. Damage to flocks caused by an animal *ferae naturae* does not seem to have been recoverable.

(iv) In order that the keeper should be liable, it was necessary to prove that the animal escaped from his control (*Rands* v. *McNeil* (1955)).

Strict Liability under the Animals Act 1971

Strict liability for dangerous animals is retained by the Animals Act. This may be welcomed, as well as the strengthening of strict liability by the abolition of the requirement of an escape by the animal and of the common law defences (if, in fact, such defences existed), of act of God and act of a third party. The Act has also left intact the common law position whereby some species of animals are conclusively presumed to be dangerous and some non-dangerous, so that in the case of the latter there is liability only where the particular animal has a known tendency to do harm. The basis chosen by the Act for classifying a species or a particular animal as dangerous seems questionable and likely to give rise to difficulties of interpretation.

Dangerous species

The dangerous species is defined by section 6 of the Act as follows: "A dangerous species is a species—

(*a*) which is not commonly domesticated in the British Islands; and
(*b*) whose fully grown animals normally have such characteristics that they are likely, unless restrained, to cause severe damage or that any damage they may cause is likely to be severe."

It may be noted that the dangerous species under this definition includes the animal such as the Colorado beetle which presents a danger only to property and also the animal likely to spread disease. Clause (*a*) of the definition shows that domestication of the species outside the British Isles is no longer relevant in determining whether it is dangerous. *McQuaker* v. *Goddard* is therefore no longer law on this point, although there would still be a question whether a camel came within section 6 (2)(*b*). The last words of section 6 (2)(*b*) cause difficulty. They require the court to take an animal not likely to cause damage, to imagine it causing damage, and to assess the probable consequences of such damage as severe or otherwise. No guidance is given by the Act as to the meaning of severe. The courts are therefore free to adopt a purely quantitative test, or perhaps to treat personal injuries as more severe than damage to property. In view of the tortuous nature of this definition it is legitimate to wonder why the Law Commission Report did not give examples of the type of animals envisaged by the words. Is a giraffe such an animal? There is no definition of species in the Act, although section 11 provides that the word includes sub-species or variety. The test is therefore presumably whether a sub-species or variety has characteristics which render it a dangerous sub-species or variety, in which case liability for its acts will be decided under section 2 (1). In *Cummings* v. *Grainger* (1975) the court considered whether alsatian dogs had characteristics which rendered them dangerous, although it was decided that they did not, so that liability for the act of such a dog, if it existed at all, did so under section 2 (2) of the Act. Presumably, therefore, the alsatian was regarded as a variety of dog, a questionable view. The lack of definition provided by the Act may here cause problems.

Liability for animals belonging to dangerous species

Section 2 (1) provides, "Where any damage is caused by an animal which belongs to a dangerous species, any person who is a keeper of the animal is liable for the damage, except as otherwise provided by this Act." It may be noted that, provided the animal has caused the damage, no further question of remoteness of damage can arise. If the animal is either likely to cause damage or if damage that it may cause is likely to be severe, it is irrelevant whether the damage it actually causes is the damage it is likely to cause or whether it is severe. While this simplifies the law it represents a considerable change.

Liability for animals not belonging to dangerous species

Section 2 (2) provides: "Where damage is caused by an animal which does not belong to a dangerous species, a keeper of the animal is liable for the damage, except as otherwise provided by this Act, if—

(*a*) the damage is of a kind which the animal, unless restrained, was likely to cause or which, if caused by the animal, was likely to be severe; and (*b*) the likelihood of the damage or of its being severe was due to characteristics of the animal which are not normally found in animals of the same species or are not normally so found except at particular times or in particular circumstances; and

(*c*) those characteristics were known to that keeper or were at any time known to a person who at that time had charge of the animal as that keeper's servant or, where that keeper is the head of a household, were known to another keeper of the animal who is a member of that household and under the age of sixteen."

The following points may be noted about this subsection:

1. It does not require the animal to inflict the damage in the course of an attack. It is thus wide enough to cover liability for infectious animals, for the animal which damages property without attacking it, and even for damage caused by a dog running into the highway and causing an accident.

2. Subsection (2)(*b*) appears to enact the common law position concerning domestic animals which cause damage through acting in a manner characteristic of the species. There is, therefore, still no strict liability for damage caused by a bull, unless that particular bull was known to have a propensity to cause that particular damage, or (*semble*) the bull was manifesting periodic sexual aggressiveness.

3. The difficulties of construing the phrase, "if caused by the animal, was likely to be severe," have already been considered in connection with the dangerous species (although the wording of section 6 is slightly different). The plaintiff's burden is increased within the context of this subsection because he must prove that the defendant knows this to be a characteristic of the particular animal. Where the animal acts in accordance with a characteristic of the species which is found only at a particular time or in particular circumstances, it is not clear whether the knowledge required of the defendant is of the characteristic of the species or of the particular animal involved.

4. The damage actually caused by the animal must be such that it is likely to cause it, or that if it did cause it, it would be likely to be severe. If the damage is of the latter type, it does not matter that it is not actually severe.

5. Subsection (*c*) is based upon the common law rules which determine whether the knowledge of one person is treated as that of its keeper.

No necessity for escape

Neither subsection requires the animal to escape from the defendant's control in order that liability be established and the Law

Commission Report makes it clear that this effect was intended. *Rands* v. *McNeil* (*supra*, p. 204) is therefore no longer law.

Liability for damage done by dogs

Section 3 of the Animals Act which replaces liability under the Dogs Acts of 1906 and 1928 provides that where a dog causes damage by killing or injuring livestock (for the definition of this, see below, p. 209), any person who is a keeper of the dog is liable for the damage except as otherwise provided by this Act. The defences in section 5 of the Act therefore apply to this form of liability. Section 3 maintains the principle of the Dogs Acts that there is liability even in the absence of *scienter* or negligence.

Section 9 provides a defence to an action for the killing of a dog which worries livestock.

Defences to actions brought under section 2 and section 3

Section 5 (1) and (2) establish the defences that the plaintiff was wholly at fault and that the plaintiff voluntarily accepted the risk. Section 6 (5) preserves the latter defence even where the risk is incidental to the plaintiff's employment. Section 10 of the Act makes it clear that the apportionment provisions of the Law Reform (Contributory Negligence) Act 1945 are applicable where the plaintiff has been contributorily negligent.

Section 5 (3) deals with the problem of whether it is a defence to an action based on section 2 that the injury was inflicted by the defendant's animal while the plaintiff was trespassing on the defendant's land. Section 5 (3) allows the defence if (a) the animal was not kept on the land for the protection of persons or property, or (b) the animal was kept there for the protection of persons or property and keeping it there for that purpose was reasonable (as to the reasonableness of keeping a savage dog for the protection of property, see *Cummings* v. *Grainger* (1975)).

The omission of the defences of act of God and of a third party from section 5 means that these defences are not available to an action under section 2.

Keeper

Liability under section 2 of the Act is imposed upon the keeper of the animal. He is defined by section 6 of the Act as the person who owns the animal or has it in his possession; or is the head of a household of which a member under sixteen owns the animal or has it in his possession. Section 6 also deals with the problem of wild animals in captivity which have escaped and returned to their wild state (particularly those indigenous to this country) by providing that the keeper of the animal at the time of its escape continues to be its keeper until another person becomes its keeper under the provisions mentioned above.

Cattle-trespass

Liability at common law

Cattle-trespass was committed at common law by one whose animals of the class of cattle entered land of the plaintiff, where the plaintiff did not permit the entry. Exceptionally it could be committed without unauthorised entry if cattle lawfully on land consumed or otherwise destroyed chattels belonging to the plaintiff on that land, for example, crops after severance from the land. "Cattle" were bulls, cows, sheep, goats, pigs, horses, asses and poultry (but not dogs and cats). The following were the chief features of liability at common law for cattle-trespass:

(i) Liability for cattle-trespass was strict.

(ii) It was actionable *per se* without proof of damage.

(iii) Liability was imposed upon the person in possession of the cattle at the time of the trespass. The owner out of possession seems not to have been liable.

(iv) The plaintiff in an action of cattle-trespass normally had to be the possessor of the land, but an exception to this has been recognised in the case of the grantee of the crops of the land, or of an exclusive right of pasture over the land. In the case of damage done to a chattel on the land the plaintiff had to be possessor of the chattel.

(v) Damages in cattle-trespass were not limited to damage to the land itself. The courts also allowed as damages consequential upon the trespass personal injuries (as in *Wormald* v. *Cole* (1954)) and damage suffered by the plaintiffs when their train was derailed by the defendant's trespassing cattle (*Cooper* v. *Ry. Executive* (*Southern Region*((1953)).

(vi) There is little authority upon defences to cattle-trespass and in view of the regulation of the general defences to the strict liability in the Animals Act it is not proposed to examine it. But two special defences must be mentioned. It was a defence to an action of cattle-trespass that the animal escaped from the highway into the plaintiff's land and that the defendant was not negligent. This defence was available whether the animal had itself escaped on to the highway or had been taken there by the defendant. But a defendant might be negligent in failing to remove his animals from the plaintiff's land after they had entered it from the highway. It is uncertain whether this liability was in negligence or cattle-trespass. It is also uncertain whether the plaintiff's land had to adjoin the highway in order that the defence be available. The better view appears to be that there was no such limitation, since if the animal could gain access to the land from the highway, that land ought to be regarded as sharing the risks of such entry.

It was also a defence that the entry occurred because of the plaintiff's failure to perform a duty owed to the defendant to fence his land.

Liability under the Animals Act

The Act makes a few important changes in the law relating to cattle-trespass but the general principles underlying the tort are left undisturbed. Thus strict liability for cattle-trespass is retained because of the necessity of providing a clear rule whereby the losses caused by marauding cattle can be automatically adjusted. But consequential loss in the form of personal injuries can no longer be recovered in cattle-trespass since such loss cannot be regarded as part of the give and take of the agricultural community. In order to establish liability for personal injuries caused by invading cattle it will therefore normally be essential to establish negligence unless the conditions of section 2 of the Act apply. The Act, however, makes it possible for the occupier to recover for damage to chattels on the land which are in his ownership or possession. Section 4 (1) (*a*) does not allow the recovery in cattle-trespass of damages where the person who suffers the damage does not own or occupy the land, and this exceptional case of cattle-trespass has therefore disappeared.

The following is a summary of the changes effected by the Act:

Livestock. Section 4 of the Act refers to livestock which is defined in section 11 to mean any animals of the bovine species, horses, asses, mules, hinnies, sheep, pigs, goats and deer not in the wild state. Livestock within the meaning of the Act appears to differ from the common law interpretation of cattle in including deer and excluding poultry.

Damage. The tort is no longer actionable *per se*; damage must be proved arising from the entry. This may take the form of damage to the land itself or to chattels on the land owned or possessed by the occupier. Section 4 (1) (*b*) also allows the recovery of expenses reasonably incurred in keeping the livestock while it cannot be restored to the person to whom it belongs or while it is detained in pursuance of section 7 of the Act (*infra*, p. 210) or in ascertaining to whom it belongs, from the person to whom the livestock belongs.

Who is liable. The person liable is the person to whom the livestock belongs but section 4 (2) provides that for the purposes of section 4 livestock belongs to the person in whose possession it is. The owner out of possession of the livestock is therefore not liable.

Who may sue. The person who may claim is the person who has ownership of or who is in occupation of the land, but if the claim is for damage to chattels on the land such person must also show that he has ownership or possession of the chattels. Under the section therefore an owner out of possession of the land may now claim, but it seems that he will only be able to claim where his reversionary interest in the land is damaged (unless his claim is for damage to his chattels).

Defences. Section 5 recognises three defences to liability under section 4. Section 5 (1) excuses the defendant where the damage is due wholly to the fault of the plaintiff. Section 5 (5) confirms the special defence formerly available to actions of cattle-trespass that the animal strayed from a highway which it was lawfully using (the subsection does not make it a requirement of the defence that the plaintiff's land should adjoin the highway). Section 5 (6) confirms and extends the defence that the entry would not have happened but for the breach by the plaintiff of his duty to fence his land. At common law it appeared that the defence was available only where the duty to fence was owed by the plaintiff to the defendant. This limitation does not appear in the subsection. Further, the defence is available where there is a breach by any person having an interest in the land, for example, to the occupier of land when the breach of the duty to fence is committed by the owner out of possession. These appear to be the only defences possible to liability under section 4, but there may be also a reduction for the plaintiff's contributory negligence.

New remedy. Section 7 abolishes the old right of distress damage feasant with regard to animals (as to objects see *supra*, p. 55), and replaces it with a new right of the occupier of any land to detain any livestock which strays on to that land.

Liability for Negligence

There may be liability for negligence both in the case of dangerous and non-dangerous animals under the existing law. Negligence is particularly important however in the case of animals which are of the class of harmless animals and which individually do not have dangerous characteristics known to their keeper. Several cases have established that there might be liability for failure to control such animals when they were taken by a person in control of them on the highway (*e.g. Deen* v. *Davis* (1935); *Aldham* v. *United Dairies Ltd.* (1940); *Gomberg* v. *Smith* (1963)). There might also be liability in negligence if such animals caused damage to other persons on the land of their keeper. There was however no duty of care, in the absence of "special circumstances" to prevent harmless animals from straying on to the highway (so held by the House of Lords in *Searle* v. *Wallbank* (1947): for a recent example of a case in which special circumstances displaced the rule in *Searle* v. *Wallbank*, see *Bativala* v. *West* (1970)).

Impressed by the evidence about accidents on the highway caused by straying animals, the Law Commission recommended the abolition of the rule in *Searle* v. *Wallbank*. The abolition of the rule is accomplished by section 8 (1). Now, therefore, an occupier of land owes a duty of care in relation to the straying of so-called harmless animals from his land on to the highway. But under section 8 (2), no breach of duty is committed by a person by reason only of the fact that he has placed animals on land if: (a) the land is common land, or is land situated in an area where fencing is not customary or is a town or village green; and (b) he had a right to place animals on that land (*cf. Davies* v. *Davies* (1975))—right to place animals on common land included a license to place animals on such land given by the person with the right to place them there.

CHAPTER 19

BREACH OF STATUTORY DUTY

THE term, "breach of statutory duty," refers particularly to those cases where a civil action in tort is available for breach of a statute which appears to impose purely criminal penalties. Whether such action is available has been based by the courts upon an inference from the words of the statute of legislative intent, but as will be seen shortly such intent appears largely a legal fiction. As a tort, breach of statutory duty is something of a hybrid. In many cases, the behaviour which constitutes it amounts also to common law negligence, and for this reason it is sometimes called statutory negligence. This is particularly so in the case of industrial safety legislation passed for the protection of workmen in factories, which is generally construed as conferring a civil action on a workman injured by its breach. The statute here serves the useful purpose of particularising the standard of reasonable conduct expected of his employer, so that the workman does not need to show that the employer acted unreasonably. But breach of statutory duty, even in those cases where the statute merely defines the employer's obligation to take reasonable care, is usually more than mere statutory negligence. If the statutory duty is construed as absolute, a non-negligent failure to comply with it will be a breach. Further, where the statute imposes an obligation which would not be required of the employer to discharge his duty of care, liability is in every sense strict. Only where the effect of the statute is to impose an obligation upon the defendant merely to take reasonable care to do that which the ordinary law of negligence would in any case compel him to do (for a case where the statute imposed a lesser duty on the employer than that required under the common law rules of negligence, see *Bux* v. *Slough Metals* (1974)) can breach of statutory duty be entirely equated with negligence.

Requirements of the tort

The plaintiff in an action for breach of statutory duty must show: (i) that the statute was intended by Parliament to confer a civil remedy for its breach; (ii) that the statute imposed a duty upon the defendant; (iii) that the defendant was in breach of this duty; (iv) that the plaintiff suffered harm or damage which was not too remote a consequence of the breach of duty.

Was the statute intended to confer a right of action in tort?

The difficulties of extracting any consistent approach from the decisions of the courts on this matter may perhaps be illustrated by indicating that though actions in tort are allowed for breach of factory legislation, the same is not true of breach of road traffic regulations (*Phillips* v. *Britannia Hygienic Laundry* (1923); *Clarke* v. *Brims* (1947); but *cf. Kelly* v. *W.R.N. Contracting* (1968) in which an action for breach of a parking regulation was allowed); or by comparing *Read* v. *Croydon Corporation* (1938), in which an action was allowed for breach of a statutory obligation to supply wholesome drinking water, with *Square* v. *Model Farms Dairies Ltd.* (1939) which held that the supply of infected bottled milk in breach of statutory duty gave no civil action. One suggested criterion is that the statutory action would be "unusual" (*cf. Atkinson* v. *Newcastle and Gateshead Waterworks Co.* (1877)—no action for breach of statutory obligation to maintain water pressure so that fire brigade could not extinguish fire; and *Cutler* v. *Wandsworth Stadium Ltd.* (1949)—no civil action for breach of statutory obligation to admit bookmaker to dog track). But in *Monk* v. *Warbey* (1935) a successful action was brought against a motorist for breach of his statutory duty to insure his car. It is arguable that if common law remedies exist, this is a reason for not adding to them—it seems unlikely that the Theft Act 1968 or the Trade Descriptions Act 1968 would be construed as conferring civil remedies. Other suggested criteria for finding that a civil remedy was intended are that the statute imposes no criminal or other sanction (*cf. Reffell* v. *Surrey County Council* (1964)), or that the statutory penalty is derisory or inadequate, or that the statute is for the protection of a distinct class of persons. The former can clearly have no general validity, and the latter two have received no general acceptance by the courts. Despite what the courts say, it seems a question of policy rather than construction whether a civil remedy exists (for a criticism of the courts' creation of new civil duties as being based on unexpressed legislative intent, see Williams (1960) 23 M.L.R. 233).

Statutory duty laid upon the defendant

The statute must impose a duty rather than a power upon the defendant. The duty must be imposed upon the defendant (*Harrison* v. *N.C.B.* (1951)—duties imposed by Coal Mines Act 1911 in relation to shot-firing were imposed upon shot-firers rather than upon defendant employer).

Breach of duty

The defendant must be in breach of his statutory duty. Whether he is or not will raise, *inter alia*, a question of statutory interpretation. The court must decide whether the duty is a strict one, or whether it is one of reasonable care only. In *Galashiels Gas Co.* v. *Miller* (1949) it was held that the defendants' statutory duty to maintain a lift in good repair was strict, so that where the lift fell to the bottom of the lift-shaft, injuring the plaintiff, there was liability even though no negligence by the defendants could be established. In *John Summers* v. *Frost* (1955) it was held that the duty to securely fence "every dangerous part of any machinery" was a strict one, so that the employers were in breach of this duty in failing to fence a grindstone, even though the effect of fencing the machine was to make it unusable. On the other hand, the duty arising under section 48 (1) of the Mines and Quarries Act 1954, to take "such steps ... as may be necessary for keeping the road or working-place secure" is a duty based upon foreseeability of danger and is therefore one of reasonable care. (*Robson* v. *National Coal Board.* (1968)). The wording "so far as reasonably practicable" qualifying the employer's obligation also means that the obligation differs little if at all from the employer's common law duty (*Levesley* v. *Thomas Firth* (1953)). The court must also be satisfied that the statutory duty, as precisely interpreted, applies to the case before it. Thus the plaintiff in *Eaves* v. *Morris Motors* (1961) failed to show a breach of section 14 (1) of the Factories Act 1937, since that section only requires fencing of dangerous parts of machinery and not of materials that are inserted into machinery. Similarly, in *British Railways Board* v. *Liptrot* (1969) it was held that there is no duty to fence when what is dangerous is the machine as a whole rather than its particular parts—otherwise there would be a duty to fence vehicles.

Plaintiff must be a person protected by the statute

In general, employees of persons other than the employer subject to the statutory duty, and self-employed persons have been held to be outside the benefit of statutory duties and regulations for the purpose of suing in breach of statutory duty. Thus in *Hartley* v. *Mayoh & Co.* (1954) the plaintiff, a fireman, was electrocuted in the course of fighting a fire at the defendants' factory, because of the defendants' breach of statutory regulations. It was held that he could not recover from the defendants for breach of statutory duty because he was not a "person employed" in the factory within the meaning of the regulation (*cf. Herbert* v. *Harold Shaw* (1959); *Kearney* v. *Eric Waller*

(1967)). Something may turn upon the interpretation of the statute in question. Thus it has been held that the phrase "any person" in section 29 of the Factories Act 1961, extends to all those who enter a factory to work for the purposes of the factory, and that, therefore, a window-cleaner who was employed as an independent contractor by the factory owner came within the ambit of the duty (*Wigley* v. *British Vinegars Ltd.* (1964)). Unless the wording of the statute appears clearly to envisage it, however, the courts will normally be reluctant to extend the benefit of statutory duties to outsiders. This may be explained either on the ground that courts believe in class benefit as the basis for allowing an action for breach of statutory duty, or as part of their general reluctance to impose duties on employers in respect of the safety of persons other than their own employees (*cf.* employers' common law liability, *supra*, p. 167).

On the other hand, if the plaintiff is within the protected class, it does not matter that he is acting outside the course of his employment (*Smith* v. *Supreme Wood Pulp Co.* (1968)), nor that he is trespassing upon his employer's machinery (*Uddin* v. *Associated Portland Cement Manufacturers* (1965)) or premises (*Wedgwood* v. *Post Office* (1973)). Where such trespass shows an unreasonable failure to look after his own safety by the plaintiff, there will be a deduction for contributory negligence (to the extent of 80 per cent in *Uddin*, though in *Westwood* no deduction was made since no danger was foreseeable to the trespassing employee).

Damage

Normally the statute will be interpreted as conferring a right of action on the plaintiff only when he has sustained actual damage. But *Ashby* v. *White* (1703) shows that a statute confer a right of action even without proof of actual damage (interference with the plaintiff's right to vote was actionable *per se*). The plaintiff must show that the damage he suffered was that against which the statutory duty was intended to guard and also that it was not too remote a result of the breach of statutory duty. These requirements must be examined in turn.

(1) *The harm suffered by the plaintiff must be that contemplated by the statute*

In *Gorris* v. *Scott* (1874) the defendant, who was transporting the plaintiff's sheep on his ship, infringed a statutory order under which animals on board ship were to be divided into pens. The sheep were washed overboard and drowned and it was found that this would not have occurred had they been penned. The plaintiff's action for breach of statutory duty failed because the purpose of the statute was to prevent the spread of disease rather than to prevent the loss of animals in the manner that occurred. It is necessary to distinguish the rule in *Gorris* v. *Scott* from the rules relating to remoteness of damage, since the loss the plaintiff suffered in that case was clearly a foreseeable result of the defendant's breach of duty. This was recognised by the House of Lords in *Close* v. *Steel Co. of Wales Ltd.* (1962). An injury to the plaintiff through fragments of a shattered drill being flung against him would have been avoided but for the defendants' breach of statutory duty in failing to fence the drill. The House of Lords held that, even had the injury been foreseeable, the plaintiff would not have recovered because the purpose of the statute was to prevent the machine operator's body coming into contact with the machine, rather than to prevent the risk of fragments being flung out. These cases emphasise a judicial tendency to confine breach of statutory duty within narrow limits. A different approach arose in *Donaghey* v. *Boulton & Paul* (1968) (plaintiff's fall through hole in roof which would have been avoided by the provision of crawling boards which defendants in breach of statutory duty failed to supply was actionable though chief purpose of crawling boards was to prevent falls through fragile material in the roof).

(2) *That the damage was not too remote*

The onus of showing that the damage was not too remote a result of the breach rests on the plaintiff (*Bonnington Castings Ltd.* v. *Wardlaw* (1956)). The normal rule of remoteness of damage applies to this tort so that the harm the plaintiff suffers must be a foreseeable consequence of the breach of duty. In *Millard* v. *Serck Tubes* (1969) the plaintiff's arm was caught in a machine which the defendants had in breach of statutory duty failed to fence. Although the way in which the plaintiff's arm became caught was unforeseeable, the defendants were held liable to him in breach of statutory duty. The result of the case would undoubtedly have been the same had the action been one for common law negligence. Where the precise harm against which the duty was intended to provide a safeguard occurs, the defendant cannot successfully argue that it occurred in an unforeseeable way (*cf. Hughes* v. *Lord Advocate* (1963), *supra*, p. 107). The principle has been pushed a little further in cases in which the plaintiff's injuries have been held not too remote a result of the breach although the way in which he received them is unexplained (*Thurogood* v. *Van Den Berghs and Jurgens* (1951); *Allen* v. *Aeroplane and Motor Aluminium Castings* (1965), discussed *supra*, p. 141).

The plaintiff must also establish causal connection between his injury and the breach (*McWilliams* v. *Arrol & Co.* (1962) in which it was held that a failure to provide safety belts in breach of statutory duty was not actionable because there was evidence that the general practice of workmen on the site was not to wear the belts and the plaintiff could not show on the balance of probabilities that he would have been an exception.

Defences to the action

Volenti non fit injuria

For reasons of public policy this defence is not available to an employer in suits against him by his workmen, since he should not be able to escape from his statutory obligations by obtaining his workman's consent. The defence is, however, available where the employer is being sued on the ground of his vicarious liability for a breach of statutory duty imposed upon and committed by his workman, provided that the workman who commits the breach is not of superior rank to and in receipt of habitual obedience from the plaintiff (*I.C.I.* v. *Shatwell* (1965)—two workmen ignored statutory safety regulations imposed upon themselves and one was injured in consequence—held that *volenti* was a defence).

There may be policy reasons for making the defence unavailable in cases other than employer and workman but there is no authority on this point.

Contributory negligence

This defence is clearly available. Special rules relating to the defence in relation to breach of statutory duty have already been discussed (*supra*, p. 128).

Statutory duty delegated to or also laid upon the plaintiff

Where the performance of the employer's statutory duty has been delegated to the plaintiff workman, and he has failed to discharge it, with the result that he has suffered injury, a difficult causal problem arises as to whether the employer is liable. On the one hand, the employer is clearly in breach of his duty, because the statutory duty is non-delegable. On the other, a person ought not to recover damages for something that is entirely his fault. In *Ross* v. *Associated Portland Cement Manufacturers Ltd.* (1964) the House of Lords attempted to solve the question whether delegation of the defendant's duty to the plaintiff was sufficient without more to enable the court to say that the plaintiff was entirely responsible for his own injuries. The employers in that case were held liable for two-thirds of the plaintiff's injuries, because they had delegated to him their statutory duty of making safe his work fence without giving him proper instructions, and he was not qualified to perform this task. The employer's fault thus was different from and went beyond that of the plaintiff in failing to make safe the work-place.

Where, however, the employer's breach of statutory duty is purely the result of the action of the plaintiff workman, no action will lie against the employer because the workman was the sole cause of his own injuries. This will be the case *a fortiori* where the statutory duty is also laid on the workman himself. Thus, in *Ginty* v. *Belmont Building Supplies Ltd.* (1959), the plaintiff failed to use a crawling-board while working on a roof, in breach of statutory regulations binding upon himself and his employers. He was injured as a result. His action for breach of statutory duty against his employers failed because he was unable to show that they had committed any breach of the statutory regulations other than that committed by himself.

The House of Lords in *Boyle* v. *Kodak* (1969) has now held that the employer's duty to instruct a workman about the steps to be taken to avoid the commission of a breach of statutory duty binding on that workman applies whenever there is a risk that the workman will not be sufficiently familiar with the regulations imposing such a duty, and even if there was no foreseeable danger as a result of any breach. It is clear, therefore, that the doctrine whereby the employer may be found liable for a breach of statutory duty where his fault is not co-extensive with that of the servant reaches beyond the case where such fault would give rise to an action for common law negligence (in the *Boyle* case, the result was an apportionment of damages between the employer and the injured plaintiff who was also at fault in not performing the statutory duty).

Extent and importance of breach of statutory duty

Statistically the tort is of very great importance today because of the large number of actions brought by workmen for breach by their employers of industrial safety legislation. Although in most of these cases the action for breach of statutory duty is duplicated by that for negligence, it has an independent importance since the statutory duty forms a particularisation of the standard of reasonable conduct expected of the employer and relieves the workman from having to prove a failure to comply with this standard. Physical safety is not, however, the only interest protected by the tort. Examples of the diverse interests that are protected are: the right to vote at a general election (*Ashby* v. *White* (1704)); the right of a shareholder to sue the company for breach of the statutory contract in the articles of the company (*Pender* v. *Lushington* (1877)); the right to compel the town clerk at the end of his term of office to hand over his accounts and books to his employers (*Lichfield Corporation* v. *Simpson* (1845)); the right of an occupier of premises who has been evicted by the owner to sue the owner for breach of section 32 (1) of the Rent Act 1965, which in certain circumstances requires the owner to take proceedings in court for the purpose of eviction (*Warder* v. *Cooper* (1970)).

Chapter 20

VICARIOUS LIABILITY

This term used in connection with the law of tort refers to the situation where one person is liable for the commission of a tort by another. The outstanding case in English law is the liability of a master for the torts of his servant committed in the course of the latter's employment. Liability for the acts of an independent contractor is based upon the breach of a personal, non-delegable duty of the employer rather than on vicarious liability.

The relationship of principal and agent is, generally speaking, irrelevant for determining questions of vicarious liability for tort. The agent is employed to bring his principal into contractual relation with third parties. He may be either a servant or independent contractor (according to principles discussed below), and upon this will turn the question of the principal's liability for the torts he commits. In one case, however, the status of agent is relevant to determining the existence of vicarious liability in tort. If the agent, by making a fraudulent misrepresentation (thus committing the tort of deceit), induces the making of a contract with the principal by a third party, the principal is liable in deceit provided the agent acted within the scope of his apparent authority. No doubt the explanation of this case is the close approximation of the liability in deceit to liability in contract (see also, *infra* pp. 229–230 for a special type of agency in tort).

Vicarious Liability in the Case of Master and Servant

Rationale

It is now recognised that the reason for imposing liability upon the master for the torts of his servant committed in the course of his employment is one of policy. Vicarious liability achieves the dual purpose of providing a financially responsible person as defendant and of providing the master with an inducement to institute maximum standards of safety within the enterprise. At the same time the limitation that the tort must have been committed during the course of the servant's employment shows that this is a form of enterprise liability, rather than that the master is an insurer of the servant's wrongdoing.

Who is a servant?

Several tests have been propounded by courts for deciding this question. But it seems that these tests are for the guidance of the court rather than principles of law, and that each case must be resolved on its own special facts. No one test has paramountcy over another and where they produce a different result, the court must make up its mind on the evidence and on its overall impression. One test that was at one time regarded almost as conclusive was whether the employer could determine the way in which the work was to be done, the test of control. With the increase in technical knowledge and skill, this test has become a great deal less useful, since in practice the employer will let the servant alone in his performance of tasks demanding such knowledge. If it is argued that the employer must be able to control the overall manner in which the work is done, this element would seem to be present also in the case of work done by independent contractors. Other factors which will enter the court's consideration are the method of payment (for example, wages or a lump sum) and who supplies tools, premises, equipment. An alternative test put forward by Lord Denning in 1952 has won some acceptance today. He contrasted the servant who is normally employed as an integral part of his employer's business (giving as examples the ship's master, the chauffeur, and the newspaper reporter) with the independent contractor whose services are accessory to the business (examples being the ship's pilot, the taxi-driver, and the freelance contributor). The two tests of control and integration may produce different results. Thus in *Morren* v. *Swinton and Pendlebury U.D.C.* (1965) an engineer employed by a local authority was held to be its servant though subject to no control by it in relation to the carrying out of his work, on the ground that the terms of his contract made him sufficiently integrated into the business of the authority. On the other hand, in *Market Investigations* v. *Minister of Social Security* (1969), a woman interviewer, employed by the plaintiffs, who was subject to exact control as to the method of conducting interviews, was held to be the plaintiffs' servant, though it seems doubtful whether she was sufficiently integrated into the employer's business to satisfy the integration test. In *Ready-Mixed Concrete Co.* v. *Minister of Pensions and National Insurance* (1968) it was stated that there must be sufficient control by the employer, and there must be no provisions in the contract inconsistent with service in order to establish a contract of service. However, it is not clear why control should be essential nor why the existence of certain terms pointing away from service should always outweigh a greater number of terms pointing towards it. The correct test of service seems to be whether a preponderance of the terms of the contract point towards it. Some may do this by establishing control, others integration, and others, such as the power of appointment and dismissal, may point to service though they establish neither control nor integration.

Cases on borrowed servants typify the problems of complicated factual analysis which have to be faced by courts. The servant may be so completely "taken over" that, at least as far as the doctrine of vicarious liability is concerned, he becomes the servant of the borrower; otherwise he will merely be his independant contractor (contractually speaking, however, he will remain throughout the servant of his original master). In *Mersey Docks and Harbour Board* v. *Coggins and Griffiths Ltd.* (1947), a crane driver employed by the Board had been hired together with his crane to another company and while with that company had by his negligence injured the plaintiff. The crane driver was held to be still a servant of the Board because of the following factors: he continued to be paid by the Board which alone had power to dismiss him; the borrower could give him directions as to the work to be done but could not instruct him in the operation of the crane. These factors outweighed the fact that the contract of hire provided that the crane driver should become the servant of the hirers, since this, as far as vicarious liability was concerned was for judicial rather than contractual determination. Other factors which may affect the decision are whether the servant lent is technically skilled (since the service of an unskilled servant is more easily transferred), and whether the servant is lent for a specific task or for the general purposes of the transferee.

Employer's personal duty

Little remains, nowadays, of the former theory of vicarious liability under which the master was liable because he had committed through his servant a breach of a duty personal to himself, although it is true that some of the older cases seem to support it (*e.g. Broom* v. *Morgan* (1953); *Conway* v. *Wimpey* (1951); *Smith* v. *Moss* (1940)). It cannot meet the insuperable difficulty that if it were correct it would not matter whether the failure to discharge the duty was through the default of a servant or independent contractor, whereas there are numerous cases in which liability exists for the acts of a servant but not an independent contractor. The correct basis for vicarious liability is therefore that the master is liable for torts committed *by the servant* in the course of his employment. This is not to say that in no case can the employer be held liable for the breach by another person of a duty personal to the employer. In fact, this is the basis for the employer's liability for the acts of an independent contractor. Where such a personal duty exists, it may help to solve difficult questions as to whether there is vicarious liability for the acts of a servant. In cases of medical negligence in the course of hospital treatment, for example, doubts may exist whether the particular person negligent is a servant of the hospital. Thus although radiographers (*Gold* v. *Essex County Council* (1942)), house-surgeons (*Collins* v. *Hertfordshire County Council* (1947)), whole-time assistant medical officers (*Cassidy* v. *Ministry of Health* (1951)) and anaesthetists (*Roe* v. *Minister of Health* (1954)) have been held to be servants of the hospital, a doubt remains about the National Health Service. An alternative approach adopted by the courts is to hold the hospital liable for breach of its own duty of care to provide proper treatment (*cf. Cassidy's* case). On this approach, it matters not whether the particular person negligent is a servant or an independent contractor.

Another example of the concept of a personal duty binding the employer easing a problem as to whether vicarious liability exists is the case of *Morris* v. *Martin* (1966). The defendants had accepted the plaintiff's mink coat for cleaning. They handed the coat to their servant to be cleaned and the servant stole it. Difficulties exist as to whether theft by a servant can be regarded as being done in the course of his employment (in fact this question was answered in the affirmative, *infra*, p. 226). The defendants were, nevertheless, held liable because they were in breach of their personal duty as bailees of the coat to look after it.

A final point needs clarification. The "servant's tort" theory of vicarious liability does not require that the plaintiff must identify the tortfeasor, provided it is clear that the tort must have been committed by one of the defendant's servants acting in the course of his employment (*cf. Grant* v. *Australian Knitting Mills* (1936)). If it is shown that the tortfeasor must have been one of a number of servants or independent contractors employed by the defendant, liability will exist only if there is a personal duty on the defendant.

Course of employment

The limitation has been established that the tort must be committed during the course of the servant's employment, and this requirement must now be examined. It may be noted that many of the decisions on whether a servant has acted in the course of his employment turn on questions of degree rather than logic. The present century has seen an extension of the limits within which the servant is recognised as acting in the course of his employment.

Substantive limits and duration of employment

The servant must be doing the work he has been employed to do.

In *Rand* v. *Craig* (1919) the defendant employed servants to carry rubbish and deposit it in a named place. Instead they deposited it on the plaintiff's land. The defendant was held not liable to the plaintiff since the servants were acting outside the course of their employment. Here the area of employment was defined by the employer's express instructions. Similarly if the servant goes on a "frolic of his own" during his working hours he will be acting outside the course of his employment. By this term is meant some action of the servant which is so totally unrelated to the work the servant is employed to do that it cannot be understood to be a part of it. Whether the servant is on such a frolic often turns on questions of degree.

If the servant is performing work that he is employed to do in an improper way, he will be acting within the course of his employment. In *Century Insurance Co. Ltd.* v. *Northern Ireland Road Transport Board* (1942) the House of Lords held that a lorry driver who caused a fire by striking a match to light a cigarette while transferring petrol from his lorry to an underground tank in the plaintiff's garage was acting in the course of his employment because he was doing in an unauthorised way that which he was employed to do. The distinction between doing an act which is no part of the servant's employment and doing authorised work in an improper manner is also relevant where the act in question has been specifically prohibited by the master. If the prohibition is regarded as delimiting the scope of the servant's employment, the prohibited act will be outside the course of employment. If what is prohibited is an improper method of carrying out the servant's authorised tasks, it will be within the course of employment (so in *Limpus* v. *London General Omnibus Co.* (1862) the defendants' bus driver who raced his bus with another belonging to a rival company despite the fact that the defendants had expressly warned their drivers not to race, was held to be acting within the course of his employment). The question of the effect of prohibitions on the servant's conduct causes difficulty in the case of the servant who gives unauthorised lifts to third parties in his employer's vehicle. If such a person is injured by the negligence of the employer, courts have based the non-liability of the employer on the fact that the servant was not acting in the course of his employment (*Twine* v. *Bean's Express* (1946); *Conway* v. *Wimpey* (1951) in which it was also explained by reason of the plaintiff's status as a trespasser on the vehicle). In *Rose* v. *Plenty* (1975) a milk roundsman had, contrary to the instructions of his employer, made use of the services of the plaintiff, a thirteen-year-old boy, for the purpose of assisting him in delivering milk. The plaintiff was injured by the negligent driving of the float by the roundsman. The Court of

Appeal by a majority held the employer of the milk roundsman vicariously liable for his negligence to the plaintiff. All three members of the Court of Appeal treated the question as turning on whether the roundsman was acting in the course of his employment —the plaintiff's status as a trespasser on the float did not affect the duties owed to him by the servant and the vicarious liability of the employer depended upon whether the servant and not the employer had committed a tort. The majority were able to distinguish the earlier cases on the ground that in them the plaintiffs were receiving gratuitous lifts whereas here the plaintiff was being used for the purpose of the employer's business. Although the case seems rightly decided, the distinction it draws is not very satisfactory. In the earlier cases, it is not clear why the employer's prohibition is regarded as delimiting the sphere of the servant's employment, since apart from the prohibited act, the servant was carrying out his duties in a normal fashion (see also *Iqbal* v. *London Transport Executive* (1974)—a bus conductor who was prohibited from driving the bus was acting outside the course of his employment when he drove it; *Stone* v. *Taffe* (1975)—a public house manager in giving an unauthorised after-hours party in the public house was not acting outside the course of his employment).

In some cases difficulty has arisen because the servant has performed some act which is not part of the servant's normal employment, but which by implication may be within the scope of his employment. Thus a servant may have an implied authority to defend his master's property, using physical force if necessary. If such a servant uses an unreasonable amount of force against one whom he reasonably suspects to be stealing from his master (so being deprived of the defence of defence of property), his master will be liable for the servant's act which is merely a wrongful way of performing something within the scope of the servant's employment (*Poland and Sons* v. *Parr* (1972)). On the other hand a servant, though he may have an implied authority to detain one whom he suspects to be obtaining his master's goods without paying for them, has no authority to do this when such payment has been made. So in *Warren* v. *Henley's Ltd.* the servant, a garage attendant, accused the plaintiff of attempting to leave without paying for petrol supplied to him. Later, after the plaintiff had paid, the servant assaulted him. The garage was held not liable because the servant had not acted in the course of his employment (for a recent illustration, see *Keppel Bus Co.* v. *Sa'ad Bin Ahmad* (1974)).

In order to be acting within the course of his employment, the servant must commit the tort during his actual hours of employment. For example, a servant who returned to his work without his master's permission after the premises had been closed would not be acting within the course of his employment. But a reasonable extension to normal working hours will be recognised by the courts as not outside the course of employment, for example, the servant who stays for a short time in order to finish a job, or one who leaves taps running in a washroom which he visits after completing his working day, so damaging the plaintiff's property (see *Ruddiman & Co.* v. *Smith* (1889)).

Criminal conduct by servant

The problem here is whether the servant who commits a crime or acts dishonestly entirely for his own benefit is acting within the course of his employment. The mere fact that the servant has committed a crime is clearly not enough to take his act outside the course of his employment—thus, the commission by a servant of a breach of statutory duty while performing his authorised work would be inside the scope of his employment. Even where the servant has acted for his own benefit the master may be held liable. Whether the servant's act will be regarded as within the course of his employment will depend upon whether it can be regarded as a wrongful performance of the work which the servant is employed to do. Thus in *Morris* v. *Martin* (1966), the master was held liable for the theft of the mink coat by the servant to whom it had been entrusted for cleaning (for this explanation of the decision based upon conventional principles of vicarious liability, see the judgment of Diplock L.J.). The Court of Appeal was in agreement that if the theft had been by a servant who had no duties in relation to the coat, the master would not have been liable. In *Lloyd* v. *Grace, Smith & Co.* (1912) the master, a firm of solicitors, was held liable for the fraud of its conveyancing clerk who had induced the plaintiff to convey two cottages, which she wished to sell, to him, representing that this was necessary for their sale. This was clearly a wrongful performance of the work the clerk was employed to do. Furthermore, the plaintiff was justified in relying on the representation of the clerk since by employing him as a conveyancing clerk the defendants had invested him with apparent authority to make representations of that sort.

Acts simultaneously inside and outside course of employment

Although there are only *obiter dicta* in support, it seems correct to say that the servant may be acting inside the course of his employment *vis-à-vis* one person, and outside it *vis-à-vis* another. In *Twine* v. *Bean's Express Ltd.* (1946) the defendants' servant, the driver of a vehicle belonging to the defendants, had given a lift to the plaintiff contrary to the defendants' instructions, and by his negligent driving of the vehicle had caused him injury. The employers were held not liable to the plaintiff because the servant's act was wholly outside the course of the servant's employment, rather than an improper means of carrying it out. But Lord Greene M.R. expressed the view that as far as persons other than the plaintiff were concerned the driving of the van was inside the course of employment, so that had they been injured by the negligent driving they would have had an action against the employer. This view appears sound in principle.

Liability for the Acts of an Independent Contractor

The liability of one who has employed a contractor to do work may be personal under the ordinary rules of tort, rather than vicarious. So, he may have instructed or authorised the contractor to commit a tort, or by his negligent instructions may have contributed to the contractor's commission of a tort, or he may have committed a tort of strict liability through the contractor (as in *Rylands* v. *Fletcher* (1868)). In certain cases there may be liability for the negligence of a contractor although the employer is not personally at fault and no tort of strict liability has been committed. Such liability has been based by English courts on a breach by the employer of a non-delegable duty of care binding on himself. Liability is therefore still personal rather than a vicarious liability for the contractor's negligence. This formulation is misleading in so far as it suggests that liability is other than strict.

Non-delegable duties

The cases in which a duty of care has been held to be non-delegable to an independent contractor are of a somewhat miscellaneous nature, and the policy reasons for their existence are various. In the first place an employer who orders the performance of extra-hazardous activities by the contractor will be liable for the contractor's negligence in carrying out these activities. The outstanding example is *Honeywill and Stein* v. *Larkin Brothers Ltd.* (1934) in which the defendants who had employed a contractor to take flash-light photographs of the interior of a cinema were held liable when the negligence of the contractor caused a fire to start in the cinema.

The notion of the extra-hazardous activity is probably also the explanation for the fact that there is liability for the negligent operations of a contractor employed to work on a highway. It remained in doubt until recently whether there was liability for work done by the contractor near the highway. This doubt was removed by *Salsbury* v. *Woodland* (1970) which held the employer not liable for the contractor's negligence. The case also held that the felling of a tree near a highway did not come within the category of extra-hazardous activities. Such work will normally involve some hazards to the public. *Holliday* v. *National Telephone Co.* (1899) is an example of employer's liability for contractor's work done on the highway. The contractor, a plumber, was engaged by the defendants to solder tubes through which the defendant's telephone wires were passed. He carried out this work negligently, using a defective benzolene lamp which exploded and scattered molten solder over the plaintiff, a passing pedestrian. The defendants were held liable for the contractor's negligence. Section 1 (3) of the Highways (Miscellaneous Provisions) Act 1961 provides that in an action for non-repair of highways or bridges it shall not be relevant to prove that the highway authority had arranged for a competent contractor to carry out or supervise the maintenance of the (highway) unless it is also proved that the authority had given proper instructions with regard to the maintenance of the highway and that he had carried out these instructions. The effect of this appears to be that the common law rule is extended to include the duties of highway authorities under this Act.

In the case of nuisance, even when liability for the nuisance is not strict, there may be liability for the negligence of a contractor in creating the nuisance, provided the work undertaken by the contractor involved a particular risk of the creation of a nuisance (*Matania* v. *National Provincial Bank Ltd.* (1936)). The employer's duty to provide proper plant, premises and staff, is not delegable to a contractor. This may be explained both for the reason that failure to perform the duty may cause serious injury, and also because the employer as a financially responsible person is able to absorb the losses he suffers by way of payment of damages. This dual explanation is also put forward for the argument that a hospital is under a non-delegable duty to provide proper treatment for its patients. But it is not yet certain that this represents the law though there are dicta in several of the cases on the liability of hospitals to support it. If this were the law, it would be unnecessary to determine the often exacting question (*supra*, p. 223) whether the particular negligent person was a servant of the hospital or an independent contractor. Nor would it matter if it was impossible to identify the particular servant or contractor who had been negligent provided it was clear that negligent treatment had been administered. Finally it may be noted that many statutory duties (*e.g.* the duty to fence dangerous machinery) are non-delegable, although in such a case, the duty being a strict one, liability will exist whether or not the contractor is negligent.

Collateral negligence by contractor

If the contractor is negligent in some matter which is an integral part of the task which has been entrusted to him, the employer is liable (assuming that on the above principles liability for the contractor's negligence exists). If, however, the negligence consists in some collateral act, not a necessary part of the contractor's function, the employer is not liable for such negligence. In *Padbury* v. *Holliday and Greenwood Ltd.* (1912) the servant of a contractor who had been employed to fit casements into windows negligently left a hammer lying on the window sill. The hammer was knocked down by the casement being blown open by the wind and the plaintiff passing by on the highway below was struck and injured by it. The employer was held not liable for the negligence of the contractor's servant because the placing of the hammer on the sill was not a necessary part of fitting the window. The case seems to turn on the fact that the negligence of the workman was collateral to his carrying out his duties, rather than that the plaintiff's injury occurred through a risk collateral to the risk created by the work commissioned (*i.e.* the danger to the highway. *Holliday* v. *National Telephone Co.*, *supra*, is an example of negligence which was not collateral to the task being performed. Since the justification for imposing a duty upon the employer of an independent contractor is that the work which the contractor is employed to do creates a risk to the public, it is suggested that the employer should be liable if that risk materialises, and that, therefore, *Padbury's* case is wrongly decided).

Liability of Car Owners

It has been established for some time that a car-owner who has delegated the driving of a car to another person while remaining a passenger in the car is liable for the negligence of the driver, on the ground that he has retained control over the vehicle. This is personal rather than vicarious liability. In *Ormrod* v. *Crosville Motor Services Ltd.* (1953) an extension to this rule was recognised, when the owner of a car which was being driven from London to Monte Carlo at the owner's request and for his benefit but in which he was not himself travelling was held liable for the driver's negligence. The ratio of the case is that where the driving is done at the request of the owner and for his purposes, the driver is the owner's agent, and the owner is vicariously liable for his negligence.

A recent case, *Launchbury v. Morgans* (1971) concerned the liability of the owner of a car whose husband borrowed it daily for work. She knew that the husband occasionally stopped out late for a drink, and acquiesced in this, provided he got someone else to drive him home if he was unfit to drive. After one such evening, the husband was killed and the plaintiffs, passengers in the car, were injured through the negligence of the husband's friend who was driving the car for the husband. In the Court of Appeal, the wife was held vicariously liable for the negligence of the friend on the ground that the car was being driven for her purposes, either on the ground that it was in the wife's interest that the husband should be driven home safely, or that in the case of a "matrimonial" car almost any journey undertaken by either spouse in it has a joint matrimonial purpose. The House of Lords refused to accept either argument. The fact that the wife had an interest in the driving did not mean that it was done for her purposes. Furthermore, the innovation of the "matrimonial" or "family" car was one for the legislature rather than the courts to make. The decision had unfortunate practical consequences for the plaintiffs since it meant that they could not recover from the wife's insurers. Now that insurance against liability to passengers in a motor vehicle is compulsory, the wife herself could be sued in similar circumstances for breach of statutory duty for permitting the car to be driven without insurance cover. More importantly, the plaintiffs would have an action against the Motor Insurers Bureau which by agreement among insurance companies pays out in cases where insurance against third party liability is compulsory but insurance cover does not exist (but only in cases of personal injury. It may therefore still be important to establish that the driver was driving the car as agent of the wife where the third party suffers damage to his property). The House of Lords did not disapprove of *Ormrod* v. *Crosville Motor Services* and presumably the doctrine laid down by that case survives intact. Some of the other cases in which owners have been held liable for the negligence of those whom they have permitted to drive their cars must, however, be of dubious authority in the light of the judgments in the House of Lords (*cf.* especially, *Parker* v. *Miller* (1926); *Carberry* v. *Davies* (1968)).

CHAPTER 21

DEFAMATION

INTRODUCTION

THE tort of defamation protects a person's interest in his reputation. Thus, if the defendant has made an untrue statement, or what amounts to a statement, which is defamatory of the plaintiff, the plaintiff has a right of action against him unless the defendant can establish one of the special defences available to an action for defamation. It is important to note that the tort protects the plaintiff's reputation as it appears to other people. This means that publication of the statement by the defendant to persons other than the plaintiff himself is an essential part of the tort—the purpose of the tort is not to protect the injured feelings of the plaintiff (on the other hand it appears to be accepted that there is defamation if the statement is made to a person who disbelieves it—see, for example, Lord Reid in *Morgan* v. *Odhams Press* (1971), the justification for this being, according to Lord Reid, the annoyance caused to the plaintiff). The tort goes beyond protecting the mere personal reputation of the plaintiff and extends to the protection of the reputation of his commercial and business undertakings.

The rules of the tort represent an attempt to strike a balance between two important and often competing interests, the public interest in freedom of speech (which is often a private interest also), and the private interest in maintaining one's reputation. The difficulty of achieving this balance is perhaps indicated by the fact that, though liability for a defamatory statement is strict and substantial damages may be recovered from one who makes such a statement, a large variety of defences exist for the protection of one who makes such a statement. It is also the case that many of the rules of the tort, though reasonably well settled as matters of law, are notoriously uncertain in their practical application. This again supports the idea of the law treading a knife-edge between two conflicting interests.

The recovery of substantial damages for a defamatory statement, especially from one who is ignorant of the defamatory nature of the statement, has led to criticism in recent years. Certain statutory defences (*infra*, pp. 241, 242) mitigate the hardship of this in the case of innocent defamation by allowing the defamer to escape liability by making, for example, an offer of amends to the plaintiff. The inequity of allowing the recovery of substantial damages by one who has suffered a mere injury to reputation remains. It is true that the remedy of damages is necessary as a deterrent to the calculated use of defamatory statements as a means of selling newspapers and periodicals. But the amount of damages recovered for defamation seems often disproportionate to the actual effect in financial terms the statement may have.

Slander and Libel

Defamation comprises two torts, slander and libel. The distinction was formerly of purely procedural effect, slander being actionable in the common law courts while libel was purely within the jurisdiction of the Star Chamber. After the common law courts succeeded to the jurisdiction of the Star Chamber over libel, the distinction was maintained and unfortunately acquired substantive force. Broadly speaking, it can now be said that slander is committed by one who publishes the defamatory statement orally, libel by one who publishes it in writing. The effect of the distinction is that in the case of slander proof of special damage is, with four exceptions, an essential part of the plaintiff's cause of action; libel is on the other hand actionable *per se*. The distinction receives some justification from the greater triviality and lesser potentiality for doing harm of spoken rather than written words. But it still seems unfortunate for several reasons. In the case of slander which is not actionable *per se*, the plaintiff often has no means at all of vindicating his reputation. The distinction can also be criticised both for the difficulties that arise in drawing it and for its arbitrary nature. The line between slander and libel may be drawn on the technical ground that slander has its impact on the aural sense, libel on the visual. Thus libel would include defamatory pictures, statues, and conduct such as hanging the plaintiff in effigy. This distinction becomes increasingly arbitrary with the development of methods of communication which, though operating through the ear, are clearly as potent in the spreading of defamatory material as the written word, the most obvious examples being films, radio and television, and gramophone records. If, on the other hand, a purely technical test is replaced by one which attempts to draw the line between slander and libel on the ground that libel is a more serious form of defamation than slander, there is again difficulty in deciding what such a test should be and how it is reconcilable with the English cases. One possibility is that slander refers to a transient statement, libel to one with some degree of permanence. Another is that for the statement to amount to libel it should have considerable potential for doing harm to reputation. Both these tests have obvious difficulties in their application.

The only English case which suggests that the test is anything other than a mechanical one depending upon the mode of publication of the statement is *Forrester* v. *Tyrrell* (1893) in which it was held that reading out a defamatory written statement is libel. It is weak authority for a test of permanency, but does not distinguish according to whether the listener to the statement realises that a written statement is being read. It is contradicted by *Osborn* v. *Boulter and Son* (1930) in which two members of the Court of Appeal thought that the dictation of a letter to a typist and the reading out of the letter aloud after dictation amount to slander alone (although the person dictating is liable in libel if the letter is subsequently published by his authority). In *Youssoupoff* v. *Metro-Goldwyn-Mayer Pictures Ltd.* (1934) it was held that a film which suggested as a matter of historical fact that the plaintiff had at one time been raped was libellous, but as the defamatory meaning was conveyed by a combination of pictorial representations and sound, the case is no support for the view that a defamatory anecdote told in a film is libel. Defamatory statements made in broadcasts whether through radio or television are, under the Defamation Act 1952, to be treated as published in permanent form by which it appears to be meant that they are libel. So, under the Theatre Act, 1968 are statements in theatrical performances. However, the uncertainty about other media such as films, gramophone records, and recorded tapes, as well as statements made through trained parrots and skywriting, remains. The abolition of the requirement of special damage in slander would appear to be the easiest way of removing these difficulties. Frivolous actions in respect of defamatory spoken statements could be dealt with as in libel by an award of nominal damages to the plaintiff and a refusal to allow him costs.

Slander actionable per se

In four cases the plaintiff does not have to prove special damage as part of his cause of action in slander:

(1) *Imputation of crime*

It is slander actionable *per se* to impute to the plaintiff the commission of a crime for which he may suffer or have suffered imprisonment.

(2) *Imputation of disease*

The disease imputed must be infectious or contagious and the imputation must be that the plaintiff is presently suffering from it.

(3) *Imputation in respect of office, profession, calling, trade or business*

At common law an imputation that a schoolteacher had committed adultery with a school cleaner was not actionable *per se* under this rubric—it reflected discredit on the schoolteacher as a man rather than on the man as a schoolteacher. But section 2 of the Defamation Act 1952 makes it slander actionable *per se* where the words are calculated to disparage the plaintiff in his office, profession, calling, trade or business, though not spoken of him in the way of such office, profession, calling, trade or business.

(4) *Imputation of unchastity to a woman under Slander of Women Act 1891*

Such imputation includes one of lesbianism (*Kerr* v. *Kennedy* (1942)).

Special damage in slander not actionable per se

Material loss such as loss of employment, loss of contracts through refusal by persons to contract with the plaintiff and loss of hospitality from friends proved to have provided food and drink on former occasions is special damage for the purpose of the tort. Nervous shock and illness arising from mental distress do not appear to be recoverable in slander, although the rule in libel is different, and no satisfactory explanation appears to exist for this difference.

Where the damage is suffered because of a third party's action, this may make it too remote (*Lynch* v. *Knight* (1861)—damage too remote where husband made wife leave home when he heard she had almost been seduced before marriage). But the third party's action must be unforeseeable; for this reason the rule that damage caused by repetition of the slander is too remote is questionable (*Ward* v. *Weeks* (1830)). There is certainly liability when the repetition is performed in the course of a legal or moral duty, or where the defendant intends the repetition.

Principles of Defamation

It now remains to consider those principles which are applicable to both libel and slander. In order to establish the defendant's liability in defamation, the plaintiff must show that the defendant has published a statement about him which is defamatory.

Defamatory nature of the statement

The requirement that the statement should bring the plaintiff into hatred, contempt or ridicule, formerly the accepted definition of a defamatory statement, is now recognised to be inadequate in the light of decisions that to impute to the plaintiff that she has been raped (*Youssoupoff's* case, *supra*, p. 233) or is insane is defamatory. The test that the statement should lower the plaintiff in the esteem of right-thinking men also fails to explain these cases. These tests fail to appreciate that the reaction of society as a whole to the statement may be irrational and emotional and may make people inclined to shun the plaintiff when what is imputed to him is a misfortune rather than a misdeed. Thus to say of the plaintiff that he is illegitimate, impotent or has cancer is almost certainly defamatory.

Another problem arises where the statement is calculated to bring the plaintiff into disfavour with a certain section of the community which is not an ordinary cross-section of the community and whose reaction to the statement is questionably right-thinking. Although there is little English authority on the point it has been held that to call a person a German in time of war with Germany is defamatory; it also seems likely that it is defamatory to call a person a Communist. These problems become more intractable when the statement imputes something to the plaintiff upon which there are deep divisions within the country. Is it defamatory to say that a worker is a non-unionist, or has worked during a strike, or that a student is a demonstrator? The answer to each question is, it is submitted, yes, on the ground that the statement is calculated to bring the plaintiff into disfavour with a sufficiently sizeable section of the community. This must receive some qualification, however, in the light of the decision of the Court of Appeal in *Byrne* v. *Deane* (1937). In that case it was held that it was not defamatory to say of a member of a club that he had supplied the police with information about an illegal gaming machine kept at the club, because a person who supplies such information ought not to be less well-thought of by his fellows. There seems no reason of policy behind this decision, since a court's decision that the statement was defamatory would not mean that the court condoned the offence. The court's preference for the ideal rather than the actual attitudes of the club members may therefore be questioned. The result of the case seems to be that where the court classifies the attitude of the section of the public concerned as anti-social or perverse it will not hold the statement defamatory.

Circumstances of time, place and occasion will often be relevant in determining whether a statement has a defamatory content. Thus it is only defamatory to say of a person that he is a German if a state of war prevails between Germany and this country. The relevance of occasion explains why mere vulgar abuse spoken in the course of quarrelling is normally not defamatory. To call another a bastard in the course of a skirmish would not be defamatory, since the listeners would understand that the statement was not intended to contain any substratum of fact. But if the statement was intended to convey that a factual basis existed for the statement, or if its listener would reasonably interpret it in this way, then the statement would be defamatory even if uttered as abuse. Thus to call a man a pansy or a turncoat might be actionable.

Statements imputing incompetence to the plaintiff in his trade or profession are actionable in the same way as attacks upon his character. Thus to suggest that the goods manufactured by the plaintiff are of inferior quality or that a film critic is an incompetent member of his profession is undoubtedly defamatory. Equally it is possible for a trading association such as a company to sue in defamation (*South Hetton Coal Co.* v. *North Eastern News Association* (1894)). It has also been held that a trade union (*Willis* v. *Brooks* (1947)), and a local authority (*Bognor Regis U.D.C.* v. *Campion* 1972)) can be defamed. It may be noted that dead persons cannot be defamed.

In order that a statement be defamatory it must be untrue, but not every untrue statement is defamatory. To say that the plaintiff has ceased to be in business is not defamatory since this can have no damaging effect upon the plaintiff's reputation (*Ratcliffe* v. *Evans* (1892)). If such a statement is made maliciously and if it causes the plaintiff actual damage, the plaintiff has another cause of action against the defendant (*infra*, p. 279).

Interpretation of defamatory statements: Innuendo

The test to be applied is whether the words of the defendant in their ordinary and natural sense defame the plaintiff. The whole of the defendant's statement must be looked at, not merely that which the plaintiff relies on as being defamatory. This is important because what follows an *ex facie* defamatory statement may qualify or explain it (as in, "Lord X, you are a thief. You have stolen my heart"). Where the plaintiff is relying on the words having a defamatory meaning which is not explicity stated, but which can be collected from the words in their ordinary and natural sense, the plaintiff does not have the burden of proving such extended meaning, and it is for the judge to decide whether the words are capable of bearing that meaning. The plaintiff does not have to allege such extended meaning in his pleadings, though in some cases it may be prudent for him to do so. In this situation the plaintiff is said to be relying on a "false" innuendo, false in the sense that the burden of proving such innuendo does not rest upon him. In *Lewis* v. *Daily Telegraph* (1964) the defendant newspaper stated that the Fraud Squad of the City of London Police were investigating the affairs of the plaintiff's company. The House of Lords held that, though the natural interpretation of these words was that the plaintiff was reasonably suspected of fraud, and were therefore prima facie defamatory, they could not bear the interpretation that the plaintiff had actually been guilty of fraud, so that the defendant could justify the statement by proving the facts stated. If the defendant has stated therefore that A reasonably suspects B of fraud, this is only defamatory if it is not true; if on the other hand he says that A has told him that B has committed fraud, this is apparently defamatory in the sense that B has actually been fraudulent (*M'Pherson* v. *Daniels* (1829)). The distinction though not difficult to draw is difficult to justify.

Where the defamatory meaning cannot be collected from the actual words used, and the plaintiff is relying upon knowledge by those who have received the statement of facts which render it defamatory, the plaintiff is said to rely on a "true" innuendo. In *Tolley* v. *J. S. Fry and Sons Ltd.* (1931) the plaintiff, a well-known amateur golfer, was depicted in cartoon likeness in the defendants' advertisement, the suggestion in the advertisement being that he had a fondness for the defendants' chocolate. The advertisement was held to be defamatory because it suggested that the plaintiff had infringed his amateur status by accepting payment for appearing in the advertisement. This meaning could not have been derived from the advertisement alone; the plaintiff therefore had to prove that there were persons who knew of him as an amateur golfer and who would read the meaning he alleged into the advertisement. Where the plaintiff is relying on facts not stated in the defendant's statement in order to prove its defamatory nature, he must give details of these facts in his pleadings. He must therefore also prove the existence of such facts on the balance of probabilities.

The interpretation of the statement is along with other matters of law for the judge rather than the jury. He must decide, *inter alia*, whether the statement is capable of being defamatory in the sense that it is capable of bearing the meaning that the plaintiff puts upon it. If it is, the jury, which decides questions of fact, then decides whether it is actually defamatory. The interpretative function of the judge allows him to exercise considerable control over the outcome of an action, and can be abused (see, for example, the surprising decision in *Capital and Counties Bank* v. *Henty* (1882) in which it was held that the defendants' statement to their customers that they would not receive in payment cheques drawn on the plaintiff bank was incapable of being defamatory, although it caused a run on the bank).

Reference to the plaintiff

There must be such sufficient reference to the plaintiff in the defendant's statement that it may reasonably be concluded that it is defamatory of the plaintiff. This does not mean that the plaintiff must actually be named in the statement. All that is required is that the defendant has supplied sufficient particulars to enable the plaintiff to be identified as the subject of the statement. Where the defendant's statement is made of a large class of people which includes the plaintiff ("All lawyers are crooked," or "All West Indians are idle") the law will not generally allow the plaintiff an action in defamation although the statement may constitute a criminal offence, for example, seditious libel, or an incitement to a breach of the peace. But if the class referred to is so small that the defendant's statement may be regarded as being defamatory of each member of it, then the defendant may be successfully sued by each such member. Thus where seventeen defendants had been indicted for murder, the defendant's statement that all took part in the murder was actionable by each of them (*Foxcroft* v. *Lacy* (1613)). Furthermore, a statement made about a class which would ordinarily be too large to allow members of the class to sue may be actionable by individual members of that class if there is evidence that the statement particularly refers to them. So in *Le Fanu* v. *Malcolmson* (1848) a statement in an article by the defendant imputing cruelties to Irish factory owners was found by the court on a reading of the article as a whole to refer to factory owners in Waterford including the plaintiff. Reference to the plaintiff by the defendant's statement need not be intentional. There is sufficient referent if the defendant has used a fictitious name to identify a person in a work intended to be fictional, provided that it was believed by certain persons to refer to the plaintiff (*cf. Hulton* v. *Jones* (1910)) in which one Artemus Jones, a churchwarden of Peckham was said in a newspaper article to be conducting an amorous liaison with a woman not his wife—the real Artemus Jones, a barrister who was not a churchwarden and who did not live at Peckham recovered £1,750 damages because several people testified to the fact that they thought the statement referred to him). Equally a true statement about one person may be defamatory of another person with the same name (*Newstead* v. *London Express Newspaper* (1931))—a newspaper statement that Harold Newstead, a thirty-year-old Camberwell man had been convicted of bigamy was true of a Camberwell barman of that name but untrue of the plaintiff, a Camberwell barber aged about thirty. The statement was held to be defamatory of the plaintiff. Finally it is clear that the statement need not expressly refer to the plaintiff, provided persons reading it or hearing it would take it as so referring. In *Cassidy* v. *Daily Mirror Newspapers* (1929), a newspaper photograph of Cassidy with a woman, together with a statement that the two had become engaged was held to be defamatory of Cassidy's wife who would have been assumed by those reading the statement who knew her to have been living in sin. The result of this case has been confirmed by *Morgan* v. *Odhams Press* (1971). In that case an article in the defendants' newspaper stated that a girl, who had been an accomplice of a dog-doping gang, had been kidnapped by members of the gang. The girl in question had, to the knowledge of people who read the article, stayed with the plaintiff during the period mentioned in the article and in the area indicated by the article. The article was held to be defamatory of the plaintiff.

Whether the statement is capable of being understood as referring to the plaintiff is a question of law for the judge; whether it in fact refers to him is a matter for the jury to decide.

Publication

Publication of the statement to persons other than the plaintiff himself is an essential requirement of defamation. This requirement is clearly satisfied where the defendant has intentionally made the statement to another person, but it is enough if the defendant should have foreseen its publication. Several cases have turned on whether the sender of a letter should foresee that it will be opened and read by someone other than its intended recipient. There is no publication when a father opens his son's letter, nor when a butler opens a letter to his employer even though it is unsealed. But it is to be expected that a postcard will be read, that clerks employed by the plaintiff will open letters addressed to him at his place of business and which appear to be business letters, and that a husband will open a letter which though sealed and addressed to his wife looks like a circular (on the last point see *Theaker* v. *Richardson* (1962)). There will also be publication if a Post Office official opens the letter in the course of his duties, for example, to check that it was the class of mail which ought to be placed in an unsealed envelope. Where the defendant has no reason to suspect that his statement is being published, as in the case where the statement is overheard by one whose presence is reasonably unsuspected by the defendant, there is no publication (*White* v. *Stone Lighting and Radio Ltd.* (1939)).

It is also relevant in deciding whether there there has been publication to consider the person to whom the statement has been made. Where a statement has been typed or printed at another's request, there is no publication when the statement is handed back to its author (*Eglantine Inn Ltd.* v. *Smith and Smith* (1948), a Northern Ireland decision—the typist or printer may be liable for its subsequent distribution under principles to be discussed below). Publication by the defendant to his wife is also not enough though publication to the wife of the plaintiff is. In general the person to whom publication is made must be able to understand the statement—there is no publication by speaking the words to a deaf person who cannot lip-read, nor to an infant who is below the age of understanding. Where the defendant's words have some special sense which can only be appreciated by one who knows of facts not stated by the defendant, it must be shown that publication has been made to such persons, though it is not necessary that any of them should be called to give evidence that he did so understand the defendant's words (*Hough* v. *London Express Newspapers Ltd.* (1940)). Publication by dictating the statement to a typist is sufficient (*Pullman* v. *Hill and Co.* (1891)).

One who repeats a defamatory statement made by another person is liable if the repetition constitutes a publication even if he does not know that the statement is defamatory. The original maker of the statement is liable for such republication if he has authorised it, or, it seems, if it is reasonably foreseeable. On these principles, the author, publisher, printer of defamatory material and even such mechanical distributors as newsagents, bookshops and libraries are liable in defamation for the dissemination of the material among the public (for the defences available in the case of innocent defamation, see pp. 241, 242). All, it seems, are principals in respect of the publication (although as between themselves one may be the agent of the other) and they will be treated as joint tortfeasors. The printers in *Eglantine Inn* v. *Smith* (*supra*) were held liable on these principles because they clearly envisaged the distribution of the defamatory material among the public, and could therefore be taken to have authorised it. More difficulty exists where the defendant has not authorised its subsequent publication, for example, where he has made a speech at which reporters are present, or has told defamatory matter to a reporter without authorising him to publish it. English law is unclear about the liability of the maker of the statement, but the question probably depends upon the foreseeability of the later publication.

Failure to remove defamatory matter may constitute publication (held *obiter* in *Byrne* v. *Deane* (*supra*) where the court considered that failure to remove the libel from the club notice-board amounted to publication). But the limits of this rule are ill-defined. There must be control by the defendant over the place where the statement appears and an expectation that he will keep it under periodic review. *Byrne* v. *Deane* was followed in the American case of *Hellar* v. *Bianco* (1952) in which failure to remove a libel from the wall of a toilet was held to be actionable defamation.

Nature of the liability for defamatory statement

Liability for publication of the statement requires, as noticed already, fault, in the form of intention or negligence on the defendant's part. Furthermore it seems clear that the defendant must intentionally make a statement (for example if the defendant's computer produced a defamatory statement through some mechanical defect, the defendant would not be liable). The defendant need not, however, know of the defamatory nature of the statement. He is liable, for example, if he does not know of facts which make the statement defamatory of the plaintiff, or if he does not realise that the statement refers to the plaintiff. Defamation is therefore in this sense a tort of strict liability (the "reference" cases, *supra*, p. 238, make it clear that liability is strict, although in all of them it is arguable that the defendant was at least negligent; in *Hulton* v. *Jones*, in failing to make it clear that the statement was intended to be fiction, in *Cassidy* and *Morgan* in failing to make proper enquiries, and in *Newstead* in failing sufficiently to identify the correct Harold Newstead).

DEFENCES TO DEFAMATION

Innocent defamation

The common law position whereby an innocent defamer could be held liable to pay substantial damages was clearly unjust. The rigour of the law has been mitigated in two respects.

(1) *Mechanical distributors*

Mechanical distributors of a libel, for example, newsagents, carriers, booksellers and circulating libraries are liable for publication of the libel despite ignorance of its existence. *Vizetelly* v. *Mudie's Select Library Ltd.* (1900) gives the mechanical distributor a defence if he can show that he neither knew nor ought to have known of the existence of the libel in the work he was distributing.

(2) *Unintentional defamation*

Printers and publishers. The printer and publisher (other than a mere mechanical distributor) (the term "publisher" no doubt covers broadcasts on radio or television) of a defamatory statement cannot make use of the defence based on *Vizetelly's* case but may establish a defence based upon section 4 of the Defamation Act 1952. Under the terms of this section the publisher may make an offer of amends to the aggrieved party. This means (a) an offer to publish or join in the publication of a suitable correction and apology; and (b) to take such steps as are reasonably practicable on his part for notifying persons to whom copies have been distributed that the words are alleged to be defamatory of the party aggrieved. If the offer of amends is accepted by the party aggrieved and duly performed, no proceedings for libel or slander may be taken against the party making the offer. If the offer of amends is not accepted by the party aggrieved, it is a defence to an action for libel or slander to prove that the words were published innocently in relation to the plaintiff. Innocent publication is defined in such a way as to include the various types of unintentional reference to the plaintiff in the cases considered above. It is also required, however, that the defendant must have exercised all reasonable care in relation to the publication and there must be some doubt whether each defendant in those cases could have established this. The defendant must also show that if he was not the author of the words, that the words were written by the author without malice. This last requirement is a particularly onerous one and infrequent use is in fact made of the procedure under section 4 because of this.

Justification

Defamation cannot be committed by telling the truth however deleterious an effect the truth may have on another's reputation. For the law protects the plaintiff against imputations about his actual character, rather than one he is generally thought to possess. The defendant, however, has the onus of establishing the truth of what he has said—he must justify the statement. The defendant justifying need only show that his statement was substantially accurate. A statement that the plaintiff had been sentenced to a fine or three weeks' imprisonment was justified by showing that he had actually been given the alternative of two weeks in prison (*Alexander* v. *North-Eastern Ry. Co.* (1865)). Further, section 5 of the Defamation Act 1952 provides that the defence will not fail if the truth of several charges is not established provided that, having regard to the truth of the remaining charges, the charge not proved does not materially injure the plaintiff's reputation. If, for example, the defendant states the plaintiff's conduct amounts to obtaining property and pecuniary advantage by deception under the Theft Act 1969, whereas in fact his conduct amounts to only one of these offences, the defendant could, it seems, justify by proving this. In such a case, however, there is nothing to prevent the plaintiff relying in his statement of claim on the one defamatory statement which the defendant cannot justify. A low award of damages might be expected here, although the defendant cannot adduce in mitigation of damages the fact that the plaintiff committed the other offence (*infra*, p. 253).

The defence of justification is vitally bound up with the interpretation of the statement (*cf.* for example, the distinction drawn in the cases discussed above (p. 237)) between a statement that X suspects Y of fraud and a statement that X says Y is guilty of fraud. The former can be justified by proof of X's suspicion; the latter only by proving that Y has committed fraud.

An extraordinary twist to the defence of justification has been provided by the Rehabilitation of Offenders Act 1974. The Act has introduced the notion of a "spent" conviction. Where a person has received a sentence for a crime, which generally speaking must not exceed 30 months' imprisonment, and where a certain period of time varying from five to 10 years has elapsed since the conviction (the rehabilitation period) the conviction becomes spent and the convicted person is entitled to be treated in law as though he had not been committed, charged with, prosecuted for, convicted of or sentenced for that offence. A person who publishes any of these facts may nevertheless rely upon the defence of justification (or any of the other defences to defamation). In the case of justification the Act expressly provides that this defence cannot succeed if the publication is proved to have been made with malice. The Act thus establishes the first infraction of the principle that truth is an absolute defence to the publication of defamatory material. It is worthy of note that section 13 of the Civil Evidence Act 1968 prevents the convicted person reopening the issue of his guilt in proceedings for defamation by providing that the conviction is conclusive evidence of this fact.

Fair comment

It is a defence to an action of defamation that the defendant's words were fair comment upon a matter of public interest. More latitude is allowed to the defendant in establishing this defence than the previous one. In so far as his words consist of comment he is not required to show the objective correctness of his views. Indeed it is the difficulty of determining what is the correct view on so many matters that has led to the recognition of this defence. But the courts have placed on the extent of the defence a number of restrictions which must now be considered.

Matter of public interest

The matter commented on must be one of public interest. Thus, it may concern the conduct of public officials, the government of the country both central and local, works of art and other matters submitted for public consideration, and other matters of public concern (such as the running of religious institutions) of which an exhaustive list cannot be given. The private life and conduct of anyone is not a matter of public interest, unless it throws light upon such matters as his fitness to hold public office.

Comment on true facts

Any comment presupposes facts upon which the comment is made. The rule is that in so far as the comment has a factual basis, the defendant must show that such factual basis exists. In this respect therefore the onus on the defendant is the same as in the defence of justification, although the defence is entirely one of fair comment, not one of justification and fair comment combined. The factual basis for the comment need not be explicitly stated as part of the comment, although it seems that there must be something in the comment to link it with the facts that are relied on as supporting it. But that this requirement is easily satisfied is shown by the case of *Kemsley* v. *Foot* (1952). In that case the defendant, a journalist, had written an article in a newspaper condemning the newspaper the *Evening Standard* for its standards of journalism in publishing a certain story. The article was headed "Lower than Kemsley." Lord Kemsley was the proprietor of other newspapers but had no connection with the *Evening Standard.* The House of Lords held that taken in conjunction with the article itself, the heading could be taken as a slur on the journalistic standards of the Kemsley newspapers, and that a sufficient substratum of fact had been stated on which a comment could be made. Where no substratum of fact exists in the defendant's statement, fair comment is not available as a defence, and the defendant must justify the truth of this statement. Thus, if the defendant has said, "Mr. X is a moral coward. He deserted from military service during the war," the original sentence might here be regarded as fair comment upon the second. If, however, the defendant merely states that Mr. X is a moral coward, he must justify the truth of this, and the fact of Mr. X's desertion is only relevant evidence of its truth.

Under the doctrine of *Kemsley* v. *Foot*, it appears that those who criticise on matters of public interest may make statements which consist entirely of vilification provided there is a minimum substratum of fact within the statement. To say of a film produced by the plaintiff that it is vulgar and degrading may be justified as comment, on the ground that the statement contains the factual content that a film produced by the plaintiff is at present on public release.

In such a case it would clearly be incumbent upon the defendant to prove facts which tend to substantiate his comment. But the necessity for this appears to be to show the fairness of the comment rather than to establish its factual basis. This was recognised by Lord Porter in *Kemsley* v. *Foot* when he said that the defendant might succeed in proving only one of twenty facts relied on by him as justifying the comment, yet the comment would be fair if that one fact gave it sufficient support. There was statutory recognition of this in section 6 of the Defamation Act 1952, which provides that a defence of fair comment shall not fail by reason only that the truth of every allegation of fact is not proved, if the expression of opinion is fair comment having regard to such of the facts alleged or referred to in the words complained of as are proved. This section relieves the defendant from proving the whole of the factual basis upon which his comment is made, provided sufficient is proved to justify the comment, even where the facts are expressly stated by the defendant. The defendant must, however, prove the truth of every fact he has stated which is defamatory of the plaintiff. Even if his comment is fair in relation to those facts he can prove, the defence of fair comment will not protect him if he cannot do this (in other words he must here establish justification—see *Truth* (*N.Z.*) *Ltd.* v. *Holloway* (1960), a New Zealand case, which held that fair comment is a defence in the case of comment only and not of defamatory statements of fact. The so-called "rolled-up plea" which attempts to combine the defences of fair comment and justification into one defence in these circumstances seems therefore to be misconceived. In so far as the statement contains defamatory factual matter, this must be justified. In so far as it consists of comment whether upon defamatory or non-defamatory statements of fact, the comment must be fair.

Because the defendant may have to prove the truth of factual allegations, whereas in the case of comment need only show that it is fair, it is clearly important to distinguish between what is fact in the defendant's statement and what is comment. This may, however, be a troublesome question. If the defendant has criticised a certain play because of the inadequacy of its plot, this is comment and it is irrelevant that the majority of leading drama critics would disagree with the defendant's views. If, however, the play is based on true events, a criticism which failed to make this clear and at the same time castigated the weakness of the plot would be factually inaccurate and the plea of fair comment would fail for this reason. The mere fact that the truth of the defendant's comment may be tested either empirically or by hearing evidence on the matter does not necessarily deprive it of the status of comment, provided it is a fair comment in the light of what is known to the defendant. This is because what the defendant is expressing is an opinion as to the truth of the fact, rather than advancing it as fact itself. The defendant runs the risk, however, that the court will treat his statement as a factual allegation and require him to justify it. This is well illustrated by *London Artists* v. *Littler* (1969) in which the defendant, relying on the fact that the owners of a theatre wished to get a certain play produced by the defendant out of their theatre by a certain time, and the fact that the actors in the play all gave notice of termination of their contracts through the same agent at the same time and in the same form, alleged the existence of a plot between the artists and the theatre owners. The Court of Appeal treated this as a factual allegation and required the defendant to justify it.

A particular instance showing the difficulty of drawing the line between fact and comment is that in which the defendant imputes motives of dishonesty or self-seeking to the plaintiff. Such an allegation is treated as one of comment, but in evaluating the fairness of such a comment the law adopts a stricter test than that applying generally in cases of fair comment. The defendant must here show a reasonable basis of fact for the making of such imputations. Such basis was not present in *Campbell* v. *Spottiswoode* (1863) in which the defendant alleged that the plaintiff's motive in attempting to organise a religious campaign to spread the doctrines of Christianity among heathens was to increase the sales of the plaintiff's own newspaper (*cf.*, however, the remarks of Lord Denning M.R., in *Slim* v. *Daily Telegraph* (1968) to the effect that even in cases where dishonesty is alleged, the only test of the fairness of the comment is whether the defendant honestly believed it).

Fairness of the comment

Given the truth of the facts on which the defendant has commented, the court must then decide on the fairness of the comment. Courts are loth to pronounce comment upon true facts unfair, since the defence of fair comment is an important bastion of freedom of speech. Lord Denning remarked in *Slim* v. *Daily Telegraph* that the defence of fair comment is available to an honest man expressing his honest opinion on a matter of public interest, no matter how wrong, exaggerated or prejudiced that opinion. The defence will only fail therefore if either the comment is so blatantly unfair that no honest man could have written it, or if it is proved that the defendant had no genuine belief in the truth of what he said. There are two exceptions to this principle. Where the defendant's comment imputes dishonesty or dishonourable motives to the defendant (as in *Campbell* v. *Spottiswoode*, *supra*), the comment must be one which could reasonably be made on the facts known to the defendant. Secondly, in the case where the defendant's comment is actuated by malice towards the plaintiff, this will render his comment unfair even if he honestly believed in the comment and even though the comment itself would have been fair if made by one who genuinely believed it to be true (*Thomas* v. *Bradbury, Agnew & Co.* (1966)). This does not preclude the person actuated by malice towards another person from commenting upon the latter or his work, provided he does not allow his views to be distorted by malice. Furthermore, it is for the plaintiff to prove malice and a distortion of view arising from that malice (the Report of the Committee on Defamation (Cmnd. 5909) made the satisfactory suggestion that the only test of the fairness of the comment should be whether the defendant genuinely believed it, whether or not he was malicious).

Burden of proof

The onus is on the defendant to establish that the facts on which he commented were true, that the comment was such as an honest man might make, and that the matter commented on was one of public interest. The plaintiff must prove malice on the part of the defendant. The judge decides whether the matter commented on is one of public interest. The other questions that arise in relation to the defence must be decided by the jury.

Privilege

It may be a defence to an action of defamation that the statement was made on a privileged occasion. Such privilege may arise in the public interest (for example, the public interest in the freedom of reporting certain matters to be considered shortly) or in the private interests of the persons between whom the statement is communicated. If the occasion is one of absolute privilege, this is a complete defence to proceedings for defamation, however irresponsible or malicious the statement may be. If the occasion is one of qualified privilege, the privilege may be defeated by proof that the defendant was malicious.

Absolute privilege

The following are subject to absolute privilege:

(i) statements made in the course of parliamentary proceedings; this privilege extends to all reports, papers, votes and proceedings published by, or under the authority of, either House of Parliament. It is not possible to refer to a speech made in Parliament in order to establish malice in relation to a speech made outside Parliament

(*Church of Scientology of California* v. *Johnson-Smith* (1973)).

(ii) communications between high-ranking officers of state;

(iii) statements made during the course of judicial proceedings, whether by the judge, counsel or witnesses;

(iv) a fair and accurate report in any newspaper or in a wireless broadcast of proceedings publicly heard before any court exercising judicial authority within the United Kingdom, if published contemporaneously with the proceedings;

(v) communications between solicitor and client; the privilege may be limited to communications made with reference to forthcoming litigation, other communications enjoying only qualified privilege.

Qualified privilege

On occasions of qualified privilege there is for various reasons not the same paramount need to protect the freedom to make the statement as in the cases considered above. Accordingly proof of malice by the maker of the statement will destroy the privilege.

Occasions of qualified privilege. Qualified privilege may arise when a statement is made for the protection of the public interest, or for the protection of the private interests of one or more persons. Examples of the former category are a statement made to the police by a member of the public giving information about the commission of a crime, and a complaint about misconduct or neglect of duty by a public officer made by a member of the public to the proper authority.

Qualified privilege in the public interest also attaches to a number of reports of the proceedings of public bodies. For example, at common law qualified privilege exists in respect of fair and accurate reports of parliamentary proceedings and of judicial proceedings. The latter privilege is wider than the statutory absolute privilege in respect of such reports in that it is available whatever form the report takes and no matter at what time it is made, and also in that it extends to the reporting of the proceedings of administrative tribunals. Various reports receive qualified privilege under section 7 of the Defamation Act 1952, for example, of public meetings, of the proceedings of a local authority, or of the proceedings at the general meeting of a public company (the privilege is forfeited if the publisher has unreasonably refused to publish a reasonable statement by the plaintiff by way of explanation or contradiction of the published statement) or, *e.g.* of public legislative proceedings in any of Her Majesty's Dominions, of proceedings of international organisations such as the United Nations or its constituent bodies, or of the proceedings in public of the International Court of Justice (in these cases the privilege is not lost by refusal to publish a statement on behalf of the plaintiff by way of explanation or contradiction). These are examples of cases where the public not only has an interest in the making of the statement but also in receiving the statement. This is not true of all statements made in the public interest. Thus information about a crime alleged to be committed by the plaintiff should normally be supplied to the police rather than to the public at large.

Qualified privilege may also be enjoyed when the statement is made for the protection of a private interest, whether that of the speaker, the listener or in the common interest of both. Where the private interest is that of the maker of the statement, the other party must be under a duty, whether legal, social or moral, to protect that interest. On the other hand, where the interest is that of the recipient of the statement, the maker of the statement must have a duty, whether legal, social or moral to protect that interest. In the case of statements made in the common interest of both parties, the element of duty is not necessarily present at all (for example, in *Hunt* v. *Great Northern Railway* (1891), a statement by an employer to his employees that the plaintiff had been dismissed because of neglect of duty was held to be privileged because it was in the common interest of employer and employees, though it is difficult to see that there was a duty of any kind to make the statement.

A case which illustrates the operation of these principles is *Watt* v. *Longsdon* (1930). In that case the defendant, a company director, received some defamatory allegations about the plaintiff, an overseas employee of the company, in a letter. The allegations were of drunkenness, dishonesty, and sexual immorality. The defendant showed the letter to the chairman of the board of directors of the company, and to the plaintiff's wife. The former communication was held to be subject to qualified privilege because of the common interest of the defendant and the chairman in the plaintiff's conduct. The communication to the wife was, however, held to be not subject to qualified privilege because although the wife had an interest in her husband's conduct, the defendant had no duty of any sort, moral, social or legal to make communications about such conduct to her. The case does not rule out the possibility of a third party having a duty to communicate to one spouse details about the behaviour of the other; on the facts however the defendant was behaving as an officious intermeddler in the plaintiff's marital affairs.

Interests protected by qualified privilege. The statement may be

made in the private interests of the statement's maker as where a creditor wrote a letter to an auctioneer who was proposing to sell the debtor's property on behalf of the debtor saying to the auctioneer that the sale was an act of bankruptcy by the debtor. The letter was held to be privileged because the creditor was merely attempting to preserve property out of which he hoped the debt would be paid (*Blackham* v. *Pugh* (1846)). The statement must be made to one who is subject to a duty to protect the interest. Thus in *Blackham* v. *Pugh* itself the auctioneer had a legal duty to abstain from making the sale if it amounted to an act of bankruptcy. The interest protected may be that of the person to whom the statement is made, examples being the supply of confidential information about an employee by an employer to a prospective employer, and information given by a solicitor to his client for the protection of the client's interests. Here, the defendant must have a duty to communicate the information. *Watt* v. *Longsdon* (*supra*) illustrates the effect of the absence of both of these requirements.
absence of both of these requirements.

Communications which do not fit easily into the requirements mentioned already may nevertheless be privileged because they are made in the common interest of the defendant and the communicand. Thus statements made by a shareholder at the general meeting of his company to other shareholders, a statement made by one creditor to examinees about cheating at the examination received qualified privilege under this head. In the first case there is no doubt some overlapping with the previous classification of interests protected on the ground that a company shareholder has a moral duty to communicate to other shareholders, who have an interest in receiving, information about the company.

Excess of privilege and malice

It is necessary to distinguish these two matters because the House of Lords decision in *Adam* v. *Ward* (1917) has made it clear that they are different. The defendant may exceed the privilege by publishing the statement to persons other than those to whom publication is necessary for the protection of an interest. For example, it will not normally be necessary for the protection of a private interest to publish a statement in the press and if this is done the privilege will be forfeited. Similarly, the privilege may be forfeited if extraneous matter not germane to the privilege is included in the defendant's statement (as in *Tuson* v. *Evans* (1840) in which the defendant's statement that the plaintiff owed him rent included the further statement that the plaintiff was dishonest). The prohibition upon publication of an otherwise privileged statement to third persons without an interest in receiving the communication does not mean that any publication of this sort automatically causes the forfeiture of the privilege. Publication to clerks and typists of the defendant is within the privilege provided it is reasonable and within the ordinary course of business. So also is a company protected if it sends a copy of its auditor's report to the printers with a view to its circulation among shareholders. In these cases there was doubt whether the privilege protecting the publication to typists was original or ancillary to the publication of the statement to a third party on a privileged occasion (the cases in which the privilege had been recognised concerned subsequent publication of the statement to a third party, for example, *Osborn* v. *Boulter* (1930)). If there was no subsequent privileged publication because, for example, the defendant decided not to send the letter or because he sent it to the plaintiff himself, a doubt remained whether publication of the statement to the typist amounted to defamation. In *Bryanston Finance Co.* v. *De Vries* (1975), the Court of Appeal, in dealing with the second of the two factual situations, decided that publication to the typist was privileged because the privilege was an original one. The conclusion has convenience if not logic to support it.

Qualified privilege may also be lost where the defendant has published a statement which does not exceed the privilege but can be proved to have been actuated by malice towards the plaintiff in making the statement. Malice for the purposes of qualified privilege means that the defendant has no honest belief in what he has said. However prejudiced, irrational or wrong-headed he may be, his belief in the truth of the statement prevents a finding of malice (recently affirmed by the House of Lords in *Horrocks* v. *Lowe* (1974), *cf.* the similar principles governing fair comment). There is an exception to this where the defendant has made use of the privilege for some improper purpose other than the legitimate protection of an interest. Here the defendant's honest belief in the truth of the statement will not protect him (*e.g.*, *Winstanley* v. *Bampton* (1943)—the defendant who in publishing the statement was motivated by feelings of spite or anger towards the plaintiff was malicious though he honestly believed its truth (*cf.* also *Angel* v. *Bushell & Co.* (1968)).

Malice and joint publication

The question of the effect upon the liability of joint publishers of the malice of one of them arises in connection with the defences of fair comment and of qualified privilege, and it may be assumed that the same considerations apply to both defences. Where each joint publisher has a separate and independent privilege, he will not be affected by the malice of one joint publisher. Thus in *Egger* v. *Viscount Chelmsford* (1965) members of the Kennel Club came to a decision that the plaintiff should not be allowed to officiate as judge at a dog show and communicated this in a letter to a third party. The letter was covered by qualified privilege but it was found that several members of the committee had been malicious in reaching their decision. The Court of Appeal held that their malice did not affect the privilege of the other members of the committee since each had a separate, independent privilege. Where the privilege of each joint publisher is not a separate privilege, but is a privilege derivative from one of their number the position is less clear. Are the printer and publisher of a work, who enjoy the same privilege as its author, affected by the malice of the author if the privilege is qualified? In *Egger* v. *Viscount Chelmsford* it was held that the secretary of the Kennel Club who wrote the letter on the instructions of the Committee and who was found to be not personally malicious was not liable, (by Lord Denning M.R. and Harman L.J. because an innocent agent should not be "infected" by his principal's malice, by Davies L.J. because the secretary had a separate and independent privilege). It may be assumed that the reasoning of the majority applies to protect all other innocent agents of the author.

Consent

It is a defence that the plaintiff consented to the publication of the defamatory material (see *Cookson* v. *Harewood* (1932)).

Apology

In order to establish the defence of apology under section 2 of the Libel Act 1845, the defendant must show that the libel was inserted in a newspaper or other periodical "without actual malice" and "without gross negligence" and that the defendant inserted a full apology for the libel either before the commencement of the action or at the earliest opportunity afterwards. The apology must be accompanied by a payment into court of money by way of amends. Apology is a complete defence to the plaintiff's action, but if it fails the defendant will be penalised in costs even though his payment into court exceeded the amount of damages awarded by the jury (though the apology may still go in mitigation of damages). This has meant that apology is an unpopular defence, since the effect of a payment into court under Order 22 of the Rules of the Supreme Court is to make the plaintiff responsible for costs incurred after the payment if the damages awarded by the jury do not exceed the payment, and this procedure is therefore preferable. It is nevertheless still advisable to publish an apology which may go in mitigation of damages.

Remedies

Damages

The primary remedy for defamation is the action for damages. Libel is actionable *per se*, as are certain forms of slander. In the case of defamation actionable *per se*, damages are at large. Therefore aggravated damages (*i.e.* increased damages arising from the circumstances of the tort's commission, *infra*, p. 305) and parasitic damages (*i.e.* for injury to interests other than reputation, for example, injured feelings, *infra*, p. 305) may be awarded. Furthermore in the case of defamation actionable *per se*, the plaintiff does not need to prove his loss—general damages may be awarded in respect of damage which is presumed to have occurred from the fact of the tort's commission (though sometimes the court will refuse to presume such damage. Contemptuous damages of a farthing were awarded to the plaintiff in the *Newstead* case, (*supra*, p. 238)). Exemplary damages can no longer be awarded in actions for defamation unless the defendant has calculated that his profit from publication of the defamatory matter will exceed the amount of damages awarded to the plaintiff, (see, for example, *Cassell* v. *Broome* (1972) confirming on this point the speech of Lord Devlin in *Rookes* v. *Barnard*)). The defendant may plead in mitigation of damages that the plaintiff's reputation was already bad (*Plato Films* v. *Speidel* (1961)) but the court is here concerned only with the plaintiff's reputation as it is and not as it ought to be. The defendant cannot therefore adduce specific events in evidence of the plaintiff's character, nor can he by delaying publication of a libel published elsewhere rely on the plaintiff's bad reputation as the result of that publication.

The courts are reluctant to issue interlocutory injunctions in cases of defamation, and will not do so when the defendant intends to plead justification or fair comment. Furthermore, the issue of a writ will not be allowed by the court to stifle further comment upon any matter—such further comment is only a contempt of court if there is a real risk, as opposed to a mere possibility, of interference with the administration of justice (*Att.-Gen.* v. *Times Newspapers* (1973)).

Report of the Committee on Defamation

The recent Report of the Committee of Defamation (Cmnd. 5909) has recommended a number of changes in the law of defamation among the more important of which are:

(i) abolition of the distinction between libel and slander so that slander would in all cases be actionable *per se*;

(ii) extension of section 5 of the Defamation Act 1952 to allow the defendant to refer to the whole of the statement in the defence of justification, so preventing the plaintiff from relying on a defamatory passage while omitting other defamatory material which the defendant can justify;

(iii) evaluation of the fairness of a comment by a test of whether the comment represented the defendant's honest opinion;

(iv) restriction of actions in defamation by corporate bodies, and governmental agencies (including local authorities) to cases where the plaintiff can establish actual damage arising from the statement, or that the statement was likely to cause such damage;

(v) abolition of the award of exemplary damages in the tort of defamation;

(vi) abolition of the rule in *Plato Films* v. *Speidel* (1961) under which the defendant cannot adduce in mitigation of damage specific events in proof of the character which the plaintiff is supposed to possess.

There are numerous, perhaps less important, substantive recommendations, and a controversial procedural recommendation which would remove the virtual right to trial by jury which exists at present in defamation actions. All these suggestions seem welcome, and it is hoped there is no undue delay before their implementation.

CHAPTER 22

THE ECONOMIC TORTS

THERE is no general principle of liability in tort for intentionally causing another economic loss. The defendant may not be liable for causing such loss even though he has been malicious (*Allen* v. *Flood* (1898) or has competed in an "unfair" manner (*Mogul S.S. Co.* v. *McGregor Gow & Co.* (1889)). English courts have attempted to solve the problem of imposing liability for causing economic loss by creating a series of exceptions to a general principle of no liability. These exceptions appear to turn on the existence of one or more of three factors:

(i) An improper motive in the defendant. Though malice is generally irrelevant, it may be so where the defendants have acted in combination.

(ii) The existence of a right in the plaintiff. The courts are more ready to give their protection when the defendant has interfered with a right of the plaintiff or something analogous to a right. The tort of interference with contract protects the plaintiff's enjoyment of his contractual rights. Intangible rights of property such as copyright, patents, and registered trade marks are protected by actions in tort. The tort of passing-off recognises a right in the name and appearance of the plaintiff's goods or services, clearly an analogous right to that of the other forms of intangible property.

(iii) The means used by the defendant. The defendant may incur liability because the means he has used are unlawful (interference with contract, conspiracy, intimidation and unlawful means) or because he has told a lie (deceit and injurious falsehood).

There may be a combination of these factors present, for example, in indirect interference with contract, the factors of the use of unlawful means and of interference with the plaintiff's right.

In many cases of liability for causing economic loss the result is achieved by influencing the plaintiff to act to his own loss. This result is inherent in the notion of an economic interest which generally presupposes an advantageous relationship with another person. However, it is possible for the economic torts to be committed otherwise than through the medium of a third party, and in the case of deceit this is invariably true. Another point of importance is that although the intention of causing the plaintiff loss is not a sufficient condition, it is generally a necessary one of liability. Negligence in relation to an economic interest is not enough unless the conditions of *Hedley Byrne* liability are fulfilled.

The economic torts have been subject to considerable legislative intervention in recent years in an attempt to regulate industrial conflict. The Industrial Relations Act 1971 took away the immunity from actions in tort which trade unions had enjoyed since 1906, and created new causes of action against them for causing economic loss. With the repeal of the Industrial Relations Act by the Trade Unions and Labour Relations Act 1974, the immunity of trade unions has been restored although some measure of tortious liability has been retained (*infra*, p. 322). Under the 1974 Act there is still the possibility of suing the union official rather than the union itself, although the effect of the Act's provisions is to considerably reduce the possibility of a successful action against him.

Interference with Contract

In *Lumley* v. *Gye* (1853) the principle was established that an action lay, at the instance of the other party to the contract, against one who induced a party to a contract to break it.

The facts in *Lumley* v. *Gye* were that the defendant persuaded a singer, who was under contract to sing at the plaintiff's theatre, to sing at the defendant's theatre instead. The defendant knew of the singer's contract with the plaintiff. The court held that these facts disclosed a cause of action in tort.

Previous to this case, although it was recognised that a master could sue one who enticed his servant away from his services, there appeared to be no general principle of protection of contractual rights. The case is, therefore, an important milestone in the recognition and protection by the courts of purely economic interests. As long as *Lumley* v. *Gye* marked the boundaries of the tort, the law was reasonably clear. Developments which have taken place since *Lumley* v. *Gye* have clouded the picture. In the first place it is now established that action lies for indirect interference causing a breach of contract, rather than direct persuasion. The probability is that in the case of indirect interference, the defendant must have used unlawful means. Secondly, it is no longer clear that the defendant must have induced a breach of contract.

Elements of the tort

Actionable interference with contract

Until recently, lip-service, at least, has been paid to the view that the defendant's act must induce a breach of contract. If, for example, A persuades B to terminate lawfully his contract with C, C could not sue A under *Lumley* v. *Gye*. The view that the defendant's act must induce a breach was difficult to reconcile with cases in which the defendant's act had made it impossible for the other party to the contract to perform (see, for example, the facts of *G.W.K. Rubber Co.* v. *Dunlop* (1926); *J. T. Stratford* v. *Lindley* (1965) (*infra*, p. 259). On facts such as these, it is arguable that no breach had been committed by the defendant. The possibility of frustration of the contract in these circumstances may also be present. That an actionable breach is not necessary is shown by *Torquay Hotel Co.* v. *Cousins* (1969). In that case the defendants were officials of the Transport and General Workers Union (T.G.W.U.). The union had a dispute over recognition with the Torbay Hotel in Torquay. The plaintiffs, who owned the Imperial Hotel in Torquay, became involved in the dispute through the act of the managing director of the Imperial Hotel, who made a statement which was reported in the press to the effect that the local Hotels Association would "stamp out" the T.G.W.U. in Torquay. As a result of this the defendants decided to stop supplies of oil reaching the Imperial Hotel. The Imperial had a contract for the supply of fuel oil, as ordered, with Esso. Esso drivers were members of the T.G.W.U. and would clearly not cross the latter's picket lines. One of the defendants telephoned Esso and informed them that because of the dispute supplies of oil to the plaintiffs would be stopped. No oil was, in fact, ordered or delivered, although Esso informed the managing director of the Imperial Hotel that they could not supply him with oil. Esso was protected from liability for breach of contract in these circumstances by reason of a *force majeure* clause in the contract. Nevertheless the Court of Appeal held that a prima facie case of inducing a breach of contract under the *Lumley* v. *Gye* principle had been established. Russell and Winn L.JJ. thought that it was sufficient that Esso were in breach of contract although protected from liability by the *force majeure* clause. Lord Denning M.R. proceeded on a broader plane. He thought that where there was direct interference with a contract, which all three members of the Court of Appeal thought to exist in this case, there was no need for a breach at all. Lord Denning's view may be seen as a logical development from the earlier cases. It would mean, however, that conduct which is perfectly lawful, in itself and in its result, might be found to be tortious. It seems doubtful whether the need to protect economic interests justifies this extension.

Act constituting an interference

In deciding what acts amount to an interference with contract, a distinction is sometimes drawn between direct interference and indirect interference. Examples of the former are persuasion of the other contracting party, and physical restraint aimed against him; of the latter, industrial action taken against him. It is suggested, however, that the more fundamental distinction is between persuasion of one of the parties to the contract to break it, and the doing of an act which, whether directly or indirectly, has the effect of preventing performance of the contract. The latter category would include both physical and industrial action against a contracting party. In the case of prevention of performance, it seems probable that the defendant is liable only if he has used unlawful means. Indeed it is possible to view the use of unlawful means to prevent the performance of a contract as part of the wider tort of causing loss by unlawful means (*infra*, p. 266). This would mean that the difficulties mentioned above of deciding whether the tort of interference with contract is limited to interference inducing a breach would disappear where the defendant had used unlawful means. This view would also make it possible to safeguard to some extent the original *Lumley* v. *Gye* principle by requiring, *pace* Lord Denning in *Torquay Hotel* v. *Cousins*, that, in cases of persuasion, the persuasion must induce a breach of contract.

(i) *Persuasion*

The defendant's persuasion must induce (*i.e.* cause) a breach of contract. It is not necessary that the defendant should stand to profit from the breach, nor is the line that is drawn between persuasion and mere advice to break the contract a sound one, since it simply restates the issue as to causation. If the defendant, whether through persuasion or advice, has induced a breach of contract, he is liable. The defendant's persuasion may take the form of a dealing with a party to the contract which the defendant knows to be a breach of that contract (as in *B.M.T.A.* v. *Salvadori* (1949)). In principle there ought to be liability only if the dealing has induced the breach. If the party to the contract had already decided to break his contract before the dealing, the latter has not caused the breach. This derives a measure of support from *Batts Combe Quarry* v. *Ford* (1943)—acceptance of a gift known to be given in breach of contract was not actionable under *Lumley* v. *Gye*.

Finally, in relation to persuasion, further mention must be made of *Torquay Hotel Co.* v. *Cousins*. In that case all three members of the Court of Appeal thought that there was direct interference with the contract because of the telephone call made by the defendants to Esso. Since, however, the purpose of the phone call was merely to inform Esso that its drivers would not be allowed to deliver oil to the plaintiffs, it seems wrong to equate this with persuasion. Such interference should have been regarded as coming within the second category of prevention of performance of the contract.

(ii) *Prevention of performance of the contract*

In the first place, the defendant may have physically prevented the performance of the contract. In *Lumley* v. *Gye*, for example, had the defendant unlawfully detained the singer, thereby falsely imprisoning her, the result in law would have been the same. In *G.W.K. Co.* v. *Dunlop Rubber Co.* (1926) a car manufacturer contracted with the plaintiff that tyres manufactured by the plaintiff should be displayed on his cars appearing at an exhibition. The defendant replaced the plaintiffs' tyres on cars on show at the exhibition with tyres of his own manufacture. He was held liable to the plaintiff under the *Lumley* v. *Gye* principle. Also coming within this category is the use of industrial action against a contracting party which has the effect of making it impossible for him to perform his contract. In *J. T. Stratford & Co.* v. *Lindley* (1965) the defendants, who were officials of the Watermen's Union, wanted negotiating rights for the union in respect of three union members employed by a company called Bowker & King. The other 45 employees of Bowker & King were members of the Transport and General Workers Union. J. T. Stratford, the chairman of Bowker & King, had refused negotiating rights in respect of these employees to both unions, but he later concluded an agreement covering all his employees with the T.G.W.U. The defendants thereupon instructed members of their union not to handle barges belonging to J. T. Stratford & Co. (of which J. T. Stratford was chairman and which was controlled by him) and which had been hired out to customers, nor to handle barges which were to be or had been repaired by that company. The result of this embargo was that the company's barge-hiring and barge-repairing businesses were crippled. The House of Lords found that a prima facie case of interference with contract had been made out in respect of the barge-hiring business, since the defendants must have realised that the barges were hired out under contracts which required their return to the company on completion of the contract. In respect of the barge-repairing business sufficient knowledge of the contracts for repair could not be proved to justify a finding that there was a prima facie case of liability under the same principle. In any case, an interlocutory injunction was issued against the defendants to cease their embargo.

Until the *Stratford* decision it had generally been thought that where the interference took the form of prevention of performance of the contract rather than direct persuasion, the defendant must have used unlawful means. The means used might be a tort (for example, the tort of trespass in *G.K.W. Co.* v. *Dunlop Rubber Co.*), or a breach of contract (assumed to be the case in *D. C. Thomson & Co.* v. *Deakin* (1952), although in that case since no breach of contract had been committed it was not possible to establish unlawful means). The judgments of the House of Lords in the *Stratford* case, however, are curiously equivocal on the question whether unlawful means are necessary in the second category of interference. Lord Pearce actually said that it was unnecessary to decide whether the refusal of union members to work the plaintiffs' barges was a breach of their contracts of employment so as to constitute unlawful means. Lord Reid and Viscount Radcliffe thought that a breach of the contract of employment had been committed, but appeared to think this was relevant only to liability for causing loss by unlawful means rather than to liability under the *Lumley* v. *Gye* principle. Viscount Radcliffe and Lord Donovan seemed to treat the case as essentially one of causing loss by unlawful means rather than of interference with contract. Only Lord Upjohn treated the case unambiguously as one of interference with contract and he clearly thought that there was a requirement of unlawful means in this tort. Admittedly the action was for an interlocutory injunction and the House of Lords had only to be satisfied that the plaintiffs had a prima facie case. Even so, the lack of clarity in the judgments is unsatisfactory. If there is no requirement of unlawful means in interference with contract coming within the second category, this surely should have been stated more explicitly.

Knowledge of the contract by the defendant

The requirement of knowledge of the contract by the defendant is illustrative of the requirement of the economic torts generally that the defendant must intend to cause loss. The rule is generally stated in terms of actual knowledge (*British Industrial Plastics* v. *Ferguson* (1940)), though there has been some relaxation of this requirement. Thus where, as in *J. T. Stratford & Co.* v. *Lindley* the existence of a contractual relationship between the company and the hirers of its barges must have been obvious to the defendants together with the fact that their action would bring about a breakdown of those contracts, sufficient knowledge existed. In *Emerald Construction Co.* v. *Lowthian* (1966) it was held that where the defendant knows of the existence of a contractual relationship, he commits the tort if he intends to bring that contract to an end even if he assumes that it can be lawfully terminated. No case yet has countenanced the possibility of "constructive knowledge" of the contract being enough.

Damage

It appears to be the law that the plaintiff must prove that he has suffered damage arising from the interference.

Only the party not in breach can sue under the *Lumley* v. *Gye* principle. Since it is clear that in the "prevention of performance" cases, the other party may also suffer economic loss, and since the tort may extend beyond interference producing a breach of contract, it is not obvious why in appropriate cases the party against whom action has been taken to produce the interference should not sue.

Defences

Trade disputes

Section 13 (1) of the Trade Union and Labour Relations Act 1974 provides that

> "An act done by a person in contemplation or furtherance of a trade dispute shall not be actionable in tort on the ground only—
>
> (*a*) that it induces another person to break a contract of employment..."

The general effect of these words is (as interpreted in *Rookes* v. *Barnard* (1964)) to prevent an action for the tort of inducement of a breach of contract of employment, where the defendant is acting in contemplation or furtherance of a trade dispute. The words "on the ground only" seem to mean that if the defendant uses other unlawful means, such as the commission of a tort, to accomplish his purpose, he is not protected by the section. Thus, if the workman is prevented from fulfilling his contract of employment by threats of violence by the defendant, section 3 will not protect the defendant.

The section does not protect the defendant when he has induced a breach of a contract other than one of employment. Where, however, the inducing of a breach of contracts of employment has led to an interference with commercial contracts made with the plaintiff, the defendant is protected by section 13 (3) (*a*) which provides that an act which by reason of section 13 (1) is not actionable shall not be regarded as the doing of an unlawful act or as the use of unlawful means for the purpose of establishing liability in tort (unless the vague expressions of certain members of the House of Lords in *J. T. Stratford & Co.* v. *Lindley* to the effect that unlawful means is not necessary for actionability under the *Lumley* v. *Gye* principle are correct. The subsection would also not be a defence where, as in *Torquay Hotel Co.* v. *Cousins*, the defendant has "directly" induced a breach of a commercial contract, whether or not he was acting in furtherance of a trade dispute).

Justification

The extent of this defence is ill-defined. It may be used by the courts to indicate disapproval of a contract which is nevertheless legally enforceable. For example, in one of the few cases in which the defence succeeded, the defendants, who were representatives of certain theatrical unions induced theatre proprietors to break their contracts with the plaintiff, a theatre manager. This was held to be justified on the ground that the plaintiff paid his chorus girls such low wages that they were compelled to turn to prostitution (*Brimdow* v. *Casson* (1924)). It seems that only in rare cases of this sort that the defence will succeed, since it is not for the courts to speculate upon whether a legally enforceable contract deserves their protection.

Conspiracy

The tort of conspiracy is committed when two or more persons conspire together to injure the plaintiff, or when they together use unlawful means with the result that the plaintiff is injured. It is a wider tort than inducement of a breach of contract in that its field of protection is not limited to rights arising under contract. Conspiracy became a potentially important tort when it was decided that it lay even where the conspiracy was to perform a lawful act, provided the defendants intended to injure or damage the plaintiff. In the sphere of economic interests in particular, conspiracy appeared to be a means of getting round the rule of English law that an act done intentionally to infringe the economic prosperity of another person was not *per se* tortious. Despite the dubious logic which accepted that what is done by one person is not actionable but will be actionable if done by two, this did seem to promise some redress in cases where people suffered damage caused intentionally by their trade competitors. However, it eventually became established that a combination to cause economic damage to another person is not actionable unless the predominant purposes of the defendants is to cause that damage. If, for example, they are acting in the furtherance of their own interests, no action for conspiracy will lie against them. Thus, in *Crofter Hand Woven Harris Tweed*

Co. Ltd. v. *Veitch* (1942) the defendant union officials instructed dockers to refuse to handle yarn sent from the mainland of Scotland for delivery to the plaintiffs' factory in the Outer Hebrides. The plaintiffs depended entirely upon these supplies in order to weave cloth. The defendants had no trade dispute with the plaintiffs but wished to reduce the competition provided by the plaintiffs' business for other mills on the island which employed union labour, so that the employers could increase wages. The House of Lords held that this was not conspiracy since the defendants' predominant purpose was the protection of members of their union. The case may be compared with *Quinn* v. *Leathem* (1901). The plaintiff had been employing non-union labour, but was willing that his men should join the union and was willing to pay their fines and entrance money. The defendant union officials refused this offer and ordered that the men be discharged and compelled to walk the streets for 12 months. The plaintiff refused to do this, and the defendants then brought pressure to bear on a customer of the plaintiff as a result of which he stopped dealing with the plaintiff. The plaintiff recovered for this loss in conspiracy. In view of the plaintiff's offer, the defendants had acted vindictively and not in protection of their legitimate interests. The interest furthered by the combination need not be economic nor need they be acting in the private interests of those combining in order to come within the protection of the *Crofter* case (*Scala Ballroom* (*Wolverhampton*) *Ltd.* v. *Radcliffe* (1958)—legitimate combination aimed against the plaintiff who operated a colour bar). But the courts have a power to say whether the interest is one that can legitimately be protected. Thus, in the *Crofter* case, Viscount Maugham thought that a conspiracy aimed against the religious views, or the politics or the race or colour of the plaintiff would be actionable; Viscount Simon thought the same would follow where those combining did so because of a bribe offered to them by a third party.

It appears that the burden of showing that the predominant intention of the defendants was to injure him, lies on the plaintiff (a majority of the law lords in the *Crofter* case were in favour of this view). Where damage disproportionate to the purpose of the defendants had been inflicted upon the plaintiff, this does not in itself make the defendants liable, but is evidence that their primary intention was to injure the plaintiff.

Conspiracy by agreement to use unlawful means

This type of conspiracy may have the advantage that it does not appear to be limited by the requirement of the *Crofter* case that the defendants' predominant purpose must be to injure the plaintiff, although it seems necessary that the defendants must have as part of their purpose the infliction of injury or damage on the plaintiff. Since, however, the individual use of unlawful means to inflict damage on another person is normally actionable, conspiracy adds little here, unless the effect of a conspiracy is to render actionable the use of unlawful means which if used by individuals would not be actionable.

Section 13 (4) of the Trade Union and Labour Relations Act 1974

This subsection gives a defence to those combining to do an act in contemplation or furtherance of a trade dispute, unless the individual acts of those combining are tortious. It appears to add nothing to the common law position, since a combination to do an act in contemplation or furtherance of a trade dispute is not an actionable conspiracy.

Intimidation

The tort of intimidation consists in a threat to commit an unlawful act (or that an unlawful act will be committed), intending as a result of the threat to produce damage to the plaintiff, and actually producing such damage. The existence of this tort, long in doubt, was finally confirmed by the House of Lords in *Rookes* v. *Barnard* (1964). The defendants were three officials of the A.E.S.D. Union, two of whom were employed by B.O.A.C. A branch of the union had, at a meeting at which the defendants were present, passed a resolution under which it was agreed that all union labour would be withdrawn unless the plaintiff, who was not a member of a union, was dismissed by B.O.A.C. The union had an agreement with B.O.A.C. providing for 100 per cent union membership. There was also in the agreement a "no strike" clause which the defendants later conceded to be incorporated in the contracts of employees subject to the agreement. The defendants notified B.O.A.C. of the union resolution and B.O.A.C. thereupon lawfully terminated the plaintiff's contract of employment. The plaintiff was held to be entitled to damages for his loss from the defendants. The ground for the decision was that the individual acts of the defendants amounted to the tort of intimidation, since each had threatened B.O.A.C. with an unlawful act, namely, a withdrawal of labour in breach of the "no strike" clause (or in the case of the official not employed by B.O.A.C. the commission of an unlawful act by other persons). The combination to utter such threats was therefore an actionable conspiracy not protected by section 1 of the Trade Disputes Act 1906 (the then equivalent of section 13 (4) of the Trade Union and Labour Relations Act 1974).

It will be noticed that three parties were involved in *Rookes* v. *Barnard*, the defendants, the plaintiff and B.O.A.C. Where only two parties are involved, *i.e.* where the plaintiff receives a threat which causes him to act to his own loss, there is less reason for the existence of the tort of intimidation since the plaintiff will normally have other remedies against the defendant. Thus if he is threatened with a breach of a contract to which he and the defendant are parties, his contractual remedies will normally protect his interest in having that contract performed. If threatened with physical violence he can sue in tort by using a *quia timet* injunction. There are cases, however, in which the existence of a tortious remedy may be useful in a two party situation. It has been held, for example, that an agreement in restraint of trade is unlawful means for the purpose of an action for causing loss by unlawful means (*Brekkes* v. *Cattel* (1971)). Yet if the plaintiff were to receive a threat from the defendant that he and another person intended to enter into such an agreement unless the plaintiff complied with the threat, the plaintiff has no remedy unless the defendant carries out the threat (in which case the agreement can be declared void under the Restrictive Trade Practices Act 1956, and damages awarded to the plaintiff). It may be that the plaintiff may here suffer no disadvantage by the absence of an immediate remedy, but the element of doubt lends support to the judgments of the House of Lords in *Rookes* v. *Barnard* in which the possibility of intimidation being available in a two party situation was not ruled out. Furthermore, even where an alternative remedy exists, there may be a case for saying that intimidation is available. Where the plaintiff is threatened with physical violence, the possibility of a *quia timet* injunction exists only until the plaintiff complies with the threat. If intimidation does not lie where the plaintiff has complied with the threat and acted to his own loss, he is without any remedy whatsoever.

Section 13 (1) (b) of the Trade Union and Labour Relations Act 1974

Section 13 (1) provides:

> "An act done by a person in contemplation or furtherance of a trade dispute shall not be actionable in tort on the ground only—
>
> (*b*) that it consists in his threatening that a contract of employment (whether one to which he is a party or not) will be broken or that he will induce another person to break a contract of employment to which that other person is a party."

The section will provide a defence on similar facts to *Rookes* v. *Barnard* since it seems clear that the defendants in seeking to enforce a closed shop agreement were acting in contemplation or furtherance of a trade dispute (Rookes's dismissal would also be fair dismissal—paragraph 6 (5) of the First Schedule to the Act of 1974, unless his refusal to join the union was based on religious or reasonable grounds. If no closed shop existed his dismissal would be unfair—paragraph 15).

The words "on the ground only" will presumably receive the same interpretation here as in section 13 (1) (*a*)—*i.e.* if the defendant's threats are accompanied by other unlawful means such as threats of violence he will forfeit the statutory protection.

Causing Loss by Unlawful Means

The question of whether liability in tort exists for the infliction of economic loss by unlawful means is a difficult one. It is probably true to say that in the case of the intentional infringement of a penal statute causing economic loss, the question is identical with the question of whether an action for breach of statutory duty will lie (although in *Williams* v. *Hursey* (1959), an Australian case, the High Court of Australia thought that a combination to violate a penal statute was actionable though no action for breach of statutory duty lay). In other cases everything depends upon whether the court concludes that the predominant purpose of the illegality is its sole purpose. In *Chapman* v. *Honig* (1963) the Court of Appeal held that a landlord who had issued a notice to quit in circumstances in which it was a criminal contempt of court (because it was designed to punish the tenant for having given evidence in court against the landlord) was not civilly liable to the tenant, since the sole purpose of the illegality was to ensure the due administration of justice. Again in *Hargreaves* v. *Bretherton* (1950) it was held for a similar reason that no civil action lay against one who had given perjured evidence. On the other hand, the mere fact that the illegality has to do with the administration of justice will not necessarily defeat the plaintiff. In *Acrow* (*Automation*) v. *Rex Chainbelt Inc.* (1971) it was held that where the defendant, in order to defeat an injunction which the plaintiff had obtained against a third party withheld supplies from the plaintiff (a civil contempt), this was the tort of causing loss by unlawful means. The distinction between this and the two earlier cases may be that the purpose of the illegality was here fairly obviously to safeguard individual rights as well as to ensure the due administration of justice.

Many of the cases in which actions have been allowed have concerned action taken against third parties with the intention of causing the plaintiff loss. In *Tarleton* v. *McGawley* (1794) the defendant fired a cannon at a canoe of natives who were trading with the plaintiff's ship as the result of which one was killed and the others returned to land. The plaintiff recovered damages for the loss of his trade from the defendant. In *J. T. Stratford & Co.* v. *Lindley* Lord Reid and Viscount Radcliffe thought that the economic loss the plaintiff suffered through loss of future contracts with barge hirers (not recoverable under interference with contract) was recoverable under this tort, since the defendants had used unlawful means in inducing breaches of the employees' contracts of employment with the barge hirers. In *Rookes* v. *Barnard* Lord Reid, speaking *obiter*, thought that a breach of contract committed with the intention of causing a third party loss is actionable by that third party if loss occurs. Privity of contract was not a fatal objection because the third party was complaining not of the non-performance of the contract, but of the intentional infliction of damage on him through its breach. *Pace* Winfield (p. 459), the cases do not bear out the suggestion that the tort of causing loss by unlawful means is limited to three party situations (*cf.* the *Acrow* (*Automation*) case). Nor is there any foundation for his suggestion that in three party situations the illegality of the means must be found to be so primarily by reference to the third party. Recent cases, for example, have held that an agreement which appears to be one which would be declared void under the Restrictive Practices Act 1956 is unlawful means for the purpose of this tort (*Daily Mirror Newspapers* v. *Gardner* (1968); *Brekkes* v. *Cattel* (1971)), though clearly such illegality is not aimed at anyone in particular (an agreement which is void as being in restraint of trade at common law is not unlawful means so as to give a civil action to persons injured by it—*Mogul Steamship Co.* v. *McGregor* (1927). The reality seems far more complex than Winfield suggests. The tort of unlawful means seems to give to courts the same sort of discretion to create new causes of action as the tort of breach of statutory duty.

Section 13 (3) of the Trade Union and Labour Relations Act 1974

This provides as follows:

"For the avoidance of doubt it is hereby declared that—

(*a*) an act which by reason of subsection (1) or (2) above is itself not actionable;

(*b*) a breach of contract in contemplation or furtherance of a trade dispute;

shall not be regarded as the doing of an unlawful act or as the use of unlawful means for the purpose of establishing liability in tort."

The effect of this is that, provided the defendant was acting in contemplation or furtherance of a trade dispute, if he has induced a breach of a contract of employment, or threatened that a breach of a contract of employment will be committed or that he will induce such a breach, or if he has actually broken a contract whether of employment or otherwise, he has statutory protection against liability in tort, whether based on interference with contract or causing loss by unlawful means. The subsection has thus confirmed the general opinion before the Act that acts which if done in contemplation or furtherance of a trade dispute were not actionable could not constitute unlawful means for the purpose of any other tort. The inclusion in section 13 (3) (*b*) of breaches of contract other than contracts of employment is odd and serves little apparent purpose. In connection with the notion of breach of a contract of employment, it has never been authoritatively determined whether, in the absence of express provision in the contract, participation in a strike is a breach of the individual contract of employment, nor whether strike notice of a length greater than that required to terminate the contract is an anticipatory breach (on the latter point Lord Denning's judgment in *Morgan* v. *Fry* (1968) suggests that there is no breach but his process of arriving at that conclusion is unsatisfactory).

The protection afforded generally by section 13 of the Trade Union and Labour Relations Act 1974 to those acting in contemplation or furtherance of a trade dispute operates only within the confines of the making use in one way or another of a breach of the contract of employment as a weapon. There is no protection, for example, where the defendants have induced or threatened a breach of a commercial contract. Furthermore, the notion of interference with contract adumbrated by Lord Denning in *Torquay Hotel Co.* v. *Cousins* might be extended by the courts beyond the tort of interference with contract to the other economic torts so as to thwart the intentions of the legislature in enacting section 13. Another possible loophole is that envisaged by some of the speeches in *J. T. Stratford & Co.* v. *Lindley* to the effect that the indirect inducement of a breach of a commercial contract does not require unlawful means. These gaps appear to be closed by clause 2 (2) of the Trade Union and Labour Relations (Amendment) Bill at present before Parliament. This provides:

"(1) An act done by a person in contemplation or furtherance of a trade dispute shall not be actionable in tort on the ground only—

(*a*) that it induces another person to break a contract or interferes or induces any other person to interfere with its performance; or

(*b*) that it consists in his threatening that a contract (whether one to which he is a party or not) will be broken or its performance interfered with, or that he will induce another person to break a contract or to interfere with its performance." (See Preface.)

"In Contemplation or Furtherance of a Trade Dispute"

The material in this chapter will have underlined the importance of deciding whether the defendant was acting in contemplation or furtherance of a trade dispute. If he is, liability under an economic tort is unlikely. Section 29 (1) of the Trade Union and Labour Relations Act 1974 provides that a

"trade dispute" means a dispute between employers and workers, or between workers and workers, which is connected with one or more of the following...

(*a*) terms and conditions of employment, or the physical conditions in which any workers are required to work;

(*b*) engagement or non-engagement, or termination or suspension of employment, or the duties of employment of one or more workers;

(*c*) allocation of work or the duties of employment as between workers and groups of workers;

(*d*) matters of discipline;

(*e*) facilities for officials of trade unions; and

(*f*) machinery for negotiation or consultation, and other procedures, relating to any of the foregoing matters, including the recognition by employers or employers' associations of the right of a trade union to represent workers in any such negotiation or consultation or in the carrying out of such procedures.

Section 29 (1) (*g*) makes clear that a dispute over union recognition by an employer is a trade dispute, a matter on which the judgments in *J. T. Stratford & Co.* v. *Lindley* threw some doubt. The defendant must prove that he was acting in contemplation or furtherance of a trade dispute to receive the protection of section 13, and on this matter the pre-Act cases remain relevant. Thus in *Huntley* v. *Thornton* (1957) the court held that, where trade union officials pursued a personal vendetta against the plaintiff who had refused to take part in a one day strike, although at one time there had been a trade dispute, the officials were acting out of spite alone and out of a desire to punish the plaintiff rather than in the furtherance of a trade dispute. Similarly, in *J. T. Stratford* v. *Lindley* although there may have been the makings of a trade dispute between the defendants and J. T. Stratford, the defendants were acting vindictively rather than in the furtherance of a trade dispute, since they had gone ahead with industrial action immediately without any attempt to negotiate after Stratford's recognition of the T.G.W.U.

Interlocutory Injunctions

The primary method of protection for a person against whom industrial action is being taken is an interlocutory injunction to prevent continuance of the action pending trial of the question whether it is tortious. The reason for the frequency of its use in the industrial sphere is that the courts recognise that the plaintiff's business may suffer irreparable damage before the trial takes place. The result has been, however, that the interlocutory proceedings have generally constituted the real trial of the action, since it has become unusual for the defendants to refuse to accept the interlocutory decision as the final one. In order to obtain an interlocutory injunction the plaintiff must show that on the balance of convenience one should be issued. In order to achieve this the plaintiff needs to prove that he would suffer irreparable damage should the injunction not be issued, and that the defendant would not suffer greater damage if it were issued. The defendant's position could generally be safeguarded by requiring the plaintiff to give an undertaking in damages (to be paid if at the trial of the action the defendant's action turns out not to be tortious. Until recently the courts also required the plaintiff to establish a prima facie case of the defendant's liability. The House of Lords' decision in *American Cyanamid Co.* v. *Ethicon* (1975) has changed this by requiring that the plaintiff need establish only that the claim was not frivolous or vexatious, *i.e.* that there is a serious question to be tried. These principles were said to be applicable to the issue of interlocutory injunctions in all cases, but in the industrial sphere, because of the peculiar characteristic of the interlocutory proceedings of being the real trial of the action, they may be unduly favourable to the plaintiff (for a judicial dissentient to the view that the *American Cyanamid* case lays down a rule of general applicability, see the judgment of Lord Denning M.R. in *Hubbard* v. *Pitt* (1975)).

CHAPTER 23

THE ECONOMIC TORTS: PASSING-OFF

THE tort known as passing-off protects primarily the person whose trade competitor passes off his goods or services as that person's. It is often said that in this tort the courts are recognising a proprietary right in the description or appearance of the goods or services, a right of intangible property akin to such things as copyright, patents, and design (which now receive the protection of statute). In a way all rights protected by the law of torts are proprietary in the sense that the protection they enjoy is universal—they are *iura in rem.* But it seems true to regard passing-off as a proprietary type of tort, in a particular sense, since in it the plaintiff is complaining not of damage inflicted upon himself or his property by the defendant, but of the defendant's unauthorised use of something which belongs to the plaintiff. In this, passing-off strongly resembles conversion, the other tort with a predominantly proprietary purpose. Passing-off is the "purest" of the economic torts. Its purpose is almost exclusively the protection of economic interests. Furthermore, passing-off has become of increasing importance since the courts by allowing numerous extensions of it have used it as a means of controlling unfair trade competition. This has meant, however, that the boundaries of the tort and its extensions are somewhat ill-defined. In order to commit passing-off, the defendant must have done something to suggest that the goods or services which he is selling to the public are those of the plaintiff. The following are some of the methods of passing-off that have been recognised by the courts.

Use of the plaintiff's trade mark

Although it is now possible to register trade marks under the Trade Marks Act 1838 and to bring a statutory action for their infringement, the action for passing-off is still available where the defendant has used the plaintiff's trade mark on his goods, and may be necessary, for example, where the plaintiff has not complied with the statutory requirements for registration.

Use of plaintiff's trade name

In *Powell* v. *Birmingham Vinegar Brewery Co.* (1896), the plaintiff sued to protect the name "Yorkshire Relish" which the plaintiff used for the sauce he manufactured. The action was successful.

The trade name may be derived from the area in which the goods are manufactured. Thus, successful actions have been brought to protect the trade names "Stone Ales," "Chartreuse" liqueurs, and "Champagne." The last case (*J. Bollinger* v. *Costa Brava Wine Co. Ltd.* (*No.* 2) (1961) concerned an action by a manufacturer of champagne against the defendants who described their wine, produced in Spain, as "Spanish champagne." It was held that the word "champagne" was still generally regarded as referring exclusively to wine produced in the Champagne district of France; that the prefix "Spanish" did not prevent the possibility of purchasers being misled into thinking they were purchasing such wine; that the plaintiff could obtain an injunction to prevent the defendant's use of the name, although he was only one of the wine producers in the Champagne district.

When the plaintiff is alleging that he alone has the right to use words which simply describe the goods or their characteristics, he has a difficult burden of proof to discharge in that he must show that these words have acquired the status of a trade name. This was achieved by the successful plaintiff in *Reddaway* v. *Banham* (*George*) *& Co. Ltd.* (1896) where an injunction was obtained to protect the name "Camel Hair Belting." It is possible, though not decided, that where the trade name ceases to be exclusively identified with the plaintiff and comes to be regarded as a description of the product itself, he can no longer sue to protect it. It may be, however, that the explanation is that this acquiescence in its use by others over a period of time allows the defendant to establish a defence of consent.

Use of plaintiff's name

It is sometimes said that there is nothing to prevent a person trading by or describing his goods by his own name. But it is clear that this is not so where the use of the name is fraudulent (*Croft* v. *Day* (1843)), nor where, though innocent, it creates avoidable confusion with that of the plaintiff (*Baume & Co. Ltd.* v. *A. H. Moore Ltd.* (1958)). Where confusion is unavoidable it seems that the defendant is entitled to use his own name, unless the plaintiff can prove that in the minds of the public the production of goods under a certain name is exclusively associated with himself (*Parker-Knoll* v. *Knoll International* (1962)).

Imitating appearance of plaintiff's goods

There are common-sense limitations to this method of committing the tort. Thus, where the similarity between the goods is in their functional rather than their decorative aspects, the courts are normally unwilling to interfere.

Action for torts analogous to passing-off

The courts have also allowed actions in some cases where no action for passing-off would lie, if the case is analogous to passing-off. For example, though no action for passing-off will lie where plaintiff and defendant are not in economic competition (see *McCulloch* v. *May Ltd.* (1947)—plaintiff, a children's broadcaster who used the name "Uncle Mac" unsuccessful in action of passing-off against defendants who manufactured a cereal, "Uncle Mac's Puffed Wheat"), it seems to be accepted that an action for a tort analogous to passing-off will lie if the defendant's act is calculated to cause damage to the plaintiff's reputation or livelihood (held so in *Sim* v. *H. J. Heinz Co. Ltd.* (1959) and *Borthwick* v. *Evening Post* (1888)—in that case an injunction by the proprietor of the *Morning Post* against the defendants to prevent them calling their evening newspaper the *Evening Post*, was refused only because the defendant's act was not calculated to cause the plaintiff damage).

An action analogous to passing-off was also available in *Sales Affiliates Ltd.* v. *Le Jean Ltd.* (1947). The plaintiffs marketed materials which were used in a permanent wave process known as "Jamal." There was evidence that this process was exclusively associated in the trade with the plaintiff's materials. The defendant hairdressers used other materials when asked by their customers for the "Jamal" treatment. This was held to be a tort analogous to passing-off, the latter not being available because the defendant had not sold goods or services to the public which they had represented as those of the plaintiffs.

Other requirements of passing-off and the analogous torts

Act calculated to deceive

It is a question of fact whether the defendant's act is calculated to deceive. Evidence may be received from persons actually deceived but such evidence is not necessary.

Defendant need not know of the infringement

It is settled that passing-off can be committed by one who is acting in complete good faith and without negligence. This emphasises the proprietary nature of the action and here also it resembles conversion.

Damage

It is unnecessary to prove damage in an action of passing-off.

Further, the court may, as in the case of libel, presume that damage will flow from the defendant's act and thus award substantial damages though no actual damage is proved. It is, however, doubtful whether damages can be claimed from the defendant for the period before he knows of the infringement. In the action for the analogous tort the plaintiff must show that the defendant's act is calculated to cause damage to his business or reputation.

Other forms of unjust trade competition

Some forms of trade competition are outside the scope of an action of passing-off or the analogous action. An example of this is *Cambridge University Press* v. *University Tutorial Press* (1928). The defendants claimed that a book published by them was the book prescribed for study by an examination board for its examination. In fact the book published by the plaintiffs had been prescribed. The plaintiffs' action against the defendants failed. Clearly, people could not have been misled into believing that they were buying the plaintiff's book; but if the use of the plaintiff's name is actionable if calculated to cause him damage (*supra*, p. 273), why should not also be the use of a quality with which the plaintiff is exclusively associated (another example would be a claim by garage A that it was the last before a motorway, whereas this was true of garage B)? There seems to be no real difference of principle between the *Cambridge University* case and *Sales Affiliates* v. *Le Jean*, in which the plaintiff was successful. For similar reasons, it seems that the law will not protect the plaintiff whose "scoop" newspaper story is published without acknowledgment by the defendant, or the dog-racing stadium broadcast commentaries of whose races are relayed from a vantage point outside the stadium (*Victoria Park Racing and Recreation Grounds Co. Ltd.* v. *Taylor* (1937)).

Where an action for passing-off, or the analogous tort, is not available, there is still a possibility of obtaining an injunction, if the court considers that the defendant is infringing a right of property of the plaintiff. The availability of the injunction depends therefore upon the extent to which courts are willing to recognise new rights of intangible property. So far, however, the courts have confined its availability to cases where the defendant is abusing information entrusted to him in confidence by the plaintiff (*cf. infra*, p. 294). Whether the protection will be extended to cases where the defendant is not breaking a confidence is a problem for the future.

CHAPTER 24

THE ECONOMIC TORTS: DECEIT AND INJURIOUS FALSEHOOD

DECEIT

THE tort of deceit is committed by one who makes a fraudulent misrepresentation to another who acts upon it to his detriment. The tort is not limited to the recovery of financial loss (in *Burrows* v. *Rhodes* (1899) the plaintiff recovered for physical injury suffered through his participation in the Jameson raid which he joined on the strength of a false representation by the defendant). Deceit has become of reduced importance since a duty of care in respect of statements was recognised by the House of Lords in *Hedley Byrne* v. *Heller and Partners Ltd.* (1963). But differences in the measure of damages in deceit (*infra*, p. 277) may mean that it is still worthwhile to attempt to prove fraud rather than negligence. It is still necessary to prove fraud in the making of the statement where either the requirements of *Hedley Byrne* or of the Misrepresentation Act 1967 (*supra*, p. 78) cannot be met.

Requirements of deceit

The requirements of deceit are as follows:

(i) the defendant must make a false representation;

(ii) he must either know that it is false or make it recklessly, not caring whether it is true or false;

(iii) he must intend that the plaintiff act or fail to act on the representation;

(iv) the plaintiff must suffer damage as a result of his reliance on the representation.

False representation

The term "representation" has acquired a restricted meaning given to it by courts of equity in deciding whether to grant the equitable remedy of rescission. Representations about the future intentions of the representor, opinions and representations of law are excluded. The term is similarly limited in the tort of deceit. But a statement of future intention is actionable if at the time of making it the defendant did not have that intention, since there is sufficient factual content in the representation, *viz*. that at the time of making it he did have that intention (*Edgington* v. *Fitzmaurice* (1885)). Similarly a statement of opinion is at least a representation that the defendant actually holds that opinion. In *West London Commercial Bank Ltd.* v. *Kitson* (1884) a representation about the effect of a private Act of Parliament was held to be actionable in deceit, but it cannot be predicated whether this would be true of a representation about the general law. There is also liability for stating half-truths, ambiguities, and for action taken to conceal the truth (*Schneider* v. *Heath* (1813)—defendant took steps to conceal from a prospective buyer that his ship had rotten timbers). There is authority in support of the view that one who knows that events subsequent to the making of a statement make it no longer true is liable, as is one who subsequently discovers the falsity of the statement, if the statement is left uncorrected (this does not extend, however, to one who changes his mind after an accurate statement of future intention).

Knowledge of the falsity

There is some difficulty where the representation is made by a person other than the defendant. Where a servant acting in the course of his employment commits deceit, the master is vicariously liable. The same applies to a principal, where his agent has committed the tort, provided the agent has authority to make representations in the relevant matter. There is also liability if a fraudulent principal makes the representation through an innocent agent. But it is not possible to make the principal liable where his agent has innocently made a misrepresentation of whose untruth the principal would have known (*Armstrong* v. *Strain* (1952)). There would, of course, be liability if the principal knew that the agent was making the misrepresentation.

Intention that plaintiff should act on the representation

It is not necessary that the representation should be made to the plaintiff himself. Thus, in *Langridge* v. *Levy* (1837), the plaintiff's father bought a gun from the defendant who knew that the father intended his sons to use it. The defendant fraudulently represented that the gun was sound. He was held liable to the plaintiff who was injured when the gun burst on firing. Clearly the defendant *intended* the sons to act upon the statement though he did not *desire* it, since whether they did or not became immaterial to him after the completion of the father's purchase. On the other hand, in *Peek* v. *Gurney* (1873) it was held that statements in a prospectus issued by the defendant were intended by him to be acted upon only by those who acquired shares by subscription from the company (to whom the prospectus would have been issued) and not by subsequent purchasers of the shares on the market. The fact that it is foreseeable that the plaintiff should act on the representation is, therefore, not enough. This rule, though satisfactory for negligent statements, seems open to criticism where fraudulent statements are concerned.

Plaintiff's reliance on the representation

It must be shown that the representation was at least one of the reasons for the plaintiff acting as he did. Thus, in *Smith* v. *Chadwick* (1884), the plaintiff had bought shares in a company on the faith of a prospectus which contained the untrue statement that a certain person was a director of the company. Since the plaintiff had never heard of this person, he could not show that he relied on the statement in the prospectus and his action therefore failed.

Plaintiff must suffer damage

The normal claim in deceit is for economic loss, but personal injury and damage to property are also recoverable.

Remedies

An action for damages is the virtually invariable remedy for deceit. In *Doyle* v. *Olby* (*Ironmongers*) *Ltd.* (1969) the plaintiff bought a business from the defendants about which the latter had made various fraudulent misrepresentations including one to the effect that all the trade was over the counter whereas, in fact, the employment of a traveller was necessary. The plaintiff recovered the following items as damages: (i) the difference between the price he paid for the business and its actual value; (ii) expenditure incurred in the course of running the business, *viz.* rent, rates, and the interest on a bank overdraft. In contract the plaintiff would have recovered only the difference between the value of the business as represented and its actual value, since in contract the plaintiff is put into the position he would have been in had the representation been made good; in tort he is put into the same position as if it had never been made. The damages awarded for the first item included the reduction in value through the plaintiff's being unable to afford to employ a traveller. This suggests that in deceit damages will be awarded even though they are caused by the plaintiff's impecuniosity, a more favourable measure than in tort generally (*cf. Liesbosch* (*Dredger*) v. *S.S. Edison* (*Owners*) (1933)). Lord Denning went so far as to say that the defendant was liable for all loss flowing directly from the fraud, whether foreseeable or not. *Mafo* v. *Adams* (1970) decided that exemplary damages may also be recovered in deceit though only if the case comes within one of the three categories laid down by Lord Devlin in *Rookes* v. *Barnard* (*infra*, p. 306).

Lord Tenterden's Act

Under the Statute of Frauds 1677 a guarantee was unenforceable unless it was in writing and signed by the guarantor or his agent. After the action for deceit was created in 1789, it became possible to circumvent the statute by suing in deceit rather than on the guarantee itself. This resulted in the passing of Lord Tenterden's Act in 1828 which provided that a false representation as to credit could not be sued upon unless made in writing and signed by the representor or his agent. The Act is limited to fraudulent representations—it does not apply where the representation is made negligently (*W. B. Anderson* v. *Rhodes* (*Liverpool*) (1967)). The curious result is produced that the defendant might be able to defeat an action brought in respect of an oral representation as to credit by establishing his own fraud, though whether the courts would allow him to succeed is not clear.

Injurious Falsehood

Injurious or malicious falsehood consists in the making of a false statement by the defendant about the plaintiff or his property which is calculated to cause him damage and as a result of which the plaintiff suffers damage. The tort is a generalisation from specific cases. It was called slander of title to make a verbal attack on another persons's title to land as a result of which the land lost value or a purchaser could not be found for it. Slander of goods consisted in a similar attack on the plaintiff's chattels. The close relationship of these torts to defamation itself is indicated by their name. In *Ratcliffe* v. *Evans* (1892), however, the Court of Appeal found that these torts formed part of a wider principle by virtue of which any intentionally false statement made by the defendant about the plaintiff or his property was actionable, even though it was not defamatory, if it resulted in damage to the plaintiff. In that case the defendant published a statement in his newspaper that the plaintiff's firm had ceased to exist, knowing that this was untrue. The plaintiff recovered damages from the defendant in injurious falsehood for the loss of custom he suffered as a result of the statement.

Elements of the tort

The following are the chief elements of the tort:

(1) *There must be a false statement about the plaintiff or his property*

Where the statement does not refer to the plaintiff or his property, this does not appear to be tortious even though the plaintiff suffers damage as a result. If, for example, on the facts of *Ratcliffe* v. *Evans*, another firm which enjoyed advantageous business relations with the plaintiff's firm had also suffered economic loss as a result of the loss of custom suffered by the plaintiff's firm, this would not have been recoverable from the defendant. This requirement of injurious falsehood appears to be the reason why statements such as that made in *Cambridge University Press* v. *University Tutorial Press* (*supra*, p. 274) are not actionable.

(2) *The statement must be calculated to cause the plaintiff damage*

Because of the courts' policy whereby they will not allow advertising campaigns by rival business men to be conducted in court, the defendant is not liable if his statement is a mere puff, extolling his own product, even at the expense of the plaintiff's. Thus, in *White* v. *Mellin* (1895), the defendant sold infant food produced by the plaintiff in his shop. He affixed to the bottles in which the food was sold, labels stating that a certain food (produced by the defendant) was better in several respects for infants than any other. This was held not to be injurious falsehood. Where, however, the defendant has made a disparaging statement about the plaintiff which goes beyond a mere puff, the requirement that it is calculated to cause damage to the plaintiff is fairly easily satisfied. In *Lyne* v. *Nichols* (1906) a statement by a newspaper proprietor that the circulation of his newspaper greatly exceeded that of the plaintiff's rival newspaper was held to be actionable. Again, in *De Beers Abrasive Products* v. *International General Electric Co. of New York* (1975), where the defendant had circulated in the international trade market a pamphlet which purported to give the findings of laboratory experiments concerning the effectiveness of an abrasive manufactured by the defendants and another manufactured by the plaintiffs, the experiments concluding that the defendants' abrasive was superior, this was held to be more than a mere puff and was capable of amounting to slander of goods.

(3) *The statement must be made to a third party or parties*

The gist of this tort is that third parties, influenced by the statement, act to the loss of the plaintiff. The plaintiff must therefore show that the statement has come to the knowledge of third parties. Whether, if this happens by the negligence of the defendant, or accidentally, the tort is committed, is uncertain. In the former case, at least, it seems there should be liability.

(4) *The statement must be made maliciously*

This requirement causes most difficulty in connection with this tort. Although malice seems originally to have been necessary only where it was necessary to rebut a "privilege" claimed by the defendant (for example, in cases of slander of title, the defendant himself might have claimed an interest in the land), it now seems to be accepted as applying to all the forms which the tort may take. But the meaning of malice here is dubious. If the defendant makes a statement knowing it to be false, and the statement is calculated to cause damage to the plaintiff, it might be thought that malice is easy to establish. Can the defendant rebut this evidence of malice by showing that he acted for the plaintiff's good? For example, if the defendant makes a false statement about the plaintiff's business to a third party causing that person not to award a profitable contract to the plaintiff, ought the defendant to be able to excuse himself on the ground that he considered it not in the plaintiff's best interest for him to undertake this contract? None of the cases seem to have gone this far, and in *White* v. *Mellin* (*supra*) the House of Lords thought (*obiter*) that either an intention to injure the plaintiff, or a knowledge of the statement's falsity would be enough. It is settled that malice may be established although the defendant was acting to further his own trade interests. Thus, in *Joyce* v. *Motor Surveys Ltd.* (1948), the defendants wished to evict the plaintiff from the tenancy of one of their garages, because they wished to sell their business with vacant possession throughout. They told the Post Office that he had changed his address, and told the tyre manufacturers' association that the plaintiff had ceased trading there (the plaintiff was a tyre dealer). This was held to constitute injurious falsehood. The burden of proving malice lies on the plaintiff.

(5) *Damage*

The plaintiff must show that he suffered damage as a result of the statement. This will normally be pecuniary, though there seems no reason to exclude a claim for physical damage where this has occurred. Where he is claiming that he suffered loss of custom as a result of the defendant's statement, it is not always necessary to call the evidence of particular customers who have ceased trading with him as a result of the statement. In *Ratcliffe* v. *Evans* (*supra*), for example, the plaintiff was allowed to succeed on proof of general business loss, rather than the loss of particular customers. Whether the plaintiff is allowed to do this will depend largely upon the type of falsehood and the circumstances of its utterance. Section 3 (1) of the Defamation Act 1952 further alleviates the position of the plaintiff by allowing him to succeed without proof of special damage at all, (a) if the words complained of are published in writing or other permanent form, and are calculated to cause pecuniary damage to the plaintiff; or (b) if the words are calculated to cause pecuniary damage to the plaintiff in respect of any office, profession, calling, trade or business carried on by him at the time of the publication.

Since most actions for injurious falsehood occur when the plaintiff has suffered such damage, and the majority of these concern damage to the plaintiff's trading interests, the necessity to prove damage will now only rarely arise. Where the requirements of the Act are fulfilled, the subsection places injurious falsehood in the same position as regards proof of damage as libel and slander actionable *per se*. *Fielding* v. *Variety Incorporated* (1967) shows both the close association between defamation and injurious falsehood and the fact that it may be advantageous to prove the defamatory nature of the statement. The defendants' magazine had published a statement that a play, "Charlie Girl," produced by the plaintiff had been a "disastrous flop." In fact the play had been a great success. The plaintiff recovered £1,500 for libel and £100 for injurious falsehood, the difference being due to the fact that damages for injury to feelings may be awarded in defamation but in injurious falsehood the plaintiff is limited to his actual loss.

Injurious falsehood and negligent misstatement

A curious position has arisen in relation to the torts of injurious falsehood and negligence. The former tort is clearly not an easy one to prove, since even if malice means only a knowledge of the falsity of the statement, there are obvious difficulties in establishing this. Furthermore, there is no particular advantage in succeeding in injurious falsehood since the plaintiff can only recover as damages his actual loss, although the faint possibility of exemplary damages exists if the defendant can be shown to have calculated to make a profit out of the commission of the tort. It seems therefore that if a duty of care could be shown to exist in respect of a statement made by A to B causing B to act to C's loss so that C could sue A in negligence, actions in injurious falsehood would virtually disappear. Whether negligence does lie in these circumstances is unclear and depends upon the interpretation that is placed on two decisions of the Court of Appeal. In *Ministry of Housing* v. *Sharp* (1970), the defendant local authority was held liable for the negligence of its clerk who issued a "clear certificate" to a purchaser of land who had applied for a search of the register of land charges. The result of the issue of the certificate was that a charge held over the land by the plaintiff, the *Ministry of Housing*, became unenforceable. The

Court of Appeal held the defendants liable for the loss the plaintiff had suffered. It is not clear whether the charge became destroyed through the actual purchase of the land (*i.e.* B's acting on A's statement to C's loss) or because the issue of the certificate itself automatically had this effect (*cf.* Winfield, p. 237). If the latter view is correct, the case has little to do with liability for negligent statements. In any case the Court of Appeal did not make anything of this distinction, and it may be possible to derive from the judgments the rule that where loss to C is clearly a foreseeable result of the statement, then A is liable in negligence. The other case is *Dutton* v. *Bognor Regis U.D.C.* (1972) (*supra*, p. 80). If the council's approval in that case were regarded as a statement, then it is clear that it was acted on to the loss of Mrs. Dutton. It is true that the Court of Appeal did not treat the case as turning on liability for misstatement, and it is possible to justify this view though on rather tenuous grounds (*supra*, p. 81). On the basis of these cases, therefore, it is too early to conclude that an action of negligence lies in the situation under review. In America it has been held that a person who has lost a benefit under a will because of the negligence of the solicitor who advised the testator could succeed against the solicitor in negligence (*Biakanja* v. *Irving* (1958)). There seems no reason why English courts should not follow the principle of this decision provided proximity between plaintiff and defendant is sufficiently close.

CHAPTER 25

INTERFERENCE WITH FAMILY RELATIONSHIPS

INTRODUCTION

THE law on the subject of torts which interfere with family relationships at one time bristled with anomalies. Most of the worst of these have been removed by the Law Reform Miscellaneous Provisions) Act 1970, which has abolished the torts of enticement, seduction (including rape) and harbouring of a child, enticement of a spouse and harbouring of a wife. Section 4 of the Act removes a husband's right to damages from a co-respondent for his adultery with his wife. The only important torts of interference with family relationships which survive are a parent's action for loss of his child's services and the husband's action for loss of his wife's consortium. Even these torts are in many respects irrational, and it is probable that there will soon be further reform in this area of the law (more sweeping changes were envisaged by the Working Paper of the Law Commission on this subject—the changes effected by the Act of 1970 are merely part of these). The Law Commission in its Report on Personal Injury Litigation-Assessment of Damages (No. 56) has recommended the abolition of the parent's action for loss of his child's services, and the husband's action for the loss of his wife's consortium.

It is noteworthy that the surviving torts supply a very incomplete protection for family relationships. A child has no action for injury to its parents, even though as a result of the injury the child has suffered loss of financial support or has incurred medical expenses on the parent's behalf. The first loss will no doubt be defrayed when the parent himself recovers tort damages, although by that time it may be too late; for example, the child may have lost a business opportunity. These remarks apply also to the case of the wife, where her husband suffers injury. She cannot obtain damages for loss of her husband's consortium (*infra*, p. 288). Where, however, the tort has caused the death of the parent or husband, before either has been able to bring his own action, dependants can obtain the full measure of their loss of financial support by taking action under the Fatal Accidents Acts 1846–1959.

Parent's Action for Loss of Child's Services

Nature of the defendant's act

The parent must prove that the defendant committed a tort against the child, leading to the loss of service, other than a tort committed in the course of rape. For example, the defendant may have injured the child by committing battery, or negligence.

Proof of loss of services

The parent in his action, which derives from the same source as the master's action for the loss of his servant's service, *i.e.* the *actio per quod servitium amisit*, must establish that he was in receipt of services from the child and that he has been deprived of these as the result of the defendant's act. In theory, therefore, the action is intended to recompense the parent for his economic loss. In practice the courts are willing to place an economic value on the most trivial of domestic services, for example, the making of a cup of tea (*Carr* v. *Clarke* (1818)) or the milking of cows (*Bennett* v. *Allcott* (1787)); indeed the presence of a child under the age of majority in the parent's household is normally enough to imply the fact of service (*Jones* v. *Brown* (1794)). Furthermore, the fact that such services will not be replaced at the parent's expense (for example, by engaging a housekeeper) is irrelevant. But the child must be of a sufficient age to be capable of rendering service—so the parent had no action when his two-year-old child suffered an illness through the defendant's tort (*Hall* v. *Hollander* (1825)). The fact that the child has attained its majority is irrelevant provided service by it is proved. The only difference appears to be that with such a child, service will not be presumed merely from the fact that the child lived in the same household as its parent (*Bennett* v. *Allcott* (*supra*))—that case is an illustration of the ease with which service may be otherwise established).

Plaintiff in the action

The parent's enjoyment of the child's services is part of his right to the custody of the child, a right which normally persists until the child reaches his majority. Custody was at one time held to be the right of the father alone. Now, however, at least where the spouses are living together, each is jointly entitled to custody, and the mother also may bring the action for loss of services (as she may also do when she alone has custody, for example, when her husband is dead). The action may also be brought by any other person who has custody of the child, and who is in receipt of its services, for example, an adoptive parent or a foster parent.

Measure of damages

The damages that can be awarded in this tort are limited to the actual pecuniary loss suffered by the parent. Aggravated damages in respect of injury to the parent's feelings or emotional distress caused by the child's condition cannot be recovered (*Flemington* v. *Smithers* (1826)). But the parent is not restricted to claiming an amount representing the value of the lost services. He is also entitled to claim any out-of-pocket expenses reasonably incurred because of the tort, *e.g.*, medical expenses (*Bates* v. *Stone Parish Council* (1954)).

Defences

Contributory negligence by the child does not appear to be a defence, since the parent's action is distinct from that of the child (so held for the analogous action by husband for loss of wife's consortium—*Mallet* v. *Dunn* (1949)). Does this mean that consent by the child will not bar the parent's action? Consent by the parent clearly does so (for example, consent to operation on child).

Conclusion

The tort by its very nature is anomalous. Its requirement that the parent must establish loss of service makes the basis of the claim extremely artificial. In the first place, it means that in many cases the parent receives a financial sum puporting to represent the economic value of the services, but in fact operating more like a payment by way of solatium for the parent's grief. In the second place, the requirement of service bars the reasonable claim of the parent who has incurred expenses on behalf of a child from whom he is not in receipt of service.

Husband's Action for Loss of Consortium

A husband may claim damages in respect of a tortious injury to the wife the result of which is that he is deprived of her consortium (which may be described as companionship and support) and her services. Although the action depends upon proof of a tort committed against the wife, the husband's action is quite distinct from that of the wife. So his action is not affected by the wife's contributory negligence (*Mallet* v. *Dunn* (1949)—*quaere*, the effect of other defences available against the wife).

There is a great deal of uncertainty about the types of damage which can be claimed in an action for loss of consortium. Three types of damage must be distinguished: (1) damage arising from loss of the wife's companionship; (2) damage arising from the loss of the services of the wife; (3) medical and other out-of-pocket expenses reasonably incurred by the husband. There is no doubt of the husband's right to claim under the third head in his action for loss of consortium. Furthermore, it does not matter that there has never been any actual loss of consortium, for example, if the wife receives medical treatment at home. For this reason, the courts have sometimes based the husband's right upon his legal obligation to maintain his wife, so necessitating expenditure by him in the event of her injury.

Under the second head of damage, it seems, it has always been recognised that the husband may claim for the expense of hiring services during a period of total loss of consortium, for example, while the wife was in hospital. There has been uncertainty about the availability of such a claim when cohabitation has been resumed. In *Best* v. *Samuel Fox & Co.* (1952) the House of Lords were equally divided on the question whether the husband could maintain an action when his consortium has merely been impaired, rather than totally lost. Recent cases, however, have favoured the husband's claim where he has been deprived of services during a period when consortium is merely impaired. So in *Cutts* v. *Chumley* (1967) where the wife was rendered totally incapable by her injuries of rendering services, the husband received £5,000 damages representing the future expense of employing a housekeeper to look after the three young children of the marriage. Even where the husband has not had to incur expense in order to replace the wife's services, the court may allow a claim by him. For example, in *Lawrence* v. *Biddle* (1966), a husband who would be required to do more work in the house because of the wife's injury was awarded £40 damages. The definition of such damage in the Australian case of *Toohey* v. *Hollier* (1955) as being of a "material and practical kind because of greatly reduced capacity of his wife to perform the domestic duties, to manage the household affairs and give him her support and assistance" expresses the matter best.

The first head creates the most difficulty. There is no doubt that the husband may claim damages for loss of consortium during the period when he has been totally deprived of his wife's society, even though during this period he has incurred no expense. The only basis for such damage is therefore loss of companionship. It seems very doubtful whether any further damages can be awarded in respect of such intangible matters as diminution of conjugal happiness after resumption of cohabitation (although in *Best* v. *Samuel Fox* (*supra*), Lord Reid, consistently with his view that the action protected impairment as well as total loss of consortium, thought that the husband would have a claim where the wife became sexually frigid as a result of the injury).

Another problem arises where the husband claims for loss of earnings arising from the fact that he has given up his employment in order to visit his wife in hospital. This loss is allowable as damages only if the visits will have the effect of shortening the wife's stay in hospital and therefore the period of loss of consortium, or of maintaining consortium between husband and wife, and thereby reducing the damages that would have to be paid for loss of it (*Kirkham* v. *Boughey* (1957); *McNeill* v. *Johnstone* (1958)).

Since the basis of the claim for loss of earnings is that they substitute damages that would otherwise be awarded for loss of consortium, it seems unlikely that loss of earnings could be recovered beyong the amount of those damages (see, for example, the judgment of Lord Devlin in *McNeill* v. *Johnstone*). Where the husband does not make loss of consortium the basis of his claim, he cannot recover loss of earnings through giving up his employment in order to be near or with his wife, even though he acted reasonably (*Kirkham* v. *Boughey*, *supra*—the husband gave up lucrative employment in Africa in order to be near to and visit his wife in hospital. Since he and his wife lived separately while he was in Africa, he could not make the maintenance of consortium the basis of his claim for loss of earnings).

Master and Servant

The torts involving a master's claim for the loss of services of his servant are survivals from the days when servants were regarded as part of the master's family circle. It remains a tort to deprive the master of the services of his servant by enticing him or harbouring him although both actions are now obsolete. The *actio per quod servitium amisit* is of rather greater importance since it allows a master to recover from a person who has deprived him of the services of his servant by tortiously injuring the servant. The tort may be one resting on proof of intention or negligence, so that in the case of the latter the action is an exception to the rule that negligence will not lie for purely pecuniary loss. The importance of this tort was, however, considerably reduced by the decision in *I.R.C.* v. *Hambrook* (1956) that it was limited to cases where the service was menial or domestic. The Law Commission's Report on Personal Injury Litigation-Assessment of Damages (No. 56) recommends the abolition of all the torts mentioned in this paragraph.

Conclusion

Apart from the cases discussed already, no relational claim (*i.e.* related to, or derived from the claim of the person injured) exists in English law, apart from the claim of the dependants under the Fatal Accidents Acts. In *Best* v. *Samuel Fox & Co.* (1952) the House of Lords held that a wife had no claim for loss of her husband's consortium, on the ground that the husband's claim was a historical anomaly, and should not be extended. The law relating to the protection of family relationships is thus both archaic (in particular, in the requirement of proof of service in the parent's claim for injury to a child and of loss of consortium in the husband's claim for injury to a wife), and fragmentary. Rather than extend rights of of this sort to wives or children, the Law Commission has recommended their abolition in the case of husbands and parents. Some mitigation of this is enshrined in the recommendation that the victim himself should be able to recover a sum representing the value of services gratuitously rendered, or expenses gratuitously incurred on his behalf by a third party, a suggestion that already appears to represent the existing law (*infra*, p. 310).

CHAPTER 26

MALICIOUS PROSECUTION AND ABUSE OF PROCESS

MALICIOUS PROSECUTION

MALICIOUS prosecution is committed by one who maliciously and without reasonable and probable cause institutes criminal or civil proceedings against the plaintiff, the result of the proceedings being in the plaintiff's favour, and the plaintiff thereby suffering damage. The formidable series of hurdles the plaintiff must surmount in order to succeed in this tort accounts both for the rarity of actions for it and for the low proportion of those which succeed. It is questionable whether the public interest in the bringing of criminal prosecutions requires such extensive protection at the expense of the private interest in not being brought unnecessarily to court.

The tort must be distinguished from false imprisonment. Clearly distinct interests are protected by the two torts. False imprisonment protects against loss of liberty by wrongful arrest, malicious prosecution against all forms of wrongful institution of legal proceedings whether or not they include an arrest. The two may overlap where the legal proceedings instituted include an arrest. But this overlap is reduced to a minimum by the requirement of directness in false imprisonment. So it is not false imprisonment but may be malicious prosecution where the defendant has obtained a warrant for the plaintiff's arrest, or has signed the charge-sheet, and his arrest follows, since in these cases an independent decision is interposed between the plaintiff's action and the arrest. If, however, the police make it clear that they will not arrest the plaintiff unless the defendant signs the charge-sheet, the defendant may commit false imprisonment (*Hopkins* v. *Crowe* (1836); *Grinham* v. *Willey* (1859)). Malicious prosecution is one of the torts in which a right to jury trial exists.

Prosecution

The defendant must be the person "actively instrumental" in causing proceedings to be brought against the plaintiff. In the large number of prosecutions brought by the police, the prosecutor is the police officer who conducts the prosecution, even though he may have acted on the advice of his superior officers in deciding to prosecute. A private person who gives information to the police or to a magistrate as the result of which a prosecution is brought is not the prosecutor, since the decision to prosecute is not his. If, however, he has signed the charge-sheet, he is then the prosecutor even though the police are not bound to bring criminal proceedings. Although it used to be thought that the mere laying of an information or bill of indictment before a magistrate was not a sufficient commencement of the proceedings to constitute a prosecution, unless the magistrate issued in consequence a summons against the plaintiff or a warrant for his arrest, it now appears to be the law that, if the magistrate has begun to inquire into the merits of the case, this may amount to a prosecution provided the plaintiff suffers damage thereby (*Mohamed Amin* v. *Jogendra Kuma Bannerjee* (1947)).

Termination of the proceedings in the plaintiff's favour

This requirement of the tort is satisfied even though the plaintiff has won on a technicality such as a defect in the indictment or excess of jurisdiction in the court.

Absence of reasonable and probable cause

The plaintiff has the difficult onus of proving the negative, that there was no reasonable and probable cause for the institution of proceedings against him. Such absence may be established in one of two ways: (i) the plaintiff may show that the prosecutor had no honest belief in the probable guilt of the plaintiff; (ii) he may show that despite the prosecutor's honest belief in the plaintiff's probable guilt, the facts which the defendant honestly believed would not lead a man of ordinary prudence and caution to that conclusion.

Both means of discharging the plaintiff's onus require the court to inquire into the prosecutor's state of mind. If dishonesty on the defendant's part is established, it is irrelevant that the facts as found by the jury would have led a man of prudence and caution to believe in the plaintiff's probable guilt. The second method involves an inquiry into the facts honestly believed by the defendant and then an objective determination whether these facts ought to have caused him to believe in the plaintiff's guilt. The jury as the tribunal of fact will answer the question whether the defendant was dishonest and if they find he was this will determine the question whether there was reasonable cause. If they find the defendant to be honest, the jury must determine what facts the defendant honestly believed, and it is for the court to decide whether these were capable of furnishing reasonable and probable cause.

The fact that the defendant took advice before instituting proceedings seems logically relevant only to whether he was dishonest, not also to whether or not the facts he believed constituted reasonable cause. But several recent cases have indicated that this fact may be sufficient to determine both issues in the plaintiff's favour (*Malz* v. *Rosen* (1966)—private person prosecuting on advice of police; *Glinki* v. *McIver* (1962)—(*obiter*)—police officer acting on advice of his superiors, for example, the legal department of Scotland Yard). To take advantage of this rule, the defendant must communicate all the facts which he knows to the other person.

Malice

The plaintiff also has the notoriously difficult task of proving malice on the defendant's part. This is most commonly achieved where criminal proceedings are involved by showing that the prosecutor acted for some ulterior purpose of his own rather than the furtherance of justice (for example, *Stevens* v. *Midland Counties Ry. Co.* (1854)—purpose of prosecuting plaintiff was to keep other persons away from the defendant's property). No doubt generalised ill-will towards the plaintiff is enough, but feelings of anger and resentment arising from the facts on which the defendant bases his decision to prosecute are not.

The judge decides whether there is evidence of malice to go to the jury. The jury decides whether there was malice in fact.

The two issues of malice and absence of reasonable and probable cause must be kept separate by the judge in advising the jury. Thus, though malice exists, there may still be reasonable cause for bringing the prosecution and no inference can be drawn of the absence of reasonable cause from the presence of malice. Where, however, reasonable cause is absent, this does not *ipso facto* establish malice but may justify an inference of malice (*Johnstone* v. *Sutton* (1786)). Such inference is particularly likely to be drawn where it is shown that the defendant has no honest belief in the plaintiff's guilt.

Damage

The tort of malicious prosecution requires proof of actual damage. Because damages are not at large, the plaintiff cannot recover for his distress or humiliation arising from the prosecution even though he has succeeded in showing malice on the part of the defendant. Actual damage may be proved under one or more of three heads established by *Savile* v. *Roberts* (1968).

These are:

(i) Damage to reputation. The charge against the plaintiff must be necessarily defamatory of him, not merely capable of being understood in a defamatory sense, malicious prosecution being narrower here than defamation. To accuse the plaintiff of pulling the communication cord in a train is not defamatory (*Berry* v. *British Transport Commission* (1962)).

(ii) Damage in respect of the personal security of the plaintiff. Mere exposure of the plaintiff to the risk of imprisonment because of the charge seems enough (*Wiffen* v. *Bailey and Romford U.C.* (1915)—*contra*, Diplock J. *obiter* in *Berry's* case).

(iii) Pecuniary loss. The plaintiff may recover the difference between actual costs awarded him and the amount of his defence costs (*Berry's* case), but unsatisfactorily this does not appear to be the rule where civil proceedings were instituted against the plaintiff.

Abuse of Process

It is the above tort maliciously and in the absence of reasonable cause to make use of a legal process against the plaintiff (other than the institution of proceedings against him, and the mere swearing of false evidence—see *Hargreaves* v. *Bretherton* (1958)) as the result of which the plaintiff suffers damage. The tort differs from malicious prosecution in that the process does not have to terminate in the plaintiff's favour, and any form of temporal loss constitutes damage. In *Roy* v. *Prior* (1970) the defendant obtained a bench warrant for the arrest of the plaintiff by swearing in evidence to the court, falsely as the plaintiff alleged, that the plaintiff was evading service of a witness summons. The House of Lords held that, by proving these facts, *i.e.* that he had suffered damage and that the defendant had acted maliciously and without reasonable cause, the plaintiff would establish a good cause of action against the defendant. It did not matter that the defendant had allegedly obtained the bench warrant by giving false evidence since the gist of the action was not the mere giving of false evidence but the defendant's institution of a legal process against the plaintiff maliciously and without reasonable cause.

CHAPTER 27

INNOMINATE AND DOUBTFUL TORTS

INNOMINATE TORTS

IN this chapter will be discussed a number of cases which cannot be classified under previously mentioned categories. Innominate torts are those which escape classification either because the interest protected is an unusual one, or because they are analogous to torts which protect a well-recognised interest. There is a large variety of torts of the former class of which only a few examples can be given. It is a tort actionable *per se* for a member of a common calling to refuse to provide services to the public. So an innkeeper is liable in tort for refusing to provide accommodation which he has available to the plaintiff (*Constantine* v. *Imperial Hotels Ltd.* (1944)). It is a tort actionable *per se* to interfere with another person's right to vote (held so far as the Returning Officer of a constituency was concerned in *Ashby* v. *White* (1703), although this person now has a statutory defence to such an action). It is tortious to interfere with a right of franchise enjoyed by another, an example of such a franchise being the exclusive right to carry for hire goods or passengers by means of boats across a river or arm of the sea.

Innominate torts which are analogous to nominate torts have been discussed in various sections of this book. So, for example, those with a reversionary interest in land or in chattels can sue in tort for damage done to such interests though they cannot comply with the strict requirements of trespass or conversion (*supra*, pp. 42, 50). Other examples discussed above are torts analogous to false imprisonment (*supra*, p. 16) or passing-off (*supra*, p. 270).

DOUBTFUL TORTS

Interference with occupation

Although the phrase "right to work" is an emotive one and although no such generalised legal right exists, it is undoubtedly true that courts will sometimes intervene to protect the plaintiff in the exercise of his occupation or profession. What is not clear is whether the type of intervention that the court makes justifies the view that the defendant has committed a tort. Many cases have concerned the expulsion of the plaintiff from membership of an association which controls the entry into or right to practice a given occupation. The courts will intervene here if the expulsion is *ultra vires* or otherwise in breach of the association's rules, by way of an injunction or a declaration that the plaintiff has been improperly expelled (*Lee* v. *Showmen's Guild* (1952); *Abbott* v. *Sullivan* (1952)). The remedy in such cases is often explained as resting on contract—the rules of the association have contractual force as between the members of the association. In *Abbott* v. *Sullivan* the Court of Appeal considered whether the expelled member had any claim in damages for breach of contract or in tort but decided against both. Since the right to claim damages is an essential characteristic of a tort, the case does not support the view that the right is based on tort. On the other hand it is clear that the situations in which the courts will protect a person's occupation are not limited to cases where there is a breach of contract. In *Nagle* v. *Feilden* (1966) the Court of Appeal refused to strike out a cause of action in which the plaintiff claimed that the Stewards of the Jockey Club had refused her a trainer's licence solely on the ground that she was a woman. In *David* v. *Abdul Cader* (1963) the Privy Council refused to hold that an allegation that the defendant had maliciously refused the plaintiff a licence to run a cinema disclosed no cause of action. Nor did they rule out the possibility of damages being recovered. These cases could not have rested on contract, and it may be therefore that a new tort, though not yet in existence is in the process of creation.

Breach of confidence

Courts have for many years been willing to restrain by injunction the disclosure of confidential information, whether of a personal (see *Gee* v. *Pritchard* (1818); *Argyll* (*Duchess*) v. *Argyll* (*Duke*) (1967)) or of a commercial character (*Cranleigh Precision Engineering* v. *Bryant* (1965)). It is possible to obtain damages in lieu of an injunction in such cases under Lord Cairns' Act 1858, but the award of damages, like that of the injunction itself, lies within the discretion of the court (*infra*, p. 313). Furthermore, as the remedy is equitable, damages could not be awarded against a bona fide purchaser of the information for value and without notice. It is clearly therefore advantageous to claim that the user of confidential information commits a tort, since in that case damages are obtainable as of right, and, perhaps, from anyone who obtains the information in whatever circumstances. *Seager* v. *Copydex* (*No.* 1) (1967) suggests that a tort is committed by one who makes use of confidential information. In that case, damages were awarded against the defendants who had made use of the plaintiff's design for a carpet grip, which the plaintiff had entrusted in confidence to the defendants. The damages awarded were tortious in character, on the analogy of conversion, rather than equitable in lieu of injunction (see *Seager* v. *Copydex* (*No.* 2) (1969)). A new tort seems therefore to have been created. Its extent, and in particular whether it is available against an innocent purchaser of the information, seems to depend upon whether its juridical basis is the existence of a property right in the information (in which case all third parties are affected) or upon the principle that an obligation of confidence should not knowingly be broken or interfered with. The courts have decided that a disclosure of a confidence which is in the public interest will not be restrained by injunction (*Fraser* v. *Evans* (1968); *Initial Services* v. *Putterill* (1968)). The Law Commission in Working Paper No. 58 has recommended that a new tort of breach of confidence should be created by statute. The details of their proposals are too complicated for treatment here and reference should be made to the working paper.

Privacy

Privacy already receives a considerable degree of incidental protection under existing legal remedies, for example, nuisance (*cf.* *Lyons* v. *Wilkins* (1899)), trespass to land (*cf.* *Hickman* v. *Maisey* (1900)), defamation (*cf.* *Tolley* v. *Fry* (1931)), infringement of copyright (*cf.* *Williams* v. *Settle* (1960)), and the action for breach of confidence. There is, however, no tort of infringement of privacy itself, despite several abortive attempts to pass legislation creating one. In this Britain is very different from the United States in which protection of privacy is comprehensive. The Younger Committee Report on Privacy (Cmnd. 5012), however, recommended no basic change in the law, although recommending that there should be a new tort of unlawful surveillance by technical device. Part of the problem with protection of privacy is that it interferes with freedom of speech, the view prevailing in this country that this should rule out a remedy for infringement of privacy altogether rather than that the publisher should be required to justify his publication on the ground that it was in the public interest or made without malice. Another problem with the protection of privacy is that there appears to be no consensus among those who support it as to the best method of achieving it and in particular whether this should be done through criminal sanctions or civil remedies. The Rehabilitation of Offenders Act 1974 is a good example of the complications that may be involved. It contains criminal penalties for the disclosure of spent convictions, a civil remedy for defamation against a person who reveals another person's spent conviction, and a number of exemptions from liability in relation to the non-disclosure or denial of a previous spent conviction.

CHAPTER 28

DEATH IN RELATION TO TORT

THE former rule was that the death of either party extinguished the defendant's tortious liability. To this there were a few minor exceptions. Apart from this, it was also a rule of the common law that a third party could not bring an action in respect of the death of another person as the result of a tort (*Baker* v. *Bolton* (1808)). Both these rules could be productive of injustice and both have now largely been abrogated by statute. The major injustice was to deny third parties such as dependants an action in respect of the death. This was remedied by a series of Acts called the Fatal Accidents Acts. The effect of these, since they allow dependants a tortious action in respect of the death of another, has been to create a new tort. The substantive effect of these Acts must be contrasted with the merely procedural significance of the Law Reform (Miscellaneous Provisions) Act 1934, which allows tortious actions to survive as part of the estate of the victim or against the estate of the tortfeasor. Despite the differing effects of these statutes, they are best treated in conjunction since claims under both are commonly made when actions are brought in respect of death as the result of a tort.

FATAL ACCIDENTS ACTS; DEATH CREATING LIABILITY

By a series of Acts beginning in 1846, the latest being 1959, it is possible for a dependant to bring an action when the death of the person upon whom the dependancy exists has been caused by the tort of another, provided the person killed would have been able to bring an action and recover damages for such tort. The relation of dependancy can only be established by certain relatives who are defined by the Acts as follows: wife, husband, children, grandchildren, father, mother, step-parents, grandparents, brothers, sisters, uncles, aunts, and their issue, adopted and illegitimate dependants and step-children. Furthermore, such persons must establish a relation of dependancy on the person killed. The nature of this will be explored later. It is still true that apart from these exceptions created by statute, it is impossible for a tortious action to be brought in respect of another's death. An employer cannot sue where his servant is negligently killed, though he has an action where the servant is merely injured. The acts have created an important exception to the general principle that negligence causing purely pecuniary loss is not actionable.

Nature of the relative's action

The Act of 1846 requires the death to be caused by the "wrongful act, neglect or default" of the defendant. These words are clearly wide enough to cover all torts, and in substance the relatives' action is an action for tortiously causing the death of another person. As such, it has been said to be "new in its species, new in its quality, new in its principle, in every way new" (words spoken by the court in an 1884 case). It is, however, a requirement of the Act that the wrongful act of the defendant could have been made the subject of a successful action for damages by the person injured had he survived to bring such action. This requirement has been interpreted by the courts to mean that anything which had the effect of extinguishing or reducing the liability of the defendant to the deceased (for example, settlement of action by deceased, expiry of limitation period on deceased's action, deceased's contributory negligence) has this effect also upon the relatives' action. In practice, thus, the relatives' action is treated as the same as that of the deceased. In *Pigney* v. *Pointer's Transport* (1957), the action of the relatives succeeded even though the deceased's death had been self-inflicted, but the court also allowed the deceased's estate to claim damages under the 1934 Act (*infra*, p. 300). The case seems to point to the defence *ex turpi causa* not arising on these facts rather than to the relatives' action being treated as distinct from that of the deceased. Again in *Burns* v. *Edman* (1970), the family of a criminal could not sue in respect of loss of their dependancy since the latter arose *ex turpi causa*. This points to an identification of the relatives' claim with that of the deceased.

Nature of the dependancy

The courts have in the absence of specific legislative provisions devised rules of their own about the interest of the relatives which is protected by the action. This interest will be described here as their dependancy, although it is not so described in the Act itself. The dependancy must be of a financial nature; the relative must suffer pecuniary loss as a result of the death. Thus the action is not available to give damages to the relatives for their mental suffering as a result of the death. The financial advantage must be a reasonable probability; if it is too speculative the courts will reject it. So where the deceased was a child of four years to whom the father intended to give a good education, the action was not allowed. Where on the other hand the deceased had gratuitously assisted his father in his business in the past, and where the deceased had made gifts of money to his father during a period of unemployment, the action was allowed because it was reasonable to expect such charity would recur (*Barnett* v. *Cohen* (1921); *Franklin* v. *S.E. Ry.* (1858); *Hetherington* v. *N.E. Ry.* (1882)).

One case (*Sykes* v. *N.E. Ry.* (1875)) holds that the dependancy must arise from a family rather than business relationship. So where a son was employed by his father under a contract of service, the father did not have an action for loss of these services when the son was killed. But an alternative explanation of the case is that the father had suffered no loss since he paid his son the normal wages for the job. It is suggested that there would be difficulties in applying the suggested distinction; and for this reason the alternative ratio of the case if preferable.

Although a pecuniary advantage is insisted on, this may be of a quite indirect nature. Thus the services of a wife or a daughter in performing ordinary domestic tasks have a financial value, even though in their absence the employment of outside help would not be considered. An unusual benefit was recognised in *Davies* v. *Whiteways Cider Co.* (1974). The deceased's dependants had in his lifetime received gifts which because of his death within seven years of the gift attracted estate duty. The amount of this was held to be recoverable in the dependants' action.

Assessment of damages

It is impossible to lay down firm rules on this matter; so much depends on the individual case and the nature of the dependancy involved. Where the deceased's resources include earnings, the amount of future earnings lost is worked out on similar lines to those governing the assessment of such loss generally (*infra*, p. 307–308). Contingencies affecting both the deceased and the relatives must be assessed by the court, but statute now prevents the assessment of the likelihood of a widow's remarriage or actual remarriage to be used as a ground for reducing damages (Law Reform (Miscellaneous Provisions) Act 1971, s. 4 (1)). The court may still have to make such an assessment in evaluating the personal claim for damages of an injured, living plaintiff. Furthermore in the case of the child's claim under the Fatal Accidents Acts, the likelihood of remarriage of the widow may be a relevant factor and is one which the court is not precluded from taking into account.

Benefits arising from the death may go in reduction of damages but the Acts themselves have prohibited deduction in the case of money paid under an insurance policy taken out against the deceased's life, pensions and gratuities. In view of this it is hard to see why any deduction should be made in respect of, for example, the deceased's own savings. The courts are generally speaking unwilling to make any deduction in respect of voluntary benefits that may be conferred on dependants by third parties, on the ground that the voluntary nature of the benefit means that it does not result from death, or that it does not adequately replace the lost dependancy. In the latest decision (*Hay* v. *Hughes* (1975)), the plaintiff children who had lost both their parents in a road accident were looked after free of charge by their grandmother. It was held that this was not a benefit resulting from death so as to be deductible from the award of damages.

In the case of inherited property, also, the courts are slow to make deductions. In the first place, if the property would in any case have been inherited by the same person, only the amount attributable to the acceleration of the benefit is deducted. Secondly, where a widow inherited a house from her husband which she would continue to use as a dwelling, no deduction was made because the continuing residential requirement of the widow meant that no real financial benefit accrued to her (*Heatley* v. *Steel Co. of Wales* (1953)).

The Law Commission Report on Personal Injury Litigation-Assessment of Damages recommended that no deductions should be made whatsoever in respect of benefits received after the death.

Survival of Causes of Action after Death

It has been already stated that the common law rule was that the death of either the tortfeasor or his victim normally rules out the possibility of an action in tort. The common law has been totally changed by the Law Reform (Miscellaneous Provisions) Act 1934 which provides that on the death of any person all causes of action subsisting against or vested in him shall survive against, or as the case may be, for the benefit of, his estate. The only tort to which the Act does not now apply is defamation. The Act applies even when death follows instantaneously upon the commission of the tort.

Action on behalf of the estate of victim

The action differs from that brought under the Fatal Accidents Acts in that it is the deceased's own action which is brought. It is therefore brought on behalf of his estate by his personal representative, the amount recovered passing as part of his estate to those entitled under the rules of succession.

What damages may be claimed

Damages are awarded to the estate under the same heads of damages as in the normal tortious action, for example, in actions for personal injury, pain and suffering, loss of amenity, loss of expectation of life, and loss of earnings. In the case of those heads of damages which have both a past and a future element, the court will take into account the death of the victim, and make no award in respect of the future element. Thus damages for pain and suffering, for loss of amenity, and for loss of earnings will be limited to the period from the injury until death. The award in respect of these heads will thus normally be small, although if the victim survives a lengthy period before his death quite a substantial sum may be awarded (for example, the award £2,000 for loss of amenity to the victim in *Andrews* v. *Freeborough* (1962) who survived for a year in an unconscious state before dying).

Damages for loss of expectation of life do not have the same built-in limitation, not having a future element, and there were signs that estates of tort victims would be awarded substantial damages under this head. This tendency received a check, however, in the House of Lords decision in *Benham* v. *Gambling* (1941) which laid down judicial policy for the award of damages under this head. The principles established by the case apply not only to actions by the victim's estate, but to actions by the victim himself. Most important there is an arbitrary ceiling upon awards of damages under this head. This was assessed in *Benham* v. *Gambling* as £200, but, inflation being taken into account, is now £500 (*Yorkshire Electricity Board* v. *Naylor* (1968)). The courts have thus administered their own corrective to the legislature's perhaps erroneous decision in allowing tortious actions to survive for the estate's benefit. Within the £500 limit, damages will vary not so much with the length of life that is lost as with the loss of future happiness that the death entailed. The character and habits of the deceased, his personal circumstances and state of health are clearly relevant matters from which this can be inferred. But the victim's own estimate of his future prospects of happiness is irrelevant—the test is to this extent objective. Actual life expectancy is relevant where the victim is very old, since the brevity of the remaining life-span will go in reduction of damages. Also where the victim is a young child the amount of uncertainty involved in assessing his future prospects will again cause a reduction. Such matters as the wealth and social status of the deceased are irrelevant, the courts recognising that wealth is not synonymous with happiness.

Damages for loss of expectation of life are objective in the sense that they do not include suffering caused by the victim's knowledge of the reduction of his life expectancy—such suffering may however be compensated in damages awarded for pain and suffering.

Funeral expenses

These may be recovered as damages from the tortfeasor if they have been met out of the deceased's estate.

Overlapping Claims under Fatal Accidents and Law Reform Acts

The persons who can claim as relatives of the deceased under the 1846 Act or as being entitled to his estate under the 1934 Act are not necessarily the same, and where this is the case, both claims will have to be met in full by the defendant. It is common, however, for the same persons to be entitled to damages and to make claims under both Acts. Where the claims overlap in this way, the courts apply the rule that no relative should have double recovery of damages and deduct the amount received under the 1934 Act from that received under the Fatal Accidents Acts (but see *Murray* v. *Shuter* (1975)—damages for deceased's loss of earnings not deductible from Fatal Accidents Acts award, since plaintiff would have been maintained out of them by deceased).

Law Commission Recommendations for reform

The Law Commission Report on Personal Injury Litigation-Assessment of Damages (No. 56) made a number of recommendations concerning claims arising on death. In the first place, they concluded that the problem of over-compensation which the 1971 Act substantially certain to is insoluble given the present method of awarding damages in a lump sum. Any change to the old practice would lead to under-compensation of some widows. In fact, an extension to the 1971 Act was recommended under which the remarriage or prospects of remarriage of the widow should not affect the claims of other dependants under the Fatal Accidents Acts, for example, the deceased's children (the likelihood is that such remarriage would not justify a deduction from the damages—*Mead* v. *Clarke Chapman & Co.* (1956); *Hay* v. *Hughes* (1975), *supra*, p. 300). The report recommended the abolition of the award of damages to the estate in respect of the deceased's loss of expectation of life, though continuing to allow damages to be claimed in respect of pain and suffering the deceased experienced through his awareness that his expectation of life had been shortened. This would mean that where the deceased was killed instantly, the estate could claim nothing at all. A new cause of action, however, was proposed under which a husband or wife could claim in respect of bereavement caused by the other's death, or a parent(s) in respect of the death of a child. The maximum that could be awarded in such actions would be £1,000.

CHAPTER 29

REMEDIES

DAMAGES

THE most common and important remedy in the law of tort is the award of damages. The principles upon which damages are awarded have, where relevant, been discussed in connection with the individual torts. In this chapter the general principles relating to damages will be set out, together with an examination of the rules governing the assessment of damages for personal injury. The fundamental principle governing the assessment of damages in nearly all cases is that the plaintiff should be compensated for the injury he has received. This point should always be remembered in considering the effectiveness of the law.

Classifications of damages

(1) *Contemptuous and nominal damages*

Both these types of damages are similar in that they signify the award of a token sum to the plaintiff equivalent in law to no damages at all. But they differ in purpose. Nominal damages are awarded in order that the plaintiff's right should be vindicated although he has not suffered anything for which substantial damages could be awarded (for example, the right to vote in *Ashby* v. *White* (1703)). Contemptuous damages are awarded where the court, though vindicating the plaintiff's right is also signifying disapproval of his having brought the action. The award is therefore of the smallest coin of the realm. Contemptuous damages are particularly appropriate in the case of torts where the damages are at large, and the court wishes to "penalise" the gold-digging plaintiff who claims a large amount of general damages (as in the award of ¼d. to Harold Newstead, *supra*, p. 238). There is the important difference between contemptuous and nominal damages that where the former are awarded the plaintiff is unlikely to be awarded costs. Neither can be awarded where the tort is not actionable *per se*, since their award is tantamount to a finding that the plaintiff has suffered no damage.

(2) *Special and general damages*

This classification of damages is used in at least three senses by the courts. The term "special damages" sometimes refers to those damages which are awarded in respect of the damage which the plaintiff must establish when suing for a tort not actionable *per se.* In this sense they contrast with general damages which are awarded in respect of damage which the court presumes to have occurred on proof of the commission of the tort. General damages can clearly only be awarded where the tort is actionable *per se*, and their award is particularly common in libel and nuisance. A second distinction follows from this but is to some extent in conflict with it. Special damages are those of which the plaintiff is required to give the defendant notice in his pleadings and is therefore required to prove strictly at the trial; general damages do not require such strict pleading and proof. Clearly the plaintiff ought to give notice of those damages which are not ordinarily presumed to occur. But foreseeable items of damage such as loss of wages up to trial and medical expenses in actions for personal injuries are special damages for this purpose, and here the two meanings are in conflict. A final distinction is that special damages are those capable of precise pecuniary estimate; general damages can only be assessed by a measure corresponding to the opinion of a reasonable man. Special damages would here include loss of earnings up to the date of the trial and loss of future earnings (which are general damages under the rules of pleadings but of which in practice the plaintiff is required to furnish proof). General damages would include damages for pain and suffering in actions for personal injuries, damages for injury to reputation and feelings.

(3) *Damages at large; aggravated damages*

In the case of torts actionable *per se*, damages are said to be at large. The court is able to award substantial damages even though no actual damage is proved by the plaintiff. Damages may be presumed to have occurred from the mere fact of the tort's commission (*cf.* particularly, defamation and nuisance). Another consequence of the damages being at large is that the court is free to award aggravated damages where the injury to the plaintiff is aggravated by such matters as the defendant's conduct or the distress or humiliation suffered by the plaintiff (see, for example, *Loudon* v. *Ryder* (*No.* 2) (1953)).

(4) *Parasitic damages*

These are damages given for the infringement of some interest which is not protected at all or not primarily protected by the tort in question. So, in an action for conversion, damages have been awarded for loss of reputation (*Thurston* v. *Charles* (1905)). In a woman's action for negligence causing her personal injuries, damages were awarded in respect of the loss of her husband's consortium, even though no action could have been brought in respect of this alone (*Lampert* v. *Eastern National Omnibus Co.* (1954)).

This case shows that the "parasitic interest" may be one not protected by other torts.

(5) *Exemplary or punitive damages*

In all the cases discussed so far, the amount of damages the court may award reflects as far as this is possible the injury or damage inflicted upon the plaintiff. In the case of exemplary or punitive damages this is not the case; extra damages are awarded in order to punish or make an example of the defendant. The House of Lords in *Rookes* v. *Barnard* (1964) confined the award of such damages to three situations:

(i) where the tortious action consists in oppressive, arbitrary or unconstitutional conduct by a government official;

(ii) where the defendant has calculated to make a greater amount out of his commission of the tort than he will have to pay in damages to the plaintiff;

(iii) where statute authorises the award of such damages. In *Cassell & Co.* v. *Broom* (1972) the House of Lords confirmed the existence of these limitations upon the power to award exemplary damages. It must be noted that aggravated damages may serve a purpose similar to exemplary damages, with the limitation that they can only be awarded where the tort is actionable *per se*, and with the difference that in theory they are compensatory, being awarded to assuage the plaintiff's injured feelings.

(6) *Damages for personal injuries*

Two types of "loss" are inflicted upon one who suffers personal injuries. He may suffer actual financial loss such as loss of wages or reduction in his earning capacity. And he may suffer reduction in his enjoyment of his life, through pain and suffering and inability to participate in his usual activites, whether of a temporary or permanent nature. It is clear that the latter loss is incompensable in monetary terms. To allow a plaintiff £1,000 for the loss of a leg is assuagement rather than replacement. Nevertheless, English law compensates the injured person for both types of loss. Many of the difficulties in the law of damages are caused by the attempt to evaluate the non-pecuniary claim.

In considering the award of damages for personal injuries, damages in respect of the non-pecuniary aspects of the plaintiff's claim will be considered first.

(i) NON-PECUNIARY DAMAGES

There are a number of recognised heads of non-pecuniary damages. These are damages for loss of expectation of life, for pain and suffering, and for loss of amenity. The first of these is considered elsewhere (*supra*, p. 301).

Pain and suffering. This is pre-eminently the head of damages which reflects the subjective effect the injury has upon the plaintiff. He is entitled to be compensated both for pain and suffering he has experienced up to the date of the trial and for such as he will experience in the future. The sum awarded may be in respect not only of the physical pain involved but also the mental anguish the plaintiff experiences, for example, in knowing that his expectation of life has been reduced or that his capacity to enjoy life has been reduced. No award for pain and suffering can be made where the plaintiff is rendered permanently unconscious by the injury and does not regain consciousness (*Wise* v. *Kaye* (1962)).

Loss of amenity. There was doubt for some time whether in the case of injury such as loss of a leg, damages were given to compensate the plaintiff's subjective appreciation of the effect of the injury, or for the injury itself. If the former, damages for loss of an amenity would be merely part of damages awarded for pain and suffering. In *Wise* v. *Kaye*, however, the Court of Appeal awarded £15,000 damages for loss of amenity although the plaintiff could have had no appreciation of the effect of her injuries upon her, and this decision was upheld by the House of Lords in *West and Son Ltd.* v. *Shephard* (1964). It is now clear, therefore, that loss of amenity is a distinct head of damages from pain and suffering. Cases such as *Wise* v. *Kaye* and *West* v. *Shephard* render the compensatory function of the award of damages almost a fiction.

(ii) PECUNIARY DAMAGES

The plaintiff will recover as special damages his loss of earnings up to the time of the trial, and medical expenses actually incurred by him (including the cost of private medical treatment). He seems also able to recover medical or other out-of-pocket expenses incurred on his behalf by a third party, provided their incurrence was reasonably necessary, and the plaintiff would feel under a moral obligation to reimburse the third party. The plaintiff is also able to recover as general damages loss of future earnings through reduction in his earning capacity. The method of assessment is to take a number of years' purchase (corresponding to the number of years of working life that would have been left to the plaintiff but for his injury), to multiply this by the annual sum of earnings lost by the plaintiff, and to adjust the sum arrived at to reflect contingencies such as the shortening of the plaintiff's working life through other events, and the benefit the plaintiff receives from receiving an immediate lump sum. Courts do not take account of inflation in making awards in respect of loss of future earnings (*Taylor* v. *O'Connor* (1971)), the reason for this given by Lord Pearson being that the capital sum received by the plaintiff should counteract inflation. But this ignores the fact that the capital sum may itself be inadequate being based on the premise that the value of a wage will remain constant over the years. Furthermore actuarial evidence will not be admitted to decide the amount of working life left to the plaintiff (*Taylor* v. *O'Connor* (1971); *Mitchell* v. *Mulholland* (1971)). This has led to considerable standardisation of awards. Even in the case of young persons, quite short periods are arrived at by courts in deciding what working life was left (for example, 16 years in the case of a child of 3½ in *Taylor* v. *Bristol Omnibus Co.* (1975)).

If the injury has shortened the plaintiff's life expectancy, no damages in respect of lost future earnings for the period beginning from the moment of the plaintiff's presumed death are awarded (*Oliver* v. *Ashman* (1961)). This case has unfortunate consequences for the dependants of the deceased who suffer an actionable loss if the deceased's working life is shortened but whose claim is barred if the deceased himself has brought an action. The plaintiff may also recover as general damages future medical expenses; again a lump sum is awarded, assessed in a similar way to future earnings.

(iii) DEDUCTIONS

The difficulty of the problem whether an incidental benefit received by the plaintiff as a result of his injuries should be deducted from the damage he receives is explained because of competing considerations of policy; fears of over-compensation and an excessive rise in liability insurance premiums if the benefit is not deducted, and of under-compensation if it is, particularly if the view is taken that the amount of damages awarded is generally inadequate. The law on this matter seems something of a compromise. If the purpose of the benefit is to compensate for those aspects of the plaintiff's loss which are capable of yielding to a precise pecuniary estimate, then it is deductible, since the function of damages is compensatory. Where, on the other hand, the benefit is not clearly directed towards any particular part of the plaintiff's loss, so that it may cover those aspects of his claim which are not capable of being precisely estimated (for example, pain and suffering) it is not deductible because it is impossible to decide whether to allow him to keep the benefit would represent over-compensation. Examples of the former class of case are the deductibility of wages—or sick pay paid by an employer to his employee while the latter is off work (*Receiver of Metropolitan Police District* v. *Croydon Corporation* (1957); and of unemployment benefit (*Foxley* v. *Olton* (1965)), although in the same case it was said that supplementary benefit was not deductible on the unsatisfactory ground that its payment was discretionary. The deductibility of income tax from awards of damages for personal injuries (*British Transport Commission* v. *Gourley* (1956)) is explicable on similar grounds. By special legislative provision (s. 2 of the Law Reform (Personal Injuries) Act 1948), half the amount of social security benefits such as industrial injury benefit, disablement benefit and sickness benefit is deductible from damages for a period of five years. The prime example of the second class of case is money payable under an accident insurance policy. This is not deductible from damages (*Bradburn* v. *G.W. Ry.* (1874)), nor are charitable gifts by third parties for the same reason.

The distinction drawn above, however, has become much blurred if not altogether erased in recent cases. Most important is the House of Lords decision in *Parry* v. *Cleaver* (1970). In that case it was held that a disability pension payable by an employer to his employee when the latter became unfit for work was not deductible from damages. The majority in the House thought that the pension was not intended to compensate for lost earnings but was more in the nature of insurance. It seems, however, difficult to argue that a pension payable by employer to employee and earnings related was not intended to compensate for loss of earnings. In *Cunningham* v. *Harrison* (1973) the Court of Appeal went even further in holding that an *ex gratia* payment of half pay for the rest of his life made by employer to employee was in the nature of a pension and not deductible. In *Daish* v. *Wauton* (1972) the Court of Appeal held that a boy of five who was so severely injured in a road accident that he would have to be housed in a National Health Service institution for the rest of his life would not lose from the award of damages the value of the benefit of free board and lodging which this conferred. In view of these cases, the principles upon which courts deduct incidental benefits have become extremely uncertain. The Law Commission is inclined to be similarly generous to the victims of torts (*infra*, p. 312).

In the *Receiver for Metropolitan Police District* case, it was held that an employer who had continued to pay his employee's wages during his absence from work had no action in quasi-contract against the third party who by his tort had caused the absence from work. The court thought that it made no difference whether or not there was a contractual obligation to make the payment. Since wages are deductible from the award of damages (though see *Cunningham* v. *Harrison* (*supra*, p. 309), it follows that the employer has no hope of being recompensed by the employee, so that the *actio per quod servitium amisit*, where available, is his only remedy. Where, on the other hand, a third party has rendered gratuitous services to the plaintiff because of the injury, it now appears to be settled that the plaintiff can recover in his own action the value of such services, even the third party has no more than a moral claim against the plaintiff to be recompensed (*Donnelly* v. *Joyce* (1973)—the plaintiff's mother gave up her job in order to care for him. The plaintiff was allowed to recover the value of the services rendered. *Roach* v. *Yates* (1938) is to similar effect).

(iv) ITEMISATION OF DAMAGES AND OVERLAP

In *Fletcher* v. *Autocar and Transporters* (1968) the Court of Appeal expressed its disapproval of a method of awarding damages under which individual amounts were assessed for the different heads of damages and the total sum was then awarded as damages. This they thought would tend to produce over-compensation, particularly if no account was taken of possible overlap between these heads of damages. Thus where the plaintiff indulged in an expensive pastime such as golf, the loss of amenity involved in not being able to play golf was to some extent compensated in the financial saving to the plaintiff. This approach was also manifested in *Smith* v. *Central Asbestos Co.* (1972) in which the Court of Appeal thought that a high award in respect of future earnings would to some extent compensate for the loss of amenity involved in asbestosis. There is some inconsistency in the Court of Appeal's approach to this problem since it is difficult to see how the question of overlap can be examined without the court making at least a notional itemisation of damages. In any case the court must now itemise its awards for the purpose of awarding interest (*i.e.* into special damages up to the date of trial, general damages in respect of future pecuniary loss and general damages for pain and suffering and loss of amenities. Different rates of interest apply to each head—*Jefford* v. *Gee* (1970)). The justice of the Court of Appeal's approach to overlap is also not readily apparent. If the plaintiff has lost one expensive amenity, this seems no reason to deprive him of the opportunity of replacing it with another expensive pastime which the injury does not prevent him from indulging.

Duty to mitigate damage

The plaintiff must not do anything to increase the amount of damage he has suffered. Nor must he omit to take reasonable action to reduce such damage (*HMS Flying Fish* (1865)—damages reduced because plaintiff refused to accept aid after a collision at sea.)

Once-and-for-all assessment of damages

Damages are awarded in a lump sum and are not subject to review. The award of damages in respect of any one cause of action is therefore final. This causes hardship in the type of case of which *Fetter* v. *Beale* (1701) is an example, where the plaintiff's injuries are greater than appears at the trial. In that case the court refused to alter its original award on subsequent application to it by the plaintiff. The principle established by this case does not apply when the plaintiff is suing in respect of a different cause of action (as in *Brunsden* v. *Humphrey* (1884) in which it was held that the defendant's negligence in causing the plaintiff personal injury and damage to his property gave rise to distinct causes of action so that action in respect of the latter did not prevent a subsequent action for the former). For the same reason, it does not apply where the defendant has committed a continuing tort since fresh causes of action arise in respect of such tort from day to day as long as it is being committed.

Law Commission recommendations on damages for personal injuries

In its Report on Personal Injury Litigation-Assessment of Damages (No. 56) the Law Commission has made a number of recommendations concerning the award of damages for personal injuries. For various reasons they rejected the introduction of periodic payments of damages as a method of dealing with the problem of inflation and of cases where the plaintiff's injuries are more serious than appeared at the time of the award. In the latter case, however, the report recommends that when the court thinks there is a chance of greater injury appearing in the future it should have a power to make a provisional award of damages, and the plaintiff should have the power to apply to the court for a further award if further injury appeared. In relation to inflation generally, the report thought the problem to be insoluble within the present system of awarding damages, but they did recommend a replacement of the "multiplier" system with a system which allowed actuarial evidence to be taken into account in assessing the life expectancy of a particular person. Itemisation of awards of damages was also recommended, together with a recommendation that the plaintiff should receive the total sum arrived at by adding the various heads, so depriving the courts of power to take account of possible overlap between different heads. After examining various methods of removing the injustice of *Oliver* v. *Ashman*, the commission thought that the best solution would be to allow the deceased himself to claim in his own action damages for loss of earnings during the period between the time when he would probably die and the time when his working life would probably have ended but for the tort committed against him. This could lead to considerable over-compensation in the event of the deceased dying without dependants. The Law Commission proposed that in the case of reasonable expenses gratuitously incurred on an injured person's behalf by a third party, or services gratuitously rendered to him, these should be recoverable in the injured person's own action, a proposal which has been anticipated in principle at least by *Donnelly* v. *Joyce* (1973). They did not consider that the policy arguments for allowing employers who continue to pay wages to an injured employee to sue the tortfeasor for their recovery were sufficiently strong. In the case of incidental benefits, the sweeping recommendation was made that no deductions whatsoever should be made except those prescribed under section 2 (1) of the Law Reform (Personal Injuries) Act 1948 and wages or sick-pay paid by employer to employee where the employee has no legal obligation to reimburse the employer.

The Injunction

A court may, in addition to awarding damages to the plaintiff, or without awarding damages, issue an injunction. This is a peremptory order to the defendant (disobedience of which is punishable by imprisonment) to abstain from (prohibitory injunction) or to take (mandatory injunction) certain action. The injunction is a discretionary remedy and will be issued only where it is "just and convenient" to do so (the words are taken from section 45 of the Supreme Court of Judicature Act 1925).

Types of injunction

A prohibitory injunction will take the form of an order to the defendant to stop committing a tort such as, commonly, trespass or nuisance. The mandatory injunction orders the defendant to perform a certain act, for example, the pulling down of a building which infringes the plaintiff's right to light. An injunction of the former type may cause less hardship to a defendant in that it may afford him a large amount of choice as to how he complies with it. So an order to discontinue a nuisance caused by fumes may be obeyed in a number of ways, which is not true of an order to pull down a building. For this reason a stronger case has normally to be made for the grant of a mandatory than a prohibitory injunction.

Interlocutory injunctions must be distinguished from *quia timet* injunctions. The former type of injunction is claimed by the plaintiff in interlocutory proceedings taking place before the actual trial of the action, the justification for its issue being that otherwise the plaintiff may suffer irreparable damage before the trial of the action takes place. The interlocutory injunction has been heavily relied on in recent years by those who have been threatened with heavy economic losses as a result of strikes (*supra*, p. 270). The interlocutory injunction is distinguishable from the *quia timet* injunction on the ground that the plaintiff is alleging that the defendant is actually committing (or has committed) a tort against him. The *quia timet* injunction is available where no tort has been committed by the defendant but the plaintiff apprehends the possible future commission of a tort by the defendant. An injunction which is a final one issued after the trial of the plaintiff's action is called perpetual.

Torts restrainable by injunction

There appears to be no tort against which an injunction will not be awarded, although some torts, notably trespass to land and nuisance, are particularly apt for the issue of the remedy, and others, such as assault and malicious prosecution, will nearly always be redressed by damages. Where it is doubtful whether the wrong committed by the defendant is a tort, this does not mean that an injunction will not be granted. Examples have already been given (*supra*, pp. 293–294) of the issue of injunctions in cases where the tortious character of the defendant's conduct is debatable. Furthermore, under Lord Cairns' Act 1858 the courts may award damages in such cases (see *infra*). Eventually the courts may award damages as of right in cases of this sort, thereby treating them as torts. If this is the case, the injunction may be seen as a way of extending the boundaries of the law of tort.

Exercise of court's discretion

The court may take a number of factors into account in deciding whether to grant an injunction, for example, whether damages are an adequate remedy (if the tort is continuing or there is a likelihood of repetition, damages are probably inadequate); the defendant's difficulty in complying with the injunction in view of the expense involved or its impracticability; the conduct of the plaintiff, in particular acquiescence on his part. Although the courts will consider the defendant's convenience in exercising their discretion, they will also consider the justice of the case. If the defendant has incurred expenditure after notice of the plaintiff's right and in wilful violation of such right, an injunction may be granted though its effect is to cause this expenditure to be wasted (*Daniel* v. *Ferguson* (1891)).

Lord Cairns' Act 1858

The court has jurisdiction under Lord Cairns' Act 1858 to award damages either in addition to or in substitution for an injunction. Although originally intended for the purely procedural purpose of giving the Court of Chancery a general power to award damages, the Act has a substantive effect also in allowing the award of damages in cases where no tort or breach of contract has been committed, provided an injunction is at least theoretically available. The award of such damages, like the injunction itself, is within the discretion of the court. Where the award is made in substitution for an injunction, it covers future damage as well as damage that has already occurred; this is not so with normal damages. Damages can even be awarded under this Act where a *quia timet* injunction is sought (*Leeds Industrial Co-operative Society Ltd.* v. *Slack* (1924)).

Other Remedies

The plaintiff may choose in some cases to sue for an account of the profits the defendant has made through committing the tort. This is particularly the case where the tort is passing-off or another of the torts involving trade competition. It has been mentioned in an earlier chapter (*supra*, p. 39), that in detinue the plaintiff may claim restitution of his property in addition to or as an alternative to a claim for damages. The remedy of self-help has already been dealt with in Chapter 5 (*supra*, pp. 55, 63–65).

CHAPTER 30

EXTINCTION OF TORTIOUS LIABILITY

TORTIOUS liability may be extinguished in any of the following ways.

DEATH

The death of the tortfeasor extinguishes his liability in the case of defamation only.

JUDGMENT

Judgment obtained against a tortfeasor has the effect of converting his liability on the cause of action into liability on the judgment, so that further actions cannot be brought against him in respect of that cause of action. So, for example, a judgment obtained in conversion bars a subsequent action in quasi-contract for the proceeds of sale of the chattel. Where the same facts give rise to distinct causes of action (*supra*, p. 311) judgment obtained on one cause of action will not bar a later action based on the other.

Satisfaction of judgment

Judgment obtained against one of several joint or concurrent tortfeasors does not release the others (*supra*, p. 119). But satisfaction of the judgment by one of them releases the rest. Where tortfeasors are neither joint nor concurrent, satisfaction by one will not normally release the others except in special circumstances. If however A and B have successively converted C's chattel, satisfaction of the judgment by A will release B since C thereafter no longer has the right to possession of the chattel.

WAIVER OF TORT

The problem here is whether the election by the plaintiff to pursue one of two alternative remedies means that he cannot go back on this decision and pursue the alternative remedy. At one time it was thought that by choosing one remedy the plaintiff must be taken to have waived the other. But the House of Lords in *United Australia Ltd.* v. *Barclay's Bank Ltd.* (1941) found that the cases relied on for this turned on the extinction of tortious liability through judgment rather than waiver. The pursuit of one remedy only constituted waiver where the remedies were inconsistent with rather than alternative to each other. So a landlord who chooses to sue for a forfeiture of the lease rather than for rent which is due, cannot sue for rent due from the date of the forfeiture proceedings even though judgment in the latter is not obtained (*Jones* v. *Carter* (1846)). On the other hand in the *United Australia* case the plaintiff company's institution and subsequent discontinuance before obtaining judgment of proceedings in quasi-contract against another company for improperly obtaining the proceeds of a cheque payable to the plaintiffs was held to be no bar to an action in conversion against the defendant bank which cashed the cheque.

Voluntary Termination

1. Accord and satisfaction

Liability in tort may be extinguished by an accord and satisfaction. This means an agreement between the parties (accord) backed up by consideration (satisfaction), the intention being that liability under the agreement should replace the liability in tort. The normal "settlement" of a tortious action operates in this way, the plaintiff agreeing to accept a certain sum and in return agreeing not to institute proceedings against the defendant. The consideration for the accord may be executory or executed; the difference is between the plaintiff's agreement to release the defendant in consideration of his promise to pay £100, and in consideration of his actual payment of that sum.

2. Release

This term signifies an agreement binding the victim of the tort whereby the tortfeasor is released from liability though he provides no consideration. The usual form of a release in English law is by deed, although this does not appear to be essential.

Limitation

The principle of limitation is that by lapse of time a right of action becomes no longer enforceable. The relevant limitation periods for tortious actions are contained in two statutes, the Limitation Act 1939 and the Limitation Act 1975. The former laid down a six-year limitation period for all torts, with the exception of an action for the recovery of land which must be brought within twelve years of the accrual of the cause of action. The latter Act has preserved a change first introduced by the Law Reform (Limitation of Actions, etc.) Act 1954, under which the period in respect of actions for damages for negligence, nuisance or breach of duty, when the damages claimed by the plaintiff include damages for personal injuries, is three years. When the plaintiff claims both for damage to property and personal injuries in the same action, the three-year period applies to both.

"Personal injuries" for the purposes of the Act include any disease and impairment of a person's physical or mental condition. It is doubtful whether the latter words include injury to feelings where the tort protects these parasitically (as in defamation). The Act's specification of negligence and nuisance seems futile in the light of the likely interpretation by the courts that breach of duty includes all torts (for example, negligent trespass in *Letang* v. *Cooper* (1965); battery in *Long* v. *Hepworth* (1968)).

Effect of limitation

The effect of the expiry of a relevant period is generally procedural rather than substantive. The right of action is rendered unenforceable rather than extinguished altogether. So, for example, a limitation defence must be pleaded. So also, the court may allow the plaintiff to amend his writ by adding a defendant against whom the limitation period has expired when satisfied that the plaintiff has made a genuine mistake (*Rodriguez* v. *Parker* (1967)). In the case of conversion, detinue and the action for recovery of land the plaintiff's title to the property is extinguished by expiry of the limitation period. Without this rule the property in question would be unmarketable.

Accrual of cause of action

Under both statutes the limitation period begins to run from the date on which the cause of action accrued. There are two requirements for determining such date. In the first place there must be a person capable of suing and being sued. Secondly, the cause of action must be complete.

(1) *Person capable of suing and being sued*

A special dispensation exists under section 22 of the Limitation Act 1939 when the potential plaintiff is a minor or of unsound mind at the time the cause of action accrued. The limitation period does not commence until the disability ceases, or he dies. In the case of an action for personal injuries, the plaintiff had under the 1954 Act to prove also that he was not at the time the right of action accrued to him in the custody of a parent. Section 2 of the Limitation

Act 1975 has removed this requirement so that the claim of persons under disability in respect of personal injuries is now governed by the same principles as claims for other damage. The dispensation granted to persons under disability by section 22 of the 1939 Act does not extend to allowing the cessation of a limitation period which had commenced before the plaintiff became subject to disability.

(2) *Completion of cause of action*

In the case of torts actionable *per se*, time runs from the moment the defendant acted; in the case of torts which require proof of damage, from the moment damage occurs. In the case of continuing torts where a fresh cause of action arises *de die in diem*, each new cause of action has its own limitation period (*Coventry* v. *Apsley* (1691)). The facts of *Dutton* v. *Bognor Regis U.D.C.* (*supra*, p. 80) show the difficulty of deciding when the damage occurs. In that case it was stated *obiter* that the cause of action accrued at the time of the council's negligence. This led to the loss of the plaintiff's claim in *Higgins* v. *Arfon B.C.* (1975), but in *Sparham-Souter* v. *Town and Country Developments* (*Essex*) (1976) the Court of Appeal changed its mind and decided that the cause of action did not accrue until the cracks appeared (it is not quite clear whether this was regarded as the moment the damage occurred, or the moment the plaintiff discovered, or should have discovered it). In an action against a negligent builder under section 3 (1) of the Defective Premises Act 1972, the cause of action runs from the time of completion of the building, so that the common law claim (*supra*, pp. 155–156) may still be advantageous. In any case, it is doubtful whether section 3 (1) covers negligent inspection by local authorities.

The law used to be that time ran even though the identity of the tortfeasor was not discoverable, and also against a person who did not know that a tort had been committed against him. In *Cartledge* v. *E. Jopling and Sons Ltd.* (1963) the House of Lords held that the rule applied even though the plaintiff could not have known that a tort had been committed (time ran when pneumoconiosis affected plaintiff's lungs though this would not have been revealed by X-ray examination). The hardship of this decision led to the passing of the Limitation Act 1963, which allowed the court in its discretion to extend the limitation period under the Act of 1954, if the plaintiff was ignorant of material facts of a decisive character (defined as ignorance either that the personal injuries resulted from a tort, of the nature and extent of the injuries, or the fact that they were attributable to the tort). The 1963 Act had numerous deficiencies. The grant of extra time was within the court's discretion whereas arguably it should have existed as of right. It was not clear whether, if the plaintiff knew the material facts in the case but neither knew nor ought to have known that they gave him a cause of action, the case fell within the Act (*cf. Central Asbestos Co.* v. *Dodd* (1973); *Harper* v. *N.C.B.* (1974)). It was also not clear whether the identity of the defendant was a material fact of a decisive character. These deficiencies appear to have been removed by section 2 (A) and (B) of the Limitation Act 1975. Section 2 (A) (4) provides that in actions for personal injuries the limitation period is three years from the date of accrual of the cause of action or from the date of the plaintiff's knowledge. Section 2 (A) (6) provides that the knowledge required is knowledge (a) that the injury in question is significant; (b) that the injury is attributable in whole or in part to the act or omission which is alleged to constitute negligence, nuisance or breach of duty; (c) of the identity of the defendant, including (d) if it is alleged that the act or omission was that of some person other than the defendant, of the identity of that person. The court has a further discretionary power to override these limitation rules in a proper case. The Act amends the Fatal Accidents Acts and the Law Reform (Miscellaneous Provisions) Act 1934 to provide that the limitation period on claims under these Acts runs either from the death or from the time of the dependant's or personal representatives' knowledge of facts coming within section 2 (A) (6). The court also has a discretion to override these limits.

The Act of 1939 makes special provision for the case of fraud. Where the plaintiff's action is based upon the fraud of the defendant, or where the right of action has been concealed by the defendant's fraud, time does not begin to run until the plaintiff has or, with reasonable diligence, could have discovered the fraud. The tort of deceit appears to be the only cause of action in tort based on fraud. But in *Beaman* v. *A.R.T.S. Ltd.* (1949) the court's interpretation of fraud in connection with the concealment of a right of action shows that a consciousness of wrongdoing rather than legal fraud is sufficient. Steps taken to conceal the right of action are also unnecessary (fraudulent concealment where bailee in time of war disposed of chattel without attempting to communicate with bailor).

In the case of successive causes of action in conversion or detinue or conversion and detinue in respect of the same chattel (whether committed by the same or different persons), the Act of 1939 provides that time runs from the first of these. This, coupled with the fact that section 3 (2) provides that the effect of the expiry of the limitation period on conversion or detinue is to extinguish completely the former owner's title, ensures that he cannot sleep on his rights for too long.

Period of limitation in respect of claims on death

Under the Proceedings against Estates Act, 1970 the normal periods of limitation apply to claims by the estate of the deceased victim of a tort. Claims by defendants under the Fatal Accidents Acts must normally be brought within three years of the death.

Chapter 31

PARTIES

Corporations

It is clear law that a corporation, as a legal person distinct from its members, may commit torts and may have torts committed against it. The commission of torts by a corporation clearly requires some action on the part of the human agents of the corporation. Thus the corporation is vicariously liable for the torts of its servants committed in the course of their employment. The corporation may incur personal liability where the human agent is so much in control of the corporation that his actions may be regarded as those of the corporation itself. In *Lennard's Carrying Co.* v. *Asiatic Petroleum Co. Ltd.* (1915) it was found that the managing director of a company was the "directing mind and will of the corporation" so that fault on his part constituted "actual fault" on the company's part for the purposes of a statute. Where the personal liability of the corporation is concerned it does not seem to matter that the act is *ultra vires* the corporation (*Campbell* v. *Paddington Borough Council* (1911)). Where, on the other hand, a servant is acting *ultra vires* the corporation his action may be outside the scope of his employment. Thus in *Poulton* v. *L. & S.W. Ry.* (1867) the defendants were held not liable for the act of a station master who had detained the plaintiff for non-payment of a fare. The railway company itself had no power to detain in these circumstances. It is unsafe to conclude from this case that corporations are never liable for the torts of their servants where the corporation is carrying out an *ultra vires* activity. In *Poulton's* case the station master clearly had no authority express or implied from his superiors to act in the way he did.

Unincorporated Associations

(i) *Generally*

Unincorporated associations in general have no legal personality distinct from that of their members. In theory, therefore, all members should be joined as co-plaintiffs or co-defendants in an action in tort. Where, however, all the members of the association have an identical interest in defending an action, it is possible to bring a representative action against certain members who are sued as representing the members as a whole. So in *Campbell* v. *Thomson* (1953) a representative action against two members of a club was held to be correctly brought, where the members were allegedly all individually in breach of their duties towards the plaintiff as his employers and as occupiers of the club premises. Where such an action succeeds, judgment can be enforced against the separate property of any member—there is no limitation to "club" property. The same considerations will determine whether members of an unincorporated association can bring a representative action in tort.

(ii) *Trade unions*

Trade unions are a special type of unincorporated association. They have since 1871 been endowed by statute with the capacity to sue and be sued in the name of the union, thus avoiding the difficulty of representative actions. Furthermore the liability of trade unions appears to be enforceable only against union property (*Bonsor* v. *Musicians' Union* (1956) though the theoretical explanation for this is still a matter of some doubt. A statutory immunity from liability in tort was conferred upon trade unions by section 4 (2) of the Trade Disputes Act 1906. This immunity briefly disappeared under the provisions of the Industrial Relations Act 1971, but has now been restored by section 14 of the Trade Union and Labour Relations Act 1974. The immunity also prevents the bringing of representative actions against trade union officials representing themselves and all the other members of the union. Such officials can, however, still be sued in their personal capacity.

The Act of 1974 has created several important exceptions to the immunity of trade unions from liability in tort. Actions in tort can be brought in respect of:

(a) any negligence, nuisance or breach of duty (whether imposed on them by any rule of law or under any enactment) resulting in personal injury to any person; or

(b) without prejudice to (a), breach of any duty so imposed in connection with the ownership, occupation, possession, control or use of property (whether real or personal).

Such liability must not arise, however, from an act done in contemplation or furtherance of a trade dispute.

The Crown

Until 1947, the Crown enjoyed virtually complete exemption from liability in tort. The Crown Proceedings Act of 1947 took away this immunity, however, with the result that the Crown's liability is now determined on the same principles as that of a private person. Whether the Crown is liable for breach of statutory duty depends upon whether the statute binds the Crown; unless the statute expressly provides that the Crown is bound or unless it is bound as a matter of necessary implication, the Crown will not be bound. Where a common law duty is replaced by a statutory duty it is therefore a matter of importance whether the statute binds the Crown (*cf.* the Occupiers' Liability Act 1957, which expressly binds the Crown).

There are still certain exemptions from liability. The Sovereign herself cannot be sued in tort in her private capacity. Section 2 (5) of the Act of 1947 prevents the Crown from being sued for acts done or omitted to be done by persons in the exercise of their judicial office, or by any person in the execution of the judicial process (*cf. infra*, for the personal immunities of participants in the judicial process). Section 10 of the Crown Proceedings Act prevents a member of the armed forces from suing another member of the armed forces in tort for death or personal injury inflicted on him in circumstances where the injury would be attributable to service for the purposes of his pension.

The Post Office

The Post Office which now has separate legal personality of its own distinct from that of the Crown has an immunity, formerly enjoyed by the Crown, from liability in tort where loss or damage has been suffered by any person by reason of anything done or omitted to be done in relation to anything in the post.

Participants in Judicial Process

A judge in a superior court of record acting within his jurisdiction is not liable in tort for acts done or words spoken in his judicial capacity even though he has acted maliciously or corruptly. In the case of judges of inferior courts, for example, county and magistrates' courts, the judge has immunity except where he has acted maliciously or corruptly or in excess of his jurisdiction. A similar immunity to that of the judge of an inferior court applies to officials who perform administrative functions. Other participants in the legal process, for example, parties, witnesses, counsel and jurors, enjoy absolute privilege from liability in defamation and other torts in respect of statements made by them in the course of the proceedings. The statement must have some relevance to the matter before the court.

Husband and Wife

The special position of spouses, both as regards liability in tort *inter se* and towards third parties, has now been almost totally abrogated by statute. The Law Reform (Married Women and Tortfeasors) Act 1935 put the wife into exactly the same position as any other person when she had committed a tort against a third party and abolished the husband's vicarious liability for his wife's torts. The Law Reform (Husband and Wife) Act 1962 removed the suriving anomaly, that of prohibiting actions in tort between the spouses. The court has power to stay the proceedings if no substantial benefit will accrue to either party or if the case can more conveniently be dealt with under section 17 of the Married Women's Property Act 1882.

Persons who are Insane

Insanity is not a recognised defence to an action in tort. Where a tort requires proof of a specific intention, it might be expected that inability to form that intention through insanity would preclude liability and this receives support from *Morriss* v. *Marsden* (1952) (schizophrenic held liable in battery because he intended to commit the attack although he did not know that what he was doing was wrong). It has been suggested that insane persons are less capable of committing torts requiring intention and a specific state of mind such as malice (Clerk & Lindsell, para. 185). Torts of strict liability can no doubt be committed by such persons, but whether they can commit negligence is an open question.

Minors

There is no minimum age of tortious responsibility. Minors, like insane persons, are judged by ordinary principles of tort. There is no authority to indicate at what age an ability to form a tortious intention is acquired. Does a minor of tender years who tears up a pound note commit conversion? Contributory negligence cases (*supra*, p. 95) indicate that a minor of quite advanced years will not be judged by the same standards as an adult. Different considerations may affect his liability for negligence—in *Gorely* v. *Codd* (1967) a sixteen-year-old boy was held liable for his negligence in the use of an air-rifle.

A minor cannot be sued in tort where the action in tort is a means of enforcing a contract which does not bind him. So, for example, in *Jennings* v. *Rundall* (1799) where the defendant hired the plaintiff's horse to be ridden for a short journey, and rode it for a much longer journey with the result that it was injured, he was held not liable in trespass. But in *Burnard* v. *Haggis* (1863) where the minor hired a mare which was not to be used for jumping, and allowed a friend to ride and jump it, he was held liable in trespass. His action was not merely a wrongful performance of the contract—it went totally outside its terms.

Parents

There is no general principle whereby a parent is vicariously liable for the torts of his children. His liability exists, if at all, under the ordinary rules of tort. So, for example, he may be liable in negligence for giving a dangerous gun to his child (*Newton* v. *Edgerley* (1959)—*cf. Donaldson* v. *McNiven* (1952)).

Bankrupts

The effect of section 30 (1) of the Bankruptcy Act 1914, which provides that demands in the nature of unliquidated damages arising otherwise than by reasons of a contract, promise or trust are not provable in the bankruptcy courts, is that most tortious claims cannot be so proved. The bankrupt himself remains liable in tort and may be sued for the full amount of the claim. The bankrupt retains the right to sue in tort where the claim is for the infringement of a purely personal interest. Where the claim is for the protection of the bankrupt's property, it vests in the trustee in bankruptcy. Examples of the former are claims in defamation, battery and false imprisonment; of the latter, conversion and passing-off.

Assignees

It is impossible for a right of action in tort to be assigned. Exceptions to this rule are recognised where the subject-matter of the tortious claim is property and in the subrogation of the insurer to the position of the insured person, having discharged his liability on the policy.

INDEX

Abatement of Nuisance, *see* Defences to the Intentional Torts to Person and Property.
Abuse of Process, 292
Accord and Satisfaction, *see* Extinction of Tortious Liability.
Account, Action for, 314
Actio per quod servitium amisit, 287
Agent,
  deceit, liability of principal, 276
  vicarious liability and, 220
Animals,
  liability for, 202–211
    cattle-trespass, 208–209
    dangerous animals, 205–206
    dogs, 207
    negligence, 210–211
    non-dangerous animals, 205–206
    scienter liability, 202–204
    trespassing livestock, 208–210
Apportionment, *see* Contributory Negligence; Joint and Concurrent Tortfeasors.
Arrest, Lawful, *see* Defences to the Intentional Torts to Person and Property.
Assault, 13–15
  apprehension, of plaintiff, 14–15
  damages, 15
  definition, 13
  state of mind of defendant, 14
  verbal, 13–14
Assignee, *see* Parties.

Bailee,
  conversion by, 36
  estoppel, 29–30
  involuntary, 33–34
  recovery of full value of chattel in conversion, 41–42
  title to sue,
    conversion, 25–27
    trespass to chattels, 22
  trespass by, 22
Bailment, meaning of, 21
Bailor,
  title to sue, conversion, 25–27
  trespass to chattels, 22
Bankrupt, *see* Parties.
Battery, 11–12
  consent, 11–12
  damages, 15
  definition, 11
  directness, 11
  method of commission, 12–13

Case, Action on, 8–9, 16, 19, 35, 36, 42
Cattle-Trespass, *see* Animals.
Causation, *see* Negligence.
Chattels, *see also* Conversion; Liability for Chattels; Trespass to Chattels.
  damage to, residual principle of liability, 42
  recaption of, *see* Defences to the Intentional Torts to Person and Property.
Children, *see also* Minor; Parent.
  occupier's liability towards, 146–148, 153–155
Consent, *see* D.I.T.P.P.
  battery, in, 11–12
Conspiracy, 262–264
Contract,
  detinue and, 38–39
  minor, 324–325
  misrepresentation, 78–80
  tort and, 2–3
Contribution, *see* Joint Tortfeasors.
Contributory Negligence, 124–130
  apportionment,
    power of, 125–130
    basis of, 127–128
  fault of defendant, 126–127
  fault of plaintiff, 125–126
  history, 123
  imputed, 129
  particular cases, 128–130
Conversion, 24–37, 39–42
  acts amounting to,
    dealing, 31–33
    demand and refusal, 35
    destruction, 31
    interference with plaintiff's exercise of his right, 34–35
    involuntary receipt, 33–34
    negligence, 36–37

Conversion—*cont.*
receipt, 33
user, 36
bailee, by, 29–30, 36
definition, 24–25
detinue and, 37–38
finder, right to possession of, 27–29
interest of plaintiff, right to possession, 25–30
state of mind of defendant, 30
judgment, effect of satisfaction of, 37
jus tertii, whether defence, 29–30
limitation of action in 316
limited interest, plaintiff with, 41–42
measure of damages, 39–41
proprietary function, 25
trespass to chattels and, 25
wrongdoer, right to possession of, 27
Corporation, *see* Parties.
Crime, Tort and, 3
Crown, *see* Parties.

Damages, *see also* the individual torts.
aggravated, 305
at large, 305
contemptuous, 304
continuing tort, 311
death, for, 299–300
deductions from personal injuries award, 308–310
duty to mitigate, 311
estate to, 301–302
exemplary, 306
future earnings, 307–308
general, 304–305
loss of amenity, 307–308
loss of earnings, 307–308
loss of expectation of life, 301–302
lump sum, 311
nominal, 304
pain and suffering, 307
parasitic, 305–306
personal injuries, 306–310
special, 304–305
Death and Tort, 297–303
Fatal Accidents Acts, liability under, 297–300
estate, survival of actions for and against, 300–302
limitation period, 320
Deceit, 275–278
damage, necessity for, 277
Deceit—*cont.*
intention that plaintiff should act on statement, 276
reliance of plaintiff, 277
representation, 275–276
Defamation, 231–254
damage, special, 234
damages as remedy, 253
defamatory nature of statement, 235–238
defences, 241–253
apology, 252–253
consent, 252
fair comment, 243–247
justification, 242–243
mechanical distribution, 241
privilege,
absolute, 247–252
qualified, 248–252
unintentional defamation, 241–242
innuendo, 236–237
interpretation of statement, 236–238
libel, 232–233
malice,
fair comment, 247
qualified privilege, 251–252
nature of liability in defamation, 241
publication of statement, 239–241
reference to plaintiff, 238–239
slander, 232–234
Defences, *see* under individual torts; *see also* Contributory Negligence; *Volenti non fit Injuria.*
Defences to the Intentional Torts to Person and Property, 52–65
abatement of nuisance, 64–65
authority of law, 60
consent, 52
contributory negligence, 61
defence of person, 53–54
defence of property, 54–55
discipline, 57
distress damage feasant, 55
illegality, 62–63
inevitable accident, 53
lawful arrest, 57–59
mistake, 53
necessity, 55–57
police powers other than arrest, 59–60
recaption of chattels, 63
re-entry on land, 64
torts which are crimes, 61

Detinue, 37–42
  conversion, 37–38
  contract and, 38–39
  demand and refusal, basis of cause of action, 37
  measure of damages, 39–41
  interest of plaintiff, 38
  specific restitution, 39
Discipline, *see* Defences to the Intentional Torts to Person and Property.
Distress Damage Feasant, *see* Defences to the Intentional Torts to Person and Property.

Economic Torts, 255–282
Ejectment, Action of, 48–50
Employer's Liability towards Workmen, 163–167
  duties,
    competent staff, 162
    delegability, 165–166
    proper plant and premises, 164–165
    reasonable care, 167
    safe system of work, 165
    tripartite division, 164–165
Extinction of Tortious Liability, 315–320
  accord and satisfaction, 316
  death, 315
  judgment, 315
  limitation, 316–320
  release, 316
  waiver, 315–316

Fair Comment, *see* Defamation.
False Imprisonment, 15–20
  act constituting, 16
arrest, defence to, 57–59
  directness, 15–16
  escape route, reasonableness, 16–17
  interest of plaintiff, 18
  justification of imprisonment, 18–19
  omission, by, 17–18
  state of mind of defendant, 15–16
Family Relationships, Interference with, 283–287
  parent and child, 284–285
  husband and wife, 285–287
  master and servant, 287
Fatal Accidents Acts, *see* Death and Tort
Fire, Liability for Escape of, 200–201
Franchise, Interference with, 293

Highway,
  animals,
    straying on, 211
    trespass from, on to adjoining land, 210
  extra-hazardous activities on, 227–228
  failure to maintain, highway authority by, 188
  obstruction to, public nuisance, 187
  projection over, public nuisance, 187
  trespass to, 45
Husband and Wife, *see* Parties; Family Relationships, Interference with.

Illegality, *see* Defences to the Intentional Torts to Person and Property.
Independent contractor, *see* Vicarious Liability.
Interference with contract, 256–262
Inevitable Accident, *see* Defences to the Intentional Torts to Person and Property.
Injunction, 312–314
  interlocutory injunction, 270
  injurious falsehood, 278–282
  damage, 280–281
    calculated to cause, 279
  false statement about plaintiff or property, 278–279
    made to third party, 279
  malice, 280
  negligence and, 281–282
Innkeeper's Liability, 293
Innominate and Doubtful Torts, 293–295
Insane persons, *see* Parties.
Intentionally Causing Physical Harm, 19–20
Intimidation, 264–266

Joint and Concurrent Tortfeasors, 118–123
  categories of, 119–120
  concurrent tortfeasors, distinguished from, 119
  contribution, 121–123
  indemnity, 123
  judgment against one, effect of, 120
Judicial Process,
  participants in, immunity of, 323

Jus tertii,
defence to conversion, 29–30
defence to trespass to chattels, 23
Justification, *see* Defamation.
defence as, interference with contract in, 262

Liability for Chattels, 158–162
dangerous chattels, 159
manufacturer, 159–162
persons other than manufacturer, 158–159

Malicious Prosecution, 289–292
damage, 291–292
prosecution, 289–290
malice, 291–292
reasonable cause, absence of, 290–291
termination of proceedings in plaintiff's favour, 290
Manufacturer, *see* Liability for Chattels.
Master and Servant, *see* Employer's Liability towards Workmen; Vicarious Liability; *Actio per quod servitium amisit.*
Mesne Profits, Action for, 48–50
Minor,
parental liability in tort for, 325
party in tort, as, 324–325
standard of care in negligence, 95–96
Mistake, *see* Defences to the Intentional Torts to Person and Property.

Necessity, *see* Defences to the Intentional Torts to Person and Property.
Negligence, 66–117, 135–139
animals, 209
breach of duty of care, 90–99
degree of risk, 91–93
expense of precautions, 94
factors involved in, 90–91
reasonable man, 95
reasonableness, 90
seriousness of injury, 93
social utility, 93–94
causation and remoteness of damage, 100–117
causation, remoteness distinguished from, 100–101
causation in fact, 101–103
causation in law, 103

Negligence—*cont.*
multiple causes and apportionment, 119–123
constituent requirements, 68
defences, *see* Contributory Negligence, *Volenti non fit injuria.*
duty of care, 68–89
duty in fact distinguished from, 68–69
necessity for concept of, 68–70
neighbour principle, 66–67
owed to plaintiff, 70–71
situations in which does not arise,
dangerous chattels, 156–157
nervous shock, 85–88
occupier and trespassers, 151–153
omissions and gratuitous undertakings, 81–83
purely pecuniary loss, 83–85
statements, 71–81
nuisance and, 170
occupier's liability and, 141–142
proof of, 136–141
burden of proof, 137
conviction, as proof of, 141
judge and jury, 136
no evidence of negligence, 136–137
res ipsa loquitur, 138–141
remoteness of damage, 100–117
breach of duty, distinguished from, 105–106
damage aggravated by peculiarity of victim, 108–110
damage aggravated by later events, 116–118
foreseeable consequences rule, 104–105
measure of damages, distinguished from, 111
rescuer, liability towards, 113–115
ulterior harm, 111–114
standard of care, 96–99
age, 96
character, 96
children, 95–96
general practice, 98–99
illness, 96
knowledge, 96–97
skill, 97
sportsmen, 98
superior qualities, 98

Negligence—*cont.*
statutory duty, breach of, distinguished from, 212
Nervous Shock,
duty of care in relation to, 85–88
intentional infliction, 19–20
Nuisance, 170–189
abatement, 64–65
authorisation of, 179–180
conduct of defendant, 173–174
creator, liability of, 179–181
damage, 177
defences to private, 183–184
highway, failure to maintain, 187–188
highway, premises adjoining, 187
interference with enjoyment of land, 171
isolated escape, 178
landlord, liability of, 182
liability for, 179–182
locality, 175
natural conditions on land, 180–181
negligence, distinguished from, 172
plaintiff, extra-sensitivity of, 176
private, 171–185
private and public, 170, 185–186
public, 185–189
remoteness of damage in, 184
Rylands v. *Fletcher*, distinguished from, 198–199
strict liability, whether tort of, 177–178
tenant, liability of, 182
unreasonableness, 172–176

Occupier of Premises; *see* Premises, Liability of Occupier for; *also* Nuisance, *Rylands* v. *Fletcher*, rule in.

Parent, *see* Parties; Interference with Family Relationships.
Parties, 321–325
assignees, 325
bankrupts, 325
corporations, 321
Crown, 322–323
husband and wife, 324
insane persons, 324
minors, 324–325
parents, 325
participants in judicial process, 323
Parties—*cont.*
Post Office, 323
trade unions, 322
unincorporated associations, 321–322
Partners,
joint tortfeasors, 120
Passing Off, 271–274
calculated to deceive, 273
damage, proof not necessary, 273–274
methods of commission, 271–272
state of mind of defendant, 273
torts analogous to, 273
Police Officer,
powers of arrest, 57–59
powers other than arrest, 59–60
Post Office, *see* Parties.
Premises, Liability of Occupier for, 142–155
activity duty, 144–145
children, allurement, 146–147
child trespassers, 153–155
very young, 147–148
common duty of care, 143–144
calling, risks incidental to, 144, 146
definition, 143–144
common law position prior to the Occupiers' Liability Act, 142–143
contract,
liability to contracting party, occupier, of, 151–152
liability to persons permitted to enter under, occupier, of, 152–153
contributory negligence of visitor, 148–150
damage to property, 144
entrant as of right, 143–144, 150
exclusion of liability by occupier, 150–151
implied licence, 153–154
independent contractor, liability of occupier for, 151
knowledge of visitor, effect of, 148–150
negligence, liability to persons in adjacent premises, 157
nuisance, distinguished from, 142, 182
occupier, who is, 145

Premises—*cont.*
premises, what are, 145–146
trespasser, liability of occupier towards, 153–155
visitors, lawful, 142–144
volenti non fit injuria, visitor, 148
warning by occupier, 148–149
Prescription, defence to nuisance, 183
Privacy, Interference with, 295–296
Privilege, *see* Defamation.

Release, *see* Extinction of Tortious Liability.
Remedies,
account, 314
damages, *see* Damages.
declaratory action, 314
injunction, *see* Injunction.
self-help, 63–65, 314
specific restitution, 39, 314
Res Ipsa Loquitur, *see* Negligence, proof of.
Reversionary Interest in Chattel,
holder of, action by, 42
Reversioner,
damage to land, action by, 50
Rylands v. *Fletcher*, Rule in, 190–199
bringing on land, 191–192
defences,
act of God, 195
act of stranger, 195–196
consent, 197–198
statutory authority, 196–197
escape, 191, 194
fire, applicability of rule, 200–201
interest of plaintiff, 194–195
non-natural use, 193-194
other torts, and, 198–199
personal injuries, whether recoverable, 194–195
remoteness of damage, 198
strict liability, 190–191

Scienter Action, *see* Animals.
Seduction, *see* Family Relationships, Interference with.
Self-defence, *see* Defences to the Intentional Torts to Person and Property.
Self-help, *see* Remedies.
Servant, *see* Employer's Liability; Vicarious Liability; *Actio per quod servitium amisit.*
Slander, *see* Defamation.
Slander of Goods; Slander of Title, injurious falsehood and, 278
Specific Restitution, *see* Detinue; Remedies.
Statutory Authority, *see* Defences to Nuisance; *Rylands* v. *Fletcher*, defences to.
Statutory Duty, Breach of, 212–219
breach of duty, 214
civil action, whether statute intended to create, 212–213
damage, contemplated by statute, 215–216
remoteness of, 216–217
defences, 217–218
plaintiff, person protected, 214–215
Strict Liability, Introduction to Torts of, 167–169
Survival of Action,s, *see* Death and Tort.

Tort,
classiffication of torts, 3–4
meaning of, 1
Trade Mark,
use of plaintiff's, 271
Trade Union, *see* Parties.
Trespass,
actionability *per se*, 8
burden of proof in, 9
case and, 8–9
cattle by, see Animals.
defences to, *see* Defences to the Intentional Torts to Person and Property.
directness, 8
false imprisonment, form of, 15
fault necessary, 9
meaning of, 8–10
negligence and, 9–10
Trespass to Chattels, 21–24
acts constituting, 23
conversion, distinguished from, 23
damages, 24
definition, 21
directness, 24
interest of plaintiff, possession, 22–23
jus tertii, no defence, 23
state of mind of defendant, 24
Trespass to Land, 44–50
ab initio, 47
airspace, interference with, 46–47

Trespass to Land—*cont.*
defences, 47–48
definition, 43
ejectment, distinguished from, 48–50
interest of plaintiff, possession, 43–45
highway, to, 45
licensee, action by, 44–45, 50
measure of damages, 48–49
mesne profits, action for, 48, 49
nature of act constituting, directness, 45
nuisance, distinguished from, 45
relation, by, 49
state of mind of defendant, 45–46
Trespass to the Person, 12–19; *see also* Assault; Battery; False Imprisonment.
Trespasser,
implied licensee, distinguished from, 153–154
non-occupier's liability towards, 157
occupier's liability towards, 154–155

Unincorporated Association, *see* Parties.
Unlawful Means, Tort of Causing Loss by, 266–269

Vicarious Liability, 220–230
course of employment, 227
driving as agent of car owner, 229–230
independent contractor, 227–229
servant, who is, 221–222
theoretical basis, 222–223
Volenti non fit Injuria, 130–135
agreement between plaintiff and defendant, distinguished from, 134–135
limits of defence, 132–134
meaning, 131
unintentional torts, 131
voluntary act by plaintiff, 134

Waiver, *see* Extinction of Tortious Liability.
Work, interference with occupation, 293–294